MW00908208

THE
SHEPHERD
KING

"David was a representative man. His history is of
interest to every soul who is striving for eternal
victories. . . . David understood what it meant to
fight against principalities and powers, against
the rulers of the darkness of this world. . . .
"The struggle that David endured, every
follower of Christ must go through."

—Ellen G. White, " 'That Your Joy Might Be Full,' "
Signs of the Times®, August 11, 1909

"David's experiences are recorded for the
instruction of the people of God in these last days."

—Ellen G. White, "David Becomes Weary in Well-Doing,"
Signs of the Times®, November 9, 1888

DAVID METZLER

Pacific Press®
Publishing Association
Nampa, Idaho | www.pacificpress.com

To order additional copies of this book or other devotional books,
call toll-free 1-800-765-6955, or visit AdventistBookCenter.com.

Library of Congress Cataloging-in-Publication Data

Names: Metzler, David, 1951- author.
Title: The Shepherd king / David Metzler.
Description: Nampa, Idaho : Pacific Press Publishing Association, [2023] |
    Series: Daily devotional | Summary: "A collection of 366 daily devotional
    readings, providing lessons from the life of King David"—Provided
    by publisher.
Identifiers: LCCN 2023017229 (print) | LCCN 2023017230 (ebook) |
    ISBN 9780816369263 (hardcover) | ISBN 9780816369270 (ebook)
Subjects: LCSH: David, King of Israel—Biblical teaching. | Church year
    meditations. | Devotional calendars.
Classification: LCC BS580.D3 M39 1996 (print) | LCC BS580.D3 (ebook) |
    DDC 222/.4092—dc23/eng/20230629
LC record available at https://lccn.loc.gov/2023017229
LC ebook record available at https://lccn.loc.gov/2023017230

November 2023

DEDICATION

To my grandsons, Jacob and Reuben
When trials come, always remember—
the Lord is *your* Shepherd too!

Contents

PREFACE

T he story of David has fascinated and inspired Christians for generations. His story comes to us as instructive of one man's lifelong struggle between good and evil. Here was a man capable of not only great heroics and tender mercies but also base crimes and poor judgment. As a gentle shepherd, faithfully leading his flocks to green pastures and courageously protecting them from danger, he plainly states, "The LORD is *my* shepherd" (Psalm 23:1; emphasis added). His psalms bring solace and inspiration. He is referred to as a man after God's "own heart" (1 Samuel 13:14). And yet knowing his failings, we ask, How can this be?

David had his share of faults and failures. His lack of truthfulness directly led to the death of Ahimelech and most of Ahimelech's family (1 Samuel 22:9–23). By aligning himself with the Philistines, David came dangerously close to having to fight his own countrymen. He coveted and eventually committed adultery with another man's wife. He conspired against and ultimately murdered her husband to hide the results of that act. He neglected his paternal duties, which resulted in dysfunctional and rebellious sons. He went against the counsel of God by numbering the warriors of Israel during a moment of self-pride and thus brought punishment upon all Israel. Before committing any of these sins, he had said, "Thy word have I hid in mine heart, that I might not sin against thee" (Psalm 119:11). But he sinned nonetheless.

David's struggles with doubt, temptation, despair, betrayal, sorrow, fear, and pride resonate with us because we face many of the same challenges and questions. Does God exist? How can I have faith in a just God when bad things happen to seemingly good people? Where is God when I pray and no answer appears to be forthcoming? Why do the wicked seem to prosper? How do I deal with overwhelming grief? How long must evil continue? Is God punishing me? Which path does God want me to choose? Does God really keep His promises?

In the story of David, we find reasons to hope, believe, and trust in the Lord. True repentance and sorrow for sin brought peace and salvation to David. God forgave him. God did not forsake him. "These things . . . are written for our admonition, upon whom the ends of the world are come" (1 Corinthians 10:11).

PSALMS OF DAVID CROSS-REFERENCE

Psalms referenced in this devotional are listed here in numerical order, facilitating rapid location for cross-reference or additional study of a particular psalm.

Psalm 1	Nov. 5	Psalm 36	Oct. 5	Psalm 80	July 7
Psalm 2	Nov. 6	Psalm 37	Oct. 8	Psalm 84	Aug. 23
Psalm 3	Sept. 7	Psalm 38	Aug. 21	Psalm 86	July 6
Psalm 4	Sept. 8	Psalm 39	Oct. 20, 21	Psalm 88	Oct. 24
Psalm 5	Sept. 9	Psalm 40	Sept. 14	Psalm 89	Sept. 16, 17
Psalm 6	Oct. 22	Psalm 41	Aug. 22	Psalm 92	June 25
Psalm 7	Aug. 24	Psalm 42	Mar. 29	Psalm 94	Sept. 13
Psalm 8	Feb. 18	Psalm 44	Oct. 10	Psalm 101	May 31
Psalm 9	Sept. 12	Psalm 45	Nov. 26	Psalm 103	Aug. 2
Psalm 10	Sept. 11	Psalm 46	July 21	Psalm 104	Feb. 20
Psalm 11	Apr. 15	Psalm 48	June 17	Psalm 108	Nov. 19
Psalm 12	Mar. 14	Psalm 50	Oct. 6	Psalm 109	Aug. 29
Psalm 13	Apr. 21	Psalm 51	July 29, 30	Psalm 110	July 5
Psalm 14	Aug. 25	Psalm 52	Apr. 11	Psalm 119	Nov. 7–15
Psalm 15	June 29, 30	Psalm 53	Aug. 25	Psalm 120	Apr. 30
Psalm 16	May 9, 10	Psalm 54	Apr. 18	Psalm 121	May 1
Psalm 17	Apr. 23, 24	Psalm 55	Aug. 26	Psalm 122	June 24
Psalm 18	July 19	Psalm 56	Mar. 26	Psalm 124	July 8
Psalm 19	Feb. 21–23	Psalm 57	Mar. 25	Psalm 131	Nov. 20
Psalm 20	July 15	Psalm 58	Aug. 30	Psalm 132	Nov. 1
Psalm 21	July 20	Psalm 59	Mar. 16	Psalm 133	Apr. 1
Psalm 22	Oct. 23	Psalm 60	July 9	Psalm 138	Oct. 17
Psalm 23	Feb. 16	Psalm 61	Aug. 17	Psalm 139	Oct. 18
Psalm 24	June 26–28	Psalm 62	Aug. 20	Psalm 140	Apr. 19
Psalm 25	Aug. 16	Psalm 63	Apr. 16	Psalm 141	May 12
Psalm 26	July 1	Psalm 64	Aug. 18	Psalm 142	Apr. 2
Psalm 27	Mar. 30, 31	Psalm 65	Oct. 4	Psalm 143	Apr. 3
Psalm 28	Aug. 27	Psalm 66	July 10, 11	Psalm 144	June 14–16
Psalm 29	Feb. 19	Psalm 68	Nov. 18	Psalm 145	Nov. 3
Psalm 30	Oct. 16	Psalm 69	Aug. 28, 31	Psalm 146	Nov. 21
Psalm 31	Apr. 22	Psalm 70	Sept. 15	Psalm 147	Nov. 22
Psalm 32	July 28	Psalm 71	Oct. 25	Psalm 148	Nov. 23
Psalm 33	Feb. 17	Psalm 72	Nov. 17	Psalm 149	Nov. 24
Psalm 34	Mar. 27	Psalm 73	Oct. 7	Psalm 150	Nov. 25
Psalm 35	Aug. 19	Psalm 77	July 31		

CREATION OF A MONARCHY

Ruth 1–4
1 Samuel 1–15

Patriarchs and Prophets, chapters 55–61

GOOD AND BAD INFLUENCES

And Ruth said, Intreat me not to leave thee, or to return from following after thee: for whither thou goest, I will go; and where thou lodgest, I will lodge: thy people shall be my people, and thy God, my God.

—Ruth 1:16

The Israelites seemed content, after forty years of wandering, to settle down in the midst of Canaan with enough room to raise a few sheep in relative security. They had no desire to conquer or live in the fortified cities of the Canaanites, but "living thus among the Canaanites the Hebrews were brought into close contact with the religion of the country and its cult system. This seemed so attractive to many that great sections of the people accepted the Canaanite religion. The repeated periods of apostasy were always followed by periods of moral weakness, a situation that provided their more powerful enemies an opportunity to oppress them. In such periods of distress a strong political leader invariably arose and, driven by the Spirit of God, led His people—in whole or in part—through repentance back to God."[1]

As the Israelites grew in numbers over the centuries, this cycle of war and peace developed between the two nations. Periods of peace existed only as long as a current judge lived. During this time, there occurred a famine in Judah. Elimelech, Naomi, and their two sons, Mahlon and Chilion, sojourned in Moab, east of the Dead Sea. There, the sons married women of Moab; "the name of the one was Orpah, and the name of the other Ruth" (Ruth 1:4). The husband and sons died, leaving Naomi and her daughters-in-law destitute. With the famine being over in Judah, Naomi decided to return to her home near Bethlehem.

Orpah chose to remain in Moab, but Ruth passionately refused (vv. 16, 17). Being poor, Ruth went out to glean the fields around Bethlehem. Here she came to the attention of Boaz, a rich relation of Elimelech. Boaz purchased Elimelech's land from Naomi, thereby gaining permission to marry Ruth, whom he had come to admire. Ruth, the converted Moabitess, gave birth to Obed—"the servant of God"—perpetuating the family line reaching to King David.

"All will have associates, and will influence and be influenced in their turn."[2]

---

1. Francis D. Nichol, ed., *The Seventh-day Adventist Bible Commentary*, vol. 2 (Washington, DC: Review and Herald®, 1976), 45.
2. Ellen G. White, *Testimonies for the Church* (Mountain View, CA: Pacific Press®, 1948), 4:587.

VIRTUE IS NOT INHERITED

Pure religion and undefiled before God and the Father is this, To visit the fatherless and widows in their affliction, and to keep himself unspotted from the world.

—James 1:27

When Israel entered Canaan the Lord had commanded them to assign cities to the Levites throughout the various tribes. Thus instruction in ways of righteousness might be given to all the people. But they seem to have paid little or no attention to the command. They did not, in fact, even drive out the Canaanites, but dwelt among them (Judges 1:21, 27, 29–33). Within a few years the Levites, who had received no specific tribal allotment, found themselves without employment. Even Jonathan, the grandson of Moses (see on Judges 18:30), visited the home of Micah the Ephraimite 'to sojourn where' he could 'find a place' (Judges 17:8), and became priest to Micah's 'house of gods' (Judges 17:5). He eventually stole the images out of Micah's house and went with the migrant Danites to be their priest (see Judges 18). Thus at a time when 'every man did that which was right in his own eyes,' Israel violated God's plan that the Levites should instruct the people in His ways, and soon lapsed into the ignorant, superstitious ways of the heathen about them."[1]

Thus, the story of David begins with Samuel, the son of Elkanah and Hannah. He was "the last of the judges, one of the greatest of the prophets, founder of the schools of the prophets . . . , and the one who led out in the establishment of the Hebrew kingdom and in the laying down of the fundamental principles on which it was to operate (see 1 Sam. 10:25)."[2] "Samuel chose to repudiate the evils of the day and to devote his life to the correction of these tendencies."[3] "The reign of judges in Israel closes with Samuel, . . . few purer or more illustrious characters are presented in the sacred record. There are few, also, whose life-history contains lessons of greater value to the thoughtful student."[4]

Position and possessions are lent to an individual to test his or her character. Helping and uplifting others purifies one's nature from selfishness.

---

1. Francis D. Nichol, ed., *The Seventh-day Adventist Bible Commentary*, vol. 2 (Washington, DC: Review and Herald®, 1976), 449.

2. Nichol, 445–447.

3. Nichol, 449.

4. Ellen G. White, "The Birth of Samuel," *Signs of the Times*®, October 27, 1881, 1.

A Mother's Influence

And [Hannah] called his name Samuel, saying,
Because I have asked him of the Lord.
—1 Samuel 1:20

Hannah had long wished for a child. Elkanah's second wife, Peninnah, had been blessed with sons and daughters, but Hannah was childless. During a yearly visit to Shiloh to offer sacrifices before God, she silently prayed that she might be blessed with a son. Should her prayer be answered, she promised God she would lend her child to His service all the days of his life. Eli, the high priest, was sitting nearby, leaning against a post of the temple. Seeing her lips moving but no sound coming out, he accused Hannah of being drunk. When her heartbreaking tale was told, Eli realized this God-fearing woman was pouring out a heartfelt desire to her Lord. His heart softened, and he said, "Go in peace: and the God of Israel grant thee thy petition that thou hast asked of him" (1 Samuel 1:17). God heard her prayer, and she gave birth to a son.

"During the first three years of the life of Samuel the prophet, his mother carefully taught him to distinguish between good and evil. By every familiar object surrounding him, she sought to lead his thoughts up to the Creator. In fulfilment of her vow to give her son to the Lord, with great self-denial she placed him under the care of Eli the high priest, to be trained for service in the house of God."[1]

"As soon as the little one was old enough to be separated from his mother, she fulfilled her vow. She loved her child with all the devotion of a mother's heart; day by day, as she watched his expanding powers and listened to his childish prattle, her affections entwined about him more closely. He was her only son, the special gift of Heaven; but she had received him as a treasure consecrated to God, and she would not withhold from the Giver His own."[2] "And the child Samuel grew on, and was in favour both with the Lord, and also with men" (1 Samuel 2:26). This text brings to mind the description of another Child who found favor with God (Luke 2:52). Hannah had done her job well.

The influence of a Christian mother in forming her children's character is soul saving brought home.

---

1. Ellen G. White, "Training Children for God—No. 1," *Review and Herald*, September 8, 1904, 7.
2. Ellen G. White, *Patriarchs and Prophets* (Mountain View, CA: Pacific Press®, 1943), 570, 571.

CALLED TO SERVICE

*But Samuel ministered before the LORD, being a child,
girded with a linen ephod. Moreover his mother made him
a little coat, and brought it to him from year to year, when
she came up with her husband to offer the yearly sacrifice.*

—1 Samuel 2:18, 19

Though Samuel's youth was passed at the tabernacle devoted to the worship of God, he was not free from evil influences or sinful example. The sons of Eli feared not God, nor honored their father; but Samuel did not seek their company nor follow their evil ways. It was his constant endeavor to become what God would have him. . . .

"Samuel had been placed under the care of Eli, and the loveliness of his character drew forth the warm affection of the aged priest. He was kind, generous, obedient, and respectful. Eli . . . found rest and comfort and blessing in the presence of his charge. Samuel was helpful and affectionate, and no father ever loved his child more tenderly than did Eli this youth. It was a singular thing that between the chief magistrate of the nation and the simple child so warm an affection should exist."[1]

Levites were called to the ministry of the Lord only after they had attained their twenty-fifth birthday. Samuel was an exception to that rule. "Every year saw more important trusts committed to him; and while he was yet a child, a linen ephod was placed upon him as a token of his consecration to the work of the sanctuary."[2] The tiny linen ephod "was a short, sleeveless garment consisting of front and back panels joined at the shoulders and drawn in at the waist with a girdle."[3]

Hannah and her husband made yearly trips to the tabernacle and would bring Samuel a new coat Hannah had made for him. I can just see her trying it on him and asking him to turn so she might gauge the fit. The bond between mother and son was unbroken.

"What is lent to the Lord is sure to be returned with compound interest. Hannah dedicated one child to the Lord and was rewarded with five others."[4]

---

1. Ellen G. White, *Patriarchs and Prophets* (Mountain View, CA: Pacific Press®, 1943), 573.
2. White, 573.
3. Francis D. Nichol, ed., *The Seventh-day Adventist Bible Commentary*, vol. 2 (Washington, DC: Review and Herald®, 1976), 463.
4. Nichol, 463.

A WARNING UNHEEDED

Wherefore . . . honourest thy sons above me, to make yourselves
fat with the chiefest of all the offerings of Israel my people?
—1 Samuel 2:29

The sons of Eli were entirely unfit to serve as priests. They showed marked disrespect for the services. Eli's lack of early discipline made them incorrigible. No amount of pleading now made any impression on their behavior. "By their vile lusts they lowered the service of the Lord in the eyes of the people to the level of the sensual orgies of the neighboring idol groves."[1] When Eli failed to act, God intervened. One day a man of God appeared at the sanctuary with a warning message for Eli (1 Samuel 2:27–36). It should have had a sobering effect, but such was not to be.

"The promise had been made that the house of Aaron should walk before God forever; but this promise had been made on condition that they should devote themselves to the work of the sanctuary with singleness of heart and honor God in all their ways, not serving self nor following their own perverse inclinations. Eli and his sons had been tested, and the Lord had found them wholly unworthy of the exalted position of priests in His service."[2] The house of Eli would cease to exist. Eli's sons would die a violent death. They would not be punished immediately nor die by the direct hand of God, but "in turning away from the angel of the Lord (Ps. 34:7), they sealed their own doom. It was the Philistines who killed them (1 Sam. 4:10, 11), yet God permitted their death because of their refusal to follow Him."[3]

God lifted the veil and showed the results of continued sin. "He did not foreordain it. He who knows the end from the beginning knows all that affects the exercise of free choice. By warning individuals of what the future holds in store for them, God proves to the universe that men go so far of their own free choice that even that knowledge will not deter them."[4]

The influence of a Christian home is best seen in the character it develops.

1. Francis D. Nichol, ed., *The Seventh-day Adventist Bible Commentary*, vol. 2 (Washington, DC: Review and Herald®, 1976), 462.
2. Ellen G. White, *Patriarchs and Prophets* (Mountain View, CA: Pacific Press®, 1943), 579.
3. Nichol, *The Seventh-day Adventist Bible Commentary*, 2:463.
4. Nichol, 464.

THE VOICE OF GOD

And ere the lamp of God went out in the temple of the LORD,
where the ark of God was, and Samuel was laid down to sleep;
that the LORD called Samuel: and he answered, Here am I.
—1 Samuel 3:3, 4

There had been no direct message from God to the Israelites for some time. Neither dreams nor visits from heavenly messengers had taken place as the nation had sunk to a spiritual low. Samuel was now twelve years of age. Eli was an obese old man with failing eyesight. The high priest had come to rely upon the young lad for assistance in his old age. "Another warning was to be given to Eli's house. God could not communicate with the high priest and his sons; their sins, like a thick cloud, had shut out the presence of His Holy Spirit. But in the midst of evil the child Samuel remained true to Heaven, and the message of condemnation to the house of Eli was Samuel's commission as a prophet of the Most High."[1]

In the silence of the dimly lit tabernacle, " 'the Lord called Samuel.' Supposing the voice to be that of Eli, the child hastened to the bedside of the priest, saying, 'Here am I; for thou calledst me.' The answer was, 'I called not, my son; lie down again.' Three times Samuel was called, and thrice he responded in like manner. And then Eli was convinced that the mysterious call was the voice of God. . . .

"No feeling of envy or jealousy was awakened in Eli's heart. He directed Samuel to answer, if again called, 'Speak, Lord; for Thy servant heareth.' Once more the voice was heard, and the child answered, 'Speak; for Thy servant heareth.' So awed was he at the thought that the great God should speak to him that he could not remember the exact words which Eli bade him say."[2] Samuel was frightened by the message of doom pronounced on Eli and his sons. As God had not told him to convey the message, he remained in silent turmoil all that morning.

God waited until He found a leader true to His calling. He never leaves us in the dark!

---

1. Ellen G. White, *Patriarchs and Prophets* (Mountain View, CA: Pacific Press®, 1943), 581.
2. White, 581.

Why Are These Leaders Not Removed?

Then Eli called Samuel, and said, Samuel, my son. And he answered, Here am I. And he said, What is the thing that the LORD hath said unto thee?
—1 Samuel 3:16, 17

Things had become so bad at the tabernacle they could no longer be tolerated. "As the men of Israel witnessed the corrupt course of the priests, they thought it safer for their families not to come up to the appointed place of worship. Many went from Shiloh . . . determined to offer their sacrifices themselves, concluding that this would be fully as acceptable to God, as to sanction in any manner the abominations practiced in the sanctuary."[1]

"Elkanah and Hannah must have had some concern as they placed their gift to the Lord in the hands of Eli, and of his two sons, Hophni and Phinehas. How much greater must have been the concern of the divine Father as He placed His Son under the influence and scrutiny of the unworthy priests of His day. Christ was 12 years of age when He came to the attention of the priests, yet His conduct upon that occasion testifies to the reality of divine protection extended even to children who seek heavenly guidance (see on Luke 2:52). Samuel's experiences testify to the same divine guidance."[2]

"Samuel lived for years in an evil environment, and could not help seeing the difference between the instructions given in the scrolls of the law and the lives of the young priests. . . . As he turned the matter over in his heart, the same question would come to him that comes to the mind of a godly youth today: If the Word of God lays down certain principles for the conduct of His work, and the leaders not only fail to follow these instructions, but are guilty of gross misconduct, why does He allow them to continue ministering in holy office?"[3]

Samuel knew he must faithfully bear the message given, no matter how painful. Eli accepted the verdict and the sentence (1 Samuel 3:18).

"Eli's sun was about to set, but that of Samuel was already rising."[4]

1. Ellen G. White, "The Sons of Eli," *Signs of the Times®*, December 1, 1881, 1.
2. Francis D. Nichol, ed., *The Seventh-day Adventist Bible Commentary*, vol. 2 (Washington, DC: Review and Herald®, 1976), 462.
3. Nichol, 467.
4. Nichol, 467.

WHY CONSULT GOD?

*Now Israel went out against the Philistines to battle, and
pitched beside Ebenezer: and the Philistines pitched in Aphek.*
—1 Samuel 4:1

The Philistines pitched camp at Aphek on the Plain of Sharon, about eleven miles northeast of Joppa on the coast. This placed them within twenty-five miles of the tabernacle at Shiloh. "Upon numerous previous occasions God had directed that the armies of Israel go forth into battle with their enemies, and when they did so in response to His command victory was theirs. This time, however, the circumstances were different. . . . [The Israelites] went forth into battle, not in humble faith trusting in God, but with pride in their own cleverness and power. When God was with them no enemy could stand before them; when He was not, defeat was certain."[1] Neither God nor His recognized prophet Samuel was consulted before the armies of Israel marched.

Things immediately went wrong for Israel. The Philistines attacked with great ferocity, and four thousand Israelites were slaughtered on the battlefield. Anciently, when a nation met with defeat in battle, it was believed "their gods were angry with them and should be more earnestly placated to avoid worse afflictions in the future. Considering the low religious condition of Israel at this time, it is little wonder that Israel had much the same attitude toward the Lord. . . . Probably past victories during Eli's judgeship had led to a feeling of self-confidence that blinded their eyes to their need of God. Because the leaders had willfully forsaken Him for the gods of the nations about them, God could do nothing but permit them to reap the harvest of their own seed sowing."[2]

Samuel had been empowered by God to be Israel's judge, prophet, and priest. His insight and resolve had thus far preserved Israel from destruction. Yet the elders felt no need to seek his counsel regarding their current course of action. This was a fatal mistake. They would soon make an even greater mistake, resulting in a horrific loss.

Refusing to consult with God before making important decisions often leads to disaster.

1. Francis D. Nichol, ed., *The Seventh-day Adventist Bible Commentary*, vol. 2 (Washington, DC: Review and Herald®, 1976), 469.
2. Nichol, 470, 471.

VICTORY IS ASSURED

*Let us fetch the ark of the covenant of the LORD out
of Shiloh unto us, that, when it cometh among us,
it may save us out of the hand of our enemies.*

—1 Samuel 4:3

The elders met and decided on a new strategy. The ark of the covenant had always brought victory. Perhaps what was needed was something to revive the troops. Remembering past triumphs might bolster Israel with fresh optimism and courage. Therefore, they sent to Shiloh for the ark, thinking, "It may save us out of the hand of our enemies" (1 Samuel 4:3). "They did not consider that it was the law of God which alone gave to the ark its sacredness, and that its presence would bring them prosperity only as they obeyed that law."[1]

"The two sons of Eli, Hophni and Phinehas, eagerly acceded to the proposal to bear the ark into the camp. Without the consent of the high priest, they ventured presumptuously into the holy of holies, and took from thence the ark of God. Filled with pride, and elated with the expectation of speedy victory, they bore it to the camp. And the people beholding, as they thought, the token of Jehovah's presence, 'shouted with a great shout, so that the earth rang again.' "[2] The Philistines heard the shout and knew exactly what it meant. God had come into the camp of the Israelites. Israel appeared unbeatable. But David tells us in Psalm 78:60, 61, 64, "[God] forsook the tabernacle of Shiloh . . . and delivered his strength into captivity; and his glory into the enemy's hand. . . . Their priests fell by the sword." It was all too true. Thirty thousand men died that day. Hophni and Phinehas were among those slain protecting the ark. It was complete chaos as men deserted and fled for home, seeking safety individually.

"The most terrifying calamity that could occur had befallen Israel. The ark of God had been captured, and was in the possession of the enemy. The glory had indeed departed from Israel when the symbol of the abiding presence and power of Jehovah was removed from the midst of them. . . . It had brought no victory. It had not proved a defense on this occasion, and there was mourning throughout Israel."[3]

Historically, when a nation rejects God's law, certain doom follows.

---

1. Ellen G. White, "The Glory Departed From Israel," *Signs of the Times*®, December 22, 1881, 1.
2. White, 1.
3. Ellen G. White, *Patriarchs and Prophets* (Mountain View, CA: Pacific Press®, 1943), 584.

ICHABOD

*And she named the child Ichabod, saying, The glory is
departed from Israel: because the ark of God was taken,
and because of her father in law and her husband.*
—1 Samuel 4:21

A ccording to Josephus, "Eli had at this time resigned his high priesthood in favor of Phinehas, but as the ark left Shiloh, he instructed
his sons that 'if they pretended to survive the taking of the ark,
they should come no more into his presence' (*Antiquities* v. 11.2)."[1] "When
the army went out to battle, Eli, blind and old, had tarried at Shiloh. It was
with troubled forebodings that he awaited the result of the conflict. . . .

"At length a Benjamite from the army, 'with his clothes rent, and with
earth upon his head,' came hurrying up the ascent leading to the city.
Passing heedlessly the aged man beside the way, he rushed on to the
town, and repeated to eager throngs the tidings of defeat and loss.

"The sound of wailing and lamentation reached the watcher beside
the tabernacle. The messenger was brought to him. And the man said
unto Eli, 'Israel is fled before the Philistines, and there hath been also a
great slaughter among the people, and thy two sons also, Hophni and
Phinehas, are dead.' Eli could endure all this, terrible as it was, for he
had expected it. But when the messenger added, 'And the ark of God is
taken,' a look of unutterable anguish passed over his countenance. The
thought that his sin had thus dishonored God and caused Him to withdraw His presence from Israel was more than he could bear; his strength
was gone, he fell, 'and his neck brake, and he died.' "[2]

The wife of Phinehas, a God-fearing woman, was pregnant and near
delivery. The news of the death of her husband and father-in-law and
the loss of the ark brought on labor. The midwives told her, "Fear not;
for thou hast born a son" (1 Samuel 4:20). With her dying breath, she
named him Ichabod, "inglorious." She believed the last hope for Israel
was gone.

*"The presence of God should always be accounted the greatest blessing, and
the loss of His presence and restraining power over evil should be dreaded as the
direst calamity."*[3]

---

1. Francis D. Nichol, ed., *The Seventh-day Adventist Bible Commentary*, vol. 2 (Washington,
DC: Review and Herald®, 1976), 471.
2. Ellen G. White, *Patriarchs and Prophets* (Mountain View, CA: Pacific Press®, 1943), 585.
3. Nichol, *The Seventh-day Adventist Bible Commentary*, 2:472.

THE SPOILS OF WAR

And the Philistines took the ark of God,
and brought it from Ebenezer unto Ashdod.

—1 Samuel 5:1

A careful study of Ps. 78:60–64 together with Jer. 7:12; 26:6, 9 indicates that God permitted the Philistines not only to discomfit the people of Israel at Ebenezer but probably also to pursue them northeast to Shiloh. The Philistines left part of their army to guard the prize they had taken from Israel, for it was from the camp of Israel (1 Sam. 5:1) that they started their return journey to the cities of the plain."[1]

The victorious Philistines took the ark back to the city of Ashdod and placed it in the temple of Dagon, their principal deity. Entering the temple the next morning, "they beheld a sight which filled them with consternation. Dagon had fallen upon his face to the earth before the ark of Jehovah. The priests reverently lifted the idol and restored it to its place. But the next morning they found it, strangely mutilated, again lying upon the earth before the ark. The upper part of this idol was like that of a man, and the lower part was in the likeness of a fish. Now every part that resembled the human form had been cut off, and only the body of the fish remained. Priests and people were horror-struck; they looked upon this mysterious event as an evil omen, foreboding destruction to themselves and their idols before the God of the Hebrews. They now removed the ark from their temple and placed it in a building by itself."[2]

Their remedy for the disaster was to be short lived. Now a plague of painful, tumorlike swellings fell upon the people of Ashdod. "Remembering the plagues that were inflicted upon Egypt by the God of Israel, the people attributed their afflictions to the presence of the ark among them. It was decided to convey it to Gath. But the plague followed close upon its removal, and the men of that city sent it to Ekron."[3]

"Wherever iniquity is cherished, there, swift and unerring, the divine judgments will follow."[4]

---

1. Francis D. Nichol, ed., *The Seventh-day Adventist Bible Commentary*, vol. 2 (Washington, DC: Review and Herald®, 1976), 473.
2. Ellen G. White, *Patriarchs and Prophets* (Mountain View, CA: Pacific Press®, 1943), 586.
3. White, 586.
4. White, 586.

DIVINE GUIDANCE

Therefore they sent the ark of God to Ekron.

—1 Samuel 5:10

N o city seemed safe from the plague that followed the ark. "Each city, in turn, sent the ark on to a neighboring city. Finally, it arrived at Ekron, the northernmost of the five principal cities of Philistia. The cry of that city was one of indignation at having something forced on them without their consent."[1] The city of Ekron thought it wise to locate the ark in an open field rather than risk placing it in their city. A plague of mice overran their fields and storerooms. Their crops were destroyed, and famine loomed. For seven months, the ark remained in Philistia, and Israel made no effort to retrieve it.

The Philistines finally consulted their astrologers, spirit mediums, and soothsayers, desperate for an answer to what literally plagued them. These wise men counseled that the ark must be returned to the Israelites with an appropriate offering to appease their offended God.

"The ark, with the golden trespass offering [1 Samuel 6:4], was placed upon a new cart, thus precluding all danger of defilement; to this cart, or car, were attached two kine [cows] upon whose necks a yoke had never been placed. Their calves were shut up at home, and the cows were left free to go where they pleased. If the ark should thus be returned to the Israelites by the way of Beth-shemesh, the nearest city of the Levites, the Philistines would accept this as evidence that the God of Israel had done unto them this great evil; 'but if not,' they said, 'then we shall know that it is not His hand that smote us; it was a chance that happened to us.'

"On being set free, the kine turned from their young and, lowing as they went, took the direct road to Beth-shemesh. Guided by no human hand, the patient animals kept on their way."[2]

If only humans would faithfully submit to follow the guiding hand of the Master as did those animals.

---

1. Francis D. Nichol, ed., *The Seventh-day Adventist Bible Commentary*, vol. 2 (Washington, DC: Review and Herald®, 1976), 474.
2. Ellen G. White, *Patriarchs and Prophets* (Mountain View, CA: Pacific Press®, 1943), 588.

IRREVERENT CURIOSITY

*[God] smote the men of Bethshemesh, because
they had looked into the ark of the LORD.*

—1 Samuel 6:19

I t was harvesttime in Israel, and men were in their fields when the cart carrying the ark came to a stop in the field of a man named Joshua. As the ark had stopped near a large stone, the Levites placed the ark upon the stone, and then, breaking up the cart, they offered the cattle as a burnt offering to the Lord. The Philistine leaders who had followed the ark now returned to a plague-free Ekron with the belief that their calamities had been a judgment from the God of Israel.

Rather than prepare a suitable place for the ark to rest, these men of Beth-shemesh allowed the ark to remain on a rock in the middle of the field. "As they continued to gaze upon the sacred chest and to talk of the wonderful manner in which it had been restored, they began to conjecture wherein lay its peculiar power. At last, overcome by curiosity, they removed the coverings and ventured to open it.

"All Israel had been taught to regard the ark with awe and reverence. When required to remove it from place to place the Levites were not so much as to look upon it. Only once a year was the high priest permitted to behold the ark of God. Even the heathen Philistines had not dared to remove its coverings. Angels of heaven, unseen, ever attended it in all its journeyings. The irreverent daring of the people at Beth-shemesh was speedily punished. Many were smitten with sudden death."[1]

Many commentators agree—seventy men from fifty families were slain. This would have constituted a large share of the male population of such a small town. The Philistines, no doubt, heard of the judgment and rejoiced that they had not been so reckless as to open the ark. Remarkably, the survivors of Beth-shemesh did not repent of their sin in opening the ark. Instead, with superstitious fear, they wanted it removed from their midst. Therefore, they sent a message to the inhabitants of Kirjath-jearim, inviting them to take it away.

"The spirit of irreverent curiosity still exists among the children of men. Many are eager to investigate those mysteries which infinite wisdom has seen fit to leave unrevealed."[2]

---

1. Ellen G. White, *Patriarchs and Prophets* (Mountain View, CA: Pacific Press®, 1943), 589.
2. Ellen G. White, "The Ark Restored," *Signs of the Times®*, January 19, 1882, 1.

FORSAKING IDOLATRY—AGAIN

And as Samuel was offering up the burnt offering,
the Philistines drew near to battle against Israel.
—1 Samuel 7:10

S amuel reenters the narrative for the first time since being mentioned at the Battle of Aphek. The ark is now safely housed in the forest city of Kirjath-jearim, near Jerusalem—a location further from the Philistine border and more easily defended—not that the Philistines want the ark returned after the ordeal they just endured. Eleazar, son of Abinadab, will tend the ark.

For forty years, during the time of Samson and Eli, Israel had been oppressed by the Philistines. Commerce and worship had so mingled the Israelites with the Canaanites that the worship of Baal and Ashtoreth, the Canaanite gods of reproduction and nature, had replaced the God of Israel. But now, a new generation turned to Samuel for guidance. "Samuel knew that if the people forsook their idolatry and refused to serve the Philistine gods, this would be interpreted as equivalent to rebellion against Philistine supremacy, and of course meant war. But Samuel had confidence in God's promises and went forward to inspire a forlorn people with hope."[1]

A large congregation representing all the tribes of Israel gathered at Mizpah and held a solemn fast. The leaders confessed their sins and appointed Samuel as judge. The congregants had assembled peacefully, but "the Philistines interpreted this gathering to be a council of war, and with a strong force set out to disperse the Israelites before their plans could be matured. . . .

"While Samuel was in the act of presenting a lamb as a burnt offering, the Philistines drew near for battle. Then the Mighty One who had descended upon Sinai amid fire and smoke and thunder, who had parted the Red Sea and made a way through Jordan for the children of Israel, again manifested His power. A terrible storm burst upon the advancing host, and the earth was strewn with the dead bodies of mighty warriors."[2]

"Anything which tends to abate our love for God, or to interfere with the service due him, becomes thereby an idol."[3]

---

1. Francis D. Nichol, ed., *The Seventh-day Adventist Bible Commentary*, vol. 2 (Washington, DC: Review and Herald®, 1976), 481.

2. Ellen G. White, *Patriarchs and Prophets* (Mountain View, CA: Pacific Press®, 1943), 590, 591.

3. Ellen G. White, "The Victory at Ebenezer," *Signs of the Times®*, January 26, 1882, 1.

AFTER THE STORM

*So the Philistines were subdued, and they came no
more into the coast of Israel: and the hand of the LORD
was against the Philistines all the days of Samuel.*

—1 Samuel 7:13

The defenseless Israelites beheld the hand of the Lord. "Having renounced their idols and confessed their departure from the Lord, in humiliation of spirit, they were to witness how readily God took them back under His protection, and demonstrated a heavenly Father's love for the returning prodigal. God neither expressed bitterness nor held aloof. . . . Immediately He spread over them His protecting arm."[1] Realizing God had accepted their repentance, the Israelites took up the weapons of the fallen Philistines and pursued them.

"Along the way they [the Philistines] were harassed by the assembled Israelites. And there, as Isaiah declared centuries later, God graciously gave them at once 'beauty for ashes, the oil of joy for mourning' (Isa. 61:3)."[2] Thus came about a complete reversal of the stunning defeat of twenty years prior that saw Israel defeated and the ark taken.

"It was the Lord's purpose so to manifest his power in delivering Israel, that they might not take the glory to themselves. He permitted them, when unarmed and defenseless, to be challenged by their enemies, and then the Captain of the Lord's host marshalled the army of Heaven to destroy the foes of his people."[3] "The Philistines were now so completely subdued that they surrendered the strongholds which had been taken from Israel and refrained from acts of hostility for many years. Other nations followed this example, and the Israelites enjoyed peace until the close of Samuel's sole administration.

"That the occasion might never be forgotten, Samuel set up, between Mizpeh and Shen, a great stone as a memorial. He called the name of it Ebenezer, 'the stone of help,' saying to the people, 'hitherto hath Jehovah helped us.' "[4]

God is ever our "Ebenezer"! In times of distress, it is comforting to recall instances of divine intervention in our past Christian experience and take heart.

---

1. Francis D. Nichol, ed., *The Seventh-day Adventist Bible Commentary*, vol. 2 (Washington, DC: Review and Herald®, 1976), 482.
2. Nichol, 482, 483.
3. Ellen G. White, "The Victory at Ebenezer," *Signs of the Times*®, January 26, 1882, 1.
4. Ellen G. White, *Patriarchs and Prophets* (Mountain View, CA: Pacific Press®, 1943), 591.

HISTORY REPEATS ITSELF

And his sons walked not in his ways, but turned aside
after lucre, and took bribes, and perverted judgment.
—1 Samuel 8:3

It is amazing how many biblical families were dysfunctional! The list begins with the death of Abel at the hands of his brother Cain. Abraham had issues with his two wives and their sons. Jacob and Esau fought over a birthright. Joseph's brothers sold him into slavery. We have seen what Eli's indulgence did to his two sons and what their evil influence did to Israel. David's family was riddled with incest, murder, deceit, and rebellion. Biblical stories were written for our admonition. Family relationships might just be the most difficult challenge facing humankind.

As Samuel aged, he took on his sons, Joel and Abiah, as assistants. "While Samuel continued the duties of his office at Ramah, the young men were stationed at Beersheba, to administer justice among the people near the southern border of the land.

"It was with the full assent of the nation that Samuel had appointed his sons to office, but they did not prove themselves worthy of their father's choice. The Lord had, through Moses, given special directions to His people that the rulers of Israel should judge righteously, deal justly with the widow and the fatherless, and receive no bribes. But the sons of Samuel 'turned aside after lucre, and took bribes, and perverted judgment.' The sons of the prophet had not heeded the precepts which he had sought to impress upon their minds. They had not copied the pure, unselfish life of their father. The warning given to Eli had not exerted the influence upon the mind of Samuel that it should have done. He had been to some extent too indulgent with his sons, and the result was apparent in their character and life."[1]

Samuel realized his two sons, Joel (Jehovah is God) and Abiah (Jehovah is my father), were failing their test of character. Separation from God took away their moral compass. The principles Samuel had tried to instill were no match for their inflated pride of position. That they were representing their earthly father and his reputation made little impact on their actions. That they were representing God as judges of His people likewise never crossed their minds.

Honoring one's parents also means preserving the family name and reputation.

---

1. Ellen G. White, *Patriarchs and Prophets* (Mountain View, CA: Pacific Press®, 1943), 604.

UNGRATEFUL ELDERS

Behold, thou art old, and thy sons walk not in thy ways:
now make us a king to judge us like all the nations.
—1 Samuel 8:5

Samuel had judged Israel from his youth. He had been a righteous and impartial judge, faithful in all his work. He was becoming old; and the people saw that his sons did not follow his footsteps. Although they were not vile, like the children of Eli, yet they were dishonest and double-minded. While they aided their father in his laborious work, their love of reward led them to favor the cause of the unrighteous."[1]

Israel's tribal elders came to Samuel and asked him to appoint a king to judge them like all the nations. God had told Moses the people would eventually ask for a king "like as all the nations" (Deuteronomy 17:14). This must have hurt Samuel deeply, for they were seeking no less than to replace him. The Israelites once again were reasoning without asking God for guidance. Samuel tried to warn them that this decision would bring upon them a curse, but they added a second reason for wanting a king. A king would fight their battles for them. Having lost sight of the times the Lord had interposed and led them to victory over their enemies, they sought tribal consolidation under a king for mutual defense against invaders.

"Israel again proceeded to do precisely what they had done for centuries—move without awaiting divine guidance. . . . Although the elders were probably moved solely by political motives, Samuel showed them the better way—seeking the Lord in prayer."[2] The elders had not considered future consequences beyond solving their immediate invasion problem. "At the beginning of his judgeship Samuel had shown the people that the real solution of their troubles was not a change of administration but rather a change of heart, a contrite turning to the Lord."[3]

Do not be too quick to judge the Israelites for failing to consult God regarding their plans. Modern-day Christians too often do the same thing.

1. Ellen G. White, *The Spirit of Prophecy*, vol. 1 (Battle Creek, MI: Seventh-day Adventist Pub. Assn., 1870), 353.
2. Francis D. Nichol, ed., *The Seventh-day Adventist Bible Commentary*, vol. 2 (Washington, DC: Review and Herald®, 1976), 485.
3. Nichol, 488.

GOD'S REPLY

The LORD said unto Samuel, Hearken unto the voice of the people in all that they say unto thee: for they have not rejected thee, but they have rejected me, that I should not reign over them.
—1 Samuel 8:7

When men choose to have their own way, without seeking counsel from God, or in opposition to His revealed will, He often grants their desires, in order that, through the bitter experience that follows, they may be led to realize their folly and to repent of their sin."[1] The decision of the elders to ask for a king was shortsighted for several reasons:

1. "Under the judges God had made each tribe virtually independent. Taxes were extremely low. . . .
2. "God had given every Israelite considerable individual freedom in earning a livelihood, in choosing his own form of worship, and in administering his own affairs in general. . . .
3. ". . . There was no such thing as hereditary succession; judges were raised up by God from time to time, on the basis of personal qualifications. . . .
4. "Over and over again when Israel had sought the Lord for counsel, He miraculously protected them from the attacks of the enemy. . . .
5. ". . . Under God's guidance mistakes could become steppingstones to a greater knowledge of God and His plan of salvation."[2]

"And still the longing to conform to worldly practices and customs exists among the professed people of God. As they depart from the Lord they become ambitious for the gains and honors of the world. Christians are constantly seeking to imitate the practices of those who worship the god of this world."[3]

Are you content to let leaders dictate your thoughts as long as they do not disturb your possessions or ease? Christians should stand apart as different (1 Peter 2:9)!

---

1. Ellen G. White, *Patriarchs and Prophets* (Mountain View, CA: Pacific Press®, 1943), 605, 606.
2. Francis D. Nichol, ed., *The Seventh-day Adventist Bible Commentary*, vol. 2 (Washington, DC: Review and Herald®, 1976), 486.
3. White, *Patriarchs and Prophets*, 607.

A Choice Young Man

And he had a son, whose name was Saul, a choice young
man, and a goodly: and there was not among the children
of Israel a goodlier person than he: from his shoulders
and upward he was higher than any of the people.
—1 Samuel 9:2

Humanity often places value on those things which are of little consequence. The people of Israel judged their king based on outward appearance. That he was tall and of regal bearing was foremost in their criteria, for he must measure up to the kings of the nations surrounding them. This human mistake was made clear to Samuel when he anointed David. God told him, "Man looketh on the outward appearance, but the LORD looketh on the heart" (1 Samuel 16:7).

"Saul was the son of a powerful and wealthy chief, yet in accordance with the simplicity of the times he was engaged with his father in the humble duties of a husbandman. Some of his father's animals having strayed upon the mountains, Saul went with a servant to seek for them. For three days they searched in vain, when, as they were not far from Ramah, the home of Samuel, the servant proposed that they should inquire of the prophet concerning the missing property."[1]

After trudging over hills and valleys for three days, any option was enticing. Saul was concerned, however, that he had no present to give to the prophet as was customary when asking a favor. The servant insisted they should go see Samuel. "Behold, I have here at hand the fourth part of a shekel of silver: that will I give to the man of God, to tell us our way" (1 Samuel 9:8).

Approaching the city, they asked where they might find the seer. Some girls informed them a religious service was about to start and Samuel would be present to offer a sacrifice. The service would be followed by a sacrificial feast. "On what apparently inconsequential incidents does the destiny of races and peoples often depend! Saul set out to find the lost asses . . . , little dreaming that the day had come for him to assume the responsibilities of a kingdom!"[2]

"Humble yourselves therefore under the mighty hand of God, that he may exalt you in due time" (1 Peter 5:6).

---

1. Ellen G. White, *Patriarchs and Prophets* (Mountain View, CA: Pacific Press®, 1943), 608.
2. Francis D. Nichol, ed., *The Seventh-day Adventist Bible Commentary*, vol. 2 (Washington, DC: Review and Herald®, 1976), 490.

FINDING THE SEER

*Then Saul drew near to Samuel in the gate, and said,
Tell me, I pray thee, where the seer's house is. And
Samuel answered Saul, and said, I am the seer.*
—1 Samuel 9:18, 19

God had revealed to Samuel that at that time the chosen king of Israel would present himself before him. As they now stood face to face, the Lord said to Samuel, 'Behold the man whom I spake to thee of! This same shall reign over My people.' "[1] "Before Saul spoke, Samuel knew that he was the man of whom the Lord had told him the previous day."[2]

Samuel first answered the pressing question on Saul's mind. The missing livestock had been found. This information convinced Saul that Samuel was indeed the seer; for how could he otherwise have answered a question before it was asked? Samuel urged Saul to remain in town for the sacrificial feast.

"Though himself a prophet and a judge, Samuel accepted the counsel of the Lord that Israel be granted the desire of their hearts. He expressed no feelings of regret or jealousy at meeting the young man who was to take over the responsibility of delivering Israel from the hand of the Philistines (v. 16). Instead, he accorded Saul evidences of honor and respect (see vs. 20–24). . . . Samuel not only indicated that he was willing to give Saul the responsibility, but also that he would do all in his power to prepare the future king for his duties."[3]

"Saul was not told of his high calling that day. Evidently Samuel spent some time in explaining to his guest the great principles of the theocratic government that had now been in operation for centuries, and the implications of the changes urged by the elders. But the unexpected events of the day did not apparently weigh heavily on the heart of Saul, for he slept until called by the prophet the next morning."[4]

Would you have been as gracious in greeting a person selected to take your place as Samuel?

---

1. Ellen G. White, *Patriarchs and Prophets* (Mountain View, CA: Pacific Press®, 1943), 609.
2. Francis D. Nichol, ed., *The Seventh-day Adventist Bible Commentary*, vol. 2 (Washington, DC: Review and Herald®, 1976), 491.
3. Nichol, 491.
4. Nichol, 492.

THE CAPTAIN OF ISRAEL

*Then Samuel took a vial of oil, and poured it upon his head,
and kissed him, and said, Is it not because the LORD hath
anointed thee to be captain over his inheritance?*
—1 Samuel 10:1

After telling Saul's servant to go on, Samuel told Saul to stop and receive a message from God: Saul would soon be king of all Israel! "As evidence that this was done by divine authority, he foretold the incidents that would occur on the homeward journey and assured Saul that he would be qualified by the Spirit of God for the station awaiting him."[1] Saul would experience three specific signs or encounters on his journey home:

The first encounter would occur by Rachel's tomb at Zelzah, where Saul would meet two men. They would tell him his father's livestock had been found, and his father was eager for his return.

In his second encounter, he would meet three men going up to worship God at Bethel. One would be carrying three young goats for a burnt offering, another three loaves of bread, and the third a skin of wine for the sacrificial feast. They would greet Saul and give him two of their loaves of bread.

The third sign would occur near the Philistine garrison at Gibeah. Saul would meet a group of prophets chanting praises to God. He would receive the Spirit of God and join them in their praises.

After these signs, Saul was to return home and wait one week for Samuel to come to him. Then Samuel would tell Saul what the Lord required of him. "Evidence of the foreknowledge of God . . . encouraged Saul to accept the responsibility to which he was now called."[2]

"To the humble and willing heart God multiplies evidence of the way in which to go. . . . And the beauty of it all is that He has a thousand ways in which to manifest these evidences."[3]

---

1. Ellen G. White, *Patriarchs and Prophets* (Mountain View, CA: Pacific Press®, 1943), 610.
2. Francis D. Nichol, ed., *The Seventh-day Adventist Bible Commentary*, vol. 2 (Washington, DC: Review and Herald®, 1976), 494.
3. Nichol, 494.

SAUL BECOMES A NEW MAN

And it was so, that when he had turned his back
to go from Samuel, God gave him another heart.
—1 Samuel 10:9

The Lord would not leave Saul to be placed in a position of trust without divine enlightenment. He was to have a new calling, and the Spirit of the Lord came upon him. The effect was that he was changed into a new man. The Lord gave Saul a new spirit, other thoughts, other aims and desires, than he had previously had."[1]

"God was ready to transform Saul's vision, ambition, and aspirations in such a way that the things of God would become to him the all-important issues of life. . . . God first answered the plea for personal guidance, and then invited Saul to accept His guidance in matters that affected the welfare of the entire nation. So it is today. God takes men where He finds them and invites them to fulfill His own glorious plan for their lives."[2]

"The reality of the transformation becomes apparent as changes occur in the thoughts, the habits, the life. Old things pass away; all things become new (2 Cor. 5:17). But it must be remembered that such a change becomes permanent only with the daily reaffirmation of the choice thus made. . . . How many men, today as in ancient times, wear the badge, 'might-have-been.' "[3]

"Saul had a mind and influence capable of governing a kingdom, if his powers had been submitted to the control of God, but the very endowments that qualified him for doing good could be used by Satan, when surrendered to his power, and would enable him to exert widespread influence for evil. He could be more sternly vindictive, more injurious and determined in prosecuting his unholy designs, than could others, because of the superior powers of mind and heart that had been given him of God."[4]

"Brethren, give diligence to make your calling and election sure: for if ye do these things, ye shall never fall" (2 Peter 1:10).

---

1. Ellen G. White, *Christ Triumphant* (Hagerstown, MD: Review and Herald®, 1999), 142.
2. Francis D. Nichol, ed., *The Seventh-day Adventist Bible Commentary*, vol. 2 (Washington, DC: Review and Herald®, 1976), 495.
3. Nichol, 495.
4. Ellen G. White, "The Death of Samuel," *Signs of the Times*®, October 19, 1888, 2.

A GATHERING OF THE TRIBES

And Samuel called the people together unto the LORD to Mizpeh.
—1 Samuel 10:17

The anointing of Saul as king had not been made known to the nation. The choice of God was to be publicly manifested by lot. For this purpose Samuel convoked the people at Mizpeh. Prayer was offered for divine guidance; then followed the solemn ceremony of casting the lot. In silence the assembled multitude awaited the issue. . . . Saul, the son of Kish, was pointed out as the individual chosen. But Saul was not in the assembly. Burdened with a sense of the great responsibility about to fall upon him, he had secretly withdrawn. He was brought back to the congregation, who observed with pride and satisfaction that he was of kingly bearing and noble form, being 'higher than any of the people from his shoulders and upward.' Even Samuel, when presenting him to the assembly, exclaimed, 'See ye him whom the Lord hath chosen, that there is none like him among all the people?' "[1]

"Many raise the question, Why did God choose Saul as king, knowing full well the life he would lead? . . . God chose in harmony with their wishes, to prove to them: (1) that He did not limit their freedom of choice, (2) that in spite of their unwise choice He would restrain the evil influences that came with the monarchy, (3) that they must learn by experience that what a man sows he must also reap, and (4) that national departure from the path of God's choosing does not prevent individuals within that nation from living in harmony with His will and receiving His blessing."[2]

"While the people in general were ready to acknowledge Saul as their king, there was a large party in opposition. For a monarch to be chosen from Benjamin, the smallest of the tribes of Israel—and that to the neglect of both Judah and Ephraim, the largest and most powerful—was a slight which they could not brook. They refused to profess allegiance to Saul or to bring him the customary presents."[3]

When a question put to God does not yield the answer you desire, how do you react?

---

1. Ellen G. White, *Patriarchs and Prophets* (Mountain View, CA: Pacific Press®, 1943), 611.
2. Francis D. Nichol, ed., *The Seventh-day Adventist Bible Commentary*, vol. 2 (Washington, DC: Review and Herald®, 1976), 497.
3. White, *Patriarchs and Prophets*, 611, 612.

THE HISTORY OF JABESH-GILEAD

So all the men of Israel were gathered against the city, knit together
as one man. And the tribes of Israel sent men through all the tribe of
Benjamin, saying, What wickedness is this that is done among you?
—Judges 20:11, 12

A brief history lesson might be in order at this point. A Levite was traveling with his servant and concubine through the area of Israel allotted to the tribe of Benjamin. Arriving at nightfall in the town of Gibeah, he sat down in the street as no rooms were available to rent. An old man, returning from working in the fields, invited him to his house for the night. As they were eating, a group of riotous young men stood outside shouting, "Bring forth the man that came into thine house, that we may know him" (Judges 19:22).

Refusing their homosexual advances, the Levite offered his concubine instead. In the morning, she was found abused and dead on the doorstep. Upon arriving home, the Levite, seeking justice, divided her body and sent a piece to each of the eleven tribes. The tribes gathered and, upon hearing the details of the outrage, swore revenge. They petitioned the people of Gibeah to deliver up the perpetrators so that they would face judgment. The tribe of Benjamin refused to surrender the guilty parties, thereby condoning their actions.

Twice the alliance of tribes attacked Gibeah, and each time suffered defeat. Their third attempt drew most of the city's defenders outside the walls. Part of the army waited until these defenders passed, then they attacked the few guards left in the city. All were slain, and the city was burned. When the warriors of Benjamin looked back and saw their city in flames, they panicked and were slaughtered. Justice had been served.

A rash oath had been taken by the armies of Israel that any city not joining the battle for justice should die (Judges 21:5), and no daughter should be given in marriage to a Benjaminite. It was discovered no warrior from Jabesh-gilead had answered the summons. Israel's armies attacked and wiped out the residents of Jabesh-gilead, saving only four hundred innocent virgins. These were offered as wives to the survivors of Benjamin to preserve the tribe (v. 14). Jabesh-gilead severed ties with all tribes west of the Jordan. The stage was now set for what happened next.

"In those days there was no king in Israel; every man did that which was right in his own eyes" (Judges 21:25).

THE PRICE OF SERVITUDE

Then Nahash the Ammonite came up,
and encamped against Jabeshgilead.

—1 Samuel 11:1

T he city of Jabesh-gilead lay east of the Jordan River in the foot-hills of Gilead. Long before Saul's time, the nation of Ammon had held Israel in slavery for eighteen years until Jephthah defeated them in battle (Judges 11:32). Now, once again, the nation of Ammon rose up, under their king Nahash, and sought to reclaim all the land east of Jordan. Jabesh was alone—outnumbered, surrounded, and apparently doomed.

Believing they could not succeed in battle, the men of Jabesh sought terms from Nahash. His response was brutal: "On this condition will I make a covenant with you, that I may thrust out all your right eyes, and lay it for a reproach upon all Israel" (1 Samuel 11:2). This would render all men of war useless as their damaged depth perception would not allow proper aiming of weapons. "It was not that Nahash had any special grudge against the elders of Jabesh more than the rest of Israel; his purpose was to show contempt for all Israel by inflicting injury on some of their number."[1] The elders of besieged Jabesh requested seven days to formulate a response. Nahash agreed, thinking a delay would not change their fate and might add prestige to the victory. But messengers slipped through the lines and made their way to the tribes west of the Jordan. They held little hope that their request for assistance would be granted, but they had to try.

"Jabesh-gilead had risen from the ruin of earlier days, but its inhabitants had probably not forgotten their brutal punishment following the affair with Benjamin. . . .

"It would seem that since Israel's servitude under the Ammonites, Jabesh had more or less withdrawn from association with even nearby tribes such as Issachar, Ephraim, and Benjamin. . . . They were not even sure that the tribes would make any response to their plea. In sheer desperation they virtually acknowledged their shortcomings and threw themselves upon the mercy of their fellow Israelites, whom they had neglected in the past."[2]

"Thank God for the thousand ways He has out of every difficulty!"[3]

1. Francis D. Nichol, ed., *The Seventh-day Adventist Bible Commentary*, vol. 2 (Washington, DC: Review and Herald®, 1976), 499.

2. Nichol, 499.

3. Nichol, 499.

SAUL PROVES HIMSELF IN BATTLE

Saul put the people in three companies; and they came into the midst
of the host in the morning watch, and slew the Ammonites until the
heat of the day: and it came to pass, that they which remained were
scattered, so that two of them were not left together.
—1 Samuel 11:11

S aul had been plowing in the fields and was returning home to Gibeah with his oxen when messengers arrived from Jabesh. When told the news, the Spirit of the Lord came upon Saul, and he was outraged. History was repeated in another call to arms accompanied by body parts. Cutting up his oxen, he sent pieces to each of the tribes, saying, "Whosoever cometh not forth after Saul and after Samuel, so shall it be done unto his oxen. And the fear of the LORD fell on the people, and they came out with one consent" (1 Samuel 11:7).

The response to Saul's call to arms was enthusiastic. Around 330,000 warriors gathered at Bezek, ten miles southwest of Jabesh-gilead. Here, Samuel and Saul would form the tribes into a cohesive unit. "From Bezek, more than 1,000 ft. above sea level, the armies would descend via the *Wadi el-Khashneh* to the Jordan, at this point about 900 ft. below sea level. . . . This gathering of armed men could be accomplished within a period of six days, and by marching from Bezek during the night Saul could reach Jabesh early in the morning of the seventh day. By the morning of the sixth day Saul had enough of an army present to assure the elders of Jabesh that they would have help on time."[1] Meanwhile, Jabesh's elders told Nahash that on the last day agreed they would surrender, and he could do with them as he wished.

"Saul did not stop to ask why the elders of Jabesh had not come to Samuel when a king was to be appointed. He did not inquire concerning their past, whatever it might be. They were in need, and the Holy Spirit took possession of him in bringing them help."[2] A rapid march brought the army to Jabesh at first light. Dividing his men into three columns, as had Gideon, Saul fell on the unprepared Ammonite camp. The battle lasted from sunrise until noon, resulting in total victory for the forces of Israel. The siege was lifted, and the citizens of Jabesh rejoiced.

With God on your side, anything is possible (see Matthew 19:26).

---

1. Francis D. Nichol, ed., *The Seventh-day Adventist Bible Commentary*, vol. 2 (Washington, DC: Review and Herald®, 1976), 500.
2. Nichol, 500.

SAUL CROWNED KING

And all the people went to Gilgal; and there
they made Saul king before the LORD.

—1 Samuel 11:15

The promptness and bravery of Saul, as well as the generalship shown in the successful conduct of so large a force, were qualities which the people of Israel had desired in a monarch, that they might be able to cope with other nations. They now greeted him as their king, attributing the honor of the victory to human agencies and forgetting that without God's special blessing all their efforts would have been in vain. In their enthusiasm some proposed to put to death those who had at first refused to acknowledge the authority of Saul. But the king interfered, saying, 'There shall not a man be put to death this day: for today the Lord hath wrought salvation in Israel.' Here Saul gave evidence of the change that had taken place in his character. Instead of taking honor to himself, he gave the glory to God. Instead of showing a desire for revenge, he manifested a spirit of compassion and forgiveness. This is unmistakable evidence that the grace of God dwells in the heart."[1]

Saul was willing to let those who initially opposed his selection as king be given a pass. "If because of recent developments an enemy could be changed into a friend, greater would be the advantage than if he were put to death. Exactly the same Spirit was now speaking through Saul as spoke through Christ in His Sermon on the Mount [Matthew 5:44]."[2] Forgiveness is a Christian virtue.

Samuel now suggested Israel gather at Gilgal to crown Saul king. "When the shouts of welcome to the king had died away, the aged prophet gave his parting words as ruler of the nation.

" 'Behold,' he said, 'I have hearkened unto your voice in all that ye said unto me, and have made a king over you. And now, behold, the king walketh before you: and I am old and gray-headed; . . . and I have walked before you from my childhood unto this day.' "[3] Samuel then called Israel to witness before God that he had been fair and defrauded no one during his ministry.

The true Christian is always honest and never vindictive.

---

1. Ellen G. White, *Patriarchs and Prophets* (Mountain View, CA: Pacific Press®, 1943), 613.
2. Francis D. Nichol, ed., *The Seventh-day Adventist Bible Commentary*, vol. 2 (Washington, DC: Review and Herald®, 1976), 501.
3. White, *Patriarchs and Prophets*, 614.

SAMUEL DEFENDS HIMSELF

And they said, Thou hast not defrauded us, nor oppressed
us, neither hast thou taken ought of any man's hand.
—1 Samuel 12:4

The kingdom of God is based upon the principle of free choice. The fact that God knows the end from the beginning does not in any way limit man's making his own decisions. . . . When God made known to the people before they entered Palestine that the time would come when they would ask for a king (Deut. 17:14), He was not expressing His will in the matter, but only unfolding to them the course events would take."[1]

Being replaced by a king, Samuel would no longer be called upon to judge the people as he had since his calling as a child. He would still be God's spokesperson and, in this way, direct the people, but much of his authority would now pass to a monarch. But Samuel would never abandon the people he served. He had a sacred mission to safeguard the nation's spirituality.

"It was a time of great crisis for Samuel, and he felt that to a large extent the convincing quality of the message he was about to present depended upon his own integrity of character. Except for this his counsel would have little weight."[2] The people were convinced that all he had done throughout his life of ministry was for the good of the nation.

"Samuel was not seeking merely to justify his own course. He had previously set forth the principles that should govern both the king and the people, and he desired to add to his words the weight of his own example. From childhood he had been connected with the work of God, and during his long life one object had been ever before him—the glory of God and the highest good of Israel."[3]

"The honor accorded him who is concluding his work is of far more worth than the applause and congratulations which those receive who are just entering upon their duties, and who have yet to be tested."[4]

---

1. Francis D. Nichol, ed., *The Seventh-day Adventist Bible Commentary*, vol. 2 (Washington, DC: Review and Herald®, 1976), 502.
2. Nichol, 503.
3. Ellen G. White, *Patriarchs and Prophets* (Mountain View, CA: Pacific Press®, 1943), 614.
4. Ellen G. White, "The Inauguration at Gilgal," *Signs of the Times®*, July 27, 1882, 1.

OBEY THE VOICE OF THE LORD

If ye will fear the LORD, and serve him, and obey his voice, and not rebel against the commandment of the LORD, then shall both ye and also the king that reigneth over you continue following the LORD your God.
—1 Samuel 12:14

S amuel needed to impress upon the people that the choice they were making was not without danger. They must remember how God had led them in the past and place their trust in Him, not in an earthly king. He, therefore, reminded them of their sinful past and God's continued care. When they turned from Him, their enemies overcame them. Without fail, God heard their prayers for deliverance and provided a liberator. With total disregard for the way God had sustained them in the past, they now wanted an earthly king like the nations around them. Samuel brought them back to their senses: "The LORD your God was your king" (1 Samuel 12:12).

Samuel now called upon the Lord to send thunder and rain upon them to show their wickedness in turning from Him to follow their own path. Since this was May or June in Palestine, the season of the wheat harvest, it was historically a time of balmy skies and no rain. The violent storm that arose caused great fear among the people. In anguish, they implored Samuel, "Pray for thy servants unto the LORD *thy* God, that we die not: for we have added unto all our sins this evil, to ask us a king" (v. 19; emphasis added). The people were asking Samuel to pray to *his* God, not to *their* God. Even in acknowledging their mistake, they still did not understand how far they had drifted from that vital connection with God.

Samuel did not leave the people without hope. "Moreover as for me, God forbid that I should sin against the LORD in ceasing to pray for you: but I will teach you the good and the right way: Only fear the LORD, and serve him in truth with all your heart: for consider how great things he hath done for you. But if ye shall still do wickedly, ye shall be consumed, both ye and your king" (vv. 23–25). Though demoted, Samuel vowed to keep praying for Israel. His love for them was unchanged!

"One of the greatest needs of men today is time for meditation—meditation on God's infinite goodness and the evidences of His care and guidance."[1]

---

1. Francis D. Nichol, ed., *The Seventh-day Adventist Bible Commentary*, vol. 2 (Washington, DC: Review and Herald®, 1976), 505.

FIGHTING THE PHILISTINES AGAIN

*And Saul blew the trumpet throughout all
the land, saying, Let the Hebrews hear.*
—1 Samuel 13:3

The Philistines still held the center of Palestine following their defeat at Ebenezer (1 Samuel 7:10, 11). They maintained strongholds in the hills and had a strong grip on the coastal areas. In an effort to deprive Israel of weapons, the Philistines had not allowed blacksmiths to ply their trade. If a farmer wanted a metal implement, he had to visit a Philistine smithy. The armies of Israel could put their hands on slings and bows, but no one, save Saul and Jonathan, possessed a sword or spear. Israel also had fewer men it could put onto the battlefield. Outnumbered, lacking adequate weaponry, strategically divided, short on equipment, and without a method to even make metal weapons, Israel was oppressed by Philistia. There was peace, but there was no liberty.

Against this backdrop, Saul disbanded his army after the victory at Jabesh-gilead. He kept only two thousand men at his headquarters at Michmash and a thousand men stationed with Jonathan at Gibeah. Saul should have attacked Israel's enemies while he had an army flush with recent victory. Now, two years into his reign, he came to the realization that if Israel was to unite, they must fight. Jonathan struck the first blow.

The Philistines reacted swiftly and raised an army at Michmash to challenge Israel. Saul, having retreated east to Gilgal, now sounded the trumpet, calling all Israel to his aid. Things went poorly from the start. "When the tidings reached Saul and his army at Gilgal, the people were appalled at [the] thought of the mighty forces they would have to encounter in battle. They were not prepared to meet the enemy, and many were so terrified that they dared not come to the test of an encounter. Some crossed the Jordan, while others hid themselves in caves and pits and amid the rocks that abounded in that region. As the time for the encounter drew near, the number of desertions rapidly increased, and those who did not withdraw from the ranks were filled with foreboding and terror."[1] It was in this atmosphere of impending doom that Saul's faith faltered. The morale of his troops hit rock bottom, and he could no longer maintain order in the camp.

Too often, men and women call upon the Lord for assistance only after they have gotten themselves into trouble.

1. Ellen G. White, *Patriarchs and Prophets* (Mountain View, CA: Pacific Press®, 1943), 617.

SACRED DUTIES USURPED

And Saul said, Bring hither a burnt offering to me, and
peace offerings. And he offered the burnt offering.

—1 Samuel 13:9

When Saul was first anointed king of Israel, he had received from Samuel explicit directions concerning the course to be pursued at this time. 'Thou shalt go down before me to Gilgal,' said the prophet; 'and, behold, I will come down unto thee, to offer burnt offerings, and to sacrifice sacrifices of peace offerings: seven days shalt thou tarry, till I come to thee, and show thee what thou shalt do.' 1 Samuel 10:8."[1] But Samuel was late! Saul could have humbly prayed for strength. He could have encouraged belief among the men that God would fight beside them and exercised faith himself. He did none of those things.

With his army now numbering only six hundred men, thousands of Philistines only 11.5 miles away, and no prophet in sight, Saul now feared not only for the nation but his own safety. "The time for the proving of Saul had come. He was now to show whether or not he would depend on God and patiently wait according to His command, thus revealing himself as one whom God could trust in trying places as the ruler of His people, or whether he would be vacillating and unworthy of the sacred responsibility that had devolved upon him."[2] "In detaining Samuel, it was the purpose of God that the heart of Saul should be revealed, that others might know what he would do in an emergency. It was a trying position in which to be placed, but Saul did not obey orders. He felt that it would make no difference who approached God, or in what way; and, full of energy and self-complacency, he put himself forward into the sacred office."[3]

"God had directed that only those consecrated to the office should present sacrifices before Him. But Saul commanded, 'Bring hither a burnt offering;' and, equipped as he was with armor and weapons of war, he approached the altar and offered sacrifice before God."[4]

When you are in a tight spot, to whom do you turn?

---

1. Ellen G. White, *Patriarchs and Prophets* (Mountain View, CA: Pacific Press®, 1943), 617.
2. White, 618.
3. Ellen G. White, "The First King of Israel—No. 2," *Youth's Instructor*, November 17, 1898.
4. White, *Patriarchs and Prophets*, 618.

REBUKED

But now thy kingdom shall not continue: the LORD hath sought him a man after his own heart, and the LORD hath commanded him to be captain over his people, because thou hast not kept that which the LORD commanded thee.

—1 Samuel 13:14

When Samuel finally arrived in the camp of the Israelites, he was deeply troubled by what he saw. To his inquiry, "What have you done?" Saul offered excuses: "The people were deserting. You did not come within the time you had promised, so I had to improvise." "I *forced* myself therefore, and offered a burnt offering" (1 Samuel 13:12; emphasis added). "Saul endeavored to vindicate his own course, and blamed the prophet, instead of condemning himself. . . .

"Had Saul been willing to see and confess his error, this bitter experience would have proved a safeguard for the future. He would afterward have avoided the mistakes which called forth divine reproof. But feeling that he was unjustly condemned, he would, of course, be likely again to commit the same sin.

"The Lord would have his people, under all circumstances, manifest implicit trust in him. Although we cannot always understand the workings of his providence, we should wait with patience and humility until he sees fit to enlighten us."[1]

Unfortunately, Saul did what any one of us might have done under similar circumstances. When rebuked, we often seek to blame others: Samuel was to blame for arriving late; the people were to blame for they were scattering and needed reassurance. Saul was "forced" to do what he did. Saul was not penitent nor did he ask forgiveness. He should have waited on the Lord.

"Saul's transgression proved him unworthy to be entrusted with sacred responsibilities. . . . Had he patiently endured the divine test, the crown would have been confirmed to him and to his house. In fact, Samuel had come to Gilgal for this very purpose. But Saul had been weighed in the balance, and found wanting. He must be removed to make way for one who would sacredly regard the divine honor and authority."[2]

The Bible is replete with stories of transgressors who failed to accept responsibility and excused their sins. Excuses only worsen our transgressions.

---

1. Ellen G. White, "Victory at Michmash," *Signs of the Times*®, August 10, 1882, 1.
2. Ellen G. White, "The Forbidden Sacrifice," *Signs of the Times*®, August 3, 1882, 1.

JONATHAN'S SCOUTING MISSION

Now it came to pass upon a day, that Jonathan the son of Saul said unto the young man that bare his armour, Come, and let us go over to the Philistines' garrison, that is on the other side. But he told not his father.

—1 Samuel 14:1

I n secret, Jonathan decided to take the battle to the Philistines. Knowing the Philistine guards were in a stronghold difficult to assail, he devised a plan. If the enemy sentries assumed he was a deserter from the armies of Israel and invited him to come up, he would take that as a sign God was with him. " 'The enemy's camp was upon a precipice which had three tops, that ended in a small but sharp and long extremity, while there was a rock that surrounded them, like lines made to prevent the attacks of an enemy' ([Josephus,] *Antiquities* vi. 6. 2). Those who have visited the site, on the north side of the precipitous wadi, say the residents still speak of it as 'the fort.' "[1]

At daybreak, upon receiving an invitation from the Philistine sentries to "come up to us" (1 Samuel 14:12), Jonathan and his armor-bearer climbed the near vertical escarpment. "It would have been an easy matter for the Philistines to kill these two brave, daring men; but it did not enter into their minds that these two solitary men had come up with any hostile intent. . . . They regarded these men as deserters, and permitted them to come without harm."[2] Jonathan dispatched the sentries and set upon the sleeping men, destroying twenty before any alarm could be raised.

The God of Israel rewarded Jonathan's courage. "Angels of heaven shielded Jonathan and his attendant, angels fought by their side, and the Philistines fell before them. The earth trembled as though a great multitude with horsemen and chariots were approaching. Jonathan recognized the tokens of divine aid, and even the Philistines knew that God was working for the deliverance of Israel. Great fear seized upon the host, both in the field and in the garrison. In the confusion, mistaking their own soldiers for enemies, the Philistines began to slay one another."[3]

Great accomplishments are possible when faith in God and trust in His guidance are exercised. Angels stand ever ready to help in our battles against sin.

1. Francis D. Nichol, ed., *The Seventh-day Adventist Bible Commentary*, vol. 2 (Washington, DC: Review and Herald®, 1976), 515.
2. Ellen G. White, "The First King of Israel—No. 3," *Youth's Instructor*, November 24, 1898.
3. Ellen G. White, *Patriarchs and Prophets* (Mountain View, CA: Pacific Press®, 1943), 623.

SAUL'S OATH

And the men of Israel were distressed that day: for Saul had adjured the people, saying, Cursed be the man that eateth any food until evening, that I may be avenged on mine enemies. So none of the people tasted any food.
—1 Samuel 14:24

The noise of battle reached the camp of Israel, yet no order had been given to attack. Saul immediately requested a muster to see who was fighting without orders. Only Jonathan and his armor-bearer were missing.

"Saul's impetuosity was developing rapidly. The apparent confusion in the enemy's camp threw him into such excitement that he could not even wait for counsel from the Lord. For days he and his fellows had stood by and heard reports of raids by the enemy upon nearby towns, and though he did not know the reason for the flight of forces across the wadi, he abruptly gave the order to attack."[1]

"Determined to make the most of his advantage, the king rashly forbade his soldiers to partake of food for the entire day [1 Samuel 14:24]. . . . He hoped to distinguish himself by the utter destruction of the vanquished army. The command to refrain from food was prompted by selfish ambition, and it showed the king to be indifferent to the needs of his people when these conflicted with his desire for self-exaltation. To confirm his prohibition by a solemn oath showed Saul to be both rash and profane. The very words of the curse give evidence that Saul's zeal was for himself, and not for the honor of God. He declared his object to be, not 'that the Lord may be avenged on *His* enemies,' but 'that *I* may be avenged on *mine* enemies.' "[2]

The Israelites pursued the fleeing Philistines, inflicting great casualties upon them. When the battle ended, those who had fought all day were exhausted and famished. Evening had come, and the curse was over. They now ate whatever was at hand.

Twice in one day, Saul failed to seek guidance from the Lord. How often do we rush into situations without consulting God?

1. Francis D. Nichol, ed., *The Seventh-day Adventist Bible Commentary*, vol. 2 (Washington, DC: Review and Herald®, 1976), 516.
2. Ellen G. White, *Patriarchs and Prophets* (Mountain View, CA: Pacific Press®, 1943), 624; emphasis original.

Jonathan Must Die!

And Saul answered, God do so and more also:
for thou shalt surely die, Jonathan.

—1 Samuel 14:44

S aul wanted to pursue the enemy during the night and complete their annihilation. Israel had chased the Philistines thirteen miles from Michmash to Aijalon and had not stopped to gather the spoils of battle. They were keen to continue the slaughter of their enemies. The priest Ahiah counseled Saul to consult with God as to any planned pursuit. There was silence in response to his proposal to pursue. Saul now decreed lots should be cast to expose the one who had sinned and cut off communication with the Lord. And the lot fell upon Jonathan.

"By permitting the lot to fall on the innocent Jonathan, God most effectively exposed the evil course of the king. Saul, who had begun his reign in all humility, had now fallen into a hopeless state of self-justification."[1]

"During the day's battle Jonathan, who had not heard of the king's command, unwittingly offended by eating a little honey as he passed through a wood. Saul learned of this at evening. He had declared that the violation of his edict should be punished with death; and though Jonathan had not been guilty of a willful sin, though God had miraculously preserved his life and had wrought deliverance through him, the king declared that the sentence must be executed. To spare the life of his son would have been an acknowledgment on the part of Saul that he had sinned in making so rash a vow. This would have been humiliating to his pride."[2]

The people recognized Saul's injustice and rebelled. "They remembered the mighty deeds of the hero of the day, and how God had given them the victory through his bravery and faith. The same God who had impressed Jonathan to make his famous exploit, now inspired the army to cry out as one man, 'There shall not one hair of his head fall to the ground.' "[3]

"Those who are most ready to excuse or justify themselves in sin are often most severe in judging and condemning others."[4]

---

1. Francis D. Nichol, ed., *The Seventh-day Adventist Bible Commentary*, vol. 2 (Washington, DC: Review and Herald®, 1976), 518.
2. Ellen G. White, *Patriarchs and Prophets* (Mountain View, CA: Pacific Press®, 1943), 624, 625.
3. Nichol, *The Seventh-day Adventist Bible Commentary*, 2:518.
4. Ellen G. White, "King Saul's Rash Oath," *Signs of the Times®*, August 17, 1882, 1.

SAUL'S HEART REVEALED

And the people said unto Saul, Shall Jonathan die,
who hath wrought this great salvation in Israel? . . .
So the people rescued Jonathan, that he died not.
                                                    —1 Samuel 14:45

S aul could not but feel that his son was preferred before him, both by the people and by the Lord. Jonathan's deliverance was a severe reproof to the king's rashness. He felt a presentiment that his curses would return upon his own head."[1] "There are many today, like Saul, bringing upon themselves the displeasure of God. They reject counsel and despise reproof. Even when convinced that the Lord is not with them, they refuse to see in themselves the cause of their trouble. How many cherish a proud, boastful spirit, while they indulge in cruel judgment or severe rebuke of others really better in heart and life than they. Well would it be for such self-constituted judges to ponder those words of Christ: 'With what judgment ye judge, ye shall be judged; and with what measure ye mete, it shall be measured to you again.' "[2]

Saul now stood before the people in a new and troubling light. He was impulsive. Israel would soon have even more reason to doubt his judgment in addition to the rash action taken against his own son. Adding to his impulsiveness was overarching pride. "Saul seemed to exult in his military genius. Instead of protecting the rights of his people he took the offensive against his neighbor nations, with the purpose of enhancing his own reputation as king."[3]

Saul was judgmental. He stood ready to accuse others for his own folly and sinful actions. He accused Samuel of being tardy, so, in the absence of the priest, he was forced to proceed without him. When God's instruction ran contrary to his own, he sought to place blame elsewhere rather than accept the error of his own opinion. Saul took any reproof as an insult and instinctively blamed the messenger. Pride, impulsiveness, and being judgmental were just a few of his faults. We will soon see he was envious, vindictive, and cruel as well.

No one is righteous enough to claim God's prerogative to judge another.
"Judge not, that ye be not judged" (Matthew 7:1).

---

1. Ellen G. White, *Patriarchs and Prophets* (Mountain View, CA: Pacific Press®, 1943), 625.
2. Ellen G. White, "King Saul's Rash Oath," *Signs of the Times*®, August 17, 1882, 1.
3. Francis D. Nichol, ed., *The Seventh-day Adventist Bible Commentary*, vol. 2 (Washington, DC: Review and Herald®, 1976), 519.

SAUL DISOBEYS GOD AGAIN

Now go and smite Amalek, and utterly destroy
all that they have, and spare them not.
—1 Samuel 15:3

Having failed one test, God sent Saul another. Samuel was very specific in the charge he gave Saul. This was to be a scorched-earth campaign. Nothing was to be spared.

"Many years before, God had appointed Amalek to utter destruction. They had lifted up their hands against God, and his throne, and had taken oath by their gods that Israel should be utterly consumed, and the God of Israel brought down so that he would not be able to deliver them out of their hands.

"Amalek had made derision of the fears of his people, and made sport of God's wonderful works for the deliverance of Israel performed by the hand of Moses before the Egyptians. They had boasted that their wise men and magicians could perform all those wonders. And if the children of Israel had been their captives, in their power as they were in Pharaoh's, that the God of Israel himself would not have been able to deliver them out of their hands. They despised Israel, and vowed to plague them until there should not be one left. . . .

"God proved Saul by intrusting him with the important commission to execute his threatened wrath upon Amalek. . . . Saul thought it would add to his greatness to spare Agag, a noble monarch splendidly attired. And to return from battle with him captive, with great spoil of oxen, sheep, and much cattle, would get to himself much renown, and cause the nations to fear him, and tremble before him. And the people united with him in this. They excused their sin among themselves in not destroying the cattle, because they could reserve them to sacrifice to God, and spare their own cattle to themselves."[1]

This battle had been the most victorious yet achieved, and Saul was immensely proud of his accomplishment. He failed to recognize the hand of the Lord in the victory. Although he had not followed the Lord's instruction to the letter, in this he saw no fault. This little transgression would surely be excused as the majority of God's command had been followed.

"The children of God should cultivate a keen sensitiveness to sin. . . . Little sins eat out the life of godliness in the soul."[2]

---

1. Ellen G. White, *Spiritual Gifts*, vol. 4 (Washington, DC: Review and Herald®, 1945), 72, 73.
2. Ellen G. White, "Humility Before Honor," *Signs of the Times®*, September 7, 1882, 1.

A LAME EXCUSE

And Samuel said, When thou wast little in thine own sight,
wast thou not made the head of the tribes of Israel,
and the LORD anointed thee king over Israel?
—1 Samuel 15:17

Saul had now been subjected to the final test. His presumptuous disregard of the will of God, showing his determination to rule as an independent monarch, proved that he could not be trusted with royal power as the vicegerent of the Lord. While Saul and his army were marching home in the flush of victory, there was deep anguish in the home of Samuel the prophet. He had received a message from the Lord denouncing the course of the king: 'It repenteth Me that I have set up Saul to be king: for he is turned back from following Me, and hath not performed My commandments.' The prophet was deeply grieved over the course of the rebellious king, and he wept and prayed all night for a reversing of the terrible sentence."[1]

The next morning Saul went out to greet the prophet, saying, "Blessed be thou of the LORD: I have performed the commandment of the LORD" (1 Samuel 15:13). Both men knew this was a falsehood. Samuel challenged Saul, saying, "What meaneth then this bleating of the sheep in mine ears, and the lowing of the oxen which I hear?" (v. 14). Saul sought to blame the people, even though it was his command that spared the livestock. "*They* have brought them from the Amalekites: for *the people* spared the best of the sheep and of the oxen, to sacrifice unto the LORD *thy* God; and the rest we have utterly destroyed" (v. 15; emphasis added). Samuel gave Saul a second chance, but he stuck by his alibi (vv. 20, 21).

"And Samuel said, Hath the LORD as great delight in burnt offerings and sacrifices, as in obeying the voice of the LORD? Behold, to obey is better than sacrifice, and to hearken than the fat of rams" (v. 22). "God required of his people obedience rather than sacrifice. All the riches of the earth were his. The cattle upon a thousand hills belonged to him. He did not require the spoil of a corrupt people, upon whom his curse rested, even to their utter extinction, to be presented to him to prefigure the holy Saviour, as a lamb without blemish."[2]

Imaginary obedience deceives few—least of all God.

---

1. Ellen G. White, *Patriarchs and Prophets* (Washington, DC: Review and Herald®, 1943), 629, 630.
2. Ellen G. White, *The Spirit of Prophecy*, vol. 1 (Battle Creek, MI: Seventh-day Adventist Pub. Assn., 1870), 365.

47

THE PENALTY FOR DISOBEDIENCE

*And Samuel said unto him, The LORD hath rent the
kingdom of Israel from thee this day, and hath given
it to a neighbour of thine, that is better than thou.*

—1 Samuel 15:28

Prior to Samuel's announcement that God had rejected Saul as king [1 Samuel 15:23], Saul stoutly defended his course of action. Only when sentence was pronounced and the penalty became known was he willing to admit erring from the divine command. . . . It was not the sincere desire to do right that impelled this admission, but the fear of forfeiting his kingdom. It was only when confronted with this prospect that he feigned repentance, with the objective of saving, if possible, his position as king."[1]

Realizing the kingdom was lost, Saul again blamed the people for his sin and begged Samuel to intercede for him with the Lord. Instead, Samuel added further punishment. "And Samuel said unto Saul, I will not return with thee: for thou hast rejected the word of the LORD, and the LORD hath rejected thee from being king over Israel" (v. 26).

Saul feared his authority would be impossible to maintain once word got out God had deserted him. He begged Samuel to honor him before the elders by publicly worshiping with him. "By divine direction Samuel yielded to the king's request, that no occasion might be given for a revolt. But he remained only as a silent witness of the service.

"An act of justice, stern and terrible, was yet to be performed. Samuel must publicly vindicate the honor of God and rebuke the course of Saul. . . . Above all who had fallen by the sword of Israel, Agag was the most guilty and merciless; one who had hated and sought to destroy the people of God, and whose influence had been strongest to promote idolatry. He came at the prophet's command, flattering himself that the danger of death was past. Samuel declared: 'As thy sword hath made women childless, so shall thy mother be childless among women. And Samuel hewed Agag in pieces before the Lord.' This done, Samuel returned to his home at Ramah, Saul to his at Gibeah. Only once thereafter did the prophet and the king ever meet each other."[2]

To reject God's leading and follow one's own inclination leads to disaster.

---

1. Francis D. Nichol, ed., *The Seventh-day Adventist Bible Commentary*, vol. 2 (Washington, DC: Review and Herald®, 1976), 526.
2. Ellen G. White, *Patriarchs and Prophets* (Mountain View, CA: Pacific Press®, 1943), 632.

SAMUEL IN SEMIRETIREMENT

*And Samuel came no more to see Saul until the day of
his death: nevertheless Samuel mourned for Saul: and the
LORD repented that he had made Saul king over Israel.*

—1 Samuel 15:35

The relation between Samuel and Saul was one of peculiar tenderness. Samuel loved Saul as his own son, while Saul, bold and ardent of temper, held the prophet in great reverence, and bestowed upon him the warmth of his affection and regard. Thus the prophet of the living God, an old man whose mission was nearly finished, and the youthful king, whose work was before him, were bound together by the ties of friendship and respect. All through his perverse course, the king clung to the prophet as if he alone could save him from himself."[1] Samuel, at the direction of the Lord, separated himself from the king. Samuel's work was not yet at an end, however. New avenues of service opened for the servant of the Most High.

"Samuel's life of purity and unselfish devotion was a perpetual rebuke both to self-serving priests and elders and to the proud, sensual congregation of Israel. . . . But the people had become weary of his piety and devotion; they despised his humble authority and rejected him for a man who should rule them as a king.

"In the character of Samuel we see reflected the likeness of Christ. It was the purity of our Saviour's life that provoked the wrath of Satan."[2]

"How many retiring from a position of responsibility as a judge, can say in regard to their purity, which of you convinceth me of sin? Who can prove that I have turned aside from my righteousness to accept bribes? I have never stained my record as a man who does judgment and justice. Who today can say what Samuel said when he was taking leave of the people of Israel, because they were determined to have a king? . . . Brave, noble judge! But it is a sorrowful thing that a man of the strictest integrity should have to humble himself to make his own defense."[3]

Israel now saw plainly what Samuel had foreseen in their request for a king. They had received what they had asked for. Samuel henceforth shunned public life and went into semiretirement at Ramah. He continued as a teacher in the schools of the prophets, which he enjoyed.

Age does not define usefulness in the Lord's service.

---

1. Ellen G. White, "The Rejection of Saul," *Signs of the Times*®, June 1, 1888.
2. Ellen G. White, *Patriarchs and Prophets* (Mountain View, CA: Pacific Press®, 1943), 607.
3. Ellen G. White, "The Unjust Judge," MS 33, 1898.

SCHOOLS OF THE PROPHETS

And Samuel judged Israel all the days of his life.

—1 Samuel 7:15

Samuel spent his remaining days preparing young minds to serve the Lord. The early training of Hebrew children was stressed so they might learn the requirements of God and understand the history of His leading in the affairs of the nation. Solomon wrote: "Train up a child in the way he should go: and when he is old, he will not depart from it" (Proverbs 22:6).

The Bible is filled with examples of godly parents training their children to obey and reverence God. "Such was the training of Moses in the lowly cabin home in Goshen; of Samuel, by the faithful Hannah; of David, in the hill dwelling at Bethlehem; of Daniel, before the scenes of the captivity separated him from the home of his fathers. Such, too, was the early life of Christ at Nazareth; such the training by which the child Timothy learned from the lips of his grandmother Lois, and his mother Eunice (2 Timothy 1:5; 3:15), the truths of Holy Writ."[1]

Additional training was provided at schools where youth were taught the Word of God by God-fearing teachers. "In Samuel's day there were two of these schools—one at Ramah, the home of the prophet, and the other at Kirjath-jearim, where the ark then was. Others were established in later times."[2] In these schools, Israel's future religious leaders were taught a skill or trade and spent a portion of the day in manual labor in God's creation. The classroom curriculum consisted of the Mosaic Law, poetry, music, and history. " 'The fear of the Lord is the beginning of wisdom: and *the knowledge of the Holy* is understanding.' Proverbs 9:10. The great work of life is character building, and a knowledge of God is the foundation of all true education."[3]

"It is a law of the mind that it gradually adapts itself to the subjects upon which it is trained to dwell. . . . As an educating power the Bible is without a rival. In the word of God the mind finds subject for the deepest thought, the loftiest aspiration."[4]

"And the education begun in this life will be continued in the life to come."[5]

---

1. Ellen G. White, *Patriarchs and Prophets* (Mountain View, CA: Pacific Press®, 1943), 592.
2. White, 593.
3. White, 596; emphasis original.
4. White, 596.
5. White, 602.

TESTS OF A PROPHET

Then came the word of the LORD unto Samuel, saying . . .
—1 Samuel 15:10

In the Garden of Eden, there was face-to-face communication between God and man. Sin ended that but did not end our Creator's desire to communicate with humanity. Old Testament scripture is filled with messages from Him. One who received a message from God and faithfully transmitted it to the people was called a *prophet*. One who was shown future events was called a *seer*. Samuel was both a seer and a prophet. "Surely the Lord GOD will do nothing, but he revealeth his secret unto his servants the prophets" (Amos 3:7; see also 2 Peter 1:21).

But how is one to know a prophetic message is from God? We are told false prophets will arise in the last days (Matthew 24:11). Fortunately, there are tests by which we may examine whether a prophet claiming a message from the Lord is, in truth, a heavenly messenger.

1. *Does the message agree with the Bible and confirm the Ten Commandments?* "To the law and to the testimony: if they speak not according to this word, it is because there is no light in them" (Isaiah 8:20). God's law does not change (James 1:17)!
2. *Do their prophecies come to pass?* "The prophet which prophesieth of peace, when the word of the prophet shall come to pass, then shall the prophet be known, that the LORD hath truly sent him" (Jeremiah 28:9; see also Deuteronomy 18:21, 22).
3. *Do they confess Jesus Christ is the Son of God come in the flesh?* "Hereby know ye the Spirit of God: Every spirit that confesseth that Jesus Christ is come in the flesh is of God: And every spirit that confesseth not that Jesus Christ is come in the flesh is not of God: and this is that spirit of antichrist" (1 John 4:2, 3).
4. *Does the prophet bear "good fruit"?* Is the prophet's life a positive influence? "Beware of false prophets. . . . Ye shall know them by their fruits" (Matthew 7:15, 16; see also vv. 18–20).
5. *Does the prophet's message bring unity to the church?* (see Ephesians 4:11–16).

"Beloved, believe not every spirit, but try the spirits whether they are of God: because many false prophets are gone out into the world" (1 John 4:1).

David and Saul

1 Samuel 16:1–18:8

Patriarchs and Prophets, chapters 62; 63

GO TO BETHLEHEM!

*And the L*ORD *said unto Samuel, How long wilt thou mourn*
for Saul, seeing I have rejected him from reigning over Israel?
fill thine horn with oil, and go, I will send thee to Jesse the
Bethlehemite: for I have provided me a king among his sons.
—1 Samuel 16:1

Reluctant as Samuel may have been in the first place to give Israel a king, once the king had been selected; Samuel remained loyal to him in spite of his mistakes. To Samuel, as later to David, Saul was 'the Lord's anointed' ([1 Samuel] 24:10). Samuel's grief over the course Saul had chosen . . . is evidence of the sincerity of Samuel's solicitude for him."[1] "As the first chief of state under a new form of administration, . . . [Saul] had almost hypnotic power over the high-spirited and independence-loving Israelite people. But he had rapidly developed into a despot—cruel, tyrannical, and unforgiving."[2] Samuel still carried a burden for Saul as a friend gone astray.

The Lord instructed Samuel to go to the home of Jesse the Bethlehemite to anoint one of his sons as the new king of Israel. God instructed him to take a heifer with him to Bethlehem and offer a sacrifice there to the Lord. During his periodic visits, Samuel would often reaffirm the plan of salvation with the residents and encourage promising young men to attend the schools of the prophets. It was routine, therefore, to hold a local meeting and should elicit no questions.

The anointing of David was done secretly in much the same manner as that of Saul. Even the elders, who were present at the feast prepared for Saul and his servant, did not know of his selection. "The only difference between Samuel's anointing of Saul and his trip to Jesse's home was that at this time there was already a king, suspicious of every move the prophet made since he had announced the Lord's rejection of Saul."[3] As Samuel's arrival was a surprise, the elders of Bethlehem were concerned that something terrible had happened. Samuel eased their minds, announcing, "Peaceably: I am come to sacrifice unto the L ORD" (1 Samuel 16:5).

Bethlehem, the City of David, would gain even greater prominence as the birthplace of our Savior—Jesus Christ.

---

1. Francis D. Nichol, ed., *The Seventh-day Adventist Bible Commentary*, vol. 2 (Washington, DC: Review and Herald®, 1976), 527.
2. Nichol, 528.
3. Nichol, 529.

THE EIGHT SONS OF JESSE

But the LORD said unto Samuel, Look not on his countenance,
or on the height of his stature; because I have refused him:
for the LORD seeth not as man seeth; for man looketh on the
outward appearance, but the LORD looketh on the heart.
—1 Samuel 16:7

Samuel invited Jesse and his sons to the sacrifice at Bethlehem. "When the sacrifice was ended, and before partaking of the offering feast, Samuel began his prophetic inspection of the noble-appearing sons of Jesse. Eliab was the eldest, and more nearly resembled Saul for stature and beauty than the others. His comely features and finely developed form attracted the attention of the prophet."[1] But Eliab did not fear the Lord and would be a proud, exacting ruler. God was looking for a teachable spirit that could be guided into righteous obedience. "It is the inner worth, the excellency of the heart; that determines our acceptance with the Lord of hosts."[2]

In rapid succession, Eliab, Abinadab, Shammah, and four other sons passed before the prophet, yet he received no sign any of these was chosen of the Lord. Samuel was perplexed. "And Samuel said unto Jesse, Are here all thy children? And he said, There remaineth yet the youngest, and, behold, he keepeth the sheep. And Samuel said unto Jesse, Send and fetch him: for we will not sit down till he come hither" (1 Samuel 16:11).

David arrived and stood before the prophet, wondering why he had been called. "And the LORD said, Arise, anoint him: for this is he" (v. 12). David "had filled the humble office of shepherd with such faithfulness and courage that God selected him to be captain of his people. . . .

"The angel of God signified to Samuel that David was the one for him to anoint, for he was God's chosen. From that time the Lord gave David a prudent and understanding heart."[3]

The anointing ceremony was carried out in secrecy. Only David's family knew. And David, unshaken by his high position, simply returned to his lonely task of guarding the sheep.

"For many be called, but few chosen" (Matthew 20:16). An intimate knowledge of God and a teachable spirit prepare one for service.

---

1. Ellen G. White, *Patriarchs and Prophets* (Mountain View, CA: Pacific Press®, 1943), 638.
2. White, 638.
3. Ellen G. White, *Spiritual Gifts*, vol. 4 (Washington, DC: Review and Herald®, 1945), 78.

WHY A SHEPHERD?

Then Samuel took the horn of oil, and anointed him in the midst of his brethren: and the Spirit of the LORD came upon David from that day forward.

—1 Samuel 16:13

When God called David from his father's sheepfold to anoint him king of Israel, He saw in him one to whom He could impart His Spirit. David was susceptible to the influence of the Holy Spirit, and the Lord in His providence trained him for His service, preparing him to carry out His purposes. Christ was the Master-builder of his character."[1] This future king developed fidelity and wisdom while faithfully guarding his father's flocks. As with Moses, who also tended flocks before becoming a leader, David learned valuable lessons by caring for sheep.

Sheep must be led; they cannot be driven. Sheep are defenseless against predators and must be guarded. Sheep wander off and must be found and returned to the safety of the flock. Sheep often follow one another blindly into difficulty. But sheep will recognize the voice of their shepherd and follow his direction. These—and lessons of equal importance—prepared both Moses and David to deal with people who, more often than not, mimic sheep in their behavior.

"As humble and modest as before his anointing, the shepherd boy returned to the hills and watched and guarded his flocks as tenderly as ever."[2]

"The communion with nature and with God, the care of his flocks, the perils and deliverances, the griefs and joys, of his lowly lot, were not only to mold the character of David and to influence his future life, but through the psalms of Israel's sweet singer they were in all coming ages to kindle love and faith in the hearts of God's people, bringing them nearer to the ever-loving heart of Him in whom all His creatures live."[3]

"All unconsciously man is tested by the common events of life until finally God can say, 'Thou hast been faithful over a few things, I will make thee ruler over many things' (Matt. 25:23)."[4]

---

1. Ellen G. White, "David's Testimony to God's Goodness," MS 163, 1902.
2. Ellen G. White, *Patriarchs and Prophets* (Mountain View, CA: Pacific Press®, 1943), 641.
3. White, 642.
4. Francis D. Nichol, ed., *The Seventh-day Adventist Bible Commentary*, vol. 2 (Washington, DC: Review and Herald®, 1976), 530.

WHO AUTHORED THE PSALMS?

*I will be glad and rejoice in thee: I will sing
praise to thy name, O thou most High.*

—Psalm 9:2

The psalms were meant to be accompanied by stringed instruments. They are poetic and lyrical in voicing praise to the Lord and lose much when simply read silently. Some psalms are still sung as part of Jewish worship. There is beauty in hearing these songs of our redemption.

While numerous musicians contributed to the assembled works, David is generally acknowledged as the author or collector of a majority of the 150 psalms found in the Bible. Approximately fifty psalms are anonymous. These are often called Orphan Psalms. Twelve psalms are attributed to Asaph, but it is likely David and Asaph collaborated on them. "Asaph was a Levite, one of David's choir leaders. Like David, Asaph was a seer and a musical composer (see 1 Chron. 6:39; 2 Chron. 29:30; Neh. 12:46). In the list of captives who returned to Jerusalem, the children of Asaph are the only singers mentioned (Ezra 2:41)."[1]

"The titles to three psalms (Ps. 39, 62, and 77) contain the name of Jeduthun, who was the head of a company of Temple musicians (see 1 Chron. 16:41, 42), and probably an arranger and compiler of Temple music."[2] Researchers cannot, with certainty, delineate all the psalms David authored or coauthored.[3]

"Man is in trouble—God gives relief. This is the theme—universal in its appeal—of the book of Psalms. In these sacred poems we hear the cry, not only of the Hebrew, but of universal man, ascending to God for help, and see the hand of Omnipotence reaching down to bring relief. No wonder that for centuries, for Jew and Gentile alike, the Psalter has supplied material for private prayer and for public devotion; it has served with equal satisfaction as the formal liturgy for the Hebrew Temple and synagogue, as the hymnbook of the Christian church, and as the prayer book of the solitary child of God, regardless of race or creed."[4]

There exists a psalm for every outlook and every desire. Praise the Lord in song!

---

1. Francis D. Nichol, ed., *The Seventh-day Adventist Bible Commentary*, vol. 3 (Washington, DC: Review and Herald®, 1977), 617.
2. Nichol, 617.
3. Using the best available information, this devotional presents psalms believed to have been written by David and others representative of his writing style.
4. Nichol, 619.

PSALM 23: THE SHEPHERD PSALM

The LORD is my Shepherd; I shall not want.

—Psalm 23:1

Probably the best known and best loved of all the psalms is Ps. 23, universally known as The Shepherd Psalm. It is at once the delight of childhood and the consolation of old age. . . .

"But it is more than The Shepherd Psalm. It paints not only the picture of the tender Shepherd, leading His flock to rest and feed 'in green pastures' 'beside the still waters' and protecting them from the perils of the wilderness, but also the picture of the gracious Host, providing superabundance of food and solicitous care for His guest. The psalm closes with a profession of absolute confidence in Jehovah to lead His child lovingly through this life and to entertain him as His guest to the end of his days."[1]

The words capture David's tender care of his flock. To appreciate this psalm, "one must know the hazardous nature of the Judean wilderness, and the intimate life of the shepherd and his sheep, especially the devotion that springs up between them during the many hours of solitude that they spend together."[2] Time spent together leads the sheep to trust the shepherd. God will never desert us or leave us in peril. We fear no evil for He has promised to walk with us, even into the dark valley of death, and will call us forth into His glory at His second coming.

"Jehovah is even more than a shepherd—He is a king, lavishing upon His guests the bounties of His table."[3] David could certainly praise God's involvement in both the pastures of his youth and the palace halls of his kingdom.

"Savior, like a Shepherd lead us, / Much we need Thy tenderest care; / In Thy pleasant pastures feed us, / For our use Thy folds prepare."[4]

---

1. Francis D. Nichol, ed., *The Seventh-day Adventist Bible Commentary*, vol. 3 (Washington, DC: Review and Herald®, 1977), 685.

2. Nichol, 686.

3. Nichol, 686, 687.

4. Anonymous, "Savior, Like a Shepherd," in *The Seventh-day Adventist Hymnal* (Hagerstown, MD: Review and Herald®, 1985), hymn 545.

Psalm 33: Six Reasons to Praise God

*By the word of the Lord were the heavens made; and all
the host of them by the breath of his mouth. . . . For he
spake, and it was done; he commanded, and it stood fast.*
—Psalm 33:6, 9

The thirty-third psalm was written by David.[1] This psalm praises God for His marvelous attributes. Praising God in song was as natural for David as breathing. Read this psalm in its entirety, then meditate on its beauty of overlapping expressions.

1. We should rejoice because God is *truthful, righteous, good,* and *merciful* (Psalm 33:1, 4, 5, 18, 22). These are the first reasons to praise God. These attributes are also stated in Psalms 25:10; 26:3; and 36:5, 6.
2. Praise God because He is the *Creator* (Psalm 33:6). By capitalizing "Word," we glimpse another truth: Christ, the "Word" made flesh (John 1:1, 3), created all things, including the heavenly bodies. Christ spoke creation into existence ex nihilo—from nothing. Creation is truly amazing (Psalm 33:8)!
3. Praise God because He is *sovereign* (vv. 10, 11). He reigns supreme and His judgments, based upon His law, are pure and right (v. 4).
4. Praise God because He is *omniscient* and *omnipresent* (vv. 6, 10, 13, 14, 18). He knows our joys and sorrows. "I will instruct thee and teach thee in the way which thou shalt go: I will guide thee with mine eye" (Psalm 32:8).
5. Praise God because He is *omnipotent* (Psalm 33:4, 6, 10, 13). "The voice of the Lord is powerful; the voice of the Lord is full of majesty" (Psalm 29:4).
6. Praise God because He is *dependable* (Psalm 33:10, 13, 16). God will protect those who put their trust in Him. "O taste and see that the Lord is good: blessed is the man that trusteth in him" (Psalm 34:8).

These six reasons to praise the Lord only begin to reveal God's character.
"Praise the Lord, His glories show. . . . / Saints within His courts below."[2]

---

1. See Ellen G. White, *Patriarchs and Prophets* (Mountain View, CA: Pacific Press®, 1943), 716.
2. Henry F. Lyte, "Praise the Lord, His Glories Show" (1834), in *The Seventh-day Adventist Hymnal* (Hagerstown, MD: Review and Herald®, 1985), hymn 25.

Psalm 8: Song of a Starry Night

*When I consider thy heavens, the work of thy fingers, the moon
and the stars, which thou hast ordained; What is man, that thou
art mindful of him? and the son of man, that thou visitest him?*
—Psalm 8:3, 4

I t is not hard to imagine that David wrote this exquisite lyric during one of those nights of his early shepherd life when, alone with his sheep, he looked up into the starry sky and felt the dignity of kinship with his Maker; or that, later in life, he composed it in recollection of the ecstasy of such early experiences." David wrote many "nature psalms"; this being the first (see also Psalms 19; 29; 104).[1]

"The psalm has also been called A Psalm in Praise of the Dignity of Man. In it the poet stands under the open canopy of the moonlit and star-studded sky, awe-struck by his contemplation of God's handiwork in nature. In the presence of all this vastness, there comes upon him a sudden realization of the insignificance of puny man. No sooner, however, is this feeling entertained than it is swallowed up in his consciousness of the true dignity of man, who is God's representative on earth, in nature a little less than divine, with all things put in subjection under his feet. No wonder that the psalmist, thus impressed by the dignified position that man holds in the universe, should extol the excellence of his Creator."[2]

The vast expanse of space, with its billions of stars and galaxies, dwarfs us when we consider God's creation. Yet God cared enough for fallen humanity to send His Son to redeem us. "Why should the infinite God, who has a universe of worlds to claim His attention, be 'mindful' of finite man? Why should He honor man by making him viceroy of the earth? Only in the realization of the worth of a human soul created in God's likeness can one answer these questions. This realization comes only in appreciation of the Saviour's death on the cross."[3]

"The worth of man is known only by going to Calvary. In the mystery of the cross of Christ we can place an estimate upon man."[4]

---

1. Francis D. Nichol, ed., *The Seventh-day Adventist Bible Commentary,* vol. 3 (Washington, DC: Review and Herald®, 1977), 648.
2. Nichol, 648.
3. Nichol, 649.
4. Ellen G. White, *Testimonies for the Church* (Mountain View, CA: Pacific Press®, 1948), 2:634, 635.

Psalm 29: Song of the Thunderstorm

Give unto the LORD the glory due unto his name;
worship the LORD in the beauty of holiness.
—Psalm 29:2

P salm 29 is another of David's nature psalms. Eighteen times David mentions Yahweh. "In this psalm a storm is thrillingly described from its beginning, through the height of its intensity, until it dies away. The structure of the poem exhibits elaborate symmetry, which appears in the prelude (vs. 1, 2), in the description of the storm with its sevenfold repetition of the phrase 'the voice of the Lord' (vs. 3–9), and in the conclusion (vs. 10, 11). It is a verbal cameo."[1] "The psalm describes the fury of a great storm originating over the sea, accompanied by gale winds, by peals of thunder, and by fiery flashes of lightning, coming in from the Mediterranean and sweeping over the Lebanon and Anti-Lebanon mountains before it loses its force in the eastern desert."[2] For those who have stood in awe at the majesty and power of a lightning storm, David's comparison of the "Song of the Thunderstorm" to God's power and grandeur is apropos.

David equates "the voice of the LORD" to thunder and sees attributes of God displayed in the storm (v. 3). Slowly, the storm gathers out at sea. Thunder rolls over the breakers and onto dry land (v. 4). Wind gusts beat the mountains of Lebanon (v. 5). Mountains reel and appear "to skip like a calf," as the wind whips trees and grasses into waves (vv. 5, 6). Mount Hermon is battered by the wind. Lightning streaks across the sky in bolts of flame (vv. 6, 7). The storm moves east, lashing the Syrian Desert (v. 8). Trees quake before the wind (v. 9). "All things—the thunder, the lightning, the crashing of the trees, the shaking of the wilderness, the leaves being stripped from the trees—declare the power and glory of God."[3] Then heavy sheets of rain fall (v. 10). Finally, the storm passes. Stillness and assurance replace tumult and anxiety (v. 11).

"O worship the Lord in the beauty of holiness, / Bow down before Him, His glory proclaim."[4]

---

1. Francis D. Nichol, ed., *The Seventh-day Adventist Bible Commentary*, vol. 3 (Washington, DC: Review and Herald®, 1977), 699.
2. Nichol, 699.
3. Nichol, 700.
4. J. S. B. Monsell, "O Worship the Lord," in *The Seventh-day Adventist Hymnal* (Washington, DC: Review and Herald®, 1985), hymn 6.

PSALM 104: HOW DIVERSE ARE THY WORKS!

O LORD, how manifold are thy works! in wisdom hast
thou made them all: the earth is full of thy riches.
—Psalm 104:24

P salm 104 rejoices in God's creation. God is represented as being robed in light (v. 2). Verses 2 and 3 are analogous to the first two days of Creation (Genesis 1:3–8). The clouds are His chariot (Psalm 104:3), and the winds, His messengers (v. 4). Verses 5–9 speak to the third day of Creation (Genesis 1:9, 10), wherein God established the earth, placing it on a firm foundation (Psalm 104:5). He then separated land from water, calling the land "earth" and the waters "sea" (vv. 6–9). The waters were placed within boundaries they could not pass (v. 9). Thus, the contours of the earth were formed, as God created mountains, valleys, rivers, and seas (v. 8).

God provided water for His creatures by sending "springs into the valleys, which run among the hills" (v. 10). He sent rain to nourish the earth (v. 13) so grass would "grow for the cattle, and herb for the service of man: that he may bring forth food out of the earth" (v. 14). He planted the trees (v. 16) in which birds build their nests (v. 17). The hills and rocks provide shelter for the wild goat and the rock badger (v. 18). God appointed the sun and the moon (v. 19; Genesis 1:14–19). He defined the seasons (Psalm 104:19). Day and night provide work and rest for humans and beasts (vv. 20–23).

Here David pauses as he can no longer restrain his praise for the wisdom and creativity of the Lord (v. 24). David resumes his account of Creation by mentioning the creatures inhabiting the seas (vv. 25, 26), which were created on the fifth day of Creation (Genesis 1:20–22). In a brief reference to humans, David applauds the skills that allow humankind to create and sail ships (Psalm 104:26). God provides for all His creatures (vv. 27–30). As David meditated on the marvelous works of our Creator, his soul was blessed (vv. 1, 35). God is certainly worthy of praise (vv. 33–35)!

"O tell of His might, O sing of His grace, / Whose robe is the light, whose canopy space; / His chariots of wrath the deep thunderclouds form, / And dark is His path on the wings of the storm."[1]

---

1. Robert Grant, "O Worship the King" (1833), in *The Seventh-day Adventist Hymnal* (Hagerstown, MD: Review and Herald®, 1985), hymn 83.

PSALM 19, PART 1: LESSONS FROM THE HEAVENS

The heavens declare the glory of God;
and the firmament sheweth his handywork.

—Psalm 19:1

I t would be hard not to date the writing of Psalm 19 sometime around the time David was a shepherd, for it extols the beauties and vast wonder of the heavens. Surely he contemplated the heavens on the nights he kept vigil over his flocks on the hills surrounding Bethlehem. God reveals Himself to us through His created works, His law, and His Son. An appreciation of the things of nature brings us to the place where we can better understand the workings of His glory. "For the invisible things of him from the creation of the world are clearly seen, being understood by the things that are made, even his eternal power and Godhead" (Romans 1:20).

"The glory of God is displayed in His handiwork. Here are mysteries that the mind will become strong in searching out. . . . All may find themes for study in the simple leaf of the forest tree, the spires of grass covering the earth with their green velvet carpet, the plants and flowers, the stately trees of the forest, the lofty mountains, the granite rocks, the restless ocean, the precious gems of light studding the heavens to make the night beautiful, the exhaustless riches of the sunlight, the solemn glories of the moon, the winter's cold, the summer's heat, the changing, recurring seasons, in perfect order and harmony, controlled by infinite power; here are subjects which call for deep thought, for the stretch of the imagination."[1]

The stars making their rounds in perfect order prove intelligent design. Each day we are reminded that God controls the movements of the natural world. The heavens speak to us, not in audible tones but in the beauty and organization they display. "No finite mind can fully comprehend the existence, the power, the wisdom, or the works of the Infinite One. Says the sacred writer: 'Canst thou by searching find out God? canst thou find out the Almighty unto perfection? It is as high as heaven; what canst thou do? deeper than hell; what canst thou know? The measure thereof is longer than the earth, and broader than the sea.' Job 11:7-9."[2]

"The mightiest intellects of earth cannot comprehend God. Men may be ever searching, ever learning, and still there is an infinity beyond."[3]

1. Ellen G. White, *Testimonies for the Church* (Mountain View, CA: Pacific Press®, 1948), 4:581.
2. Ellen G. White, *Patriarchs and Prophets* (Mountain View, CA: Pacific Press®, 1943), 116.
3. White, 116.

PSALM 19, PART 2: GOD'S LAW IS PERFECT

*Moreover by them [God's statutes, commandments, and judgments]
is thy servant warned: and in keeping of them there is great reward.*
—Psalm 19:11

Yesterday we considered the first six verses of Psalm 19, which
deal with God's glory as seen in the works of His hands. Nature is His second handbook. Psalm 19:7–10 speaks to the glory
of God as found in His law. Most of us rarely, if ever, contemplate the
completeness and beauty of God's law. For David, the law was a revelation of God's ability to transform a sinner's character. "Beautiful as the
manifestations of God's glory in the heavens may be; magnificent as the
splendor of the sun, moon, and stars may appear; still more beautiful,
more magnificent, is the picture of a character directed by God's law."[1]

The structure of this psalm has a threefold cross parallelism: (1) the
name for the law; (2) the nature of that law; and (3) the results obtained
by a follower of the law.[2] These are laid out as subject, description, and
effect: "The *law* of the LORD is *perfect, converting the soul.*" "The *testimony*
of the LORD is *sure, making wise the simple*" (v. 7). "The *statutes* of the LORD
are *right, rejoicing the heart.*" "The *commandment* of the Lord is *pure, enlightening the eyes*" (v. 8). "The *fear* of the LORD is *clean, enduring for ever.*"
"The *judgments* of the LORD are *true* and *righteous altogether*" (v. 9).

"What a God is our God! He rules over His kingdom with diligence
and care, and He has built a hedge—the Ten Commandments—about
His subjects, to preserve them from transgression. In requiring obedience to the laws of His kingdom, God gives His people health and happiness, peace and joy. He teaches them that the perfection of character
He requires can only be attained by becoming familiar with His Word.
The psalmist declares, 'The entrance of thy word giveth light; it giveth
understanding to the simple.' "[3]

God has chosen multiple ways to reveal Himself to us. Nature shows
us glimpses of His creative glory. Keeping His law shows us how He
creates a new heart in sinful man. God surrounds us, but to glimpse
Him, we must be open to His disclosures.

"Nature and revelation alike testify of God's love."[4]

---

1. Francis D. Nichol, ed., *The Seventh-day Adventist Bible Commentary*, vol. 3 (Washington, DC: Review and Herald®, 1977), 676.
2. See Nichol, 677.
3. Ellen G. White, "The Bible as Our Study-Book," MS 96, 1899.
4. Ellen G. White, *Steps to Christ* (Washington, DC: Review and Herald®, 1956), 9.

PSALM 19, PART 3:
CONTROL YOUR THOUGHTS

*Let the words of my mouth, and the meditation of my heart, be
acceptable in thy sight, O LORD, my strength, and my redeemer.*
—Psalm 19:14

P salm 19:14 contains a subtle but profound idea: one may sin simply by meditating on impure thoughts. Even if we do not act upon
those thoughts, we have committed sin. How, then, can anyone be
saved if our own thoughts betray us? "The Lord would have us awake to
our true spiritual condition. He desires that every soul shall humble heart
and mind before him. The words of inspiration found in the nineteenth
and twentieth psalms are presented to me for our people. It is our privilege to accept these precious promises, and to believe the warnings."[1]

"As God works upon the heart by his Holy Spirit, man must co-operate
with him. The thoughts must be bound about, restricted, withdrawn
from branching out and contemplating things that will only weaken and
defile the soul. The thoughts must be pure, the meditations of the heart
must be clean, if the words of the mouth are to be words acceptable to
Heaven, and helpful to your associates. . . .

"In the sermon on the mount, Christ presented before his disciples the
far-reaching principles of the law of God. He taught his hearers that the
law was transgressed by the thoughts before the evil desire was carried
out in actual commission. . . .

"Let every one who desires to be a partaker of the divine nature, appreciate the fact that he must escape the corruption that is in the world
through lust. There must be a constant, earnest struggling of the soul
against the evil imaginings of the mind. There must be a steadfast resistance of temptation to sin in thought or act. The soul must be kept from
every stain, through faith in him who is able to keep you from falling."[2]

Too often we allow the trials and tribulations of our lives to occupy every waking moment. We do not take time to pray. We do not guard what
our eyes see and our minds contemplate. Once an image is imprinted in
the brain, it is almost impossible to erase it.

There is the old saying: by beholding you are changed. What are you watching?

---

1. Ellen G. White, "A Revival Needed," *Review and Herald*, August 5, 1909, 9.
2. Ellen G. White, "The Renewing of the Mind," *Review and Herald*, June 12, 1888, 1.

BACKGROUND: THE SONS OF ANAK

And there we saw the giants, the sons of Anak.
—Numbers 13:33

The Philistines, those residents of Canaan who were not eradicated when the Israelites took possession of the country under Joshua, continued to war against the twelve tribes. These warriors from the sea occupied coastal lands along the Mediterranean Sea, including what is now the Gaza Strip. Shortly after the time of Gideon, the Philistines again oppressed the Israelites. These depredations continued for four decades, and Samson was ineffective in delivering Israel.

We saw earlier how the Philistines oppressed the Israelites, forbidding them to have blacksmiths who might fashion metal into weapons of war (1 Samuel 13:19, 20). Over the decades, Israel was defeated in battle time and again, being kept in virtual servility. The ark of the covenant was even taken (1 Samuel 4:1–11), and Shiloh was all but destroyed. Samuel rallied the Israelites and defeated the Philistines at Ebenezer (1 Samuel 7:5–14), but Philistia rebounded and took the foothills of Canaan, establishing garrisons on the hilltops.

Before the conquest and occupation of Canaan, the Lord had instructed Moses to send spies into the land. The report of these spies is found in Numbers 13:25–33. Only Joshua and Caleb returned with a positive report, urging immediate action with the real prospect of victory. The other ten spies were intimidated by what they had seen and did not hold anything back when they reported to Moses (vv. 27, 28). They saw men of large stature, who were fierce warriors. "And there we saw the giants, the sons of Anak, which come of the giants: and we were in our own sight as grasshoppers, and so we were in their sight" (v. 33).

The sons of Anak had originally come from the deserts east of the Jordan River and migrated to the foothills of Judea. Then they were driven from there by Joshua and settled in the coastal cities of Gath, Gaza, and Ashdod (Joshua 11:21, 22)—Philistine cities where they formed a loose defensive alliance with the Philistines. The Israelites eventually subjugated most of Canaan, dividing the land among the twelve tribes and settling down to domesticity. But they had not completed the task set before them by God.

By failing to displace the original inhabitants of Canaan, as God directed, Israel was forced into a contentious association with these nations, which continues to this day.

SEND OUT YOUR CHAMPION!

And there went out a champion out of the camp of the Philistines, named Goliath, of Gath, whose height was six cubits and a span.
—1 Samuel 17:4

War with the Philistines resumed, and the armies drew themselves up on either side of a valley called Elah. In the middle of the valley was a steeply sided ravine that could be crossed only at certain narrow spots. It formed an effective barrier between the two camps. As a frontal attack would be difficult to mount, the Philistines decided that rather than commit to a pitched battle, they would seek trial by combat to determine the outcome. The losers would become slaves.

Goliath was their challenger. He was a resident of Gath and probably not a Philistine by birth, being a descendant of Anak, but he was their best fighter. The exact height of Goliath is not known. Some say he was 9.5 feet tall, basing their estimate on his given height of "six cubits and a span" (1 Samuel 17:4). A cubit might be anywhere from 17.5 to 20.5 inches. Ellen White writes, "The Philistines propose their own manner of warfare, in selecting a man of great size and strength, whose height is about twelve feet, and they send this champion forth to provoke a combat with Israel, requesting them to send out a man to fight with him. He was terrible in appearance, and spoke proudly, and defied the armies of Israel and their God."[1]

Goliath's torso was covered with bronze armor weighing around 125 pounds. He carried a javelin with an iron head weighing around fifteen pounds. His armor-bearer carried a shield before him. Every day for forty days, he came out and dared Saul to send someone to fight. "Here Saul, an egotistical despot, was confronted by another braggart, and knew not what to do. Furthermore, Saul was a giant among his own people, and was the logical one to accept the challenge. He stood head and shoulders above his fellows and had a bronze helmet and coat of mail ([1 Samuel 17:38]), yet trembled before Goliath. Although he had forfeited the presence and protection of the Spirit of God, he realized that he must win this stalemate or lose face with his people."[2]

How often do you place yourself in tight spots without having first taken God into your plans?

---

1. Ellen G. White, *Spiritual Gifts*, vol. 4 (Washington, DC: Review and Herald®, 1945), 79, 80.
2. Francis D. Nichol, ed., *The Seventh-day Adventist Bible Commentary*, vol. 2 (Washington, DC: Review and Herald®, 1976), 535.

DAVID ARRIVES IN CAMP

And David rose up early in the morning, and left the sheep with a keeper,
and took, and went, as Jesse had commanded him; and he came to the
trench, as the host was going forth to the fight, and shouted for the battle.
—1 Samuel 17:20

David was at home, tending his father's flocks, while his three eldest brothers—Eliab, Abinadab, and Shammah—were with Saul's army at Elah. The scene of the standoff, being only fifteen miles from Bethlehem, was certainly not hidden from their father, Jesse. "The fact that during this time the Philistines had made no attempt to outflank the army of Israel implies that since their disastrous defeat at Michmash the Philistines had not been strong enough for a full-scale attack. They were now relying on intimidation and the possibility of victory through single combat."[1]

"By his father's direction he [David] was to carry a message and a gift to his elder brothers and to learn if they were still in safety and health. But, unknown to Jesse, the youthful shepherd had been entrusted with a higher mission. The armies of Israel were in peril, and David had been directed by an angel to save his people."[2] David therefore rose early and probably took what shortcuts he knew to reach the Valley of Elah by late morning. He took with him some corn and ten loaves of bread. He also took ten cheeses as a gift for the commander. This gift might guarantee the commander's goodwill in the placement of his brothers during battle.

"David ran to the army, and came and saluted his brothers. While he was talking with them, Goliath, the champion of the Philistines, came forth, and with insulting language defied Israel and challenged them to provide a man from their ranks who would meet him in single combat. He repeated his challenge, and when David saw that all Israel were filled with fear, and learned that the Philistine's defiance was hurled at them day after day, without arousing a champion to silence the boaster, his spirit was stirred within him. He was fired with zeal to preserve the honor of the living God and the credit of His people."[3]

God calls for courageous men and women to defend truth today.

---

1. Francis D. Nichol, ed., *The Seventh-day Adventist Bible Commentary*, vol. 2 (Washington, DC: Review and Herald®, 1976), 536, 537.
2. Ellen G. White, *Patriarchs and Prophets* (Mountain View, CA: Pacific Press®, 1943), 645.
3. White, 645.

JUST WHO DO YOU THINK YOU ARE, LITTLE BROTHER?

And Eliab his eldest brother heard when he spake unto the men; and Eliab's anger was kindled against David, and he said, Why camest thou down hither? and with whom hast thou left those few sheep in the wilderness? I know thy pride, and the naughtiness of thine heart; for thou art come down that thou mightest see the battle.

—1 Samuel 17:28

The Bible is filled with stories of dysfunctional families. Cain's jealousy of Abel ended in murder (Genesis 4:8). Abraham's marriage to two wives—Hagar who bore him Ishmael and Sarah who bore him Isaac—tore his family apart. One wife suffered exile (Genesis 21:9–14). Jacob and Esau nearly came to blows over the paternal blessing (Genesis 27:41). The deviousness of Jacob in robbing his older brother of the birthright resulted in his exile. He was never to see his mother, Rebekah, again. Joseph was sold into slavery by his brothers (Genesis 37:28) but escaped death only because Reuben refused to see him killed (vv. 20–36). Eli did not control his sons, and they made a mockery of the tabernacle and its services (1 Samuel 2:12). These few examples are representative of many found in Holy Scripture. Relationships within families are hard!

David's older brother slandered and belittled him, and he did so in public. "David's eldest brother, Eliab, whom God would not choose to be king, was jealous of David, because he was honored before him. He despised David, and looked upon him as inferior to himself. He accused him before others of stealing away unknown to his father to see the battle. He taunts him with the small business in which he is engaged, in tending a few sheep in the wilderness."[1]

The brothers' "jealousy had been aroused as they saw David honored above them, and they did not regard him with the respect and love due to his integrity and brotherly tenderness. They looked upon him as merely a stripling shepherd, and now the question which he [David] asked was regarded by Eliab as a censure upon his own cowardice in making no attempt to silence the giant of the Philistines."[2]

David was not intimidated either by the boastful blasphemy of Goliath or the jealous slander of Eliab. Do you cower when someone calls you out as a Christian?

---

1. Ellen G. White, *Spiritual Gifts*, vol. 4 (Washington, DC: Review and Herald®, 1945), 80, 81.
2. Ellen G. White, *Patriarchs and Prophets* (Mountain View, CA: Pacific Press®, 1943), 645.

I Can Do This Thing

And David said to Saul, Let no man's heart fail because
of him; thy servant will go and fight with this Philistine.
—1 Samuel 17:32

S aul knows not what to do. He imagines Israel as Philistine slaves. He can see no way of escape. In his trouble he offers great reward to any one who will slay the proud boaster. But all feel their weakness. They have a king whom God does not instruct, who dare not engage in any perilous enterprise, for he expects no special interposition from God to save his life. . . . The armies of Israel seemed paralyzed with terror."[1]

"The words of David were repeated to the king, who summoned the youth before him. Saul listened with astonishment to the words of the shepherd, as he said, 'Let no man's heart fail because of him; thy servant will go and fight with this Philistine.' Saul strove to turn David from his purpose, but the young man was not to be moved. He replied in a simple, unassuming way, relating his experiences while guarding his father's flocks. And he said, 'The Lord that delivered me out of the paw of the lion, and out of the paw of the bear, He will deliver me out of the hand of this Philistine. And Saul said unto David, Go, and the Lord be with thee.' "[2]

Saul was in a quandary. "If he refused to let David fight, the army would expect him, as king, to champion their cause. If he let David fight, and Goliath killed him, the battle would be lost and Israel would again be in bondage to the Philistines."[3]

"What a contrast—a humble shepherd lad encouraging an experienced and successful warrior of Israel! Saul, the only giant of Israel ([1 Samuel] 10:23), realized that he should have been the one to accept Goliath's challenge. But a guilty conscience left him fearful and trembling. . . . David was as courageous as Saul was cowardly."[4]

"The angel of the Lord *encampeth round about them that fear him, and delivereth them"* (Psalm 34:7).

---

1. Ellen G. White, *Spiritual Gifts*, vol. 4 (Washington, DC: Review and Herald®, 1945), 80.

2. Ellen G. White, *Patriarchs and Prophets* (Mountain View, CA: Pacific Press®, 1943), 646.

3. Francis D. Nichol, ed., *The Seventh-day Adventist Bible Commentary*, vol. 2 (Washington, DC: Review and Herald®, 1976), 538.

4. Nichol, 538.

Preparing for Battle

And Saul armed David with his armour, and he put an helmet
of brass upon his head; also he armed him with a coat of mail.
—1 Samuel 17:38

Saul was a coward! He had armor, but knew he could not meet Goliath in his own physical strength. With ostensible prudence he at first refused David permission to fight because of his youth. Then he gave further evidence of his folly by attempting to give his own armor to David."[1] "Though Saul had given David permission to accept Goliath's challenge, the king had small hope that David would be successful in his courageous undertaking. Command was given to clothe the youth in the king's own armor. The heavy helmet of brass was put upon his head, and the coat of mail was placed upon his body; the monarch's sword was at his side. Thus equipped, he started upon his errand, but erelong began to retrace his steps. The first thought in the minds of the anxious spectators was that David had decided not to risk his life in meeting an antagonist in so unequal an encounter. But this was far from the thought of the brave young man. When he returned to Saul he begged permission to lay aside the heavy armor, saying, 'I cannot go with these; for I have not proved them.' He laid off the king's armor, and in its stead took only his staff in his hand, with his shepherd's scrip [pouch] and a simple sling."[2]

It must be remembered David was of average stature, while Saul stood over six feet tall. The king's armor would have been heavy, but more than that, it would have been oversized and awkward on David. While Saul hoped David would be successful, he trusted his armor to protect the lad. When David respectfully asked to remove the king's armor, his concern was twofold: (1) he had not trained while wearing it, and it hampered his movements; and (2) more importantly, the armor showed distrust in the power of God to protect him. "David could not fight in Saul's armor—he must be himself. . . . God wants men who will be themselves, men who will learn from each day's experience what they need to know in order to solve tomorrow's problems."[3]

Saul trusted his armor; David trusted his God.

---

1. Francis D. Nichol, ed., *The Seventh-day Adventist Bible Commentary*, vol. 2 (Washington, DC: Review and Herald®, 1976), 538.

2. Ellen G. White, *Patriarchs and Prophets* (Mountain View, CA: Pacific Press®, 1943), 646, 647.

3. Nichol, *The Seventh-day Adventist Bible Commentary*, 2:538, 539.

DAVID SLAYS GOLIATH

Then said David to the Philistine, Thou comest to me with a sword, and with a spear, and with a shield: but I come to thee in the name of the LORD of hosts, the God of the armies of Israel, whom thou hast defied.
—1 Samuel 17:45

Moving through the ravine, David chose five smooth stones and placed them in the shepherd's pouch at his side. Goliath advanced to meet his opponent, but when he saw it was a mere lad without armor, he was amazed and angered. "Am I a dog, that thou comest to me with staves [sticks]?" (1 Samuel 17:43). All Israel heard David's truthful reply found in 1 Samuel 17:45–47.

"There was a ring of fearlessness in his tone, a look of triumph and rejoicing upon his fair countenance. . . . The anger of Goliath was roused to the very highest heat. In his rage he pushed up the helmet that protected his forehead and rushed forward to wreak vengeance upon his opponent. The son of Jesse was preparing for his foe. 'And it came to pass, when the Philistine arose, and came and drew nigh to meet David, that David hasted, and ran toward the army to meet the Philistine. And David put his hand in his bag, and took thence a stone, and slang it, and smote the Philistine in the forehead, that the stone sunk into his forehead; and he fell upon his face to the earth.' [1 Samuel 17:48, 49.]

"Amazement spread along the lines of the two armies. They had been confident that David would be slain; but when the stone went whizzing through the air, straight to the mark, they saw the mighty warrior tremble, and reach forth his hands, as if he were struck with sudden blindness. The giant reeled, and staggered, and like a smitten oak, fell to the ground. David did not wait an instant. He sprang upon the prostrate form of the Philistine, and with both hands laid hold of Goliath's heavy sword. A moment before, the giant had boasted that with it he would sever the youth's head from his shoulders and give his body to the fowls of the air. Now it was lifted in the air, and then the head of the boaster rolled from his trunk, and a shout of exultation went up from the camp of Israel."[1]

"With God all things are possible" (Matthew 19:26).

---

1. Ellen G. White, *Patriarchs and Prophets* (Mountain View, CA: Pacific Press®, 1943), 648.

DAVID'S THREE VICTORIES

So David prevailed.
—1 Samuel 17:50

D avid had defeated Goliath in single combat, center stage, in full view of both armies. Thousands witnessed his act of bravery and the humility he expressed in crediting God with the victory. "The perfidy of the Philistines became apparent the moment their champion was slain. They had promised to become the servants of the Israelites in the event that Goliath should be killed ([1 Samuel 17:9]). By running away they forfeited the consideration proposed in their own challenge to the army of Saul, and demonstrated, furthermore, that had Goliath been victorious they would have dealt unmercifully with Israel."[1] The Israelites charged the panicked Philistines and struck them down as they fled. For more than ten miles, the slaughter continued until, finally, the army of Saul returned to plunder the tents of their enemies.

David triumphed three times that day. "His first victory came when he was taunted by Eliab as being unfit for aught but caring for sheep. He might have made a justly sharp retort, but refused to reply in kind. Calmly composed, he merely said, 'What have I now done? Is there not a cause?' (v. 29). Such a character is not born in a moment. Had he not learned patience with his sheep, he could not have been shown patience with his jealous brothers. By ignoring the opportunity of entering into a petty quarrel, David showed himself a master of his own spirit. . . .

"David won his second victory when he was escorted into the presence of his king. . . . Saul planted seeds of doubt in David's mind, and tempted him to wear the king's own armor. But again with courteous deference, David won the victory over doubt by adhering to his Heaven-inspired purpose of maintaining faith in, and total dependence on, the Lord.

"All of this prepared him well for his third victory—that over the Philistine, who was the very personification of blasphemy."[2]

"A simple stone from the brook plus a lad's skill and his confiding trust in the eternal God gave the Israelites a lesson they were never to forget, even though they seldom emulated it."[3]

---

1. Francis D. Nichol, ed., *The Seventh-day Adventist Bible Commentary*, vol. 2 (Washington, DC: Review and Herald®, 1976), 539.

2. Nichol, 539.

3. Nichol, 539.

TRUST BRINGS VICTORY!

And the men of Israel and of Judah arose,
and shouted, and pursued the Philistines.

—1 Samuel 17:52

How astonishing! A mere boy had defeated Goliath. To all appearances, the boy possessed no discernible armor. He carried no real weapons. From a distance, it looked as though he were unarmed. He was not trained in warfare, being too young to have fought in previous conflicts. And as to his strategy—why it was no strategy at all! He just walked toward Goliath, shouted, "I come to thee in the name of the LORD of hosts, the God of the armies of Israel, whom thou hast defied" (1 Samuel 17:45), and slew him with a shepherd's sling.

With the sudden realization that the tables had been turned, the Israelites rushed forward. "The Philistines were smitten with terror, and the confusion which ensued resulted in a precipitate retreat. The shouts of the triumphant Hebrews echoed along the summits of the mountains, as they rushed after their fleeing enemies."[1] The once proud Philistines scattered. The wounded were ignored as the survivors fled for safety. What a turn of events! Where the future had looked dark and foreboding for Israel, now a great victory had been won.

Israel had simply forgotten that God has solutions to "giant" problems. It is all too easy for Christians to make that same mistake. "Some are always fearing, and borrowing trouble. Every day they are surrounded with the tokens of God's love; every day they are enjoying the bounties of His providence; but they overlook these present blessings. . . .

". . . We should not allow the perplexities and worries of everyday life to fret the mind and cloud the brow. . . .

". . . Cast your care upon God, and remain calm and cheerful. . . . Do all you can on your part to bring about favorable results. Jesus has promised His aid, but not apart from our effort."[2] "It is better to trust in the LORD than to put confidence in man" (Psalm 118:8).

A humble heart and trust in the Lord will give you victory over your "giant" problems.

---

1. Ellen G. White, *Patriarchs and Prophets* (Mountain View, CA: Pacific Press®, 1943), 648.
2. Ellen G. White, *Steps to Christ* (Washington, DC: Review and Herald®, 1956), 121, 122.

WHO IS THIS YOUNGSTER?

And when Saul saw David go forth against the Philistine, he said unto Abner, the captain of the host, Abner, whose son is this youth? And Abner said, As thy soul liveth, O king, I cannot tell.

—1 Samuel 17:55

Today's text has puzzled some Bible scholars. How could Saul not know the identity of the musician who played harp in his own court? First Samuel 17:15 says, "But David *went and returned* from Saul to feed his father's sheep at Bethlehem" (emphasis added). Was David already playing before Saul part time, or was he ferrying food from Bethlehem to Saul's camp? He was doing both!

"In the providence of God, David, as a skillful performer upon the harp, was brought before the king. His lofty and heaven-inspired strains had the desired effect. The brooding melancholy that had settled like a dark cloud over the mind of Saul was charmed away.

"*When his services were not required at the court of Saul, David returned to his flocks among the hills* and continued to maintain his simplicity of spirit and demeanor. Whenever it was necessary, he was recalled to minister before the king, to soothe the mind of the troubled monarch till the evil spirit should depart from him. . . .

". . . [David] had been in the court of the king and had seen the responsibilities of royalty. . . . He had seen the glory of royalty shadowed with a dark cloud of sorrow, and he knew that the household of Saul, in their private life, were far from happy. All these things served to bring troubled thoughts to him who had been anointed to be king over Israel. But while he was absorbed in deep meditation, and harassed by thoughts of anxiety, he turned to his harp, and called forth strains that elevated his mind to the Author of every good, and the dark clouds that seemed to shadow the horizon of the future were dispelled."[1]

Once Saul realized David, the hero of the hour, was also the humble harp player he had taken little notice of during his periods of abstraction, he refused to allow David to return to his father's home. He reasoned that if God was with David, keeping him close might be beneficial!

Beware! Some, calling themselves Christians, only associate with a church to gain short-term benefits and fleece the flock.

---

1. Ellen G. White, *Patriarchs and Prophets* (Mountain View, CA: Pacific Press®, 1943), 643, 644; emphasis added.

DAVID AND JONATHAN

*And it came to pass, when [David] had made an end
of speaking unto Saul, that the soul of Jonathan was knit with
the soul of David, and Jonathan loved him as his own soul.*
—1 Samuel 18:1

I t is rare indeed for two persons to recognize in each other a kindred spirit. Intrigued by David's character and drawn to his expressed devotion to God, Jonathan vowed to learn more about this shepherd from Bethlehem. The hero of Michmash needed a friend who shared his own standards. Jonathan had already shown an aversion to his father's actions (1 Samuel 14:29).

Gradually, a friendship developed as the two young men shared thoughts and adventures. In time, a covenant was made between them, binding each to the other in defense of their lives. This was no small pact between the two warriors. "The pact of friendship must have been the result of conversations unnumbered, of expeditions carried out together, of mature affection."[1]

As the eldest son, Jonathan was heir to the throne. "His love for David was so great that he was prepared to say, as John the Baptist did centuries later, 'He must increase, but I must decrease' (John 3:30). He beheld in David what he had once dreamed he might become. All the commendable traits of the two characters were cemented together by true affection, and Jonathan awoke to the fact that happiness consists in loving rather than in being loved. Christ so loved us that He voluntarily divested Himself of every divine prerogative (Phil. 2:6–8) that He might plant the leaven of truth in every man (John 1:9)."[2]

"In the lovely friendship of these two devoted, ardent spirits it is our privilege to behold something of the feelings of Christ as one day He beholds in the lives of His redeemed ones the same spiritual vision, the same humility of soul, the same calmness of spirit, the same obedience to eternal principles of truth, that possessed His own heart while here on earth. Seeing thus the intense travail of His soul, He will be satisfied (Isa. 53:11)."[3]

"What a joy heaven will be for kindred souls, with an eternity for companionship."[4]

---

1. Francis D. Nichol, ed., *The Seventh-day Adventist Bible Commentary*, vol. 2 (Washington, DC: Review and Herald®, 1976), 542.
2. Nichol, 542.
3. Nichol, 542.
4. Nichol, 542.

DAVID IN SAUL'S SERVICE

*And David came to Saul, and stood before him: and he
loved him greatly; and he became his armourbearer.*
—1 Samuel 16:21

D avid now entered the service of Saul. "In the providence of God, David was thus brought into a situation where he would have contact with the leading men of the nation—who might thus learn to appreciate his talents—and with the affairs of government. . . .

". . . Even Saul came to honor and respect the naturally attractive personality of David, and to esteem in him those qualities implanted there by the Holy Spirit."[1]

As Saul's armor-bearer, David became, for all intents and purposes, his bodyguard. Serving Saul could not have been easy. Saul's periods of melancholy were interspersed with those of mania, making him unpredictable. "Saul at times realized his own unfitness for the government of Israel, and he felt that the kingdom would be more secure if there could be connected with him one who received instruction from the Lord. Saul hoped also that his connection with David would be a safeguard to himself. Since David was favored and shielded by the Lord, his presence might be a protection to Saul when he went out with him to war."[2] David was, in effect, looked upon as a good-luck talisman by Saul.

"Like Moses in the courts of Pharaoh, David received training in administrative affairs that was to stand him in good stead in years to come. He was placed in a position where he could see life from all its varied angles, and was given spiritual insight that he might distinguish between right and wrong. Like Daniel, David maintained his integrity in an environment not of his own choosing; nor did he fear contamination. God does not hesitate to place His servants in the very vortex of human selfishness, knowing that the darker the night, the brighter their light will shine forth. David, who had been a dutiful son in the house of his father, Jesse, now proved his worth as a loyal ambassador for the king."[3]

Integrity is vital in any Christian's battle against evil influences.

---

1. Francis D. Nichol, ed., *The Seventh-day Adventist Bible Commentary*, vol. 2 (Washington, DC: Review and Herald®, 1976), 531.
2. Ellen G. White, *Patriarchs and Prophets* (Mountain View, CA: Pacific Press®, 1943), 649.
3. Nichol, *The Seventh-day Adventist Bible Commentary*, 2:542.

TO SOOTHE A TROUBLED SOUL

And it came to pass, when the evil spirit from God was upon Saul, that David took an harp, and played with his hand: so Saul was refreshed, and was well, and the evil spirit departed from him.

—1 Samuel 16:23

From the time Samuel departed Saul's presence, never to return (1 Samuel 15:35), Saul had no peace of mind. He knew he had been forsaken by God for his actions and his lack of willingness to conscientiously obey the Lord. He knew the kingdom would be removed violently from his family and the throne given to another more deserving (v. 28). Future disaster was certain. Thus, he became mentally and physically tense. He constantly watched for signs of a successor. He believed his associates might harbor an assassin. While he had a premonition David might be the chosen one, he was not without some doubt, for the lad expressed no interest in gaining power and seemed utterly loyal.

Saul "had recently proved powerless before the Philistines, and had it not been for the courageous exploit of this shepherd lad he might have lost his own life. Yet, he resented the thought that this lad whom he had honored and associated closely with himself might be winning away from him the affections of the people and the army as well. . . . Saul again gave way to feelings of discontent and evil surmisings until his jealous mind finally became deranged."[1]

Saul was able to fool his courtiers by exhibiting sham holiness, but it was all a frenzied act. "The monarch of Israel was opposing his will to the will of the Infinite One. Saul had not learned, while ruling the kingdom of Israel, that he should rule his own spirit. He allowed his impulses to control his judgment, until he was plunged into a fury of passion. He had paroxysms of rage, when he was ready to take the life of any who dared oppose his will. From this frenzy he would pass into a state of despondency and self-contempt, and remorse would take possession of his soul."[2] The music of David seemed to still the bipolar mind of Saul. He enjoyed the brief periods of peace that these interludes brought to his troubled mind.

Music still has power. Some music soothes and calms the mind, and some intensifies evil thoughts and passions. What does your choice of music say about you?

---

1. Francis D. Nichol, ed., *The Seventh-day Adventist Bible Commentary*, vol. 2 (Washington, DC: Review and Herald®, 1976), 542.

2. Ellen G. White, *Patriarchs and Prophets* (Mountain View, CA: Pacific Press®, 1943), 650.

PRAISE FOR THE WARRIORS

And the women answered one another as they played, and said,
Saul hath slain his thousands, and David his ten thousands.

—1 Samuel 18:7

Saul's initial friendship with David soon turned to envy. "The demon of jealousy entered the heart of the king. He was angry because David was exalted above himself in the song of the women of Israel. In place of subduing these envious feelings, he displayed the weakness of his character, and exclaimed, 'They have ascribed unto David ten thousands, and to me they have ascribed but thousands: and what can he have more but the kingdom?'

"One great defect in the character of Saul was his love of approbation. This trait had had a controlling influence over his actions and thoughts; everything was marked by his desire for praise and self-exaltation. His standard of right and wrong was the low standard of popular applause. No man is safe who lives that he may please men, and does not seek first for the approbation of God. . . .

". . . It was envy that made Saul miserable and put the humble subject of his throne in jeopardy. What untold mischief has this evil trait of character worked in our world! . . . Envy is the offspring of pride, and if it is entertained in the heart, it will lead to hatred, and eventually to revenge and murder. Satan displayed his own character in exciting the fury of Saul against him who had never done him harm."[1]

David had been placed in the court of Saul for two reasons. As already mentioned, he was exposed to the administration of a government and met the key individuals who imparted to him knowledge of how to govern. He was also positioned to be a positive influence on Saul. Saul had chosen to follow his own path, and his character flaws had deepened, yet God had not forsaken him. "Through David's ministry, the Lord was appealing to the hardened heart of Saul, inviting him to return and realize the healing power of God in his behalf. Though Saul had irretrievably disqualified himself as king, he might yet find salvation as an individual."[2]

When we are tempted, a pathway is always provided for escape (1 Corinthians 10:13).

---

1. Ellen G. White, *Patriarchs and Prophets* (Mountain View, CA: Pacific Press®, 1943), 650, 651.
2. Francis D. Nichol, ed., *The Seventh-day Adventist Bible Commentary*, vol. 2 (Washington, DC: Review and Herald®, 1976), 543.

A Fugitive From King Saul

1 Samuel 18:9–2 Samuel 1:27
1 Chronicles 10

Patriarchs and Prophets, chapters 64–68

SAUL TURNS AGAINST DAVID

And Saul cast the javelin; for he said, I will smite David even to the wall with it. And David avoided out of his presence twice.
—1 Samuel 18:11

S aul "loved to hear David play upon his harp, and the evil spirit seemed to be charmed away for the time; but one day when the youth was ministering before him, and bringing sweet music from his instrument, accompanying his voice as he sang the praises of God, Saul suddenly threw his spear at the musician, for the purpose of putting an end to his life. David was preserved by the interposition of God, and without injury fled from the rage of the maddened king."[1] Such swift mood changes made life at court very difficult. "Angels of God preserved the life of David. They made him to understand what was the purpose of Saul, and as the instrument was hurled at him, he sprang [to] one side, and received no harm, while the instrument was driven deep in the wall where David had been sitting. . . .

"David had obeyed Saul as a servant, and his conduct was humble. His life was irreproachable. His faithfulness in doing the will of God was a constant rebuke to Saul's extravagant, rebellious course. Saul determined to leave no means untried, that David might be slain. As long as Saul lived, this was the great object of his life, notwithstanding he was compelled to ascribe to the providence of God the escape of David from his hands. Yet his heart was destitute of the love of God, and he was a self-idolater. To his pride and ambition, true honor, justice, and humanity were sacrificed. He hunted David as a wild beast."[2]

This would not be the last time Saul would attempt to take the life of God's anointed with a lance. He decided to bide his time and watch for another opening to strike. He needed to be cautious, lest this favorite of the people be seen as a martyr, killed because he was perceived to be a threat to the irrationality of a jealous king. It must have taken great courage for David to return to the throne room to play for the king after this violent outburst.

David placed supreme trust in the Lord's ability to protect his servant in every circumstance.

---

1. Ellen G. White, *Patriarchs and Prophets* (Mountain View, CA: Pacific Press®, 1943), 650, 651.
2. Ellen G. White, *Spiritual Gifts*, vol. 4 (Washington, DC: Review and Herald®, 1945), 83.

A BACKHANDED GIFT

And Saul said to David, Behold my elder daughter Merab,
her will I give thee to wife: only be thou valiant for me, and fight
the LORD's battles. For Saul said, Let not mine hand be upon
him, but let the hand of the Philistines be upon him.
—1 Samuel 18:17

Saul could be cunning when he felt it necessary. He still desired to rid himself of David yet must avoid another violent attack upon the young man. This presented a problem, for David was beloved by the people, and Saul feared his own subjects. Saul's first move was to separate himself from David's association, removing the appearance of any plot to kill him by promoting him to be "captain over a thousand" (1 Samuel 18:13). But by depriving himself of David's music and removing his visible presence beside the king at public events, Saul made life harder for himself.

"David accepted his demotion—for such it seems to have been—in all humility, and in his new role won the admiration of all Israel. There were no recriminations, nor was there self-pity due to the unjust treatment. David remained the same bright, spiritual-minded soul he had always been. Greatly beloved by the Lord, he was, in spite of the wrath of the king, receiving just the training he needed before stepping into the responsibilities of leadership. God adapts the discipline of life to the peculiar needs of each individual who purposes to be true to duty."[1]

Next, Saul skillfully positioned David to be killed. If the Philistines should slay him on the field of battle, people could hardly blame Saul for his death. Saul promised his oldest daughter Merab would be David's bride if he fought valiantly. The promise of marriage to the king's daughter had already been made to anyone who might slay Goliath (1 Samuel 17:25). Apparently, Saul had not fulfilled that promise, for the princess Merab was still single. Saul had no intention of honoring this promise either. David was likewise reluctant to accept a betrothal.

David responded by saying, "Who am I? and what is my life, or my father's family in Israel, that I should be son in law to the king?" (1 Samuel 18:18). Saul was offended! How dare David refuse marriage to his daughter! Saul voided the offer, and Merab was married to another.

"A little that a righteous man hath is better than the riches of many wicked" (*Psalm 37:16*).

---

1. Francis D. Nichol, ed., *The Seventh-day Adventist Bible Commentary*, vol. 2 (Washington, DC: Review and Herald®, 1976), 543.

ANOTHER PLAN TO GET DAVID KILLED

And Saul saw and knew that the LORD was with David, and that Michal Saul's daughter loved him. And Saul was yet the more afraid of David; and Saul became David's enemy continually.
—1 Samuel 18:28, 29

No dowry had been mentioned as being necessary for the man who would receive Saul's daughter for slaying Goliath. Saul changed the rules once David was victorious. It was nothing for a king without honor. Another scheme to do away with David came to Saul. His servants told him that Michal, another of his daughters, was in love with David. "In his daughter Michal the scheming Saul saw an opportunity yet to carry out his nefarious plan for David's destruction. He would require such a dowry as would in all probability accomplish his purpose in an even better way than would have been possible had he given Merab to David. Saul was greatly pleased but had to move carefully, for David must not know that Michal was in love with him."[1]

Using unsuspecting servants as go-betweens, Saul hinted that since David was well thought of by the king, it might be possible to marry another of Saul's daughters. David was not convinced. He again replied, "Seemeth it to you a light thing to be a king's son in law, seeing that I am a poor man, and lightly esteemed?" (1 Samuel 18:23). The subject of a dowry again came up. Saul instructed his servants to tell David he would settle for one hundred Philistine foreskins. Saul hoped to have David die at the hands of the Philistines while trying to earn the dowry.

Destroying Israel's enemies was something David could do. He killed not one hundred but two hundred men. Saul had made his dowry request public knowledge, thinking to gain sympathy from the people when David fell to their enemies. Trapped by his own cunning, Saul had no choice but to honor the promise and make Michal David's wife.

"Chagrin at the failure of his evil scheme intensified Saul's hatred of David. But instead of yielding to God, Saul grieved over wounded pride. David's prestige was greater than ever. Now, fully possessed by an evil spirit, Saul's darkly brooding mind assiduously sought a new snare for his enemy, now his own son-in-law."[2]

"Deliver my soul, O LORD, from lying lips, and from a deceitful tongue" (Psalm 120:2).

---

1. Francis D. Nichol, ed., *The Seventh-day Adventist Bible Commentary*, vol. 2 (Washington, DC: Review and Herald®, 1976), 544.
2. Nichol, 544.

JONATHAN SECURES AN UNSTABLE PEACE

And Saul hearkened unto the voice of Jonathan:
and Saul sware, As the LORD liveth, he shall not be slain.
—1 Samuel 19:6

Saul now dropped all pretenses and ordered his men to kill David. More than ever, he was convinced David was the man who would replace him on the throne, for God was with David.

"This was Saul's fifth attempt to do away with David: (1) He threw his javelin at David ([1 Samuel] 18:10, 11). (2) Then he tried to accomplish his evil design by placing David at the front in the hope that he would be killed (ch. 18:17). (3) Next, Saul deceived him by promising him Merab but giving her to another, perhaps hoping that David would act rashly as a result and might be punished (ch. 18:19). (4) After that, he gave David permission to earn the dowry for Michal by a dangerous mission (ch. 18:25). (5) Now, it being evident that the Lord was with David, Saul sought the help of others to kill him."[1]

"Jonathan revealed the king's intention to David and bade him conceal himself while he would plead with his father to spare the life of the deliverer of Israel. He presented before the king what David had done to preserve the honor and even the life of the nation, and what terrible guilt would rest upon the murderer of the one whom God had used to scatter their enemies."[2] Jonathan could no longer straddle the fence. He had to maintain loyalty to a father who was obviously unhinged, and he had a duty to his best friend, David, to protect him from harm.

Jonathan displays amazing diplomacy as an advocate for justice. He could easily have pointed out that killing David would be another bad decision and thus angered the king with criticism. He could have argued that David was no threat to the throne and tried to change the stubborn king's mind. Instead, he pointed out David's unique value and the benefits he brought to the nation and further delineated David's many acts of loyalty to Saul personally. Jonathan's tact and wise counsel softened the heart of Saul, and he vowed to stop seeking the life of David.

"Blessed are the peacemakers: for they shall be called the children of God" *(Matthew 5:9).*

---

1. Francis D. Nichol, ed., *The Seventh-day Adventist Bible Commentary*, vol. 2 (Washington, DC: Review and Herald®, 1976), 545.
2. Ellen G. White, *Patriarchs and Prophets* (Mountain View, CA: Pacific Press®, 1943), 652.

Javelin, Round Two

And Saul sought to smite David even to the wall with the javelin: but he slipped away out of Saul's presence, and he smote the javelin into the wall: and David fled, and escaped that night.
—1 Samuel 19:10

Another of the interminable wars between Israel and Philistia broke out soon after Saul made his pact with David. David led the armies of Israel against the Philistines and won a great victory. Once again David was acclaimed by the people as a great warrior and the people's hero. This reignited Saul's flame of anger and kindled another outburst of rage.

"Saul had rejected the Spirit of God—committed the unpardonable sin—and there was nothing more God could do for him. . . . It was not that the Spirit of Jehovah withdrew from Saul arbitrarily; but rather that Saul rebelled against His guidance, and deliberately withdrew himself from the influence of the Spirit. This must be understood in harmony with Ps. 139:7 and with the fundamental principle of free choice. . . .

". . . The Scriptures sometimes represent God as doing that which He does not specifically prevent. In giving Satan an opportunity to demonstrate his principles, God, in effect, would limit His own power. Of course, there were limits beyond which Satan could not go (see Job 1:12; 2:6), but within his limited sphere he did have divine permission to act. Thus, although his acts are contrary to the divine will, he can do nothing except what God permits him to do, and whatever he and his evil spirits may do, is done with God's permission. Therefore when God withdrew His own Spirit from Saul (see on 1 Sam. 16:13, 14), Satan was free to have his way."[1]

Saul could not control his emotions toward David when it came to evil surmising. "While the young man was playing before the king, filling the palace with sweet harmony, Saul's passion overcame him, and he hurled a javelin at David, thinking to pin the musician to the wall; but the angel of the Lord turned aside the deadly weapon. David escaped and fled to his own house."[2]

"The wicked watcheth the righteous, and seeketh to slay him. The LORD will not leave him in his hand, nor condemn him when he is judged" (Psalm 37:32, 33).

---

1. Francis D. Nichol, ed., *The Seventh-day Adventist Bible Commentary*, vol. 2 (Washington, DC: Review and Herald®, 1976), 530, 531.
2. Ellen G. White, *Patriarchs and Prophets* (Mountain View, CA: Pacific Press®, 1943), 652, 653.

PSALM 12: HELP FOR THE FAITHFUL

*Help, LORD; for the godly man ceaseth; for the faithful fail from among
the children of men. They speak vanity every one with his neighbour:
with flattering lips and with a double heart do they speak.*

—Psalm 12:1, 2

P salm 12 is a plea to the Lord for deliverance from those who are
deceitful. Saul, the epitome of a two-faced individual, spoke
soothing things to David's face while scheming to kill him behind his back. "No confidence can be placed in a person who has one
heart to speak his words and another heart to conceal his purposes."[1]
David deplored people who felt they were not accountable for their
words or the actions their words encouraged. While feigning friendship,
these people slandered, gossiped, and destroyed reputations. But those
who use words as weapons will be held accountable. "Many who admit
responsibility for their actions are unwilling to take any responsibility
for their words."[2] However, "by thy words thou shalt be justified, and
by thy words thou shalt be condemned" (Matthew 12:37). We shall be
judged by our words because they reveal the desires of our hearts. God
understands motives and unspoken desires as well as our words, for the
Lord looks on the heart. Motives matter!

The second half of Psalm 12 expresses faith in God to make all things
right in the end. The Lord preserves the righteous, even amid flatterers,
oppressors, and liars. "Evildoers abound when those who rule over them
are corrupt. Corruption penetrates from rulers to those who are ruled by
them. In spite of this realistic close to the poem, the general tenor of the
psalm is one of confidence that God will defend the innocent."[3] One can
almost feel David's sense of betrayal by false friends. Yet his faith in
God's ultimate justice stands firm!

*"I have a Friend so precious . . . / I love to feel Him nigh, / And so we dwell
together, / My Lord and I."*[4]

---

1. Francis D. Nichol, ed., *The Seventh-day Adventist Bible Commentary*, vol. 3 (Washington,
DC: Review and Herald®, 1977), 659.

2. Nichol, 659.

3. Nichol, 659.

4. Mary Anne Shorey, "My Lord and I" (1890), in *The Seventh-day Adventist Hymnal* (Hagerstown, MD: Review and Herald®, 1985), hymn 456.

MICHAL WARNS DAVID

And Michal took an image, and laid it in the bed, and put a
pillow of goats' hair for his bolster, and covered it with a cloth.
—1 Samuel 19:13

D avid reached the safety of his home, but he was still in mortal danger. Whether David confided in his wife concerning the attempt on his life or she witnessed the officers of the court at their front door, Michal immediately realized the peril and urged David to flee certain death by escaping out a window. It seems strange that David would run rather than stand and fight. "There are times when the cause of right can be advanced better by flight than by fighting. Some may think that inasmuch as God had anointed David, and Saul had so far departed from right as to attempt murder, it would have been better for David to stand his ground. Heretofore he had never turned his back to an enemy. Had he faced Saul in the same spirit that he met Goliath, he could not have failed to draw many of the people to his side; but such an action would have led to civil war, for Saul was also popular and many obeyed him implicitly. As events later proved, it was seven years after the death of Saul before David was accepted by all Israel."[1]

Michal placed bedclothes in such a manner that they would resemble a reclining figure. She refused to allow the officers to disturb David or come close to the bed, saying he was ill. When they reported this to Saul, he sent them back with orders to return with David—sick or not. The officers were admitted to the house this time and discovered they had been tricked.

"Saul had been pleased to use Michal as a decoy to lure David on to his death; now he was highly incensed that his own daughter should be loyal to David rather than to him. Outwitted, he feared lest he lose face with his officers. Michal had evidently inherited some of her father's traits; she did not hesitate to offer the excuse that her husband had threatened to kill her. This falsehood gave Saul an excuse to pursue with increased vigor his purpose to slay David, who, it appeared, had now threatened his daughter."[2]

"Many are the afflictions of the righteous: but the LORD *delivereth him out of them all" (Psalm 34:19).*

---

1. Francis D. Nichol, ed., *The Seventh-day Adventist Bible Commentary*, vol. 2 (Washington, DC: Review and Herald®, 1976), 546, 547.
2. Nichol, 547.

PSALM 59: GOD IS MY DEFENSE

Deliver me from mine enemies, O my God:
defend me from them that rise up against me.
—Psalm 59:1

Psalm 59 can be accurately assigned to a specific event in the life of David. The psalm was written when Saul sent men to watch David's house and kill him. David vividly paints a picture of his enemies lying in wait. He asserts his innocence as he has done nothing to warrant such action. He knows God will protect him and show his foes no mercy. Court officers came to the house repeatedly to carry out the orders of Saul, as seen in verses 6 and 14: "They return at evening" (v. 6). To make sure David did not escape, patrols went "round about the city" (v. 14).

The guards think no one can hear them (v. 7), but God knows their every move. They think they can secretly advance on David, but God laughs at their feeble attempts. David is willing to wait for God to intervene rather than fight the current battle in his own strength. He is convinced God eventually will allow him to see the retribution awaiting these officers. Perhaps in time, they might see the error of their ways and repent, so he asks they not be slain outright.

David abhors Israel's lawlessness, which allows such a travesty of justice. He wants these merchants of death, so confident of success, to be confounded. The men surrounding Saul are proud. They routinely curse and lie as befits men with no moral compass. Eventually, they will see "that God is the universal sovereign, punishing wickedness and rewarding righteousness."[1]

Expanding the imagery of hungry dogs howling for prey (v. 14), David asks God to "let them wander up and down for meat, and grudge if they be not satisfied" (v. 15). Though they search all night, David will not be found. While the wicked do their deeds in the black of night, David offers his gratitude "in the morning" (v. 16), in the light of day, for all to see. The psalm ends with David attributing his deliverance to God, even though he used the skills given to him to effect a successful retreat (v. 17).

"Father, lead me day by day, / Ever in Thine own sweet way; / Teach me to be pure and true; / Show me what I ought to do."[2]

1. Francis D. Nichol, ed., *The Seventh-day Adventist Bible Commentary*, vol. 3 (Washington, DC: Review and Herald®, 1977), 773.

2. John P. Hopps, "Father, Lead Me Day by Day" (1876), in *The Seventh-day Adventist Hymnal* (Hagerstown, MD: Review and Herald®, 1985), hymn 482.

DAVID FLEES TO SAMUEL

*So David fled, and escaped, and came to Samuel to
Ramah, and told him all that Saul had done to him. And he
and Samuel went and dwelt in Naioth [the schoolhouse].*
—1 Samuel 19:18

D avid was doubtless greatly perplexed over the conduct of God's appointed leader, Saul. Why did God permit Saul to continue as king? Was God particular? Had He deserted the nation?"[1] These questions and many others must have swirled around in the mind of David as he fled to the only place he could feel safe. He certainly could not return to his father in Bethlehem. That would be the first place Saul would search. He obviously could not trust those who served Saul, knowing they would betray him. "Thoroughly frightened because of Saul's attempt on his life, David naturally sought counsel from the one who had called him from the sheepfold to a place of responsibility in Israel, and had, possibly, taught him at Ramah. With Samuel he would feel as safe from Saul as if there had been a sanctuary to which he might flee."[2]

Samuel welcomed David and, heedless of incurring the wrath of Saul, offered him sanctuary. When Saul learned David was with the prophet, he was further angered. If Samuel should lend his support to David, the people might rally to David and make him Saul's successor. Saul sent officers to Ramah to arrest David and return him to Gibeah, where Saul planned to have him put to death.

A strange thing happened to these men on their way to arrest David. As with Balaam before them, the Holy Spirit came upon them, and they prophesied of future events, praising God and forgetting their mission. Frustrated, Saul sent more men. These joined the first group in prophesying. A third group was sent, and when they arrived at Ramah, they, too, were thwarted. Finally, Saul determined to go in person and kill David. Saul was also held back by the power of the Spirit, and laying aside his royal robes, he came before Samuel with prayer, song, and prophecy. While Saul remained at Ramah, David sought counsel from his friend Jonathan.

"But I will sing of thy power; yea, I will sing aloud of thy mercy in the morning: for thou hast been my defence and refuge in the day of my trouble" *(Psalm 59:16).*

---

1. Francis D. Nichol, ed., *The Seventh-day Adventist Bible Commentary*, vol. 2 (Washington, DC: Review and Herald®, 1976), 547.
2. Nichol, 547.

DAVID AND JONATHAN MAKE A PACT

So Jonathan made a covenant with the house of David, saying,
Let the LORD even require it at the hand of David's enemies.
—1 Samuel 20:16

While Saul was occupied at Ramah, David retraced his steps to Gibeah to meet secretly with Jonathan. David had seen Saul's bizarre behavior firsthand, and he wanted another opinion as to how serious the threat to his life might be. He asked Jonathan, "How have I come up short? Where have I failed in service to king and country?" Jonathan assured him his father would take no action against David without telling him first. David was not so sure. Saul certainly knew the young men were friends, and though Jonathan had been able to reason with his father thus far, that might change in the future. Together they came up with a plan to evaluate the risk.

An annual Jewish sacrificial feast was coming up, and David would be expected to sit at the king's table. Knowing his absence would be questioned, Jonathan was to tell his father David had asked to be excused so that he might go home to Bethlehem to share the feast with family. The reaction of Saul to this news would reveal his purpose. Jonathan and David took a solemn oath to never betray one another.

"There is a valuable lesson in this experience. Men do not have the same heredity and environment, and consequently do not approach the problems of life in the same way. . . . Saul, in his impatient tyranny and bigotry, felt that he must be first, and that what he said was correct and final. Anyone disagreeing had to be eliminated, regardless of the means taken to do it. Yet his own son approached life from an entirely different angle. Why the difference between father and son when both had had much the same surroundings and training? . . .

"The solution to these questions is found in the words of Paul: 'to whom ye yield yourselves servants to obey, his servants ye are' (Rom. 6:16). Because of his free choice, man gives his service, his thoughts, and his outlook on life to either one or the other of two masters—two leaders who represent diametrically opposite standards."[1] Saul chose to walk in the darkness of his own pride and ego. Jonathan chose to humble himself and follow God's light.

Do you feel the need to always be first? (Matthew 20:16).

---

1. Francis D. Nichol, ed., *The Seventh-day Adventist Bible Commentary*, vol. 2 (Washington, DC: Review and Herald®, 1976), 552.

SAUL ATTACKS HIS OWN

And Saul cast a javelin at him to smite him: whereby Jonathan knew that it was determined of his father to slay David.
—1 Samuel 20:33

T he king sat down on the first day of the feast with Abner by his one hand and an empty seat reserved for David on the other. Thinking perhaps David was delayed for cause, he said nothing. On the second day, turning to Jonathan, Saul asked after David. Jonathan replied that David had requested that he might observe the festival and sacrifice with his family in Bethlehem. To this, Jonathan had given consent. Saul was enraged. Hurling insults at Jonathan and his mother, Saul publicly accused Jonathan of choosing David's friendship over loyalty to the throne. Taking up his spear, Saul threw it at his own son! Jonathan had felt David was wrong in his evaluation of Saul's attitude toward him. Now that Saul's anger was directed at him, he knew otherwise.

"The experience was a shocking disillusionment for Jonathan. The open break with his father was most painful to him. His decision to cast his lot with the 'son of Jesse' was being tested, but he refused to swerve from the right. Like Moses, who turned his back upon the throne of Egypt, Jonathan chose 'rather to suffer affliction with the people of God, than to enjoy the pleasures of sin for a season' (Heb. 11:25). He knew by experience the truth Christ later spoke, 'He that loveth father . . . more than me is not worthy of me' (Matt. 10:37)."[1]

"Jonathan chose of his own free will to affiliate himself with the house that God had indicated would replace the decadent family into which he had been born. In Jonathan's heart God's plan took precedence over family ties. This was not because of his desire for personal safety, but because he understood that truth must finally triumph."[2] Jonathan's approach to life did not mirror that of his father. He realized God had a planned destiny for David, and he refused to forsake him in order to gain the throne for himself. His life shines forth as an example for all who put God first in their lives.

"Behold, how good and how pleasant it is for brethren to dwell together in unity!" (Psalm 133:1).

1. Francis D. Nichol, ed., *The Seventh-day Adventist Bible Commentary*, vol. 2 (Washington, DC: Review and Herald®, 1976), 553.
2. Nichol, 552.

THREE ARROWS

And Jonathan cried after the lad, Make speed, haste, stay not. And Jonathan's lad gathered up the arrows, and came to his master.
—1 Samuel 20:38

Jonathan was angry he had misread his father's intentions. As prearranged, David had hidden near a field where Jonathan routinely practiced with his bow. Taking a lad with him, Jonathan set off for the spot. By bringing along a servant, it appeared that Jonathan was simply going for archery practice to settle his emotions. Telling the lad to fetch the arrows he would shoot, Jonathan shot an arrow beyond him. When the lad reached the spot where the arrow had landed, Jonathan waved him farther off, saying, "Is not the arrow beyond thee? . . . Make speed, haste, stay not" (1 Samuel 20:37, 38). Gathering the arrows, the boy returned and was told to take them back to town. Jonathan then waited for David to show himself.

Coming out of hiding, David fell to the ground and bowed down three times. He and Jonathan kissed one another and wept. David now knew Saul was an immediate and serious threat. At the risk of his own life, Jonathan had brought that message to David. Neither knew whether this would be the last time they would ever meet on this earth. The friendship between Jonathan and David exceeded that of most friends. Each was willing to lay down his life for the other, bound by loyalty to protect each other as brothers. Jonathan was willing to give up his position as successor to the throne so that his friend David might claim it. Together they had campaigned against the enemies of Israel. No finer example of stalwart selflessness is to be found in the Old Testament.

"Jonathan's last words fell upon the ear of David as they separated to pursue their different paths, 'Go in peace, forasmuch as we have sworn both of us in the name of the Lord, saying, The Lord be between me and thee, and between my seed and thy seed forever.'

"The king's son returned to Gibeah, and David hastened to reach Nob, a city but a few miles distant, and also belonging to the tribe of Benjamin."[1]

"The name of Jonathan is treasured in heaven, and it stands on earth a witness to the existence and the power of unselfish love."[2]

---

1. Ellen G. White, *Patriarchs and Prophets* (Mountain View, CA: Pacific Press®, 1943), 655, 656.
2. Ellen G. White, *Education* (Mountain View, CA: Pacific Press®, 1952), 157.

DAVID HIDES IN NOB

Then came David to Nob to Ahimelech the priest: and
Ahimelech was afraid at the meeting of David, and said
unto him, Why art thou alone, and no man with thee?
—1 Samuel 21:1

Here is the first in a series of disappointing scenarios in David's life. "David knew not whither to flee for refuge, except to the servant of God. The priest looked upon him with astonishment, as he came in haste and apparently alone, with a countenance marked by anxiety and sorrow. He inquired what had brought him there. The young man was in constant fear of discovery, and in his extremity he resorted to deception. David told the priest that he had been sent by the king on a secret errand, one which required the utmost expedition. Here he manifested a want of faith in God, and his sin resulted in causing the death of the high priest. Had the facts been plainly stated, Ahimelech would have known what course to pursue to preserve his life. God requires that truthfulness shall mark His people, even in the greatest peril."[1]

Observing this conversation was Doeg, an Edomite, who was head herdsman for the king. David must have thought things simply could not get worse. David had to assume Doeg would tell the king of his visit and conversation with Ahimelech. Seeking to deceive Doeg as to why he had come to Nob, David requested bread for his journey. Ahimelech replied there was no bread other than the shewbread, which had been replaced that day with freshly baked bread. Of this bread, David was welcome as long as his men were ceremonially clean. Five loaves were hardly enough for David and his men. It was quite obvious food was not the reason for David's visit to Nob. Furthermore, no "captain of a thousand" (1 Samuel 18:13) would leave on a sanctioned mission without supplies for his men. Something was very wrong with David's story!

"Doeg had embraced the Hebrew religion and was at the tabernacle paying his vows. . . . The circumstances of these vows are not known. Evidently he had committed some trespass which merited the rebuke of Ahimelech, for this action of the priest was one of the primary reasons why Doeg later turned informer against Ahimelech."[2]

"Remove from me the way of lying: and grant me thy law graciously" (Psalm 119:29).

---

1. Ellen G. White, *Patriarchs and Prophets* (Mountain View, CA: Pacific Press®, 1943), 656.
2. Francis D. Nichol, ed., *The Seventh-day Adventist Bible Commentary*, vol. 2 (Washington, DC: Review and Herald®, 1976), 557.

GOLIATH'S SWORD

And David said unto Ahimelech, And is there not here under thine hand spear or sword? for I have neither brought my sword nor my weapons with me, because the king's business required haste.
—1 Samuel 21:8

When David left Gibeah, he failed to take any weapons. When David asked for a weapon, Ahimelech said, "The sword of Goliath the Philistine, whom thou slewest in the valley of Elah, behold, it is here wrapped in a cloth behind the ephod: if thou wilt take that, take it: for there is no other save that here. And David said, There is none like that; give it [to] me" (1 Samuel 21:9).

"All Goliath's armor had become David's own personal property. It is probable that previously he had himself presented the sword to the tabernacle as a thank offering to God. David was well aware that the tabernacle was not an armory, but probably thinking of the possibility of the sword's still being there, he asked in an offhand manner whether the priest had any weapons he could borrow.

". . . David appeared happy over the thought of securing this sword, perhaps not so much for its military value as for the constant reminder it would be of the protective guidance of the Lord. He needed such encouragement at this moment."[1] Ellen G. White further states, "His courage revived as he grasped the sword that he had once used in destroying the champion of the Philistines."[2]

If only David had remembered the Lord had sheltered him in the past, he would have had little to fear for the future and certainly needed no weapon to defend himself. God could marshal the legions of heaven to fight for David if needed. David had panicked and lost sight of his advantages in the face of seemingly insurmountable difficulties. Yet God always possessed unlimited ways to deliver him that he had not even considered. David eventually realized what his sin had cost and repented with sincere contrition. Even in this, God did not forsake him and stood ready to forgive true repentance.

"For thou, Lord, art good, and ready to forgive; and plenteous in mercy unto all them that call upon thee" (Psalm 86:5).

---

1. Francis D. Nichol, ed., *The Seventh-day Adventist Bible Commentary*, vol. 2 (Washington, DC: Review and Herald®, 1976), 557.
2. Ellen G. White, *Patriarchs and Prophets* (Mountain View, CA: Pacific Press®, 1943), 656.

DAVID, THE ACTOR

*And he changed his behaviour before them, and
feigned himself mad in their hands, and scrabbled on the
doors of the gate, and let his spittle fall down upon his beard.*

—1 Samuel 21:13

It was a common practice for fugitives to hide among the enemies of their own people. Knowing he would not be safe in Israel, David fled to the Philistine town of Gath, less than thirty miles from Nob. Here he sought sanctuary with Achish, the king of Gath. David's fame as a warrior had spread beyond the borders of Israel. He had conquered Goliath and recently slain two hundred Philistine men to obtain the dowry for Michal. Yet here we see an example of the ancient proverb "The enemy of my enemy is my friend." Achish and Saul were mortal enemies.

David might prove a valuable mercenary. On the other hand, he also might be a spy and should not be trusted. David knew he was on shaky ground with Achish, and there was a good chance he would not live to see Bethlehem or his family again. Seeking refuge with the Philistines was perhaps not a good idea. David decided to act as if he had lost his mind, making him of no use to the Philistine king. Apparently, David was a very good actor, for Achish said, "Lo, ye see the man is mad: wherefore then have ye brought him to me?" (1 Samuel 21:14).

"The first error of David was his distrust of God at Nob, and his second mistake was his deception before Achish. David had displayed noble traits of character, and his moral worth had won him favor with the people; but as trial came upon him, his faith was shaken, and human weakness appeared. He saw in every man a spy and a betrayer. In a great emergency David had looked up to God with a steady eye of faith, and had vanquished the Philistine giant. He believed in God, he went in His name. But as he had been hunted and persecuted, perplexity and distress had nearly hidden his heavenly Father from his sight.

"Yet this experience was serving to teach David wisdom; for it led him to realize his weakness and the necessity of constant dependence upon God."[1]

"Every failure on the part of the children of God is due to their lack of faith."[2]

---

1. Ellen G. White, *Patriarchs and Prophets* (Mountain View, CA: Pacific Press®, 1943), 656, 657.
2. White, 657.

THE CAVE AT ADULLAM

David therefore departed thence, and escaped to the cave Adullam.
—1 Samuel 22:1

D avid sought a remote area where he might take refuge. The cave at Adullam is thought to have been one of many located near the eastern end of the Valley of Elah, where David had met Goliath. Several caves are so located that they may be held with a small force against large numbers of assailants. Adullam was near Bethlehem, and David knew the ground. Shepherds had kept their flocks in this area for years and used the caves for shelter.

David's family joined him in this mountain retreat. "The family of David could not feel secure, knowing that at any time the unreasonable suspicions of Saul might be directed against them on account of their relation to David. They had now learned—what was coming to be generally known in Israel—that God had chosen David as the future ruler of His people; and they believed that they would be safer with him, even though he was a fugitive in a lonely cave, than they could be while exposed to the insane madness of a jealous king. . . .

"It was not long before David's company was joined by others who desired to escape the exactions of the king. There were many who had lost confidence in the ruler of Israel, for they could see that he was no longer guided by the Spirit of the Lord. 'And everyone that was in distress, and everyone that was in debt, and everyone that was discontented,' resorted to David, 'and he became a captain over them: and there were with him about four hundred men.' . . . But even in his retreat in the mountains he was far from feeling secure, for he received continual evidence that the king had not relinquished his murderous purpose."[1]

"While in the cave of Adullam David wrote the 57th psalm, according to its heading. Recovering his faith and courage, he now expressed his confidence in God's deliverance, even though he found himself 'among lions: and even among . . . men, whose teeth are spears and arrows, and their tongue a sharp sword' (Ps. 57:4)."[2]

"He that dwelleth in the secret place of the most High shall abide under the shadow of the Almighty" (Psalm 91:1).

---

1. Ellen G. White, *Patriarchs and Prophets* (Mountain View, CA: Pacific Press®, 1943), 657, 658.
2. Francis D. Nichol, ed., *The Seventh-day Adventist Bible Commentary*, vol. 2 (Washington, DC: Review and Herald®, 1976), 560.

PSALM 57: GOD IS MY REFUGE

Be merciful unto me, O God, be merciful unto me:
for my soul trusteth in thee: yea, in the shadow of thy wings
will I make my refuge, until these calamities be overpast.

—Psalm 57:1

Psalms 56 and 57 echo one theme: God "would sooner send every angel out of glory to the relief of faithful souls, to make a hedge about them, than have them deceived and led away by the lying wonders of Satan."[1] David likens his place of refuge to that of baby birds resting safely under the shadow of the protective wings of a parent (Psalm 57:1). Protection from his present calamities is likewise assured, for he trusts the Lord to shield him from his enemies. While at peace, David still outlines his predicament. He is surrounded by enemies. He compares them to wild lions seeking their prey (v. 4). While these lions are human soldiers and militia, armed with spears, swords, and arrows, they are no less dangerous. They seek to trap him (v. 6), but time and time again, he has evaded them. David sees the hand of the Lord in these rescues, and for that, he is grateful.

David rises every morning, and before anything else, he takes time to talk with the Lord (v. 8). His worship at dawn is a time of sustenance and hope. During this time alone, he sings praises to the Lord, accompanied by his harp. He shares his most intimate thoughts and deepest troubles with his Lord, asking for those things he cannot himself attain without divine aid.

Psalm 57:11 repeats verse 5. Together, these verses are similar to the structure of Psalm 56, in which verse 11 repeats verse 4. The verses in these companion psalms have the appearance of a chorus. " 'Heaven and earth have . . . a mutually interwoven history, and the blessed, glorious end of this is in the sunrise of the Divine glory over both.' "[2] David's trust in God is increasing! Though a fugitive in a wilderness cave, he feels secure in God's arms. We see in these psalms a complete reversal of David's early unbelief. He now praises God for His goodness and mercy.

"My God, is any hour so sweet, / From blush of morn to evening star, / As that which calls me to Thy feet, / The hour of prayer?"[3]

---

1. Ellen G. White, *Early Writings* (Washington, DC: Review and Herald®, 1957), 88.

2. Franz Delitzsch, quoted in Francis D. Nichol, ed., *The Seventh-day Adventist Bible Commentary*, vol. 3 (Washington, DC: Review and Herald®, 1977), 769.

3. Charlotte Elliott, "My God, Is Any Hour So Sweet?" (1835), in *The Church Hymnal: The Official Hymnal of the Seventh-day Adventist Church* (Washington, DC: Review and Herald®, 1941), hymn 325.

Psalm 56: Trust in God

*Be merciful unto me, O God: for man would
swallow me up; he fighting daily oppresseth me.*
—Psalm 56:1

D avid wrote several beautiful psalms praising God for His protection. These come to us as encouragement when facing peril. Psalms 56 and 57 "have been called 'twin psalms,' because of similarities in content and in development of theme. . . . Written under circumstances of grievous trouble, they both express the complete confidence in God that overcomes all fear."[1]

David is surrounded by enemies seeking his life. Everyone has turned against him (Psalm 56:1, 2), but with God at his side, he has nothing to fear (vv. 4, 11). Previous friends are twisting his words and plotting evil deeds against him (v. 5). They are seeking to skillfully arrange an ambush so that David might be taken unawares (v. 6). Will these enemies find safety in their wickedness (v. 7)? Is God not aware that the innocent suffer? Why does He allow it?

Yet God *does* know David's wanderings (v. 8). How beautifully David sings of God collecting his tears in a bottle and noting his anguish. "In the book of God's remembrance," "every act of sacrifice, every suffering and sorrow endured for Christ's sake, is recorded."[2] David is sure he will triumph. "[For] this I *know*; that God is for me" (v. 9; emphasis added).

Christians may rest secure, having assurance that the promise of salvation comes from the Lord, and He keeps His promises (Job 19:25; Psalms 20:6; 135:5; 140:12; 2 Timothy 1:12). Psalm 56:11 echoes the sentiment of verse 4. Why be afraid of what humans can do when one trusts in an omnipotent Lord? David ends his short psalm by thanking God for answering his request for protection. The Lord has kept David from death in the past, and he trusts He will allow him to continue to "walk before God in the light of the living" (v. 13).

"O let me walk with Thee, my God, / As Enoch walked in days of old; / Place Thou my trembling hand in Thine, / And sweet communion with me hold; / E'en though the path I may not see, / Yet, Jesus, let me walk with Thee."[3]

---

1. Francis D. Nichol, ed., *The Seventh-day Adventist Bible Commentary*, vol. 3 (Washington, DC: Review and Herald®, 1977), 765.

2. Ellen G. White, *The Great Controversy* (Mountain View, CA: Pacific Press®, 1950), 481.

3. Mrs. L. D. Avery Stuttle, "O Let Me Walk With Thee," in *The Seventh-day Adventist Hymnal* (Hagerstown, MD: Review and Herald®, 1985), hymn 554.

PSALM 34: TRUST THE WORD OF THE LORD

The angel of the LORD encampeth round about them
that fear him, and delivereth them. O taste and see that
the LORD is good: blessed is the man that trusteth in him.
—Psalm 34:7, 8

Psalm 34 is an acrostic psalm, utilizing the Hebrew alphabet in order, with variations (see also Psalms 9; 10; 37; 119). This often occurs in songs of praise (see Psalms 25; 111; 112; 145). Psalm 34:3 is still recited during contemporary synagogue services as the reader "takes the Torah from the ark":[1] "O magnify the LORD with me, and let us exalt his name together."

"They looked unto him, and were lightened: and their faces were not ashamed" (v. 5). Christians should be joyful! " 'Turn your eyes upon Jesus, look full in His wonderful face.' Nothing is more beautiful than the radiant countenance of a real Christian. When God looks our way, all the world is sunlit."[2] Verse 7 is powerful and worth memorizing. How comforting to know angels are ever present, protecting those who love the Lord and do His will.

Psalm 34:8 employs wonderful imagery; we must not merely look at God's Word but taste it for ourselves. "The surest proof of religion is found in personal experience. Without Christian experience the religion of Christ is only theory, and as mere theory it has no saving power."[3] Having experienced salvation, you are to awaken others to taste the goodness of the Lord.

Verse 14 is instructional for all who would live a Spirit-filled life: "Depart from evil, and do good; seek peace, and pursue it." How much better this world would be if everyone pursued peace! "Christian living is both negative and positive; we must go away from evil, and we must do good. Merely refraining from evil is not enough. We must be active in doing good."[4] Christians are not free from this world's trials and afflictions (v. 19), but hope in the Lord gives endurance. Christ also suffered. Verse 20 is a prophetic vision of His crucifixion.

" 'Tis so sweet to trust in Jesus, / Just to take Him at His word."[5]

---

1. Francis D. Nichol, ed., *The Seventh-day Adventist Bible Commentary*, vol. 3 (Washington, DC: Review and Herald®, 1977), 711.
2. Nichol, 713.
3. Nichol, 713.
4. Nichol, 713.
5. Louisa M. R. Stead, " 'Tis So Sweet to Trust in Jesus," in *The Seventh-day Adventist Hymnal* (Hagerstown, MD: Review and Herald®, 1985), hymn 524.

WATER FROM BETHLEHEM

And David longed, and said, Oh that one would give me drink
of the water of the well of Bethlehem, that is at the gate!
—1 Chronicles 11:17

One day while he [David] was hidden in the cave of Adullam, his thoughts turning back to the untroubled freedom of his boyhood life, the fugitive exclaimed, 'Oh that one would give me [a] drink of the water of the well of Bethlehem, which is by the gate!' 2 Samuel 23:13-17. Bethlehem was at that time in the hands of the Philistines; but three mighty men of David's band broke through the guard, and brought of the water of Bethlehem to their master. David could not drink it. 'Be it far from me,' he cried; 'is not this the blood of the men that went in jeopardy of their lives?' And he reverently poured out the water as an offering to God. David had been a man of war, much of his life had been spent amid scenes of violence; but of all who have passed through such an ordeal, few indeed have been so little affected by its hardening, demoralizing influence as was David."[1]

This brave foray behind enemy lines is recounted in passing during a listing of the mighty men of valor who served in David's army. Three of those men were the ones who broke through the guard at the well of Bethlehem to secure for their commander the water he wished to taste once again. David was so beloved he only had to suggest a desire, and his men responded with alacrity. We are not told how many Philistines were faced to accomplish this bold feat.

Silently slipping through the lines, passing the guards around the city, furtively drawing water from the community well, and returning undetected to their own men—this was a mission requiring stealth and courage. I imagine it was with a great deal of pride in their accomplishment that they presented the water to David. He poured it out on the ground as an offering to God! His men must have been shocked. It appeared their efforts were not appreciated. This was the furthest thing from David's mind. He valued their courage, their loyalty, and their love! He, therefore, thanked God for the brave men who stood beside him during these trying times.

"Greater love hath no man than this, that a man lay down his life for his friends" (John 15:13).

---

1. Ellen G. White, *Patriarchs and Prophets* (Mountain View, CA: Pacific Press®, 1943), 736, 737.

Psalm 42: I Will Remember Thee!

As the hart panteth after the water brooks,
so panteth my soul after thee, O God.

—Psalm 42:1

D avid was a fugitive from Saul when the words of Psalm 42 were penned. As he hid in the mountain depths, his greatest lament was that he could no longer worship with others in the house of the Lord. In two sections of Psalm 42, each concluding with a similar chorus (vv. 5, 11), David expresses his heartfelt need to commune with God.

Having spent a good deal of time in the arid portions of Israel, David knew water could be scarce during the summer. His graphic comparison of a deer panting from thirst to his need to connect with God is powerful (vv. 1, 2). He longs to meet God in the sanctuary, but as a fugitive, it is impossible (v. 2). His enemies taunt him, claiming God has forsaken him (v. 3). When he remembers the joy of worshiping together with the congregation of the Lord, his troubles seem even worse (v. 4). Yet why should he be depressed? Has God not protected him? Is there not hope he might once again worship in the house of the Lord (v. 5)?

Verse 6 begins the second stanza of the psalm. Though driven from communal worship, David vows to remember God (v. 6). Here among the mountains of the north (v. 6), where snows melt into rushing streams flowing down in cataracts to the Jordan, he feels as if the waters mirror his sinking feelings (v. 7). "David sinks down in momentary disappointment and discouragement, like a drowning man (see Ps. 88:7), but rises immediately in faith and confidence that God will do all things well."[1] God will help David overcome whatever affliction comes (v. 8). Because of his trust in the Lord, David plans to continue asking God to explain why he is suffering (v. 9). Why does there seem to be some truth to the words of his enemies? They ask, "Where is thy God?" (v. 10). David vows, "I shall yet praise him, who is the health of my countenance, and my God" (v. 11; see also Psalm 43:5).

"I will follow Thee, my Savior, / Wheresoe'er my lot may be. / Where Thou goest I will follow; / Yes, my Lord, I'll follow Thee."[2]

1. Francis D. Nichol, ed., *The Seventh-day Adventist Bible Commentary*, vol. 3 (Washington, DC: Review and Herald®, 1977), 736.
2. James L. Elginburg, "I Will Follow Thee" (1886), in *The Seventh-day Adventist Hymnal* (Hagerstown, MD: Review and Herald®, 1985), hymn 623.

PSALM 27, PART 1: WHOM SHALL I FEAR?

The LORD is my light and my salvation; whom shall I fear?
the LORD is the strength of my life; of whom shall I be afraid?
—Psalm 27:1

Psalm 27 was also written by David as he was taking refuge in caves and mountain strongholds. Many of the psalms written during this period in his life express total confidence in the ability of the Lord to save, no matter the circumstances. This psalm has been called the Tonic Psalm because David misses communal worship, the music of choirs, and the sacred service.

The psalm is divided into three parts: Verses 1–6 place confidence in God to deliver His servant. Verses 7–12 are a cry for help from present trouble. Verses 13, 14 bring the psalm to a triumphant close with the assurance that trust in God is not misplaced.[1]

David is fearless because God is his light and salvation (vv. 1–3). Psalm 27:4 and Psalm 23:6 are very close in wording and express the same sentiment. David longs to make a closer, more vibrant connection with his Savior. He wants a close relationship that will never end. He writes, "Surely goodness and mercy shall follow me all the days of my life: and I will dwell in the house of the LORD for ever" (Psalm 23:6). "One thing have I desired of the LORD, that will I seek after; that I may dwell in the house of the LORD all the days of my life, to behold the beauty of the LORD, and to enquire in his temple" (Psalm 27:4). David longs to be in the presence of the Lord at all times. He wants to wrap himself in the love and kindness he feels when connected with his Creator. David feels safest in the presence of God, his rock and salvation (v. 5).

"There is joy and consolation for the true-hearted, faithful Christian, that the world knows not of. To them it is a mystery. The Christian's hope is big with immortality and full of glory. It reacheth to that within the veil, and is as an anchor to the soul, both sure and steadfast. And when the storm of God's wrath shall come upon the ungodly, this hope will not fail them, but they are hid as in the secret of His pavilion."[2]

"And now shall mine head be lifted up above mine enemies round about me: therefore will I offer in his tabernacle sacrifices of joy; I will sing, yea, I will sing praises unto the LORD" (Psalm 27:6).

---

1. Francis D. Nichol, ed., *The Seventh-day Adventist Bible Commentary*, vol. 3 (Washington, DC: Review and Herald®, 1977), 695, 696.

2. Ellen G. White, *Sons and Daughters of God* (Washington, DC: Review and Herald®, 1955), 354.

PSALM 27, PART 2: GOD'S LOVE NEVER WAVERS

When my father and my mother forsake me,
then the LORD will take me up.

—Psalm 27:10

T he second half of Psalm 27 is a plea for help (vv. 7–10) and the relief found in trusting God (vv. 13, 14). When all others have failed him, David knows the Lord will be there for him and will deliver him. "This verse is the dialogue of a beautiful fellowship between David and his God. God had said to him: 'Seek ye my face.' David reminds God of His command, and from the depths of his heart replies, 'I will seek thy face.' Here is intimacy indeed, resembling the friendship that existed between Moses and God (see Ex. 33:11). Precious is that fellowship with God which, in time of need, finds the soul speaking to itself the counsel of God."[1]

David wants nothing more than to continue his close relationship with God. He remembers how God had led him in the past and longs for assurance he is not forsaken (v. 9). "Past mercies are always a reason for continued blessings. As God has saved us hitherto, we may plead the continuance of His saving power."[2] Even though some parents abandon their children, God is faithful to abide with His chosen ones (v. 10). God's love is binding in that He gave us the most precious of gifts, His Son, to redeem us from sin and bring us back into His family.

With the assurance that he will not be abandoned, David does not want to follow the course of those who reproach him. This is a theme he returns to repeatedly in his psalms. Those who slander David and tell falsehoods about him are worrisome, but he refuses to sink to their level.

David wonders, " 'What would have become of me, if I had not believed in the goodness of God!' So many and formidable are his enemies that he would collapse were it not for his sure belief that he will ultimately see a revelation of God's goodness on earth. . . . Faith could lapse into fear, if hope did not keep aflame."[3]

"Gracious Father, guard Thy children / From the foe's destructive power."[4]

---

1. Francis D. Nichol, ed., *The Seventh-day Adventist Bible Commentary*, vol. 3 (Washington, DC: Review and Herald®, 1977), 696.
2. Nichol, 697.
3. Nichol, 697.
4. Anonymous, "Gracious Father, Guard Thy Children," *The Seventh-day Adventist Hymnal* (Hagerstown, MD: Review and Herald®, 1985), hymn 621.

Psalm 133: On Fellowship

Behold, how good and how pleasant it
is for brethren to dwell together in unity!

—Psalm 133:1

In the cave of Adullam the family were united in sympathy and affection. . . . [David] had tasted the bitterness of distrust on the part of his own brothers; and the harmony that had taken the place of discord brought joy to the exile's heart. It was here that David composed the fifty-seventh psalm."[1] (See March 25.)

Family was important to David. Though his elder brother had mocked him before others when David questioned the courage of Israel's army, now all were united in the realization that David was chosen of the Lord to do great things.

The fact that David's brothers now supported him was not lost on those who rallied to the defense of the fugitive. "Christian unity is a mighty agency. It tells in a powerful manner that those who possess it are children of God. It has an irresistible influence upon the world, showing that man in his humanity may be a partaker of the divine nature, having escaped the corruption that is in the world through lust. We are to be one with our fellow men and with Christ, and in Christ one with God. . . .

". . . The work of God's people may and will be varied, but one Spirit is the mover in it all. All the work done for the Master is to be connected with the great whole. . . .

"He in whose heart Christ abides recognizes Christ abiding in the heart of his brother."[2]

Psalm 133's three short verses extol the benefits of close companionship with those of like faith. "Brotherly love born of heaven refreshes and revives. It is a foretaste of the fellowship enjoyed in the heavenly home. Because of the sympathy and affection which his associates showed him, David could sing this psalm while he was in the cave of Adullam."[3]

"Jesus where'er Thy people meet, | There they behold Thy mercy seat; |
Where'er they seek Thee, Thou art found, | And every place is hallowed ground.[4]

---

1. Ellen G. White, *Patriarchs and Prophets* (Mountain View, CA: Pacific Press®, 1943), 658.

2. Ellen G. White, *My Life Today* (Washington, DC: Review and Herald®, 1980), 276.

3. Francis D. Nichol, ed., *The Seventh-day Adventist Bible Commentary*, vol. 3 (Washington, DC: Review and Herald®, 1977), 919.

4. William Cowper, "Jesus, Where'er Thy People Meet," in *The Church Hymnal: Official Hymnal of the Seventh-day Adventist Church* (Washington, DC: Review and Herald®, 1941), hymn 515.

Psalm 142: A Persistent Prayer

When my spirit was overwhelmed within me, then thou knewest my path. In the way wherein I walked have they privily laid a snare for me.
—Psalm 142:3

Psalm 142 was written in an unnamed cave. It was probably composed during this difficult time in the life of David. As such, it fits well with Psalms 27 and 42. This psalm is yet another appeal for deliverance from overwhelming odds. David knows God is aware of his predicament. He wants to share his deepest concerns with his closest Friend. God seems to be his *only* Friend. David can pour out his heart to no one else and be assured the listening one is truly interested in his plight (v. 4).

Wherever David looks, trouble lurks. "There are times when the spirit is wrapped in perplexity and distraught by false accusations. Under the stress of emotion the intellectual powers of good judgment are often confused, and the soul knows not which way to turn. At such a time one can open the heart to God and place full confidence in His overruling providence. Then the life will be filled with the bounties of the Lord, and the depression and consternation that formerly harassed the soul depart."[1]

Spies lurk everywhere. It is not safe to visit Bethlehem. Saul is actively hunting David and has undoubtedly placed a bounty on his head. Even venturing forth to obtain food from the surrounding sympathetic villages is dangerous, for anyone might turn him in for a reward. He can trust no one. Yet the Lord is his refuge (v. 5). In the depths of despair, not knowing who to trust, David is surprisingly optimistic. He can still sing praises to his God (v. 7). He has loyal men around him. His family is safe. "Though the present may be difficult and the future foreboding, the psalmist looks forward with confidence to the time of his deliverance."[2]

"Under His wings I am safely abiding; / Though the night deepens and tempests are wild, / Still I can trust Him; / I know He will keep me; / He has redeemed me, and I am His child."[3]

---

1. Francis D. Nichol, ed., *The Seventh-day Adventist Bible Commentary*, vol. 3 (Washington, DC: Review and Herald®, 1977), 930.

2. Nichol, 931.

3. W. O. Cushing, "Under His Wings," in *The Seventh-day Adventist Hymnal* (Hagerstown, MD: Review and Herald®, 1985), hymn 529.

PSALM 143: SHOWERS OF BLESSING

Cause me to hear thy lovingkindness in the morning;
for in thee do I trust: cause me to know the way wherein
I should walk; for I lift up my soul unto thee. Deliver me,
O LORD, from mine enemies: I flee unto thee to hide me.
—Psalm 143:8, 9

David needs assurance from God that he has committed no sin worthy of exile. With confidence, he asks God to judge him, even though he knows he is a sinful being. He relies on God's mercy and justice to render a righteous verdict (Psalm 143:1, 2). "Although the Scriptures frequently call men 'righteous' (see Gen. 18:23, 24; etc.), the psalmist recognizes that in the absolute sense, when compared with God, no man is righteous (see Job 9:2). Man can obtain the righteousness of Christ only through faith. Human effort can never make a man righteous (Eph. 2:8, 9)."[1]

David is feeling dejected and alone (Psalm 143:3, 4). He remembers times past when God answered his prayers. Spending time alone, tending his father's flocks amid the wonders of nature, he gained an intimate knowledge of the workings of the Creator (v. 5). And now he trusts the Lord will continue to answer his prayers. With hope, he begs for deliverance.

David thirsts for the showers of Heaven (v. 6). David's need is desperate. He feels that without God, he is doomed (v. 7). Things certainly look bleak in the dead of night. Worse yet, he feels cut off from God, who currently does not seem to answer his prayers.

Perhaps with the light of a new day, things will look more promising (v. 8). As the morning sun brightens the landscape, David likewise wants an answer from the Lord to brighten his soul and light his path (v. 8). He wants God to hide him (v. 9). David wants to be shown God's will so that he might walk uprightly in the path of righteousness (v. 10). He stresses the reason God should answer his prayer is because God is holy (v. 11). Because David is a servant of the Lord, God should destroy those who trouble him (v. 12).

" 'There shall be showers of blessing;' / This is the promise of love; / There shall be seasons refreshing, / Sent from the Savior above."[2]

1. Francis D. Nichol, ed., *The Seventh-day Adventist Bible Commentary*, vol. 3 (Washington, DC: Review and Herald®, 1977), 931.

2. Daniel W. Whittle, "Showers of Blessing," in *The Seventh-day Adventist Hymnal* (Hagerstown, MD: Review and Herald®, 1985), hymn 195.

DAVID CARES FOR HIS PARENTS

*And David went thence to Mizpeh of Moab: and he said unto
the king of Moab, Let my father and my mother, I pray thee,
come forth, and be with you, till I know what God will do for me.*
—1 Samuel 22:3

Many had joined David in his mountain refuge. "And every one that was in distress, and every one that was in debt, and every one that was discontented, gathered themselves unto him" (1 Samuel 22:2). David knew Saul might even use his parents as hostages to lure him from his hiding place. "David's anxiety was not all for himself, although he realized his peril. He thought of his father and mother, and he concluded that he must seek another refuge for them. He went to the king of Moab, and the Lord put it into the heart of the monarch to courteously grant to the beloved parents of David an asylum in Mizpeh, and they were not disturbed, even in the midst of the enemies of Israel. From this history, we may all learn precious lessons of filial love."[1]

The kingdom of Moab lay east of the Dead Sea. Watchtowers (*Mizpeh*) had been placed upon the mountains of Moab. These hillside fortresses were within sight of each other so they might communicate. This defensive line was constructed partly to keep the armies of Israel from attacking. "Saul had warred against Moab after coming to the throne (1 Sam. 14:47). Therefore anyone outlawed by Saul would find refuge in that country. Also, David may have been influenced by the fact that Ruth, his great-grandmother was a Moabitess."[2]

"The experience through which David was passing was not unnecessary or fruitless. God was giving him a course of discipline to fit him to become a wise general as well as a just and merciful king. With his band of fugitives he was gaining a preparation to take up the work that Saul, because of his murderous passion and blind indiscretion, was becoming wholly unfitted to do. Men cannot depart from the counsel of God and still retain that calmness and wisdom which will enable them to act with justice and discretion."[3]

In the midst of his own troubles, David's thoughts unselfishly turned to the safety of his parents. Thinking of others leaves less time to dwell on one's own problems.

---

1. Ellen G. White, "In the Cave of Adullam," *Signs of the Times®*, September 7, 1888.
2. Francis D. Nichol, ed., *The Seventh-day Adventist Bible Commentary*, vol. 2 (Washington, DC: Review and Herald®, 1976), 560.
3. Ellen G. White, *Patriarchs and Prophets* (Mountain View, CA: Pacific Press®, 1943), 658.

THE PROPHET GAD

And the prophet Gad said unto David, Abide not
in the hold; depart, and get thee into the land of Judah.
Then David departed, and came into the forest of Hareth.
—1 Samuel 22:5

I t seemed certain to him [David] that he must, at last, fall into the hands of his pursuer and persecutor. But could his eyes have been opened, he would have seen the angels of the Lord encamped round about him and his followers. The sentinels of Heaven were waiting to warn them of impending danger, and to conduct them to a place of refuge when their peril demanded it. God could protect David and his followers; for they were not a band in rebellion against Saul. David had repeatedly proved his allegiance to the king."[1]

Now a man who will figure prominently in the life of David enters the narrative. "Perhaps it was Samuel who dispatched Gad to connect himself with David. The future king of Israel would be greatly benefited by the presence of a divinely inspired seer. As long as David lived, Gad was his seer (2 Sam. 24:11–19). Gad, along with Nathan the prophet, was the compiler of David's biography (1 Chron. 29:29). Since he survived his lifelong friend and king, the indications are that he came to David while yet a young man. . . .

"What God did for David in providing prophetic guidance He had done for Saul. These two lives are placed in contrast and demonstrate that God is no respecter of persons. Those who fall short of the divine standard fail, not because the Lord does not do everything that Heaven can devise to make true success possible, but because Heaven's plan is persistently rejected."[2]

Saul was headstrong and so preoccupied with his vendetta against David that he neglected Israel's defense. The Philistines were raiding settlements, and someone needed to defend the innocent shepherds. "God, who had protected him [David] so many times in the past, would not now forsake him, but would shape events in such a way through hardship and suffering that he would receive the training necessary for future leadership."[3]

Though we may not see it, God has a plan for each of us. Ask Him to reveal yours.

---

1. Ellen G. White, "In the Cave of Adullam," *Signs of the Times*®, September 7, 1888.
2. Francis D. Nichol, ed., *The Seventh-day Adventist Bible Commentary*, vol. 2 (Washington, DC: Review and Herald®, 1976), 560.
3. Nichol, 560, 561.

EVIL SURMISING

All of you have conspired against me, and there is none
that sheweth me that my son hath made a league with the
son of Jesse, and there is none of you that is sorry for me.

—1 Samuel 22:8

T he spirit of evil was upon Saul. He felt that his doom had been sealed by the solemn message of his rejection from the throne of Israel. His departure from the plain requirements of God was bringing its sure results. He did not turn, and repent, and humble his heart before God, but opened it to receive every suggestion of the enemy. He listened to every false witness, eagerly receiving anything that was detrimental to the character of David, hoping that he might find an excuse for manifesting his increasing envy and hatred of him who had been anointed to the throne of Israel. . . .

"What an example was Saul giving to the subjects of his kingdom in his desperate, unprovoked persecution of David! What a record he was making to be placed upon the pages of history for future generations! He sought to turn the full tide of the power of his kingdom into the channel of his own hatred in hunting down an innocent man. All this had a demoralizing influence upon Israel. And while Saul was giving loose reign to his passion, Satan was weaving a snare to compass his ruin, and the ruin of his kingdom. . . . While imaginary foes were constantly presented before the minds of the people, the real enemies were strengthening themselves without arousing suspicion or alarm."[1]

"Saul had been preparing to ensnare and capture David in the cave of Adullam, and when it was discovered that David had left this place of refuge, the king was greatly enraged. The flight of David was a mystery to Saul. He could account for it only by the belief that there had been traitors in his camp, who had informed the son of Jesse of his proximity and design.

"He affirmed to his counselors that a conspiracy had been formed against him, and with the offer of rich gifts and positions of honor he bribed them to reveal who among his people had befriended David."[2]

Power corrupts. "Pride goeth before destruction" (Proverbs 16:18).

---

1. Ellen G. White, "In the Cave of Adullam," *Signs of the Times*®, September 7, 1888.
2. Ellen G. White, *Patriarchs and Prophets* (Mountain View, CA: Pacific Press®, 1943), 658, 659.

DOEG, THE SPY

*Then answered Doeg the Edomite, which was set
over the servants of Saul, and said, I saw the son of
Jesse coming to Nob, to Ahimelech the son of Ahitub.*
—1 Samuel 22:9

Doeg the Edomite turned informer. Moved by ambition and avarice, and by hatred of the priest, who had reproved his sins, Doeg reported David's visit to Ahimelech, representing the matter in such a light as to kindle Saul's anger against the man of God."[1] "He virtually told Saul that Jonathan and the Benjamites were not so much in the wrong as the priest, who not only gave David food but inquired of the Lord for him, and gave him a weapon (v. 10). Doeg apparently did not volunteer this information until bribed by offers of rich rewards and high position."[2]

"The priest thought that in doing a kindness to an ambassador of his [Saul's] court, he was showing respect to the king. He was altogether innocent of any evil intention toward Saul or his realm. David had not taken a straightforward course before the priest, he had dissimulated, and on this account he had brought the whole family of the priesthood into peril.

"But Doeg was a slanderer, and Saul had such a spirit of envy and hatred and murder, that he desired the report to be true. The partial and exaggerated statement of the chief of the herdsmen, was suited for the use of the adversary of God and man. It was presented to the mind of Saul in such a light that the king lost all control of himself, and acted like a madman. If he had but calmly waited until he could have heard the whole story, and had exercised his reasoning faculties, how different would have been the terrible record of that day's doings!

". . . Ahimelech was not present on this occasion to vindicate himself, and to state the facts as they existed; but Doeg cared not for this. Like Satan his father, he read the mind of Saul, and improved the opportunity of increasing the misery of the king by the words of his mischievous tongue, which was set on fire of hell."[3]

"Lying lips are [an] abomination to the LORD: but they that deal truly are his delight" (Proverbs 12:22).

---

1. Ellen G. White, *Patriarchs and Prophets* (Mountain View, CA: Pacific Press®, 1943), 659.
2. Francis D. Nichol, ed., *The Seventh-day Adventist Bible Commentary*, vol. 2 (Washington, DC: Review and Herald®, 1976), 561.
3. Ellen G. White, "Doeg the Edomite," *Signs of the Times®*, September 21, 1888.

AHIMELECH STANDS TALL

Then Ahimelech answered the king, and said, And who is so faithful among all thy servants as David, which is the king's son in law, and goeth at thy bidding, and is honourable in thine house?
—1 Samuel 22:14

Saul sent for the entire family of Ahimelech, commanding they present themselves before him. Once they arrived, he accused them of aiding and abetting in a conspiracy against the throne. These were serious charges. Ahimelech did not pretend the events being discussed had never happened. He admitted that he had indeed given David food and a weapon, but he stressed his actions had been in support of a member of the king's own retinue, and he had not known of the rift between David and Saul. He was, therefore, innocent of the charges but rather had only sought to aid David in the commission of a task designed by the king.

"And who is so faithful among all thy servants as David, which is the king's son in law, and goeth at thy bidding, and is honourable in thine house? Did I then begin to enquire of God for him? be it far from me: let not the king impute any thing unto his servant, nor to all the house of my father: for thy servant knew nothing of all this, less or more" (1 Samuel 22:14, 15).

Ahimelech stated, "Did I then begin to enquire of God for him?" (v. 15). What is the meaning of his response? "The implication is that if he had begun now, after knowing David's status, to seek divine guidance for David, that would be giving aid to a recognized enemy of Saul, but that what he had done before he learned of the controversy between Saul and David should have no bearing on the question of his loyalty. With quiet dignity Ahimelech answered Saul's charge that he had used the Urim and the Thummim in a way contrary to Saul's ideas by stating that he had inquired for the one closest to Saul, one who had ever been loyal and devoted, and he had rendered his service to the messenger *for the king*. His last word was a denial that he had known anything of the situation."[1]

Who would Saul believe—Doeg, a foreigner with a reputation for deceit, or Ahimelech, his own high priest? The man of God uttered the truth, and that made Saul even more furious.

Are you guilty of rash and hasty decisions when you feel wronged? Anger can blind us.

---

1. Francis D. Nichol, ed., *The Seventh-day Adventist Bible Commentary*, vol. 2 (Washington, DC: Review and Herald®, 1976), 562; emphasis original.

SAUL'S WORST PASSIONS AROUSED

And the king said unto the footmen that stood about him,
Turn, and slay the priests of the LORD: because their hand
also is with David, and because they knew when he fled,
and did not shew it to me. But the servants of the king would
not put forth their hand to fall upon the priests of the LORD.

—1 Samuel 22:17

S aul commanded that Ahimelech and his entire family be slain because none had come to inform him of David's presence at Nob.
"The inconsistency of jealousy was shown in this verdict. Without
proving the guilt of any one of the priests, the king commanded that all the
line of Eli should be slain. He had determined upon this course of action
before he had sent for them or heard their side of the case. And no amount
of proof could undo his malignant purpose. To vent his wrath upon one
man seemed too small a matter to satisfy the fury of his revenge."[1]

Saul's bodyguard refused to carry out his order. This further enraged the
king, for he now thought even his palace guards were against him. "And
the king said to Doeg, Turn thou, and fall upon the priests" (1 Samuel 22:18).

"Now that he had permission from the king of Israel, Doeg did not
hesitate to lift his hand against the servant of God, even disregarding
the sacred vestments of Ahimelech as well as those of his associates.
Eighty-five men fell that day before the lust of selfish greed. What a contrast here between Saul's professed religious fervor that kept Agag alive
([1 Samuel] 15:20) and his frenzy that enabled him to perpetrate an act
unparalleled in Jewish history for its barbarity."[2]

"Saul's rage was not appeased by the noble stand of his footmen, and he
turned to the man whom he had connected with himself as a friend, because
he had reported against the priests. Thus this Edomite, who was as base a
character as was Barabbas, slew with his own hand eighty-five priests of
the Lord in one day; and he and Saul, and he who was a murderer from the
beginning, gloried over the massacre of the servants of the Lord."[3]

The depth to which men and women will sink to retain power is appalling!

1. Ellen G. White, "Doeg the Edomite," *Signs of the Times*®, September 21, 1888.
2. Francis D. Nichol, ed., *The Seventh-day Adventist Bible Commentary*, vol. 2 (Washington,
DC: Review and Herald®, 1976), 562.
3. White, "Doeg the Edomite."

ABIATHAR, LONE SURVIVOR

And one of the sons of Ahimelech the son of Ahitub,
named Abiathar, escaped, and fled after David.
—1 Samuel 22:20

Not satisfied with his revenge, Saul destroyed Nob. "The innocent suffered with the supposedly guilty. The inhabitants of
Nob probably had had nothing to do with the removal of the
tabernacle and the priestly families to Nob (see on [1 Samuel] 21:1), yet
Saul's senseless and satanic fury wiped out the entire town."[1]

One survivor escaped to the safety of David and his men. Upon being
informed of the destruction of the town and all the priests, David recognized his part in the tragedy. "And David said unto Abiathar, I knew
it that day, when Doeg the Edomite was there, that he would surely tell
Saul: I have occasioned the death of all the persons of thy father's house"
(1 Samuel 22:22).

This deed of Saul "filled all Israel with horror. It was the king whom
they had chosen that had committed this outrage, and he had only done
after the manner of the kings of other nations that feared not God. The
ark was with them, but the priests of whom they had inquired were slain
with the sword. What would come next?"[2]

David immediately offered sanctuary to Abiathar (v. 23). "What
encouragement it must have been to see the Urim and the Thummim
([1 Samuel] 23:6) and to know that in spite of the devastation of Nob, the
hand of God had been over the ephod and the priest who guarded it. Yet
when David learned the awful facts of the tragedy, he was filled with
remorse as he realized that he had been responsible for the death of the
high priest and those who had perished with him. He now wished that
he had refused to stoop to duplicity. Gladly would he have done differ-
ently could he have had the year to live over again! But the past could
not be undone. Dreadful as was his self-reproach there was nothing to
do but to reach 'forth unto those things which are before' (Phil. 3:13)."[3]

Some duplicitous actions have dire, unforeseen consequences.

---

1. Francis D. Nichol, ed., *The Seventh-day Adventist Bible Commentary*, vol. 2 (Washington, DC: Review and Herald®, 1976), 562.
2. Ellen G. White, *Patriarchs and Prophets* (Mountain View, CA: Pacific Press®, 1943), 659.
3. Nichol, *The Seventh-day Adventist Bible Commentary*, 2:563.

PSALM 52: I WILL TESTIFY

I will praise thee for ever, because thou hast done it: and I will wait on thy name; for it is good before thy saints.

—Psalm 52:9

I t was after hearing of Doeg's deed that David wrote the [fifty-second psalm]. . . . He stood amazed that any man could set himself up in arrogant antagonism to God's plan instead of resting upon the Lord's eternal mercy. By a tongue sharp as a razor Doeg had sown deceit and calamity to such an extent that he became the very personification of fraud and evil. But the day was coming when he would reap that which he had sown."[1] Psalm 52 "denounces the unscrupulous talebearer, or mischief-maker, who trusts in his wealth rather than in righteousness. The psalmist is firm in the knowledge that such a one shall be plucked up, but that the righteous may rest secure under the protection of God."[2] God's goodness will overshadow and triumph over those who prolong evil (v. 1).

We are responsible for the words we speak. The Bible repeatedly counsels we should control our words and shun evil communication (Psalms 12:3; 55:9; 78:36; 109:2). "Even so the tongue is a little member, and boasteth great things. Behold, how great a matter a little fire kindleth! . . . But the tongue can no man tame; it is an unruly evil, full of deadly poison" (James 3:5, 8). Those who spread rumors, gossip, assassinate another's character, lie to create dissension, gain pleasure from destroying others, or live for intrigue will meet those same words one day and be found guilty of perpetuating evil in the world (Psalm 52:2–6).

Money and power were more important to Doeg than truth and honor (v. 7). He had confidence in his ability to advance in position and increase in wealth. David, however, placed his trust in the Lord. Because God spared David's life, despite the treachery of Doeg (v. 9), David vowed to praise God by publicly sharing his testimony. By sharing a personal example of God's deliverance from evil, David hoped to strengthen other believers.

Sharing a story of God's protection might just encourage others to rely upon the Almighty as they struggle against evil. Do not be reluctant to praise God in public for His goodness to you!

---

1. Francis D. Nichol, ed., *The Seventh-day Adventist Bible Commentary*, vol. 2 (Washington, DC: Review and Herald®, 1976), 563.

2. Francis D. Nichol, ed., *The Seventh-day Adventist Bible Commentary*, vol. 3 (Washington, DC: Review and Herald®, 1977), 757.

David Fights for Keilah

So David and his men went to Keilah, and fought with the Philistines, and brought away their cattle, and smote them with a great slaughter. So David saved the inhabitants of Keilah.

—1 Samuel 23:5

The Philistines were attacking Israel again. News reached David that the town of Keilah, southwest of Bethlehem, was being raided, and harvested grain was being stolen. David "had been anointed as king, and he thought that some measure of responsibility rested upon him for the protection of his people. If he could but have the positive assurance that he was moving in the path of duty, he would start out with his limited forces, and stand faithfully at his post whatever might be the consequences."[1]

David sought assurance from the Lord that defending this town was his responsibility. When David's men were told the Lord wanted them to fight the Philistines and defend the people of Keilah, they were frightened (1 Samuel 23:3). "Should David's men as much as show themselves at this time, they would be in danger of immediate detection. As soon as Saul would discover their hiding place he would send a force against them. Fearful for their lives among their own tribe, they hesitated to face a strong foreign enemy. . . . Despite Saul's weaknesses, the majority of the people were obedient to the crown. David and his counselors were in a real dilemma, and they felt the only wise course was to present their problem before the Lord."[2]

David asked a second time if this action was God's pleasure. "And the Lord answered him and said, Arise, go down to Keilah; for I will deliver the Philistines into thine hand" (v. 4). David's men now knew they were fighting on the side of the Lord. "Keilah was a walled town (v. 7), but the unprepared inhabitants had no chance against the experienced soldiers of Philistia. Saul was many miles away, but David and his men were removed only a short distance. Action was immediate, and the surprised Philistines were routed."[3] This showed the people of the region that David stood in defense of the nation and not in revolt against it.

Consulting God before making a critical decision is always proper.

---

1. Ellen G. White, "David's Flight From Keilah," *Signs of the Times*®, October 5, 1888.
2. Francis D. Nichol, ed., *The Seventh-day Adventist Bible Commentary*, vol. 2 (Washington, DC: Review and Herald®, 1976), 565.
3. Nichol, 565.

CAN THESE PEOPLE BE TRUSTED?

And David knew that Saul secretly practised mischief against him;
and he said to Abiathar the priest, Bring hither the ephod.
—1 Samuel 23:9

David, having left the forest of Hareth, now enjoyed the hospitality of Keilah with trepidation. David knew this could not last, for Saul, who finally knew where David was, decided to immediately besiege the city and destroy his nemesis (1 Samuel 23:7, 8). Prior to undertaking the defense of Keilah, David probably sought the counsel of Gad, the seer who had attached himself to David's band, rather than Abiathar. Abiathar, the only surviving member of the house of Eli, had brought the sacred ephod, worn by the high priest, to David, and he now asked the Lord whether the residents of Keilah would betray him to Saul.

"The men of Keilah realized they would be forced to decide, on the one hand, between loyalty to Saul, with the retention of their status in Israel, and on the other hand, the implied rejection of Saul through their befriending of the outlawed David, with the consequent destruction of their city."[1] "Although a great deliverance had been wrought for Keilah, and the men of the city were very grateful to David and his men for the preservation of their lives, yet so fiendish had become the soul of the God-forsaken Saul, that he could demand from the men of Keilah that they yield up their deliverer to certain and unmerited death. Saul had determined that if they should offer any resistance they would suffer the bitter consequences of opposing the command of their king. The long-desired opportunity seemed to have come, and he determined to leave nothing undone in securing the arrest of his rival. . . .

". . . The inhabitants of the city did not for a moment think themselves capable of such an act of ingratitude and treachery; but David knew, from the light that God had given him, that they could not be trusted, that in the hour of need they would fail."[2] David, not wanting to incite a full-scale revolution, and taking into consideration the welfare of the people, chose to withdraw his six hundred men from the city.

God still quickens our conscience to do those things that are right.

---

1. Francis D. Nichol, ed., *The Seventh-day Adventist Bible Commentary*, vol. 2 (Washington, DC: Review and Herald®, 1976), 566.
2. Ellen G. White, "David's Flight From Keilah," *Signs of the Times*®, October 5, 1888.

THE WILDERNESS OF ZIPH

And David saw that Saul was come out to seek his life:
and David was in the wilderness of Ziph in a wood.
—1 Samuel 23:15

David moved his men eastward from Keilah to the wilderness of Ziph. This area is four miles southeast of Hebron and extends eastward toward the Dead Sea. "This district is a barren, sun-scorched desert, full of deep wadies that make excellent hiding places. The 'strong holds,' or fortresses, were lookouts commanding large areas of country, and placed near enough together so that it was impossible for anyone to traverse this section without being noticed. Probably David placed his men at various strategic positions, and every day word reached him of the location of Saul's forces. Water and food were almost unobtainable."[1]

First Samuel 23:15 states David was "in a wood" in this wilderness. As the wilderness of Ziph is a barren wasteland, the location of this site has been more closely linked with a spot on the main road south of Ziph, between Hebron and En-gedi, where forage was available. Saul's search for David had been unsuccessful. Jonathan, on the other hand, found David. It is not hard to imagine David's men being told to let the king's son through their lines as he was a friend.

"At this time, when there were so few bright spots in the path of David, he was rejoiced to receive an unexpected visit from Jonathan, who had learned the place of his refuge. Precious were the moments which these two friends passed in each other's society. They related their varied experiences, and Jonathan strengthened the heart of David, saying, 'Fear not: for the hand of Saul my father shall not find thee; and thou shalt be king over Israel, and I shall be next unto thee; and that also Saul my father knoweth' [1 Samuel 23:17]. As they talked of the wonderful dealings of God with David, the hunted fugitive was greatly encouraged. 'And they two made a covenant before the Lord: and David abode in the wood, and Jonathan went to his house.'

"After the visit of Jonathan, David encouraged his soul with songs of praise, accompanying his voice with his harp as he sang: [Psalm 11:1–5 quoted]."[2]

"The Lord trieth the righteous: but the wicked and him that loveth violence his soul hateth" (Psalm 11:5).

---

1. Francis D. Nichol, ed., *The Seventh-day Adventist Bible Commentary*, vol. 2 (Washington, DC: Review and Herald®, 1976), 566, 567.

2. Ellen G. White, *Patriarchs and Prophets* (Mountain View, CA: Pacific Press®, 1943), 660, 661.

PSALM 11: GOD PROTECTS THE RIGHTEOUS

In the LORD put I my trust: how say ye to my soul, Flee as a bird to your mountain? For, lo, the wicked bend their bow, they make ready their arrow upon the string, that they may privily shoot at the upright in heart.
—Psalm 11:1, 2

A fugitive in the Wilderness of Ziph, David was encouraged by an unexpected visit from Jonathan. The two men freely talked together and 'made a covenant before the Lord' (1 Sam. 23:16–18). After the visit, David sang Psalm 11. . . . By this psalm David expressed his absolute confidence in God's protection at a time when his life was threatened and he was urged to continued flight."[1]

The imagery of the psalm is striking: "How say ye to my soul, Flee as a bird to your mountain?" (Psalm 11:1). David wonders aloud how well-meaning counselors can advise him to flee when he trusts God to deliver him from any predicament. He is at peace, even in these dire times, because God is his refuge and strength. Many of David's psalms express this total trust even in the face of seemingly insurmountable obstacles.

David laments the failure of governments to protect the righteous. "If the foundations be destroyed, what can the righteous do?" (v. 3). "These may here be thought of as the principles upon which good government rests: respect for truth and righteousness. If these are destroyed, what further can the righteous do? If the king and his counselors show contempt for that which they should uphold, collapse is inevitable. The righteous, helpless in such a case, can seek safety only in flight. But the psalmist does not accept such counsel. Verses 4–6 are his reply."[2]

God tests all, and the upright He protects. Those who do evil will be destroyed at the end of time. David believes the wicked will ultimately meet a fate worthy of their evil thoughts and actions (vv. 4–6). God will defend those who honor and obey Him and preserve them. In heaven, the saints will see the face of God (v. 7; see also Psalm 4:6; 1 John 3:2; Revelation 22:4).

"What a fellowship, what a joy divine, / Leaning on the everlasting arms."[3]

---

1. Francis D. Nichol, ed., *The Seventh-day Adventist Bible Commentary*, vol. 3 (Washington, DC: Review and Herald®, 1977), 656, 657.

2. Nichol, 657.

3. E. A. Hoffman, "Leaning on the Everlasting Arms" (1887), in *The Seventh-day Adventist Hymnal* (Hagerstown, MD: Review and Herald®, 1985), hymn 469.

119

PSALM 63: MY SOUL THIRSTETH

O God, thou art my God; early will I seek thee: my soul thirsteth for thee, my flesh longeth for thee in a dry and thirsty land, where no water is.
—Psalm 63:1

David composed [Psalm] 63 when he was in the Wilderness of Judah, a fugitive from the wrath of King Saul. . . . [Psalm] 63 is one of the tenderest of the psalms. . . . The hymn has three parts: David's hunger for God (vs. 1–4), his joy in communion with God (vs. 5–8), his confidence in the ultimate destruction of the wicked and his own triumph in the hands of God (vs. 9–11)."[1]

David was hiding in a sun-scorched, desolate place. He understandably compared his need for God to his need for water. God was just as essential to his welfare as the water that kept him alive (v. 1). Even before sunrise (v. 1), he longed to bond with his Savior. For David, the love of God was more important than life itself (v. 3). Because of this, he freely acknowledged the gifts God bestows are really unmerited blessings (v. 4). Although David continually thirsted for communion with God, he acknowledged God's blessings had already satisfied his hunger. God's presence and blessings were as food and drink to his soul (v. 5).

In verse 1, David seeks God "early." In verse 6, he remembers Him "in the night." "David doubtless spent much time thinking about God during the anxious nights in the wilderness. We would do well to turn our thoughts toward God during our sleepless hours."[2] David knows he can rely on God during coming trials because God has upheld him in the past. Under His wing, he can safely abide, for God has never failed (vv. 7, 8).

Verses 10, 11 vividly describe the fate awaiting David's enemies. "Those who seek to triumph by falsehood will be confounded. David is confident that he will be protected against the murderous designs of Saul and that his enemies will be destroyed."[3]

"Beneath the cross of Jesus / I fain would take my stand, / The shadow of a mighty rock / Within a weary land."[4]

---

1. Francis D. Nichol, ed., *The Seventh-day Adventist Bible Commentary*, vol. 3 (Washington, DC: Review and Herald®, 1977), 779.
2. Nichol, 780.
3. Nichol, 780.
4. Elizabeth C. Clephane, "Beneath the Cross of Jesus" (1872), in *The Seventh-day Adventist Hymnal* (Hagerstown, MD: Review and Herald®, 1985), hymn 303.

THE ZIPHITES BETRAY DAVID

*Now therefore, O king, come down according to all the desire of thy soul
to come down; and our part shall be to deliver him into the king's hand.*
—1 Samuel 23:20

David was finding it increasingly hard to know who was a friend
and who was a foe. He had saved the citizens of Keilah from the
Philistines, only to have them turn him out for fear of personal
loss. Such ingratitude was stupefying. Now he was betrayed by supposed friends, who hid their hatred under a cloak of pretended friendship. "The citizens of Keilah, who should have repaid the interest and
zeal of David in delivering them from the hands of the Philistines, would
have given him up because of their fear of Saul rather than to have suffered a siege for his sake. But the men of Ziph would do worse; they
would betray David into the hands of his enemy, not because of their
loyalty to the king, but because of their hatred of David. Their interest
for the king was only a pretense. They were of their own accord acting
the part of hypocrites when they offered to assist in the capture of David.
It was upon these false-hearted betrayers that Saul invoked the blessing
of the Lord. He praised their Satanic spirit in betraying an innocent man,
as the spirit and act of virtue in showing compassion to himself. Apparently David was in greater danger than he had ever been before. Upon
learning the perils to which he was exposed, he changed his position,
seeking refuge in the mountains between Maon and the Dead Sea."[1]

One must remember the distances under discussion are small. Israel
does not encompass a large geographic area, and hiding six hundred men
and their families from a king, with spies everywhere, was some trick.
David's men needed water and supplies, food and accommodation—
things not easily procured from a suspicious populace encouraged to
report such transactions. While Saul sought to slay David, David refused
to lift his hand against God's anointed king. The odds were certainly
not in David's favor, yet God was on his side, and that made all the difference. David's remarkable faith in God's power to save shines forth in
our next psalm.

"There is a place of quiet rest, / Near to the heart of God."[2]

---

1. Ellen G. White, "David and Saul at En-Gedi," *Signs of the Times*®, October 12, 1888.
2. Cleland B. McAfee, "Near to the Heart of God," in *The Seventh-day Adventist Hymnal*
(Hagerstown, MD: Review and Herald®, 1985), hymn 495.

PSALM 54: CAST YOUR BURDENS ON THE LORD

Hear my prayer, O God; give ear to the words of my mouth.
For strangers are risen up against me, and oppressors seek
after my soul: they have not set God before them.

—Psalm 54:2, 3

P salm 54, a rather short psalm, was written after David learned he was being betrayed by the Ziphites. "The psalm consists of two parts, with an abrupt change from the first to the second. Verses 1–3 are an earnest prayer for deliverance; vs. 4–7 an expression of gratitude for deliverance which the psalmist sees with all the certainty of accomplished fact."[1] "Save me, O God, by thy name, and judge me by thy strength" (v. 1). David is relying on the character of God as expressed in His name—Jehovah. He pleads for salvation and asks the Lord to hear his cry for help. When we are in trouble, how often do we, as Christians, forget God is waiting to render assistance? But for His help, we must ask.

"For strangers are risen up against me" (v. 3). The Ziphites were not of the tribe of Benjamin and therefore were strangers to David's tribe. These were men who did not fear God and had no concept of honor. They sought to have David handed over to an executioner and even went so far as to aid and abet the crime of murder.

The psalm shifts dramatically from outlining the problem to a strong statement of faith in God's power to deliver. Even though certain men are against David, seeking to betray him, God is still with him, and he places his trust in the One who will never fail. Truth will ultimately triumph! "Behold, God is mine helper: the Lord is with them that uphold my soul. He shall reward evil unto mine enemies: cut them off in thy truth" (vv. 4, 5). David is so certain God will save him that he is ready to offer freewill offerings of thanks for God's loving care. "I will freely sacrifice unto thee: I will praise thy name, O LORD; for it is good. For he hath delivered me out of all trouble: and mine eye hath seen his desire upon mine enemies" (vv. 6, 7). God is our Protector and Best Friend when weighed down by the cares of life.

"Oh, the best friend to have is Jesus; / When the cares of life upon you roll, /
He will heal the wounded heart, / He will strength and grace impart."[2]

---

1. Francis D. Nichol, ed., *The Seventh-day Adventist Bible Commentary*, vol. 3 (Washington, DC: Review and Herald®, 1977), 762.

2. P. P. Bilhorn, "Oh, the Best Friend to Have Is Jesus," in *The Church Hymnal: Official Hymnal of the Seventh-day Adventist* Church (Washington, DC: Review and Herald®, 1941), hymn 528.

PSALM 140: A PRAYER FOR DELIVERANCE

I know that the LORD will maintain the cause of the afflicted,
and the right of the poor. Surely the righteous shall give
thanks unto thy name: the upright shall dwell in thy presence.
—Psalm 140:12, 13

D avid was no stranger to betrayal. He had seen the actions of Doeg, which had resulted in the death of Ahimelech and eighty-five members of his family. Now he had witnessed the duplicity of the Ziphites, who promised protection but secretly betrayed David and his men to Saul. It seemed no one could be trusted. Wherever David turned, he was met with smiles and promises, but behind his back, these same men plotted his downfall.

David wrote Psalm 140 as a request for deliverance from duplicitous people. While he could not discern who was upright and honest, God certainly knew whom he should trust. There will always be evil men and women who seek to undermine the righteous. Using slander, lies, and gossip, they drive wedges between friends and cause conflict within churches. Playing one side against the other during contentious theological issues is enjoyable for them. They revel in their ability to sway opinions and unleash emotions, thus creating controversy between friends.

James speaks of the evil that an unholy tongue can accomplish. "The tongue can no man tame; it is an unruly evil, full of deadly poison" (James 3:8). Paul also uses descriptive language to describe the unrighteous (Romans 3:13, 14). Paul and David both employ the imagery of a snake when describing an evil tongue. All three writers label the abuse of speech as a poison.

David wanted to avoid the traps being set by his enemies (Psalm 140:5). He longed for the protection that only God could provide (v. 7). He wanted God to keep the evil schemes of his enemies from being successful and wanted them to have no reason to exult in his downfall at their hands (v. 8). Eventually, duplicitous people will have their own words rebound upon their heads; they will be seen for who they really are, and integrity will be served (vv. 9, 10). David ends his psalm with confidence that God will protect His servants and ultimately bring justice to all, for he is a child of the King. And "the upright shall dwell in thy presence" (v. 13).

"A tent or a cottage, / O why should I care? / They're building a palace for me over there."[1]

---

1. Hattie E. Buel, "A Child of the King," in *The Seventh-day Adventist Hymnal* (Hagerstown, MD: Review and Herald®, 1985), hymn 468.

THE WILDERNESS OF MAON

Saul also and his men went to seek him. And they told David: wherefore he came down into a rock, and abode in the wilderness of Maon. And when Saul heard that, he pursued after David in the wilderness of Maon.
—1 Samuel 23:25

The Ziphites, into whose wild regions David went from Keilah, sent word to Saul in Gibeah that they knew where David was hiding, and that they would guide the king to his retreat. But David, warned of their intentions, changed his position, seeking refuge in the mountains between Maon and the Dead Sea."[1] Maon was a small town approximately eight miles south of Ziph, and such a move by David's men was easily made in one day. East of the town was a wilderness of gorges, caves, and cliffs. This area offered defensive positions difficult to circumvent.

When Saul caught up with David's band, David and his men stood on one side of a deep gorge, and Saul stood on the other. Saul ordered his men to flank David's position. Things looked bleak for David and his men until unexpected news upset Saul's plans. "But there came a messenger unto Saul, saying, Haste thee, and come; for the Philistines have invaded the land" (1 Samuel 23:27). "The disappointed king was in a frenzy of anger to be thus cheated of his prey; but he feared the dissatisfaction of the nation; for, if the Philistines should ravage the country while he was destroying its defender, a reaction would be likely to take place, and he would become the object of the people's hate. So he relinquished his pursuit of David, and went against the Philistines, and this gave David an opportunity to escape to the stronghold of En-gedi."[2]

"Between the ridge of El Kôlah [the ancient hill of Hachilah] and the neighbourhood of Maon there is a great gorge called 'the Valley of Rocks,' a narrow but deep chasm, impassable except by a detour of many miles, so that Saul might have stood within sight of David, yet quite unable to overtake his enemy." This gorge was probably "the scene of the wonderful escape of David, due to a sudden Philistine invasion."[3]

The plans of evil men and women are often defeated by events little anticipated or appreciated for what they are—heaven-sent deliverance.

---

1. Ellen G. White, *Patriarchs and Prophets* (Mountain View, CA: Pacific Press®, 1943), 661.
2. Ellen G. White, "David and Saul at En-Gedi," *Signs of the Times®*, October 12, 1888.
3. C. R. Conder, *Tent Work in Palestine*, vol. 2 (London: Richard Bentley & Son, 1878), 91, 92.

PSALM 13: A PRAYER WHEN IN DISTRESS

But I have trusted in thy mercy; my heart shall rejoice in thy salvation.
I will sing unto the LORD, because he hath dealt bountifully with me.
—Psalm 13:5, 6

P salm 13 "begins with protest (vs. 1, 2), passes through prayer (vs. 3, 4), and concludes with praise (vs. 5, 6). In it the psalmist, seemingly forsaken of God, despairs over his daily persecution at the hands of the enemy, prays earnestly that God will come to his help, and realizes the answer to his prayer in a fresh measure of faith and hope. . . . It is probable that David composed this psalm out of the constant trial that he suffered at the hands of Saul. The psalm is an encouraging example of the fact that when good men feel forsaken of God, it is their privilege to cry to Him and realize the sweet assurance of His care."[1]

David's expressions are those of a man who has endured trouble and sees no end in sight. Martin Luther "is reported to have said: 'Hope despairs and yet despair hopes.' "[2] David feels God has forgotten him because his trials have seemingly gone on forever. The phrase "how long" is used four times in the first two verses. Perhaps he thought that God had hidden His face from him, and if that were the case, he really was on his own against his enemies. David had constantly devised methods to avoid Saul yet, seemingly, to no avail (v. 2). It was becoming hard to think strategically because David's anxiety and sense of abandonment were taking over his thoughts. Surrendering to these feelings of hopelessness was not an option, and yet there seemed no way to get beyond his difficulties (vv. 3, 4). Where was God?

But David's trust in the Lord stands firm! God has led in the past, and God is still his salvation (v. 5). Despair turns to song (v. 6). "Out of sadness through supplication he emerges singing. The golden thread of thanksgiving runs throughout the fabric of the psalms."[3]

"I will sing of Jesus' love, / Sing of Him who first loved me."[4]

---

1. Francis D. Nichol, ed., *The Seventh-day Adventist Bible Commentary*, vol. 3 (Washington, DC: Review and Herald®, 1977), 660.

2. Nichol, 660.

3. Nichol, 661.

4. F. E. Belden, "I Will Sing of Jesus' Love" (1886), in *The Seventh-day Adventist Hymnal* (Hagerstown, MD: Review and Herald®, 1985), hymn 183.

Psalm 31: Redeemed!

For thou art my rock and my fortress; therefore
for thy name's sake lead me, and guide me.

—Psalm 31:3

Psalm 31 "is a heartfelt prayer for deliverance from trouble, enlivened by a sincere trust in God's ability to deliver. It is characterized by a galaxy of rich figures describing the distress of the persecuted and the hope that comes in time of trouble. Some suggest as its background the experience of David in the Wilderness of Maon (see 1 Sam. 23:19–26)."[1]

David trusts God, for he has been redeemed (Psalm 31:5). Jesus likewise trusts His Father completely when He cries, "Father, into thy hands I commend my spirit" (Luke 23:46). "We too, in the hour of extremity, can safely trust our case to God."[2] David knows God is aware of his troubles, yet he stresses to the Lord just how trying his mental predicament is and the physical toll it is taking (Psalm 31:9, 10). He is cut off by friends and neighbors who fear being seen in his presence (v. 11). Rejected by society, he has been slandered and fears trusting anyone (v. 13). Yet he maintains faith in the Lord (v. 14). "Verses 14–18 are an expression of great trust, in which, despite the anguish expressed in vs. 9–13, the psalmist says, 'Thou are my God.' This is the triumph of faith."[3]

David implores the Lord to turn His face toward him and be merciful, for this is in keeping with God's character (v. 16). How great is God that He offers sanctuary to those who trust in Him (v. 19)! "Thou shalt hide them in the secret of thy presence from the pride of man: thou shalt keep them secretly in a pavilion from the strife of tongues" (v. 20). Beset by troubles, David, in a moment of despair, feels cut off from God; nevertheless, God still hears his plea for help (v. 22). David concludes by inviting all saints to be of good courage during adversity (vv. 23, 24). "Hope is a tonic to Christian experience."[4]

"Redeemed! how I love to proclaim it! | Redeemed by the blood of the Lamb."[5]

---

1. Francis D. Nichol, ed., *The Seventh-day Adventist Bible Commentary*, vol. 3 (Washington, DC: Review and Herald®, 1977), 704.
2. Nichol, 704.
3. Nichol, 705.
4. Nichol, 705.
5. Fanny J. Crosby, "Redeemed!" (1882), in *The Seventh-day Adventist Hymnal* (Hagerstown, MD: Review and Herald®, 1985), hymn 337.

PSALM 17, PART 1: GUARD MY FOOTSTEPS

Hold up my goings in thy paths, that my footsteps slip not.
—Psalm 17:5

D avid was a representative man. His history is of interest to every soul who is striving for eternal victories. In his life two powers struggled for the mastery. Unbelief marshaled its forces, and tried to eclipse the light shining upon him from the throne of God. Day by day the battle went on in his heart, Satan disputing every step of advance made by the forces of righteousness. David understood what it meant to fight against principalities and powers, against the rulers of the darkness of this world. At times it seemed that the enemy must gain the victory. But in the end, faith conquered, and David rejoiced in the saving power of Jehovah. "The struggle that David endured, every follower of Christ must go through."[1]

"You need not be surprised if everything in the journey heavenward is not pleasant. There is no use in looking to our own defects. Looking unto Jesus, the darkness passes away, and the true light shineth. Go forth daily, expressing the prayer of David, 'Hold up my goings in thy paths, that my footsteps slip not.' All the paths of life are beset with peril, but we are safe if we follow where the Master leads the way, trusting the One whose voice we hear saying, 'Follow me.' 'He that followeth me shall not walk in darkness, but shall have the light of life.' "[2]

In Psalm 17, David "asserts confidence in his appeal [v. 1], prays to be kept in an evil world [v. 5], and muses on his ultimate satisfaction in seeing God face to face [v. 15]."[3] David is sure God has found him innocent of the accusations brought against him and knows God will judge him fairly. Following God's Word, David keeps himself from sin. The path of righteousness is narrow, and David does not want to slip (v. 5). "My beloved brethren, be ye stedfast, unmoveable, always abounding in the work of the Lord" (1 Corinthians 15:58).

"All the way my Savior leads me; / What have I to ask beside?"[4]

---

1. Ellen G. White, " 'That Your Joy Might Be Full,' " *Signs of the Times*®, August 11, 1909.
2. Ellen G. White, Letter 120, 1898.
3. Francis D. Nichol, ed., *The Seventh-day Adventist Bible Commentary*, vol. 3 (Washington, DC: Review and Herald®, 1977), 667, 668.
4. Fanny J. Crosby, "All the Way" (1875), in *The Seventh-day Adventist Hymnal* (Hagerstown, MD: Review and Herald®, 1985), hymn 516.

PSALM 17, PART 2: RAISE ME UP

As for me, I will behold thy face in righteousness:
I shall be satisfied, when I awake, with thy likeness.
—Psalm 17:15

Davidknew Jesus Christ as his Redeemer and had explicit faith in His ability to preserve and protect his life. Many in David's time, and even today, find their sense of fulfillment in material possessions. "With respect to the object for which they live, the wicked are successful. They live only for this world, and are prosperous in the things of this world. The future life is not in their thinking. They have forfeited eternal satisfaction for merely temporal gratification. Herein lies a partial answer to one of the deepest questions of philosophy: 'Why do the wicked prosper?' Their prosperity is but for the moment of this fleeting life; it is therefore inconsequential compared with the eternal prosperity of the righteous."[1]

David realized life was fleeting and that the things attained in this world are temporary. Job learned this lesson when all his earthly wealth was removed, and he was left destitute of this world's treasure. Yet Job and David knew where their treasure was stored up, and it was not here on earth. "For I know that my redeemer liveth, and that he shall stand at the latter day upon the earth: And though after my skin worms destroy this body, yet in my flesh shall I see God" (Job 19:25, 26).

David also believed in the resurrection of the righteous at the second coming of the Lord. "As for me, I will behold thy face in righteousness: I shall be satisfied, when I awake, with thy likeness" (Psalm 17:15). "Instead of envying the transient pleasures of the wicked, the psalmist longs for the joy of seeing God face to face."[2] "Beloved, now are we the sons of God, and it doth not yet appear what we shall be: but we know that, when he shall appear, we shall be like him; for we shall see him as he is" (1 John 3:2).

"Face to face with Christ my Savior, / Face to face, what will it be, / When with rapture I behold Him, / Jesus Christ, who died for me?"[3]

---

1. Francis D. Nichol, ed., *The Seventh-day Adventist Bible Commentary*, vol. 3 (Washington, DC: Review and Herald®, 1977), 669.
2. Nichol, 669.
3. Mrs. Frank A. Breck, "Face to Face" (1898), in *The Seventh-day Adventist Hymnal* (Hagerstown, MD: Review and Herald®, 1985), hymn 206.

THE CAVE IN EN-GEDI

And it came to pass, when Saul was returned from following the Philistines, that it was told him, saying, Behold, David is in the wilderness of Engedi.
—1 Samuel 24:1

Saul had not given up his quest to kill David. Once the Philistine threat was neutralized, he recommenced hunting the man whom he considered a threat to his throne. On being told David was in the wilderness of En-gedi, he assembled three thousand men and proceeded to search this remote and rugged area systematically. En-gedi itself is an oasis on the western shore of the Dead Sea, but to the west is a maze of dead-end paths and steep-walled canyons, forming a perfect place to hide. Saul still had informers, and hiding men from prying eyes was not easy!

"The precipitous cliffs of the wilderness, about 2,000 ft. (610 m.) high, approach to within 1 ½ mi. (2.4 km.) of the sea. . . . In the sides of the wadi are many caves, both natural and artificial."[1] "Portions of the wilderness west of the oasis are so badly eroded as to be almost hopelessly impassable. But there is a road from Carmel in Judah that crosses the Wilderness of Maon and En-gedi and descends through the *Wadi el-Kelb* to this oasis. Saul probably took this road in his determined search for David."[2]

During the search, Saul went into a sheepcote to "cover his feet" (1 Samuel 24:3)—a euphemism for relieving himself. A *sheepcote*, in this case, was a cave with a rock or thorny wall built around the front entrance to protect sheep and shepherds from the weather. Seeking privacy, Saul did not ask even his bodyguards to accompany him into the cave. How was Saul to know David and his men were hiding in the lateral branches of that very cave? Because he had just entered from the bright sunlight, his eyes did not penetrate the darker recesses of the cave, but David could see Saul plainly. His men urged him to slay his tormenter, for surely God had delivered Saul into his hands. This argument seemed like common sense. Now was the time to strike!

This golden opportunity was presented to David as a test of his character. What would you have done?

---

1. Francis D. Nichol, ed., *The Seventh-day Adventist Bible Commentary*, vol. 2 (Washington, DC: Review and Herald®, 1976), 568.
2. Nichol, 568, 569; emphasis original.

THE LORD'S ANOINTED

And David said to Saul, Wherefore hearest thou men's
words, saying, Behold, David seeketh thy hurt?
—1 Samuel 24:9

D avid could reach out and touch Saul. What should he do? "With his enemy in his hand, he not only refused to harm him personally but restrained his men from committing any untoward act in his name."[1] "The course of David made it manifest that he had a Ruler whom he obeyed. He could not permit his natural passions to gain the victory over him; for he knew that he that ruleth his own spirit, is greater than he who taketh a city. If he had been led and controlled by human feelings, he would have reasoned that the Lord had brought his enemy under his power in order that he might slay him, and take the government of Israel upon himself."[2]

"David's men were still unwilling to leave Saul in peace, and they reminded their commander of the words of God, 'Behold, I will deliver thine enemy into thine hand, that thou mayest do to him as it shall seem good unto thee. Then David arose, and cut off the skirt of Saul's robe privily.' But his conscience smote him afterward, because he had even marred the garment of the king."[3] Saul left the cave none the wiser for his close encounter with death.

David followed and called out after Saul, "My lord the king. And when Saul looked behind him, David stooped with his face to the earth, and bowed himself" (1 Samuel 24:8). Saul must have been shocked. David's next words are those of today's text and follow in verses 10–15. Basically, David said, "Had I wanted to kill you, I could have easily done so. I hold here a piece of your robe. Does this not prove to you my loyalty?" "When he saw the edge of his robe held up before his eyes, and realized how close he had come to death, he trembled before the material evidence of David's innocence. It was the triumph of spiritual force over physical prowess."[4]

"Love your enemies, bless them that curse you, do good to them that hate you, and pray for them which despitefully use you, and persecute you" (Matthew 5:44).

---

1. Francis D. Nichol, ed., *The Seventh-day Adventist Bible Commentary*, vol. 2 (Washington, DC: Review and Herald®, 1976), 569.
2. Ellen G. White, "David and Saul at En-Gedi," *Signs of the Times*®, October 12, 1888.
3. Ellen G. White, *Patriarchs and Prophets* (Mountain View, CA: Pacific Press®, 1943), 661.
4. Nichol, *The Seventh-day Adventist Bible Commentary*, 2:570.

SAUL CALLS OFF THE SEARCH

And it came to pass, when David had made an end of speaking these words unto Saul, that Saul said, Is this thy voice, my son David? And Saul lifted up his voice, and wept.
—1 Samuel 24:16

Saul had come close to death. "David's men were willing to love their friends, but they still cherished hatred for their enemies. In the midst of such attitudes David revealed respect for his worst enemy."[1] "When Saul heard the words of David [1 Samuel 24:9–15] he was humbled, and could not but admit their truthfulness. His feelings were deeply moved as he realized how completely he had been in the power of the man whose life he sought. David stood before him in conscious innocence. With a softened spirit, Saul exclaimed, 'Is this thy voice, my son David? And Saul lifted up his voice, and wept.' Then he declared to David: 'Thou art more righteous than I: for thou hast rewarded me good, whereas I have rewarded thee evil. . . . For if a man find his enemy, will he let him go well away? wherefore the Lord reward thee good for that thou hast done unto me this day. And now, behold, I know well that thou shalt surely be king, and that the kingdom of Israel shall be established in thine hand.' And David made a covenant with Saul that when this should take place he would favorably regard the house of Saul, and not cut off his name."[2]

"Compare David's respect for Saul both as a father-in-law and as a king, and his reverence for Saul as the Lord's anointed, with Saul's impetuous selfishness in bargaining by means of Michal to have David slain, his jealous hatred that turned him into a demon, and his unsatisfied thirst for the blood of the man who had spared his life."[3] The king was humbled. He acknowledged David had returned good for evil. Had the tables been turned, Saul would have slain David. "Knowing what he did of Saul's past course, David could put no confidence in the assurances of the king, nor hope that his penitent condition would long continue. So when Saul returned to his home David remained in the strongholds of the mountains."[4]

Beware of sudden "changes of heart" when dealing with those who harbor evil intentions.

---

1. Francis D. Nichol, ed., *The Seventh-day Adventist Bible Commentary*, vol. 2 (Washington, DC: Review and Herald®, 1976), 570.
2. Ellen G. White, *Patriarchs and Prophets* (Mountain View, CA: Pacific Press®, 1943), 662.
3. Nichol, *The Seventh-day Adventist Bible Commentary*, 2:571.
4. White, *Patriarchs and Prophets*, 662.

SAMUEL: PROPHET, PRIEST, LAST JUDGE OF ISRAEL

And Samuel judged Israel all the days of his life.
—1 Samuel 7:15

*And all Israel from Dan even to Beersheba knew that
Samuel was established to be a prophet of the LORD.*
—1 Samuel 3:20

The death of Samuel was regarded as an irreparable loss by the nation of Israel. A great and good prophet and an eminent judge had fallen in death, and the grief of the people was deep and heartfelt. From his youth up Samuel had walked before Israel in the integrity of his heart; although Saul had been the acknowledged king, Samuel had wielded a more powerful influence than he, because his record was one of faithfulness, obedience, and devotion. . . .

"As the people contrasted the course of Saul with that of Samuel, they saw what a mistake they had made in desiring a king that they might not be different from the nations around them. Many looked with alarm at the condition of society, fast becoming leavened with irreligion and godlessness. The example of their ruler was exerting a widespread influence, and well might Israel mourn that Samuel, the prophet of the Lord, was dead.

"The nation had lost the founder and president of its sacred schools, but that was not all. It had lost him to whom the people had been accustomed to go with their great troubles—lost one who had constantly interceded with God in behalf of the best interests of its people. . . . The people felt now that God was forsaking them. The king seemed little less than a madman. Justice was perverted, and order was turned to confusion.

"It was when the nation was racked with internal strife, when the calm, God-fearing counsel of Samuel seemed to be most needed, that God gave His aged servant rest. Bitter were the reflections of the people as they looked upon his quiet resting place, and remembered their folly in rejecting him as their ruler; for he had had so close a connection with Heaven that he seemed to bind all Israel to the throne of Jehovah. It was Samuel who had taught them to love and obey God; but now that he was dead, the people felt that they were left to the mercies of a king who was joined to Satan, and who would divorce the people from God and heaven."[1]

The impact for good, exhibited by a devout Christian example, cannot be overestimated.

1. Ellen G. White, *Patriarchs and Prophets* (Mountain View, CA: Pacific Press®, 1943), 663, 664.

THE WILDERNESS OF PARAN

And David arose, and went down to the wilderness of Paran.
—1 Samuel 25:1

D avid could not be present at the burial of Samuel, but he mourned for him as deeply and tenderly as a faithful son could mourn for a devoted father. He knew that Samuel's death had broken another bond of restraint from the actions of Saul, and he felt less secure than when the prophet lived. While the attention of Saul was engaged in mourning for the death of Samuel, David took the opportunity to seek a place of greater security; so he fled to the wilderness of Paran. It was here that he composed the one hundred and twentieth and twenty-first psalms."[1]

The wilderness of Paran and the wilderness of Zin are well named. The desert landscape stretches south from Judah into the Sinai. Here nomads follow their flocks of sheep and goats, looking for pasture in the barren wastes. "Since the tribes inhabiting this region were predatory in nature, David would find a very cold reception as he fled to Paran, and doubtless recognized his mistake. This reception, together with the knowledge that Saul's enmity would be more bitter after the death of Samuel, made David sense the need of definite help from on high."[2]

Among the tablelands and the sand dunes, rainfall is scarce, and springs of water are valued like gold. The Amalekites and Edomites both sought to control the caravan routes. David's men numbered only around six hundred, yet they were a formidable force that would cause raiders to think twice before attacking. Even so, David felt the need to be constantly on guard.

With Samuel dead, David realized he needed an even closer connection with his Maker. "When death claims esteemed friends and valued counselors, then it is that men realize anew that their trust must not be placed in princes, but in the ever-living, ever-watchful Lord. Though the voice of earlier advisers seemed indispensable and the watchful warnings invaluable, they cannot be compared with the promised guidance by One who never slumbers or sleeps."[3]

"God is as desirous of manifesting His beneficent guidance today as He was in David's day."[4]

---

1. Ellen G. White, *Patriarchs and Prophets* (Mountain View, CA: Pacific Press®, 1943), 664.
2. Francis D. Nichol, ed., *The Seventh-day Adventist Bible Commentary*, vol. 2 (Washington, DC: Review and Herald®, 1976), 572, 573.
3. Francis D. Nichol, ed., *The Seventh-day Adventist Bible Commentary*, vol. 3 (Washington, DC: Review and Herald®, 1977), 906.
4. Nichol, 906.

Psalm 120: A Plea for Peace

Deliver my soul, O Lord, from lying lips, and from a deceitful tongue.
—Psalm 120:2

D avid knew Saul would pursue him with even greater fury with Samuel dead. He also knew no matter what the trying circumstances, God hears and answers prayer. It is difficult to understand why some things are allowed to happen when we trust in God for protection. It is a fallacy to expect there will never be hardships or troubles just because one is a Christian. If we have this erroneous, privileged attitude, it is easier to lose faith when tribulations do come our way.

The life of a Christian will not always be a bed of roses. Troubles come to everyone. It is especially hard to bear slander. Jesus knew persecution would come to His followers just as it befell Him. He, therefore, encouraged His listeners in His sermon on the mount: "Blessed are ye, when men shall revile you, and persecute you, and shall say all manner of evil against you falsely, for my sake. Rejoice, and be exceeding glad: for great is your reward in heaven: for so persecuted they the prophets which were before you" (Matthew 5:11, 12).

David wondered what God would do concerning those who were slandering his good name. "What shall be given unto thee? or what shall be done unto thee, thou false tongue?" (Psalm 120:3). He answers himself in verse 4: "Sharp arrows of the mighty, with coals of juniper." "These sharp arrows represent the retribution the Lord brings upon the slanderer."[1] The juniper is a tree and shrub that burns exceptionally hot, much like manzanita or madrone wood. The evil slanderer will ultimately be consumed in the intense heat of the lake of fire when final justice is meted out (Revelation 20:12–15).

Finally, David laments living in exile: "Woe is me, that I sojourn in Mesech, that I dwell in the tents of Kedar!" (Psalm 120:5). Saul does not want peace, and David cannot change his mind (v. 6). "David's attempts to live peaceably with Saul and his evil advisers, were answered with hatred and hostility [v. 7]."[2]

"If it be possible, as much as lieth in you, live peaceably with all men" (Romans 12:18).

---

1. Francis D. Nichol, ed., *The Seventh-day Adventist Bible Commentary*, vol. 3 (Washington, DC: Review and Herald®, 1977), 907.
2. Nichol, 907.

PSALM 121: GOD, OUR HELP

*I will lift up mine eyes unto the hills, from whence cometh my help.
My help cometh from the LORD, which made heaven and earth.*
—Psalm 121:1, 2

Psalm 121 "is a beautiful song of trust and confidence in God. It is one of the most cherished of Bible poems in the entire heritage of Hebrew poetry. . . . When David realized that his last influential earthly friend was gone, he turned to the Lord for his sole remaining help. The psalm has been a great blessing to countless thousands who at one time or another have found themselves in circumstances more or less similar to those in which the psalmist finds himself."[1]

This short eight-verse psalm is a marvelous statement of trust in our heavenly Father. "I will lift up mine eyes unto the hills, from whence cometh my help. My help cometh from the LORD, which made heaven and earth" (Psalm 121:1, 2). "God's vigilance is unwearied. The Eternal is never exhausted and is always attentive to the needs of His earthly children."[2] "He will not suffer thy foot to be moved: he that keepeth thee will not slumber. Behold, he that keepeth Israel shall neither slumber nor sleep" (vv. 3, 4).

David was living in the desert of Paran, surrounded by raiders, when he penned these lines: "The LORD is thy keeper: the LORD is thy shade upon thy right hand. The sun shall not smite thee by day, nor the moon at night. The LORD shall preserve thee from all evil: he shall preserve thy soul" (vv. 5–7). These verses take on new meaning when one realizes David was comparing God to the relief of shade in a desert land.

Furthermore, "the LORD shall preserve thy going out and thy coming in from this time forth, and even for evermore" (v. 8). The Lord continually watches over His children. The evil one cannot steal away the redeemed from the palm of His hand.

"O God, our help in ages past, / Our hope for years to come, / Our shelter from the stormy blast, / And our eternal home!"[3]

---

1. Francis D. Nichol, ed., *The Seventh-day Adventist Bible Commentary*, vol. 3 (Washington, DC: Review and Herald®, 1976), 907, 908.

2. Nichol, 908.

3. Isaac Watts, "O God, Our Help" (1719), in *The Seventh-day Adventist Hymnal* (Hagerstown, MD: Review and Herald®, 1985), hymn 103.

NABAL

And Nabal answered David's servants, and said, Who is
David? and who is the son of Jesse? there be many servants
now a days that break away every man from his master.
—1 Samuel 25:10

W hile camped in the wilderness of Paran, David and his men defended the flocks of those around them from marauding bands
of thieves. They provided this protective service at no expense
to the owners. David, therefore, sent ten men to request supplies from
Nabal—a wealthy man who was shearing his flocks at Carmel. The harvest-
ing of wool was a time of generosity to others. "Sheep owners would normally be happy to reward those helping them against loss. David's request
for supplies was legitimate and in harmony with the customs of his time."[1]

Today's scripture is Nabal's insulting reply to David's request. "David
and his men had been like a wall of protection to the shepherds and
flocks of Nabal; and now this rich man was asked to furnish from his
abundance some relief to the necessities of those who had done him such
valuable service. David and his men might have helped themselves from
the flocks and herds, but they did not. They behaved themselves in an
honest way. Their kindness, however, was lost upon Nabal."[2] "Nabal
thought nothing of spending an extravagant amount of his wealth to
indulge and glorify himself; but it seemed too painful a sacrifice for him
to make to bestow compensation which he never would have missed,
upon those who had been like a wall to his flocks and herds. Nabal was
like the rich man in the parable. He had only one thought—to use God's
merciful gifts to gratify his selfish animal appetites. He had no thought
of gratitude to the giver. . . . Present luxury, present gain, was the one
absorbing thought of his life. This was his God."[3]

David immediately gathered four hundred men and set out for a
showdown. "This impulsive movement was more in harmony with the
character of Saul than with that of David, but the son of Jesse had yet to
learn of patience in the school of affliction."[4]

Generosity should be second nature to a follower of Christ.

---

1. Francis D. Nichol, ed., *The Seventh-day Adventist Bible Commentary*, vol. 2 (Washington, DC: Review and Herald®, 1976), 574.
2. Ellen G. White, *Patriarchs and Prophets* (Mountain View, CA: Pacific Press®, 1943), 665.
3. Ellen G. White, "The Work of a Peace-Maker," *Signs of the Times®*, October 26, 1888.
4. White, *Patriarchs and Prophets*, 665.

ABIGAIL'S GOOD COUNSEL

*And when Abigail saw David, she hasted, and lighted off
the ass, and fell before David on her face, and bowed herself
to the ground, and fell at his feet, and said, Upon me, my lord,
upon me let this iniquity be: and let thine handmaid, I pray thee,
speak in thine audience, and hear the words of thine handmaid.*
—1 Samuel 25:23, 24

Alarmed at the way David's men had been treated, one of Nabal's servants hastened home to Abigail, Nabal's wife, and related the encounter. Abigail immediately knew she must apologize. "Without consulting her husband or telling him of her intention, Abigail made up an ample supply of provisions, which, laded upon asses, she sent forward in the charge of servants, and herself started out to meet the band of David. She met them in a covert of a hill."[1]

Blaming herself, she said, "Let not my lord, I pray thee, regard this man of Belial [son of wickedness], even Nabal: for as his name is, so is he; Nabal is his name, and folly is with him: but I thine handmaid saw not the young men of my lord, whom thou didst send. Now therefore, my lord, as the LORD liveth, and as thy soul liveth, seeing the LORD hath withholden thee from coming to shed blood, and from avenging thyself with thine own hand, now let thine enemies, and they that seek evil to my lord, be as Nabal. . . . I pray thee, forgive the trespass of thine handmaid: for the LORD will certainly make my lord a sure house; because my lord fighteth the battles of the LORD, and evil hath not been found in thee all thy days" (1 Samuel 25:25, 26, 28).

Abigail pointed out three things to David: (1) Nabal had not insulted David personally; that was the way he treated everyone. (2) Obviously, David had not consulted God, and God had delayed him, thereby saving innocent lives. (3) "David would be incurring guilt, from which his life had been reasonably free up till the present. . . . But had he carried out his purposes against Nabal, the incident would have raised serious queries in the minds of the people as to David's fitness for being their future king. If he was to continue his policy of exterminating those of the citizens of his realm who dared oppose his will, his administration would be quite undesirable."[2]

God often sends a messenger at exactly the right time and place to turn aside rash acts.

---

1. Ellen G. White, *Patriarchs and Prophets* (Mountain View, CA: Pacific Press®, 1943), 666.
2. Francis D. Nichol, ed., *The Seventh-day Adventist Bible Commentary*, vol. 2 (Washington, DC: Review and Herald®, 1976), 575.

GOD SETS THINGS RIGHT

And it came to pass about ten days after,
that the LORD smote Nabal, that he died.
—1 Samuel 25:38

D avid received the rebuke of Abigail in all humility, recognizing the wisdom of the godly woman who bowed before him. "The ready acceptance of rebuke is to be commended. David had accustomed himself to witnessing the mysterious workings of Providence, and he saw the divine handiwork in the happenings before him. He thanked God for starting the train of events that culminated in Abigail's meeting him at precisely the right place and moment, and for the encouragement of such a spiritual-minded soul as Abigail."[1] Abigail not only recognized when an injustice had been done but also actively took steps to right the wrong. "Would that there were many more like this woman of Israel, who would soothe the irritated feelings, prevent rash impulses, and quell great evils by words of calm and well-directed wisdom."[2] "Blessed are the peacemakers: for they shall be called the children of God" (Matthew 5:9).

"When Abigail returned home she found Nabal and his guests in the enjoyment of a great feast, which they had converted into a scene of drunken revelry. Not until the next morning did she relate to her husband what had occurred in her interview with David. Nabal was a coward at heart; and when he realized how near his folly had brought him to a sudden death, he seemed smitten with paralysis. Fearful that David would still pursue his purpose of revenge, he was filled with horror, and sank down in a condition of helpless insensibility. After ten days he died."[3] Thus, vengeance was the Lord's (see Romans 12:19), and David's hands were clean.

"The Lord had returned the wickedness of the wicked upon his own head. In this dealing of God with Nabal and David, men may be encouraged to put their cases into the hands of God; for in his own good time he will set matters right."[4]

Patience and peacekeeping are virtues Christians must cultivate. "Lead me in thy truth, and teach me: for thou art the God of my salvation; on thee do I wait all the day" (Psalm 25:5).

---

1. Francis D. Nichol, ed., *The Seventh-day Adventist Bible Commentary*, vol. 2 (Washington, DC: Review and Herald®, 1976), 575.
2. Ellen G. White, *Patriarchs and Prophets* (Mountain View, CA: Pacific Press®, 1943), 667.
3. White, 667, 668.
4. Ellen G. White, "The Work of a Peace-Maker," *Signs of the Times*®, October 26, 1888.

MARRYING AGAIN

And when the servants of David were come to Abigail to Carmel, they spake unto her, saying, David sent us unto thee, to take thee to him to wife.
—1 Samuel 25:40

When David heard Nabal was dead, he sent servants to Abigail with a proposal of marriage. Abigail did not hesitate to accept his proposal (1 Samuel 25:42). David "was already the husband of one wife, but the custom of the nations of his time had perverted his judgment and influenced his actions. Even great and good men have erred in following the practices of the world. The bitter result of marrying many wives was sorely felt throughout all the life of David."[1]

We are told: "David also took Ahinoam of Jezreel; and they were also both of them his wives.

"But Saul had given Michal his daughter, David's wife, to Phalti the son of Laish, which was of Gallim" (vv. 43, 44). Ahinoam would soon be the mother of Amnon (2 Samuel 3:2), David's firstborn son. The next son in line for the throne would be Abigail's son, Chileab. Multiple wives meant multiple sons of nearly the same age vying for the throne of their father. As we shall see, this created serious rivalries between the sons, their father, and their mothers.

Polygamy was never God's plan for humankind. It "was practiced at an early date. It was one of the sins that brought the wrath of God upon the antediluvian world. Yet after the Flood it again became widespread."[2] During the time of Abraham, "polygamy had become so widespread that it had ceased to be regarded as a sin, but it was no less a violation of the law of God, and was fatal to the sacredness and peace of the family relation. Abraham's marriage with Hagar resulted in evil, not only to his own household, but to future generations."[3]

"The kingly idolatrous nations considered it an addition to their honor and dignity to have many wives, and David regarded it an honor to his throne to possess several wives. But he was made to see the wretched evil of such a course by the unhappy discord, rivalry and jealousy among his numerous wives and children."[4]

When the sanctity of marriage is violated, Satan claims more than one victim.

---

1. Ellen G. White, *Patriarchs and Prophets* (Mountain View, CA: Pacific Press®, 1943), 668.
2. White, 338.
3. White, 145.
4. Ellen G. White, *Spiritual Gifts*, vol. 4 (Washington, DC: Review and Herald®, 1945), 86.

A SPEAR AND A JUG OF WATER

*Then Saul arose, and went down to the wilderness
of Ziph, having three thousand chosen men of Israel
with him, to seek David in the wilderness of Ziph.*
—1 Samuel 26:2

Saul's promise to leave David in peace did not last long. The Ziphites again reported his presence to Saul. David, informed by spies of the location of Saul's camp, asked for a man to accompany him and move closer. Abishai, David's nephew by his sister Zeruiah, volunteered.

With great stealth, hiding in shadows, David and his nephew snuck into Saul's camp. During their reconnaissance, they found Saul sleeping beside Abner, the commander of his forces. Saul had placed a jug of water near his pillow and had stuck his spear in the ground close beside it. Abishai saw an immediate opportunity. "Then said Abishai to David, God hath delivered thine enemy into thine hand this day: now therefore let me smite him, I pray thee, with the spear even to the earth at once, and I will not smite him the second time" (1 Samuel 26:8).

"Abishai had not learned the difficult lesson of exercising magnanimity toward an enemy. Saul had started an intertribal feud between Benjamin and Judah, and Abishai evidently concluded that such an action called for retaliation. Saul had thrown his spear at David, but had missed. Now, according to Abishai's judgment, it was David's turn, and as his bodyguard, Abishai was offering to act on behalf of his uncle."[1]

Refusing to take the life of God's anointed (vv. 9–11), David left Saul in God's hands, allowing Him to choose what course to follow. Telling Abishai to take the cruse of water and the spear, David and his nephew threaded their way back through the sleeping army. "The miracle that enabled these men to move back and forth through the lines of 3,000 men, to the very center of the group, without detection, was evidence as to which side of the controversy Providence was on. The intervention was a condemnation of Saul's changeable nature in pledging himself to one thing, and a short time later violating his word and doing exactly the opposite."[2]

"In all thy ways acknowledge him, and he shall direct thy paths" (Proverbs 3:6).

---

1. Francis D. Nichol, ed., *The Seventh-day Adventist Bible Commentary*, vol. 2 (Washington, DC: Review and Herald®, 1976), 577.
2. Nichol, 578.

DAVID CALLS OUT ABNER

*And David cried to the people, and to Abner the son
of Ner, saying, Answerest thou not, Abner? Then Abner
answered and said, Who art thou that criest to the king?*
—1 Samuel 26:14

D avid, upon reaching a safe distance from Saul's camp, stood on the top of a hill and shouted a rebuke at Abner for his dereliction of duty in protecting his king. "Art not thou a valiant man? and who is like to thee in Israel? wherefore then hast thou not kept thy lord the king? for there came one of the people in to destroy the king thy lord. This thing is not good that thou hast done. As the LORD liveth, ye are worthy to die, because ye have not kept your master, the LORD's anointed. And now see where the king's spear is, and the cruse of water that was at his bolster" (1 Samuel 26:15, 16). How this taunt must have infuriated Abner! The one he was seeking to kill had stood just feet from him, and he had been asleep at his post. Now he was being ridiculed before his men.

Saul's life had been placed in the hands of David again, and again David had refused to take that life. Why did David not avail himself of the opportunity to rid himself of his tormentor? David had been promised the kingdom, and these chances to speed along that accomplishment must have seemed heaven-sent. Why, then, did he or his men not slay Saul? David understood the Mosaic Law prohibiting him from harming God's anointed—the king of Israel (Exodus 22:28). Additionally, David had the respect of his men. When he gave an order, it was obeyed, even if every fiber of their bodies wanted to disobey him, his men respected his wishes.

David had physical evidence to prove he had penetrated the camp. Looking about, Saul suddenly realized his spear and water jar were missing. It would have been interesting to eavesdrop on the whispered discussion between Saul and his general at that moment. What excuse could Abner raise to explain his inattention? Sleeping on guard duty was a crime punishable by death. It was an unforgivable lapse, bringing the entire host into danger. Being embarrassed in front of his men was equally horrific. Abishai, as he stood beside his uncle David on that hill, must have loved every minute of this exchange.

"Correction is grievous unto him that forsaketh the way: and he that hateth reproof shall die" (Proverbs 15:10).

RETURNING GOOD FOR EVIL

And he said, Wherefore doth my lord thus pursue after his
servant? for what have I done? or what evil is in mine hand?
—1 Samuel 26:18

Saul, hearing David's voice coming out of the darkness, called out, "Is this thy voice, my son David? And David said, It is my voice, my lord, O king" (1 Samuel 26:17). David wanted to know why Saul pursued him without cause (v. 18) and offered two valid possibilities (v. 19), both without merit: "(1) If because of a sin on my part, ignorantly committed against you or against all Israel, over which you are the anointed king, God has impressed you to execute judgment against me, permit me to follow the instructions in the Torah and seek forgiveness in the divinely constituted manner (Lev. 4). (2) But if through vile, slanderous gossip, if through whispered calumnies, you have been urged to hunt me down as a rebel, feeling I am trying to usurp your place, the evidence at En-gedi and again here proves the falsity of such words and actions. Therefore those who are urging you on are cursed before God according to the regulations of the same Torah (Deut. 27:24–26), and you should not follow them, nor be guided by their counsel."[1]

David had been driven from the land and from worshiping God with his family. He had been forced to hide out in desolate places and seek refuge among the enemies of Israel. He had committed no crime yet was being treated as a rebel. "Saul found himself completely overcome for the moment when he saw that his life had once more been precious in the eyes of David. The magnanimity of this outlawed patriot forced from his lips several noteworthy confessions: (1) 'I have sinned' in secretly planning the death of a neighbor; (2) 'I have played the fool' in repeating my attempt to kill the one who has graciously spared my life; (3) I 'have erred exceedingly' in giving way to self-pity and the passion of the lower nature."[2]

Saul invited David to return with him to Gibeah and pledged his protection. David instead wisely chose not to place himself in the hands of Saul. Telling Saul to send a man over to reclaim the king's spear, David again turned back into the wilderness with his men.

"Deliver my soul, O LORD, from lying lips, and from a deceitful tongue" (Psalm 120:2).

---

1. Francis D. Nichol, ed., *The Seventh-day Adventist Bible Commentary*, vol. 2 (Washington, DC: Review and Herald®, 1976), 578.
2. Nichol, 579.

PSALM 16, PART 1: INSTRUCT ME IN THE NIGHT

Preserve me, O God: for in thee do I put my trust.
—Psalm 16:1

Many believe Psalm 16 was written after David's encounter with Saul, recounted in 1 Samuel 26:19. Psalm 16 "is an expression of complete happiness such as springs from complete submission to God. The psalmist progresses from the thought of God as his sole protector to a declaration of faith in life everlasting, a declaration rarely so clearly expressed in the OT [Old Testament]. The last verses of the psalm have Messianic import [see Acts 2:25–31]."[1]

David is not pleading for help in verse 1 so much as requesting continued care and protection. Recognizing God as the source of all goodness, David puts his trust in Him and seeks to continue their relationship. Those who worship Jehovah and obey His law are an earthly joy to associate with (Psalm 16:3). Those that follow other gods will have nothing but continual sorrow (v. 4). David maintains that his destiny rests in the hands of the Lord (v. 6). He knows God will apportion out a choice inheritance in the best of locations, and for that reason, he gives thanks to the Lord for His generosity and goodness (vv. 5, 6).

During the night's stillness, it is easier to hear the counsel of God. Listening for the answer to prayer is as important as prayer itself. Too often, we eagerly tell God our troubles and ask for help but then fail to listen and watch for His answer. An honest conscience, fortified by reading God's Word, reins in improper actions and emotions, helping us walk in the path of life (v. 7).

"In David's eyes, God was no mere abstraction, but a Person actually at his side. Enoch walked with God (Gen. 5:22; . . .). Moses kept a vision of God before him. . . . We need a consciousness of the constant presence of God. Not only will a sense of God's presence be a deterrent to sinning, but it will gladden the heart, brighten the life, and give meaning to circumstances."[2]

"Speak, Lord, in the stillness, / While I wait on Thee; / Hushed my heart to listen, / In expectancy."[3]

---

1. Francis D. Nichol, ed., *The Seventh-day Adventist Bible Commentary*, vol. 3 (Washington, DC: Review and Herald®, 1977), 664.
2. Nichol, 665.
3. E. May Grimes, "Speak, Lord, in the Stillness," in *The Church Hymnal: The Official Hymnal of the Seventh-day Adventist Church* (Washington, DC: Review and Herald®, 1941), hymn 329.

PSALM 16, PART 2:
A PROMISE OF RESURRECTION

For thou wilt not leave my soul in hell; neither
wilt thou suffer thine Holy One to see corruption.

—Psalm 16:10

Christ's crucifixion, burial, and resurrection fulfilled the prophecy of Psalm 16. Christ is the only Being who can be described as God's "Holy One." "In Christ's deliverance from the tomb and in His resurrection the full meaning of these verses became clear."[1]

What was David's understanding of the state of the dead? He uses the Hebrew word *nephesh* in verse 10 to describe a soul. "A definition for *nephesh* may be derived from the Bible account of the creation of man (Gen. 2:7). The record declares that when God gave life to the body He had formed, the man literally 'became a soul of life.' The 'soul' had not previously existed, but came into existence at the creation of Adam. . . . This uniqueness of individuality seems to be the idea emphasized in the Hebrew term *nephesh*."[2]

The word *nephesh* (root *naphash*) means "to breathe." When God created man, He "breathed into his nostrils the breath of life; and man became a living soul" (Genesis 2:7). Ecclesiastes 9:5 says, "For the living know that they shall die: but the dead know not any thing, neither have they any more a reward; for the memory of them is forgotten." "For in death there is no remembrance of thee: in the grave who shall give thee thanks?" (Psalm 6:5). "All flesh shall perish together, and man shall turn again unto dust" (Job 34:15). Upon death, the body returns to dust, and consciousness ceases.

The Bible calls death a sleep.[3] The grave is the "hell" of which David speaks. All dead go to this place, but they are not conscious (Genesis 37:35; Numbers 16:30; Psalms 30:3; 89:48; Acts 2:27, 31). The grave—*Sheol*, Hades, hell—will surrender its dead at the last trumpet!

"Attended by all the shining angels, / Down the flaming sky / The Judge will come, and will take His people / Where they will not die."[4]

---

1. Francis D. Nichol, ed., *The Seventh-day Adventist Bible Commentary*, vol. 3 (Washington, DC: Review and Herald®, 1977), 665.

2. Nichol, 666.

3. In the Old Testament, see 1 Kings 2:10; 11:43; 14:20, 31; 15:8; 2 Chronicles 21:1; 26:23; Job 14:10–12; Psalm 13:3; Jeremiah 51:39, 57; Daniel 12:2. In the New Testament, see Matthew 9:24; 27:52; Mark 5:39; Luke 7:60; John 11:11–14; 1 Corinthians 15:51, 52; 1 Thessalonians 4:13–17; 2 Peter 3:4.

4. S. J. Graham, "The Golden Morning Is Fast Approaching," in *The Church Hymnal: The Official Hymnal of the Seventh-day Adventist Church* (Washington, DC: Review and Herald®, 1941), hymn 547.

DAVID LACKS FAITH

*And David said in his heart, I shall now perish one day
by the hand of Saul: there is nothing better for me than
that I should speedily escape into the land of the Philistines.*

—1 Samuel 27:1

In spite of all David had done for his own countrymen, they manifested but little sympathy for him now that he was in disfavor with the king. The men of Keilah would have turned him over to Saul ([1 Samuel] 23:1–13). The Ziphites twice informed Saul of his hiding place ([1 Samuel] 23:19; 26:1), and Nabal proved as unfriendly as Doeg had been ([1 Samuel] 25:10, 11). Twice he had extended the hand of mercy to the jealously insane tyrant who openly sought his life ([1 Samuel] 24:6–11; 26:8–12). From the very people who should have shown him every courtesy he had received only censure and ingratitude, and his life among them had been one continuous nightmare. Living on short rations in caves and forests, in deserts and on mountain crags, he had been treated as an outlaw."[1]

David became discouraged. He again sought refuge with Achish, the king of Gath. "David's conclusion that Saul would certainly accomplish his murderous purpose was formed without the counsel of God. . . . David looked on appearances, and not at the promises of God. He doubted that he would ever come to the throne. Long trials had wearied his faith and exhausted his patience.

"The Lord did not send David for protection to the Philistines, the most bitter foes of Israel. This very nation would be among his worst enemies to the last, and yet he had fled to them for help in his time of need."[2]

David continued to worship God, but instead of trusting in God's ability to protect him, he now placed his faith in an earthly king. Achish was glad to welcome David and his men into his land and promised them protection. "At David's request for a residence in the country, removed from the royal city, the king graciously granted Ziklag as a possession."[3]

"Trust in the LORD with all thine heart; and lean not unto thine own understanding" (Proverbs 3:5).

1. Francis D. Nichol, ed., *The Seventh-day Adventist Bible Commentary*, vol. 2 (Washington, DC: Review and Herald®, 1976), 580.
2. Ellen G. White, *Patriarchs and Prophets* (Mountain View, CA: Pacific Press®, 1943), 672.
3. White, 673.

PSALM 141: RETURNING GOOD FOR BAD

Keep me from the snares which they have laid for me,
and the gins [traps] of the workers of iniquity. Let the
wicked fall into their own nets, whilst that I withal escape.
—Psalm 141:9, 10

P salm 141 repeats David's request for direction and security but with poetic imagery. "The psalmist begins with an appeal for acceptance by the Lord (vs. 1, 2), begs that his speech may be kept pure (vs. 3, 4), expresses his desire to be censured by the righteous rather than to receive deceitful flattery from the ungodly (vs. 5, 6), and closes with a request that he may be rescued from the cruel schemes of his enemies (vs. 7–10)."[1] Invoking the imagery of priests lifting their hands and offering prayers with rising incense at the evening sacrifice (vv. 1, 2), David likewise wants his prayers to be acceptable to God. The incense of the earthly tabernacle represented "the merits and intercession of Christ, His perfect righteousness, which through faith is imputed to His people, and which can alone make the worship of sinful beings acceptable to God."[2]

David "prayed earnestly that the Lord would keep him from the practices of evil men. We must not infer from the language of this verse that God ever inclines a man's heart to evil. . . . The psalmist was simply using the nontechnical language of Bible writers, by which God is presented as doing that which He does not prevent. The familiar expression in the Lord's prayer, 'lead us not into temptation' (Matt. 6:13), should be understood in the same light."[3]

David asks God to help him accept rebuke from persons who are righteous and have his best interests at heart (vv. 5, 6). David had accepted Abigail's rebuke, knowing it was true and sincere (1 Samuel 25:29–31). To accept reproof, even from a friend, is often difficult.

Closing the psalm, David returns to his oft-voiced request for protection from the snares of his enemies (Psalm 141:7–10). He trusts the Lord to lead and deliver him and cause his enemies to be caught up in their own traps.

"He leadeth me! O blessed thought! / O words with heavenly comfort fraught! / Whate'er I do, where'er I be, / Still 'tis God's hand that leadeth me."[4]

---

1. Francis D. Nichol, ed., *The Seventh-day Adventist Bible Commentary*, vol. 3 (Washington, DC: Review and Herald®, 1977), 928.
2. Ellen G. White, *Patriarchs and Prophets* (Mountain View, CA: Pacific Press®, 1943), 353.
3. Nichol, *The Seventh-day Adventist Bible Commentary*, 3:928
4. J. H. Gilmore, "He Leadeth Me" (1862), in *The Seventh-day Adventist Hymnal* (Hagerstown, MD: Review and Herald®, 1985), hymn 537.

THE ENEMY OF MY ENEMY

And David and his men went up, and invaded the Geshurites, and the Gezrites, and the Amalekites: for those nations were of old the inhabitants of the land, as thou goest to Shur, even unto the land of Egypt.
—1 Samuel 27:8

D avid, his men, and their families settled in the border town of Ziklag. This outpost placed David beyond the reach of Saul, who would not dare bring about a war by invading the land of the Philistines to capture him. "Ziklag bordered on the territory of desert marauders who had troubled Israel ever since their entrance into Canaan. The Lord had ordered the complete annihilation of such predatory tribes as the Amalekites . . . , and as the anointed heir to the throne David felt responsible to carry out what Saul had failed to accomplish. David no doubt intended thus to merit the loyalty of his own nation."[1]

"Earlier, when Saul 'utterly destroyed' all the Amalekites . . . , it is likely that many of them disappeared into the desert, and in a short time reappeared to continue their raids. The wandering Bedouin peoples have a mysterious way of disappearing suddenly, only to reappear in time."[2]

David and his men systematically waged war against the Geshurites, Gezrites (Girzites), and Amalekites, almost annihilating those tribes. It appeared there were no survivors left to tell the tale, so David lied to King Achish, telling him that he and his men had been at war with Judah. Achish was eager to believe David had allied himself with Philistia and was fighting battles for them. He told his kinsmen, "He [David] hath made his people Israel utterly to abhor him; therefore he shall be my servant for ever" (1 Samuel 27:12). "David knew that it was the will of God that those heathen tribes should be destroyed, and he knew that he was appointed to do this work; but he was not walking in the counsel of God when he practiced deception."[3]

"Great and good men, men with whom God has worked, will make grievous mistakes when they cease to watch and pray, and to fully trust in God."[4]

1. Francis D. Nichol, ed., *The Seventh-day Adventist Bible Commentary*, vol. 2 (Washington, DC: Review and Herald®, 1976), 581.
2. Nichol, 581.
3. Ellen G. White, *Patriarchs and Prophets* (Mountain View, CA: Pacific Press®, 1943), 673.
4. Ellen G. White, "David Becomes Weary in Well-Doing," *Signs of the Times*®, November 9, 1888.

IN A TIGHT SPOT

*And it came to pass in those days, that the Philistines
gathered their armies together for warfare, to fight
with Israel. And Achish said unto David, Know thou assuredly,
that thou shalt go out with me to battle, thou and thy men.*
—1 Samuel 28:1

D avid now found himself in a tight spot. He had led Achish to
believe he and his men had fought against Israel rather than
the nomadic tribes. Naturally, when war with Israel broke out,
Achish expected David to readily agree to take up arms against Saul
once again. "David had no intention of lifting his hand against his people; but he was not certain as to what course he would pursue, until
circumstances should indicate his duty. He answered the king evasively,
and said, 'Surely thou shalt know what thy servant can do.' Achish understood these words as a promise of assistance in the approaching war,
and pledged his word to bestow upon David great honor, and give him
a high position at the Philistine court."[1]

"David's faith in God had been strong, but it had failed him when he
placed himself under the protection of the Philistines. He had taken this
step without seeking the counsel of the Lord; but when he had sought
and obtained the favor of the Philistines, it was poor policy to repay their
kindness by deception. In the favor they had shown him they had been
actuated by selfishness. . . . [They] were glad of an opportunity to separate
David's forces from the army under Saul. They hoped that David would
avenge his wrongs by joining them in battle against Saul and Israel."[2]

"Saul had learned that David and his force were with the Philistines,
and he expected that the son of Jesse would take this opportunity to
revenge the wrongs he had suffered. . . . While he had been engrossed in
pursuing David he had neglected the defense of his kingdom."[3]

David had placed himself and his men in a position from which it
appeared there was no way out. To take up arms against his country was
not an option. Neither was failing to honor a pledge to those who had
given him sanctuary. If only he had asked the Lord for instruction!

*How often we place ourselves in difficult situations by not asking the Lord
for guidance.*

1. Ellen G. White, *Patriarchs and Prophets* (Mountain View, CA: Pacific Press®, 1943), 674.
2. Ellen G. White, "David's Experience in Philistia," *Signs of the Times*®, November 16, 1888, 1.
3. White, *Patriarchs and Prophets*, 675.

THE WITCH OF ENDOR

Then said Saul unto his servants, Seek me a woman that hath a familiar spirit, that I may go to her, and enquire of her. And his servants said to him, Behold, there is a woman that hath a familiar spirit at Endor.
—1 Samuel 28:7

On the morrow Saul must engage the Philistines in battle. The shadows of impending doom gathered dark about him; he longed for help and guidance. But it was in vain that he sought counsel from God. 'The Lord answered him not, neither by dreams, nor by Urim, nor by prophets.' The Lord never turned away a soul that came to Him in sincerity and humility. Why did he turn Saul away unanswered? The king had by his own act forfeited the benefits of all the methods of inquiring of God. He had rejected the counsel of Samuel the prophet; he had exiled David, the chosen of God; he had slain the priests of the Lord. Could he expect to be answered by God when he had cut off the channels of communication that Heaven had ordained?"[1]

"Spiritism was a common practice among the nations round about, but Israel had been forbidden to have anything to with it (Deut. 18:9–14)."[2] "During the life of Samuel, Saul had commanded that all wizards and those that had familiar spirits should be put to death; but now, in the rashness of desperation, he had recourse to that oracle which he had condemned as an abomination."[3] Now he ordered his men to find a woman who supposedly could contact the dead. Interestingly, his servants knew the location of just such a person.

The Philistine army was camped just north of the plain of Jezreel on the south side of the hill of Moreh. Across that plain to the southeast was the camp of the Israelites at the foot of Mount Gilboa. The witch Saul wished to see had hidden near the village of Endor on the north side of the hill of Moreh. Saul had to evade the Philistine army to his west and travel nine miles in a northwest direction to reach Endor. To seek counsel from an emissary of Satan meant traversing enemy lines. But worse than that, Saul had crossed over to Satan's side.

Willfully separating oneself from God to pursue one's own path is a recipe for disaster.

1. Ellen G. White, *Patriarchs and Prophets* (Mountain View, CA: Pacific Press®, 1943), 675, 676.
2. Francis D. Nichol, ed., *The Seventh-day Adventist Bible Commentary*, vol. 2 (Washington, DC: Review and Herald®, 1976), 584, 585.
3. White, *Patriarchs and Prophets*, 676.

SPEAKING TO THE "DEAD" IS FORBIDDEN

*For the living know that they shall die: but the dead know
not any thing, neither have they any more a reward; for the
memory of them is forgotten. Also their love, and their hatred,
and their envy, is now perished; neither have they any more
a portion for ever in any thing that is done under the sun.*
—Ecclesiastes 9:5, 6

The Israelites were forbidden to deal in any fashion with those who purported to speak with the dead. God made it plain that the dead "know not any thing" (Ecclesiastes 9:5). Whomever the Israelites thought they were talking with, it was certainly not their dead relatives. "His breath goeth forth, he returneth to his earth; in that very day his thoughts perish" (Psalm 146:4). Those who sought wizards were to be cut off from among the people of Israel (Leviticus 20:6).

"The 'familiar spirits' were not the spirits of the dead, but evil angels, the messengers of Satan. Ancient idolatry, which, as we have seen, comprises both worship of the dead and pretended communion with them, is declared by the Bible to have been demon worship. . . .

"Modern spiritualism, resting upon the same foundation, is but a revival in a new form of the witchcraft and demon worship that God condemned and prohibited of old. It is foretold in the Scriptures, which declare that 'in the latter times some shall depart from the faith, giving heed to seducing spirits, and doctrines of devils.' 1 Timothy 4:1."[1]

"Under the name of spiritualism the practice of communicating with beings claiming to be the spirits of the departed has become widespread. It is calculated to take hold of the sympathies of those who have laid their loved ones in the grave. Spiritual beings sometimes appear to persons in the form of their deceased friends, and relate incidents connected with their lives and perform acts which they performed while living. In this way they lead men to believe that their dead friends are angels, hovering over them and communicating with them. Those who thus assume to be the spirits of the departed are regarded with a certain idolatry, and with many their word has greater weight than the word of God."[2]

God has warned us not to place any credence in spiritualism (Isaiah 8:19, 20).

---

1. Ellen G. White, *Patriarchs and Prophets* (Mountain View, CA: Pacific Press®, 1943), 685, 686.
2. White, 684, 685.

THE DANGER OF SPIRITUALISM

For in death there is no remembrance of thee:
in the grave who shall give thee thanks?

—Psalm 6:5

The Bible plainly states the dead are asleep and not disembodied spirits or souls floating about heaven, looking down on the living. The dead in Christ will be raised at His second coming to join Him in the air and live with Him for eternity (1 Thessalonians 4:16–18). The redeemed will sit in judgment of the lost during the millennium (Revelation 20:4–6). The wicked will be raised, following that millennium, to face judgment and final destruction in the lake of fire that cleanses the earth (Revelation 20:11–15). Until Christ's second advent, all those who have died rest in the grave, awaiting either the first resurrection of the righteous (v. 6) or the second resurrection of the wicked (vv. 12, 13).

"The teaching that the spirits of the dead return to communicate with the living is based on the belief that the spirit of man exists in a conscious state after death, that indeed this spirit is the real man. The Bible *does* teach that the spirit [the breath of life], at death, returns unto God, who gave it (Eccl. 12:7), but the OT [Old Testament] emphatically denies that this spirit is a conscious entity (Job 14:21; Ps. 146:4; Eccl. 9:5, 6). The NT [New Testament] teaches the same doctrine. Jesus pointed forward to His second coming and not to death as the time when the believer will be reunited with his Lord (John 14:1–3). . . . In speaking solace to those who had laid their loved ones to rest, Paul significantly declared that there was to be no precedence on the part of the living over the dead, but all would be reunited with their Lord at the same moment (1 Thess. 4:16, 17). . . .

"Although much of the phenomena of spiritistic séances involves trickery and sleight of hand, not all phenomena can be explained on this basis."[1] Since it is clear the dead cannot communicate with the living, who is impersonating them? Scripture reveals Satan and his angels have the ability to impart familiar information and change their appearance (Matthew 4:1–11; 2 Corinthians 11:13, 14).

"The dead praise not the LORD, neither any that go down into silence" (Psalm 115:17).

---

1. Francis D. Nichol, ed., *The Seventh-day Adventist Bible Commentary*, vol. 2 (Washington, DC: Review and Herald®, 1976), 587; emphasis added.

SAUL CUTS HIS LAST LINK

*Then said the woman, Whom shall I bring up
unto thee? And he said, Bring me up Samuel.*
—1 Samuel 28:11

The witch of Endor had escaped the decree to destroy all wizards, witches, and necromancers (those who claim to speak to the dead). Yet "disguised as he was, Saul's lofty stature and kingly port declared that he was no common soldier. The woman suspected that her visitor was Saul, and his rich gifts strengthened her suspicions."[1] "Little did she realize that Saul himself had long been troubled by evil spirits ([1 Samuel] 16:14–16), and was now completely at their mercy."[2]

"And the woman said unto him, Behold, thou knowest what Saul hath done, how he hath cut off those that have familiar spirits, and the wizards, out of the land: wherefore then layest thou a snare for my life, to cause me to die?" (1 Samuel 28:9). Saul quickly granted immunity so that he might consult the dead prophet. "But a communication from Samuel, speaking as a prophet, would indirectly be a communication from God, and it is expressly stated that the Lord refused to communicate with Saul (1 Sam. 28:6). Saul was slain, 'for asking counsel of one that had a familiar spirit, to enquire of it; and enquired not of the Lord' (1 Chron. 10:13, 14)."[3]

"Saul knew that in this last act, of consulting the witch of Endor, he cut the last shred which held him to God. He knew that if he had not before willfully separated himself from God, this act sealed that separation, and made it final. He had made an agreement with death, and a covenant with hell. The cup of his iniquity was full."[4]

"The Scriptures predict an increase in supernatural manifestations in the last days (Matt. 7:22, 23; 2 Thess. 2:9; Rev. 13:13, 14; 16:14). The only safeguard against these delusive devices is to have the mind so well fortified with the truths of the Bible that the tempter will be recognized in his guise."[5]

Rejecting the Word in small steps leads steadily further from the path of righteousness.

---

1. Ellen G. White, *Patriarchs and Prophets* (Mountain View, CA: Pacific Press®, 1943), 679.
2. Francis D. Nichol, ed., *The Seventh-day Adventist Bible Commentary*, vol. 2 (Washington, DC: Review and Herald®, 1976), 586.
3. Nichol, 587.
4. Ellen G. White, *The Spirit of Prophecy*, vol. 1 (Battle Creek, MI: Seventh-day Adventist Pub. Assn., 1870), 376, 377.
5. Nichol, *The Seventh-day Adventist Bible Commentary*, 2:587.

SATAN IMPERSONATES SAMUEL

And he said unto her, What form is he of? And she said,
An old man cometh up; and he is covered with a mantle.
And Saul perceived that it was Samuel, and he stooped
with his face to the ground, and bowed himself.
—1 Samuel 28:14

Saul's questions, together with the woman's replies, are in themselves evidence that he did not see the apparition himself. . . . When she described the apparition, Saul 'perceived that it was Samuel.' "[1] "When Samuel was living, Saul had despised his counsel and had resented his reproofs. But now, in the hour of his distress and calamity, he felt that the prophet's guidance was his only hope, and in order to communicate with Heaven's ambassador he vainly had recourse to the messenger of hell!"[2]

"When Saul inquired for Samuel, the Lord did not cause Samuel to appear to Saul. He saw nothing. Satan was not allowed to disturb the rest of Samuel in the grave, and bring him up in reality to the witch of Endor. God does not give Satan power to resurrect the dead. . . . Satan knew Samuel well, and he knew how to represent him before the witch of Endor, and to utter correctly the fate of Saul and his sons."[3] "That supernatural appearance was produced solely by the power of Satan. He could as easily assume the form of Samuel as he could assume that of an angel of light, when he tempted Christ in the wilderness."[4]

This episode is filled with contradictions. If, as many today believe, the spirits of the good go to heaven and the evil to hell, why would Saul ask the witch to "bring me *up* Samuel" (1 Samuel 28:11; emphasis added)? Why did he not ask for Samuel to be brought *down*? And Samuel would have asked, "Why have you brought me *down*?" Instead, "Samuel" asks, "Why hast thou disquieted me, to bring me *up*?" (v. 15; emphasis added)

"For false Christs and false prophets shall rise, and shall shew signs and wonders, to seduce, if it were possible, even the elect" (Mark 13:22).

---

1. Francis D. Nichol, ed., *The Seventh-day Adventist Bible Commentary*, vol. 2 (Washington, DC: Review and Herald®, 1976), 587.
2. Ellen G. White, *Patriarchs and Prophets* (Mountain View, CA: Pacific Press®, 1943), 680.
3. Ellen G. White, *The Spirit of Prophecy*, vol. 1 (Battle Creek, MI: Seventh-day Adventist Pub. Assn., 1870), 376.
4. White, *Patriarchs and Prophets*, 679.

SATAN REVELS IN DELIVERING BAD NEWS

Moreover the LORD will also deliver Israel with thee into the hand of the Philistines: and to morrow shalt thou and thy sons be with me: the LORD also shall deliver the host of Israel into the hand of the Philistines.
—1 Samuel 28:19

C ompletely taken in by the false Samuel, Saul immediately got to the point of his visit. "I am sore distressed; for the Philistines make war against me, and God is departed from me, and answereth me no more, neither by prophets, nor by dreams: therefore I have called thee, that thou mayest make known unto me what I shall do" (1 Samuel 28:15).

"The devil took this opportunity to taunt Saul with the irony of his fate. The very man who had once persecuted the exponents of this black art was now on his knees before that power, pleading for help."[1] "Wherefore then dost thou ask of me, seeing the LORD is departed from thee, and is become thine enemy?" (v. 16). Satan taunted Saul further with words purporting to be from Samuel: "And the LORD hath done to him, as he spake by me: for the LORD hath rent the kingdom out of thine hand, and given it to thy neighbour, even to David: Because thou obeyest not the voice of the LORD, nor executedst his fierce wrath upon Amalek, therefore hath the LORD done this thing unto thee this day" (vv. 17, 18). Saul was well aware the kingdom had been given to David. "Satan, by his bewitching power, had led Saul to justify himself in defiance of Samuel's reproofs and warning. But now, in his extremity, he turned upon him, presenting the enormity of his sin and the hopelessness of pardon, that he might goad him to desperation."[2]

Satan had worse news and reveled in it. "Moreover the LORD will also deliver Israel with thee into the hand of the Philistines: and to morrow shalt thou and thy sons be with me: the LORD also shall deliver the host of Israel into the hand of the Philistines" (v. 19). "Saul had placed himself fully in the power of Satan; and now he whose only delight is in causing misery and destruction, made the most of his advantage, to work the ruin of the unhappy king."[3]

God is not the enemy of humankind (v. 16)! Yet Satan paints Him as a heartless tyrant.

---

1. Francis D. Nichol, ed., *The Seventh-day Adventist Bible Commentary*, vol. 2 (Washington, DC: Review and Herald®, 1976), 588.
2. Ellen G. White, *Patriarchs and Prophets* (Mountain View, CA: Pacific Press®, 1943), 680.
3. White, 680.

WHOSE SIDE ARE THESE HEBREWS ON?

Then said the princes of the Philistines, What do these
Hebrews here? And Achish said unto the princes of the
Philistines, Is not this David, the servant of Saul the king of
Israel, which hath been with me these days, or these years, and
I have found no fault in him since he fell unto me unto this day?

—1 Samuel 29:3

It should have been no surprise that on the eve of battle, the Philistine princes would question the presence of David and his men. The question of where his loyalties lay should have awakened in David the same question. "He should not have sought refuge among the Philistines in the first place. The step had been taken without seeking divine guidance. Now the crisis was approaching. David was in great straits. He had no desire to take up arms against his brethren."[1]

David's men were marching at the end of the Philistine column, accompanying the Philistine king and his entourage. Even though Achish attempted to allay the fears of his men, his vote of confidence in David was not accepted. Under these circumstances, it would be better not to trust David. Although delighted at this turn of events, David responded with feigned hurt: "But what have I done? and what hast thou found in thy servant so long as I have been with thee unto this day, that I may not go fight against the enemies of my lord the king?" (1 Samuel 29:8).

"In a moment of discouragement, and not knowing which way to turn, David had taken steps that placed him in a dilemma from which he was totally unable to escape without outside help. . . . How merciful was the Lord in using the ill will and animosity of the Philistines to open the door for his release from disgrace, whichever way the battle turned!"[2]

Achish excused David from participating in the coming battle (vv. 9, 10) and tactfully admonished him to leave the Philistine camp before dawn, lest the princes kill him. "Heavenly messengers moved upon the Philistine princes to protest against the presence of David and his force with the army in the approaching conflict."[3]

Often an error in judgment places us in desperate need of God's intervention.

---

1. Francis D. Nichol, ed., *The Seventh-day Adventist Bible Commentary*, vol. 2 (Washington, DC: Review and Herald®, 1976), 590.
2. Nichol, 591.
3. Ellen G. White, *Patriarchs and Prophets* (Mountain View, CA: Pacific Press®, 1943), 690.

MEANWHILE, BACK HOME . . .

And it came to pass, when David and his men were come to
Ziklag on the third day, that the Amalekites had invaded the south,
and Ziklag, and smitten Ziklag, and burned it with fire; And had
taken the women captives, that were therein: they slew not any,
either great or small, but carried them away, and went on their way.
—1 Samuel 30:1, 2

After three days' travel David and his band of six hundred men
reached Ziklag, their Philistine home. But a scene of desolation
met their view. The Amalekites, taking advantage of David's
absence, with his force, had avenged themselves for his incursions into
their territory. They had surprised the city while it was left unguarded,
and having sacked and burned it, had departed, taking all the women
and children as captives, with much spoil. . . .

". . . David's followers turned upon him as the cause of their calamities.
He had provoked the vengeance of the Amalekites by his attack upon them;
yet, too confident of security in the midst of his enemies, he had left the city
unguarded. Maddened with grief and rage, his soldiers were now ready
for any desperate measures, and they threatened even to stone their leader.

"David seemed to be cut off from every human support. All that he held
dear on earth had been swept from him. Saul had driven him from his
country; the Philistines had driven him from the camp; the Amalekites had
plundered his city; his wives and children had been made prisoners; and
his own familiar friends had banded against him, and threatened him even
with death. In this hour of utmost extremity David, instead of permitting his
mind to dwell upon these painful circumstances, looked earnestly to God
for help. He 'encouraged himself in the Lord.' He reviewed his past eventful
life. Wherein had the Lord ever forsaken him? His soul was refreshed in
recalling the many evidences of God's favor. The followers of David, by
their discontent and impatience, made their affliction doubly grievous; but
the man of God, having even greater cause for grief, bore himself with for-
titude. 'What time I am afraid, I will trust in Thee' (Psalm 56:3), was the
language of his heart. Though he himself could not discern a way out of the
difficulty, God could see it, and would teach him what to do."[1]

When afraid and in difficulty, whom do you trust for guidance?

---

1. Ellen G. White, *Patriarchs and Prophets* (Mountain View, CA: Pacific Press®, 1943), 692, 693.

SHALL I PURSUE THEM?

And David enquired at the LORD, saying, Shall I pursue after this troop? shall I overtake them? And he answered him, Pursue: for thou shalt surely overtake them, and without fail recover all.
—1 Samuel 30:8

D avid made no rash decision this time. He asked what the Lord would have him do. Should he pursue the raiders and recover what was lost? He must have desperately wanted a positive answer to his question, for Ahinoam and Abigail, "David's two wives," were among those taken captive (1 Samuel 30:5). David wisely sent for Abiathar, the priest, asking him to bring forward the ephod so that he might ask God for guidance (v. 7). The ephod of the high priest had the Urim and Thummim (which start with the first and last letters of the Hebrew alphabet), which were encircled with light when a question was asked of the Lord (Exodus 28).

Upon receiving God's instruction, "David and his soldiers at once set out in pursuit of their fleeing foe. So rapid was their march, that upon reaching the brook Besor, which empties near Gaza into the Mediterranean Sea, two hundred of the band were compelled by exhaustion to remain behind. But David with the remaining four hundred pressed forward, nothing daunted."[1]

Moving rapidly, they came upon an Egyptian slave left in the desert to die by his cruel Amalekite master. Upon being revived, the Egyptian related the story of the raid and agreed to lead David's band to the camp of the raiders. The encampment that greeted their eyes was deep in celebration. Obviously, the marauders expected no one to be on their trail. An attack was planned, and David's four hundred rushed the camp. The fighting continued all night and into the next day. In the end, only a band of four hundred nomads, mounted on camels, made their escape.

"The word of the Lord was fulfilled. 'David recovered all that the Amalekites had carried away: and David rescued his two wives. And there was nothing lacking to them, neither small nor great, neither sons nor daughters, neither spoil, nor anything that they had taken to them: David recovered all.' "[2]

God stands ever ready to counter the workings of evil.

---

1. Ellen G. White, *Patriarchs and Prophets* (Mountain View, CA: Pacific Press®, 1943), 693.
2. White, 693.

DIVIDING THE SPOILS OF BATTLE

For who will hearken unto you in this matter? but as
his part is that goeth down to the battle, so shall his
part be that tarrieth by the stuff: they shall part alike.
—1 Samuel 30:24

The battle had gone well for David and his men. They recovered not only their own flocks and herds but also those taken by the Amalekites in other raids. The Amalekites had not harmed their captives, intending instead to sell them as slaves. Their liberation was cause for celebration. "Upon reaching their companions who had remained behind, the more selfish and unruly of the four hundred urged that those who had had no part in the battle should not share the spoils; that it was enough for them to recover each his wife and children. But David would permit no such arrangement. 'Ye shall not do so, my brethren,' he said, 'with that which the Lord hath given us. . . . As his part is that goeth down to the battle, so shall his part be that tarrieth by the stuff; they shall part alike.' Thus the matter was settled, and it afterward became a statute in Israel that all who were honorably connected with a military campaign should share the spoils equally with those who engaged in actual combat."[1]

This statute did not originate with David. "A definite system for the distribution of spoils was imposed at the time Israel first fought the Midianites. Only a portion of the encampment went forth to war, but immediately after the battle the Lord instructed Moses to divide the booty into two parts, so that the warriors and those remaining with the stuff might share equally; definite amounts were also to be set aside for the Levites and for an offering to the Lord (see Num. 31:25–54). The plan was not always adhered to, but from David's time on it appeared to be an established ordinance."[2]

The flocks belonging to the Amalekites were David's share of the spoils. "During the years of his wanderings, not only had many in Judah joined him, but many others had given him provisions. Up to the present he had been unable to repay their kindnesses. Now at the first opportunity he sent liberal portions from his abundant spoil."[3]

Liberality is the currency of heaven.

---

1. Ellen G. White, *Patriarchs and Prophets* (Mountain View, CA: Pacific Press®, 1943), 694.
2. Francis D. Nichol, ed., *The Seventh-day Adventist Bible Commentary*, vol. 2 (Washington, DC: Review and Herald®, 1976), 594, 595.
3. Nichol, 595.

A PROPHECY FULFILLED

So Saul died, and his three sons, and his armourbearer,
and all his men, that same day together.
—1 Samuel 31:6

While David was defeating the Amalekites, "the armies of Israel appeared to have the tactical advantage in choosing Mt. Gilboa for their stand. . . . Nevertheless Israel fell. The apostasy of Saul, who sought help from a familiar spirit, had precipitated the disaster. Israel had been forewarned that in the day of their refusal to be guided by the Lord's statutes and covenant, they would 'flee when none pursueth' (Lev. 26:17)."[1]

"Why did the Lord permit Jonathan to be slain along with his father when his attitudes were totally contrary to those of Saul? Why could not he, a spiritual-minded soul, disavowing his father's ideals, and sympathetically knitting himself with David in following the opening providences of the Lord, have been permitted to live? . . . This is a question beyond the ability of man to answer. . . . The records of sacred history reveal that persecution and death have been the lot of the righteous in all ages. Because of the implications of the great controversy Satan must be granted an opportunity to afflict the righteous. But the Christian's comfort is that though the adversary may be able to destroy the body, he is not able to destroy the soul (Matt. 10:28). Once the relationship of the soul to God has been unalterably decided upon, the continuance or discontinuance of this present life is not of prime importance."[2]

Being wounded by Philistine archers, Saul feared he would be tortured if captured in a wounded state (1 Samuel 31:4). He fell on his own sword (v. 4) and possibly begged an Amalekite to slay him (2 Samuel 1:1–10). Thus, Saul died an ignominious death.

"Saul, by his own volition, had invited the prince of darkness to control him. His master had paid him his wages."[3]

Whose side do you choose to be on in the great controversy between Christ and Satan?

---

1. Francis D. Nichol, ed., *The Seventh-day Adventist Bible Commentary*, vol. 2 (Washington, DC: Review and Herald®, 1976), 596.
2. Nichol, 596.
3. Nichol, 597.

Philistine Revenge, Israelite Homage

*All the valiant men arose, and went all night, and took
the body of Saul and the bodies of his sons from the wall
of Bethshan, and came to Jabesh, and burnt them there.*
—1 Samuel 31:12

The Philistines were quick to follow up on their victory over the defeated Israelites. "On the north side of the Valley of Jezreel were the tribes of Naphtali and Zebulun, and part of the tribe of Issachar. East of the Jordan were the half tribe of Manasseh and the tribe of Gad. By occupying the valleys of Esdraelon, Jezreel, and Jordan, the Philistines had made a complete line of cleavage through the center of Israel's domain."[1] The inhabitants of villages along this line fled before the approach of the Philistines, who now occupied their villages and towns.

The day following the battle, Philistine soldiers picked their way through the battlefield, stripping the dead of weapons and valuables. "And it came to pass on the morrow, when the Philistines came to strip the slain, that they found Saul and his three sons [Jonathan, Abinadab, and Malchishua] fallen in mount Gilboa. And they cut off his head, and stripped off his armour, and sent into the land of the Philistines round about, to publish it in the house of their idols, and among the people" (1 Samuel 31:8, 9). Saul's head was probably placed in the temple of Dagon (v. 9), and his armor was put "in the house of Ashtaroth" (v. 10), thus symbolizing that these pagan gods had triumphed and given the Philistines victory over the God of Israel (1 Chronicles 10:10).

Near the eastern end of the Valley of Jezreel stood the small village of Bethshan. It was here the Philistines nailed the bodies of Saul and his sons to the village wall. The valiant men of Jabesh-gilead, remembering their deliverance from Nahash the Ammonite when they petitioned Saul for help (1 Samuel 11:1–11), "took the body of Saul and the bodies of his sons from the wall of Bethshan, and came to Jabesh, and burnt them there. And they took their bones, and buried them under a [tamarisk] tree at Jabesh, and fasted seven days" (1 Samuel 31:12, 13).

"Misfortune, defeat, and death all bring to light the hidden sympathies in the hearts of men, and reveal their noblest sentiments."[2]

---

1. Francis D. Nichol, ed., *The Seventh-day Adventist Bible Commentary*, vol. 2 (Washington, DC: Review and Herald®, 1976), 597.
2. Nichol, 598.

DAVID LEARNS OF SAUL'S DEATH

And David said unto him, How went the matter?
I pray thee, tell me. And he answered, That the people are
fled from the battle, and many of the people also are fallen
and dead; and Saul and Jonathan his son are dead also.
—2 Samuel 1:4

I t was the third day since David and his warriors returned to Ziklag. As they labored to restore their ruined homes, they watched with anxious hearts for tidings of the battle which they knew must have been fought between Israel and the Philistines. Suddenly a messenger entered the town, 'with his clothes rent, and earth upon his head.' He was at once brought to David, before whom he bowed with reverence, expressing recognition of him as a powerful prince, whose favor he desired."[1] "The messenger was an Amalekite . . . , of the same race as the people who had attacked the camp of David and whom David had recently smitten (1 Sam. 30:1, 17, 18). . . . His act of obeisance was presumably in recognition of David's new position as leader in Israel."[2]

The messenger stated Saul and his sons were dead. David wanted confirmation. "How knowest thou that Saul and Jonathan his son be dead?" (2 Samuel 1:5). The messenger explained, "As I happened by chance upon mount Gilboa, behold, Saul leaned upon his spear; and, lo, the chariots and horsemen followed hard after him. And when he looked behind him, he saw me, and called unto me. And I answered, Here am I. And he said unto me, Who art thou? And I answered him, I am an Amalekite. He said unto me again, Stand, I pray thee, upon me, and slay me: for anguish is come upon me, because my life is yet whole in me. So I stood upon him, and slew him, because I was sure that he could not live after that he was fallen" (vv. 6–10). "The story of the young man does not agree with the account of Saul's death found in 1 Sam. 31:3–6. . . . The Amalekite invented his tale for the purpose of securing a reward, thinking that his alleged deed would be highly acclaimed by David."[3]

"Boast not thyself of to morrow; for thou knowest not what a day may bring forth" (Proverbs 27:1).

---

1. Ellen G. White, *Patriarchs and Prophets* (Mountain View, CA: Pacific Press®, 1943), 694, 695.
2. Francis D. Nichol, ed., *The Seventh-day Adventist Bible Commentary*, vol. 2 (Washington, DC: Review and Herald®, 1976), 602.
3. Nichol, 602.

DAVID MOURNS SAUL AND JONATHAN

How are the mighty fallen in the midst of the battle!
O Jonathan, thou wast slain in thine high places.
—2 Samuel 1:25

D avid was deeply affected by the news of Saul's and Jonathan's deaths. He had lost friends and comrades in the battle. For a time, he had led Saul's army, and many of the slain were brethren. David and his men tore their clothes and wept as they mourned those lost. "This act revealed the true greatness of Israel's future king. David mourned with genuine sorrow. Even though Saul had sought to take the life of his supposed rival, David entertained no malice toward him. . . . As a true Israelite, David mourned the death of the king, and as a personal friend he mourned the loss of Jonathan, whom he regarded with deep affection."[1]

David composed a poem honoring those fallen in battle. It loses nothing by translation into English and is found in 2 Samuel 1:19–27. The first part of the epic relates to both Saul and Jonathan (vv. 19–24), while the last part deals specifically with Jonathan (vv. 25, 26). "The beauty of Israel is slain upon thy high places: how are the mighty fallen!" (v. 19). Not wanting the news to be cause for celebration in the land of the Philistines, David pronounces a curse on the site of the battlefield: "Ye mountains of Gilboa, let there be no dew, neither let there be rain, upon you, nor fields of offerings: for there the shield of the mighty is vilely cast away, the shield of Saul, as though he had not been anointed with oil" (v. 21).

Verse 23 is especially poignant: "Saul and Jonathan were lovely and pleasant in their lives, and in their death they were not divided: they were swifter than eagles, they were stronger than lions." Jonathan stood shoulder to shoulder with his father on the battlefield and died at his side. Three times (vv. 19, 25, 27) David laments: "How are the mighty fallen!" He ends by grieving for his late friend. "I am distressed for thee, my brother Jonathan: very pleasant hast thou been unto me: thy love to me was wonderful, passing the love of women" (v. 26).

"True love consists in thinking of others, caring for others, and doing for others. . . . To Jonathan, the friendship of David meant more than fame and fortune."[2]

---

1. Francis D. Nichol, ed., *The Seventh-day Adventist Bible Commentary*, vol. 2 (Washington, DC: Review and Herald®, 1976), 602, 603.
2. Nichol, 604.

KILL THE MESSENGER!

And David said unto him, How wast thou not afraid to
stretch forth thine hand to destroy the LORD's anointed?
—2 Samuel 1:14

W hile David mourned for Saul, the Amalekite stood idly by, unable to understand the significance of the scene he was witnessing. Recovering from his first shock of grief, David turned to the young man before him, desiring further details concerning the crime of which he had already confessed himself guilty."[1] "David had twice had the opportunity to take the life of Saul but had refused to lift up his hand against the Lord's anointed. He regarded the act of murdering a king a base crime against the nation as well as against God."[2]

The Amalekite had lied concerning the part he had played in the death of Saul in order to be rewarded for what he claimed was a mercy killing. Most commentators believe Saul was already dead (1 Samuel 31:3–6), and the young man simply lifted the crown and bracelet from Saul's body and concocted a story to gain favor for freeing David from his callous enemy.

"Evidently supposing that David must cherish enmity toward his relentless persecutor, the stranger hoped to secure honor to himself as the slayer of the king. With an air of boasting the man went on to relate that during the battle he found the monarch of Israel wounded, and sore pressed by his foes, and that at his own request the messenger had slain him. The crown from his head and the golden bracelets from his arm he had brought to David. He confidently expected that these tidings would be hailed with joy, and that a rich reward would be his for the part that he had acted."[3]

Instead, David ordered his death, saying, "Thy blood be upon thy head; for thy mouth hath testified against thee, saying, I have slain the LORD's anointed" (2 Samuel 1:16). Justice was thus swiftly applied to the messenger who had pronounced his own guilt, whether or not a lie. Claiming to have committed regicide, he stood condemned and paid with his life.

It is amazing how often things do not turn out as expected when one falsifies the facts.

---

1. Francis D. Nichol, ed., *The Seventh-day Adventist Bible Commentary*, vol. 2 (Washington, DC: Review and Herald®, 1976), 603.
2. Nichol, 603.
3. Ellen G. White, *Patriarchs and Prophets* (Mountain View, CA: Pacific Press®, 1943), 695.

DAVID'S REIGN

2 Samuel 2–24
1 Kings 1:1–2:11
1 Chronicles 11–29

Patriarchs and Prophets, chapters 69–73

DAVID ANOINTED KING OVER JUDAH

And the men of Judah came, and there they
anointed David king over the house of Judah.
—2 Samuel 2:4

With Saul's death, the way was open for David to return to Judah. Having learned during his exile how important it was to consult the Lord before making decisions, he sought to know God's will about this one. "Shall I go up into any of the cities of Judah? And the LORD said unto him, Go up. And David said, Whither shall I go up? And he said, Unto Hebron" (2 Samuel 2:1).

Hebron had been the home of Abraham, and his tomb was located there, along with that of his wife Sarah, their son Isaac, and grandson Jacob. "David had maintained friendly relations with this city during the lifetime of Saul. It was well suited for the temporary capital of David's southern kingdom, not only being situated in a strong position in the mountains of Judah, amid people who were friendly to David, but having the sacred associations of the early patriarchs."[1]

"David and his followers immediately prepared to obey the instruction which they had received from God. The six hundred armed men, with their wives and children, their flocks and herds, were soon on the way to Hebron. As the caravan entered the city the men of Judah were waiting to welcome David as the future king of Israel. Arrangements were at once made for his coronation. 'And there they anointed David king over the house of Judah.' But no effort was made to establish his authority by force over the other tribes."[2]

David had already been anointed privately by Samuel (1 Samuel 16:13). His coronation at Hebron was a public declaration by the tribe of Judah that they accepted him as the anointed of the Lord and the next king of Israel. One of the first acts of the new king was to send an emissary to Jabesh-gilead with a message of gratitude for the respect they had shown the bodies of Saul and Jonathan (2 Samuel 2:5–7). "David pledged that he would be the friend and protector of the inhabitants of Jabesh-gilead even as Saul had been before him."[3]

David wished the friends of Saul no ill will. In fact, he applauded their loyalty and devotion.

---

1. Francis D. Nichol, ed., *The Seventh-day Adventist Bible Commentary*, vol. 2 (Washington, DC: Review and Herald®, 1976), 606.
2. Ellen G. White, *Patriarchs and Prophets* (Mountain View, CA: Pacific Press®, 1943), 697.
3. Nichol, *The Seventh-day Adventist Bible Commentary*, 2:607.

Psalm 101: Rules to Govern By

I will sing of mercy and judgment: unto thee, O Lord, will I sing.
I will behave myself wisely in a perfect way. O when wilt thou
come unto me? I will walk within my house with a perfect heart.
—Psalm 101:1, 2

Psalm 101 was composed early in David's reign. It sets forth principles of conduct for a ruler. The first part of the psalm deals with personal objectives (vv. 1–4), while the second part deals with those actions that are public in nature (vv. 5–8). These few verses show us the decency of David and the justice of his views. David vows to conduct himself wisely in all things—a tall order for one who will soon be surrounded by sycophants and self-serving ministers. It will take great strength of will not to succumb to pride and ego. Eschewing the pomp and riches of the court will require humility and remembrance that all one possesses comes from the Lord.

First and foremost, David praises God for His mercy and judgment toward all humankind. He longs for closer fellowship with his God, which alone can keep him centered and focused on what is important (vv. 1, 2). David further pledges not to look upon evil, for he fears the influence it might have. He vows to avoid evil and not linger in its presence long enough to be affected (v. 3). A perverted heart is to be shunned, as is association with wicked people (v. 4).

David next turns to his choice of officials. He will not tolerate among his counselors those who are proud or slander others for their own advancement (v. 5). Rather, he will surround himself with those who have the well-being of Israel as their focus. "David resolves to keep on the watch for faithful men who will make worthy members of his court." "David desires his official associates to be like him [v. 6]."[1] Those who practice deceit or tell lies will have no place among his officials (v. 7). And he will do his best to make his capital city an example for the rest of the country (v. 8). These were certainly lofty aspirations. Unfortunately, resolutions often fail to materialize under everyday trials and temptations. Staying connected to God is vital if one wants to reach his or her highest potential.

"Praise to the Lord, who doth prosper thy work and defend thee; / Surely His goodness and mercy here daily attend thee."[2]

---

1. Francis D. Nichol, ed., *The Seventh-day Adventist Bible Commentary*, vol. 3 (Washington, DC: Review and Herald®, 1977), 858.

2. Joachim Neander, "Praise to the Lord," in *The Seventh-day Adventist Hymnal* (Hagerstown, MD: Review and Herald®, 1985), hymn 1.

ISH-BOSHETH—FORGOTTEN KING OF ISRAEL

Ishbosheth Saul's son was forty years old when he began to reign over Israel, and reigned two years. But the house of Judah followed David.
—2 Samuel 2:10

When Saul became king he made his uncle Abner commander in chief of his army (1 Sam. 14:50). Abner was thus, by the ties of blood and of office, strongly attached to the house of Saul. He had been with Saul in the pursuit of David, and was not now willing that the man he had so long hunted should succeed to the kingdom over which Saul had reigned. Abner never forgot the rebuke David gave him for sleeping on guard (1 Sam. 26:7–16). He was proud, vengeful, and ambitious, determined to have his own way rather than to allow David to rule as the anointed of the Lord."[1] It was his aim to install Saul's son Ish-bosheth as king. Ish-bosheth's three older brothers died with Saul on Mount Gilboa (1 Samuel 31:2), leaving him heir to Saul's throne.

"Ishbosheth was but a weak and incompetent representative of the house of Saul, while David was pre-eminently qualified to bear the responsibilities of the kingdom."[2] "God selected David, a humble shepherd, to rule his people. He . . . distinguished himself by his boldness and unwavering trust in God. He was remarkable for his fidelity and reverence. His firmness, humility, love of justice, and decision of character, qualified him to carry out the high purposes of God . . . and to rule them as a generous and wise monarch."[3]

Abner knew the Lord had chosen David to be the next king of Israel. This made little difference. Saul's hatred of David had become Abner's own, and he could not release the loathing that drove him to destroy the son of Jesse. Abner would rather tear the kingdom apart than accept David as king. In fighting David, Abner lost sight of the fact he was fighting God's anointed. This was a battle he could not win. Yet war seemed inevitable.

Human emotions and personal agendas can cloud judgment (Proverbs 14:12).

---

1. Francis D. Nichol, ed., *The Seventh-day Adventist Bible Commentary*, vol. 2 (Washington, DC: Review and Herald®, 1976), 607.
2. Ellen G. White, *Patriarchs and Prophets* (Mountain View, CA: Pacific Press®, 1943), 698.
3. Ellen G. White, *Spiritual Gifts*, vol. 4 (Washington, DC: Review and Herald®, 1945), 85.

CIVIL WAR

And there was a very sore battle that day; and Abner was
beaten, and the men of Israel, before the servants of David.
—2 Samuel 2:17

A bner, seeking to extend the rule of Ish-bosheth, led an armed incursion to the border claimed by David. He and his men gathered at a spring near Gibeon, which lay northwest of Jerusalem. Joab, the commander of David's forces, gathered his men at the same spring but on the opposite side of the large pool. Here was to be a battle between families—Abner, Ish-bosheth's great-uncle, versus Joab, David's nephew.

Once again, a method of warfare was played out that has become obsolete in modern times. As with Goliath's challenge to the armies of Israel, Abner challenged Joab to combat between chosen champions prior to engaging in a larger battle between entire armies. This vicious contest was to pit a dozen men representing Ish-bosheth and a dozen representing David against each other (2 Samuel 2:15). The contestants each grabbed the other by the head and thrust swords through their respective bodies. It would seem all perished (v. 16). *Helkath-hazzurim* means " 'field of flints' or 'field of [sword] edges,' "[1] which is an appropriate name for the action that took place at this site. The larger battle was then joined.

Battles during the time of David were mainly fought with bows, arrows, and slings from a distance and with swords and spears once the armies met in hand-to-hand conflict. Battles routinely involved little or no strategy other than to overpower one's opponent and move on to the next until one side or the other fled the field. Such was the case for the army of Abner. "The numbers engaged were probably not large, since the total of those slain was only 20 on the side of David and 360 on the side of Israel (vs. 30, 31), but the contest was fought out with a fierceness that brought a decisive victory to the forces of Judah."[2]

Abner might have been a great commander, but he saw the battle was going against his men and fled the field.

Issuing challenges is not the way for Christians to settle disputes. "Blessed are the peacemakers: for they shall be called the children of God" (Matthew 5:9).

---

1. Francis D. Nichol, ed., *The Seventh-day Adventist Bible Commentary*, vol. 2 (Washington, DC: Review and Herald®, 1976), 608.
2. Nichol, 608.

A RECKLESS RACE

And there were three sons of Zeruiah there, Joab, and Abishai,
and Asahel: and Asahel was as light of foot as a wild roe.
—2 Samuel 2:18

T he battle had gone badly for the forces of Abner, and he fled
the scene. Asahel, Joab's brother, saw Abner leave and quickly
decided to pursue him. "Abner was the backbone of the resistance against David. If he could be put out of the contest, the cause of
Ish-bosheth would collapse, and the entire kingdom would quickly be
united under David. Understanding this, Asahel persistently kept on the
heels of Israel's commander in chief.

". . . Recognizing that the foe who was pursuing him was the brother of
Joab, Abner was unwilling to injure him and urged that he turn aside and
content himself with some meaner antagonist. Though light of foot (v. 18),
Asahel was no match for a probably more robust and seasoned warrior."[1]
"And Abner said to him, Turn thee aside to thy right hand or to thy left,
and lay thee hold on one of the young men, and take thee his armour. But
Asahel would not turn aside from following of him" (2 Samuel 2:21).

Again Abner warned Asahel to desist from following him, or he would
have no choice but to slay him. Nevertheless, Asahel refused to give up
the chase (v. 22).

Seeing Asahel would not turn aside, Abner stopped, turned, and
stabbed his pursuer in the abdomen with the sharpened back end of his
spear. The force of Asahel's forward motion drove the spear through his
body and out his back. Such a wound would eventually be fatal but not
immediately. While Abner continued on his way, those of Joab's warriors who had lagged behind Asahel came up and found him mortally
wounded. This only served to further enrage the pursuers, and they
redoubled their efforts to catch Abner and the fleeing forces of their enemy. Asahel had been warned twice to cease the chase, but he recklessly
refused. Why? His death could only serve to deepen the feud between
Joab and Abner.

How many times are we warned against danger yet continue on our reckless
course toward disaster? Why?

---

1. Francis D. Nichol, ed., *The Seventh-day Adventist Bible Commentary*, vol. 2 (Washington,
DC: Review and Herald®, 1976), 608.

A Belated Appeal for Peace

And the children of Benjamin gathered themselves together after Abner, and became one troop, and stood on the top of an hill.
—2 Samuel 2:25

A bner assembled his troops on a hilltop and formed a defensive line. Joab's forces had Abner's force surrounded. "The forces of Abner had lost heavily in the struggle, but in their present hilltop position they would have been able to inflict heavy losses upon the troops of Joab if the latter had persisted in the attack. Knowing that he was in no position to win, and knowing also that Joab would be aware of the heavy price he would have to pay if he was determined to rout him from his strong defensive position, Abner now made an appeal to the opposing forces to stop pursuing their fellow Hebrews. Abner had laid down a challenge to war, and he now set forth an appeal for peace. In this appeal Abner was motivated largely by his own defeat and present danger, and not by a sincere desire to terminate the struggle with the house of David. His conciliatory proposal was dictated by a change in circumstances, not by a change of heart."[1]

Joab replied, "As God liveth, unless thou hadst spoken, surely then in the morning the people had gone up every one from following his brother" (2 Samuel 2:27). Joab's meaning is not clear. Perhaps he wished to make clear that if not for Abner's challenge that morning, there would not have been civil war, and both sides would have returned home. He might have meant his men were willing to continue the fight until the next morning had Abner not just called for a truce. "On the whole, it seems that Joab was endeavoring to place the blame upon Abner, whose rash challenge at Gibeon had brought on the struggle that day between brother and brother. To engage in civil war was most unfortunate, and Joab sought to clear himself of responsibility for what had occurred."[2]

"It is sometimes difficult to understand the motives that prompt a man to take a certain course of action that seems, in retrospect, to have been ill-advised."[3]

---

1. Francis D. Nichol, ed., *The Seventh-day Adventist Bible Commentary*, vol. 2 (Washington, DC: Review and Herald®, 1976), 608, 609.
2. Nichol, 609.
3. Nichol, 609.

ABNER GOES OVER TO DAVID

And Abner sent messengers to David on his behalf, saying, Whose is the land? saying also, Make thy league with me, and, behold, my hand shall be with thee, to bring about all Israel unto thee.
—2 Samuel 3:12

I t seemed inevitable that Abner and Ish-bosheth would eventually have a falling out. This came when Ish-bosheth accused Abner of sleeping with his father's concubine. "There is nothing in the record to indicate that Abner, if guilty of the act of which he was charged, had any design on Ish-bosheth's throne, but the king nevertheless preferred to regard the alleged conduct as an act of treachery, and it was this that aroused the anger of Abner. Ish-bosheth's words of reproach are understandable, for Abner's alleged deed violated the rights of the king."[1] Abner resented the insinuation because he had placed Ish-bosheth on the throne. For the nephew he had supported to falsely accuse him of treason was deeply offensive.

In his anger, Abner swore to place David on the throne of all Israel. "Abner's resolve to transfer the kingdom of Saul to David was probably not the result of hasty judgment. The commander may long have pondered the advisability of giving up the attempt to maintain the tottering house of Saul."[2] What could Ish-bosheth do? He realized Abner was the power behind his throne. The weakness of Ish-bosheth and the power of Abner are shown in 2 Samuel 3:11: "And he could not answer Abner a word again, because he feared him." Abner sent messengers to David, offering to join him and deliver Israel in the bargain. "Abner recognized that he was in a position to bargain with David. He would bring about the transfer of the land on one condition, that David make a league with him, giving him definite assurance of proper consideration for himself. In this proposal the narrow, haughty, self-seeking spirit of Abner was clearly revealed. He would throw in his lot with David, but only at a price, and he wanted first to make certain that the price would be paid."[3]

"Pride goeth before destruction, and an haughty spirit before a fall" (Proverbs 16:18).

---

1. Francis D. Nichol, ed., *The Seventh-day Adventist Bible Commentary*, vol. 2 (Washington, DC: Review and Herald®, 1976), 612.
2. Nichol, 612, 613.
3. Nichol, 613.

A DEAL IS STRUCK

And Abner said unto David, I will arise and go, and will gather all Israel unto my lord the king, that they may make a league with thee, and that thou mayest reign over all that thine heart desireth. And David sent Abner away; and he went in peace.
—2 Samuel 3:21

David had one stipulation before accepting Abner's defection. He wanted his first wife, Michal, returned to him (1 Samuel 18:20, 21, 27). This reinforced David's claim to the throne among Saul's supporters. "The messengers were sent to Ish-bosheth and not to Abner, probably because the negotiations between Abner and David were then still secret. On the other hand it was Ish-bosheth who as king would have to issue the orders for Michal's return. Without the support of Abner, Ish-bosheth would be in no position to resist David's demand. In complying with that demand, Ish-bosheth would reveal his own weakness, acknowledge the wrong that had been done to David, and the justice of David's demand. For Ish-bosheth publicly to accede to this demand would give evidence to all in both Judah and Israel that his days were numbered and that David would soon take over the entire kingdom."[1]

Abner personally carried out the order, and Phaltiel, Michal's second husband, followed behind, weeping. Abner ordered him home (2 Samuel 3:16). Lest one feel too much sympathy for Phaltiel, remember that he had no qualms about taking another man's wife as his own. Then Abner reminded the elders of Israel that originally, they supported David, but he persuaded them to support Ish-bosheth instead. Now Abner encouraged them to honor their original decision (vv. 17, 18).

As Saul had come from the tribe of Benjamin, Abner personally went to that tribe to negotiate. These would be the toughest to convince to swear allegiance to David. "They felt bound to Saul by ties of kinship and had enjoyed great advantages by virtue of their connection with him."[2] Abner and twenty of his men met David at Hebron with an update. Leaving Hebron, Abner went forth in peace on his final mission to align the rest of Israel with David.

"When a man's ways please the LORD, he maketh even his enemies to be at peace with him" (Proverbs 16:7).

1. Francis D. Nichol, ed., *The Seventh-day Adventist Bible Commentary*, vol. 2 (Washington, DC: Review and Herald®, 1976), 613.
2. Nichol, 614.

VENGEANCE

*And when Abner was returned to Hebron, Joab took him aside
in the gate to speak with him quietly, and smote him there under
the fifth rib, that he died, for the blood of Asahel his brother.*

—2 Samuel 3:27

Evidently, Joab had been away on a raid when David entertained Abner. "The raid had probably been against the Amalekites, the Philistines, or some other enemy of Judah. It is possible that the expedition had been planned by David, so that Joab would not be present during Abner's visit. Joab returned, elated with his victory and the great spoil."[1] It would have been imprudent for the two generals to meet at the outset of negotiations, for they were rivals, not allies.

Needless to say, Joab was not happy with David's course of action (2 Samuel 3:24, 25). Joab remonstrated with his king for allowing a spy to escape. "Joab may have had an honest suspicion of Abner's integrity, but in addition there existed a feeling of personal enmity, due partly to the fact that in the famous old warrior Joab would find a formidable rival, and partly to the blood feud between him and Abner for the slaying of Asahel (2 Sam. 2:22, 23)."[2]

Joab sent messengers after Abner, recalling him to Hebron—perhaps he sent the request in the name of David; regardless, Abner came immediately. Joab met him at the gate to Hebron and stabbed him in the stomach with a hidden knife. "Joab slew Abner for blood revenge. He may have justified his retaliation by the provision of Num. 35:26, 27. Interestingly enough, Hebron was a city of refuge (Joshua 20:7) and in view of that fact, Joab may have carried out his deed in the city gate. The death of Asahel, however, took place in battle, and the slaying was an unwilling and reluctant act of self-defense on the part of Abner. Joab may not have been familiar with these details. But he should have studied the far-reaching effect of his deed, delaying as it did the formation of a united kingdom for some time."[3]

"He that is slow to anger is better than the mighty; and he that ruleth his spirit than he that taketh a city" (Proverbs 16:32).

1. Francis D. Nichol, ed., *The Seventh-day Adventist Bible Commentary*, vol. 2 (Washington, DC: Review and Herald®, 1976), 614.
2. Nichol, 614.
3. Nichol, 614.

DAVID MOURNS ABNER

And the king lamented over Abner, and said, Died Abner
as a fool dieth? Thy hands were not bound, nor thy feet put into
fetters: as a man falleth before wicked men, so fellest thou.
—2 Samuel 3:33, 34

When David heard of the treachery against Abner, he immediately disavowed any responsibility for the act (2 Samuel 3:28). "David had evidently given his word that the person of Abner would be inviolate. The action of Joab cast suspicion on David's integrity. David wanted all to know that he had had no part in this perfidious deed and that he abhorred with all his soul such a violation of honor."[1]

David could not adequately punish the crime because Joab's popularity with the army would lead to an uprising. With his hands tied, David instead cursed the entire household of Joab forever. "And I am this day weak, though anointed king; and these men the sons of Zeruiah be too hard for me: the LORD shall reward the doer of evil according to his wickedness" (v. 39). The act had been planned and carried out with premeditation.

David arranged a public funeral for Abner in Hebron. He ordered Joab and the entire army to wear sackcloth and follow Abner's body to the grave. This showed all that while Joab might not regret his act, he was forced by David to condemn it. The king walked behind the casket in his royal robes as chief mourner and openly wept at the tomb (vv. 31–33). David's tribute made clear he considered the murderer to be wicked (vv. 33, 34). "David's magnanimous recognition of one who had been his bitter enemy won the confidence and admiration of all Israel."[2]

However, Abner had expected to gain a better position under David. "Had he succeeded in his purpose, his talents and ambition, his great influence and want of godliness, would have endangered the throne of David and the peace and prosperity of the nation."[3]

"The integrity of the upright shall guide them: but the perverseness of transgressors shall destroy them" (Proverbs 11:3).

---

1. Francis D. Nichol, ed., *The Seventh-day Adventist Bible Commentary*, vol. 2 (Washington, DC: Review and Herald®, 1976), 614.
2. Ellen G. White, *Patriarchs and Prophets* (Mountain View, CA: Pacific Press®, 1943), 700.
3. White, 700.

More Bloodshed—When Will It End?

And when Saul's son heard that Abner was dead in Hebron, his hands were feeble, and all the Israelites were troubled.
—2 Samuel 4:1

With Abner's decision to support David's reign, Ish-bosheth's rule was significantly weakened. During the heat of the day, as Ish-bosheth lay down upon his bed to rest, two of his captains entered his room, severed his head, and then carried it to David in Hebron. "They appeared before David with the gory witness to their crime, saying, 'Behold the head of Ishbosheth the son of Saul thine enemy, which sought thy life; and the Lord hath avenged my lord the king this day of Saul, and of his seed.' But David, whose throne God Himself had established, and whom God had delivered from his adversaries, did not desire the aid of treachery to establish his power. He told these murderers of the doom visited upon him who boasted of slaying Saul. 'How much more,' he added, 'when wicked men have slain a righteous person in his own house upon his bed? shall I not therefore now require his blood of your hand, and take you away from the earth? And David commanded his young men, and they slew them. . . . But they took the head of Ishbosheth and buried it in the sepulchre of Abner in Hebron.'"[1]

These men had slain Ish-bosheth for what they thought would be a personal reward. David did not need criminals to assist in gaining the throne of a united Judah and Israel. Time and time again, the Lord had shaped events and delivered David from danger. Murder was not to be countenanced (Exodus 20:13). By their own words, they stood condemned. Their actions had no legal defense.

"They pretended to be friends of David, but in being traitors to the man they served, they proved themselves to be unworthy citizens of the nation of Israel. Let some turn of events place David in an unfavorable situation, and they would not hesitate to slay him exactly as they had slain Ish-bosheth. Such men could not be trusted."[2]

"Whoso boasteth himself of a false gift is like clouds and wind without rain" (Proverbs 25:14).

1. Ellen G. White, *Patriarchs and Prophets* (Mountain View, CA: Pacific Press®, 1943), 701.
2. Francis D. Nichol, ed., *The Seventh-day Adventist Bible Commentary*, vol. 2 (Washington, DC: Review and Herald®, 1976), 617.

DAVID BECOMES KING OVER ISRAEL

*So all the elders of Israel came to the king to Hebron;
and king David made a league with them in Hebron before
the LORD: and they anointed David king over Israel.*
—2 Samuel 5:3

With the death of Ish-bosheth, the leading men of Israel decided David should become king of all Israel (2 Samuel 5:1–3). However, the shift in allegiance from Ish-bosheth to David was not as rapid as one might think. All of Israel had experienced the leadership qualities and outstanding abilities of David while he served Saul. He had gained great popularity through his protection of the land from Philistine hordes and Amalekite raiders. His wisdom and skill had gained the confidence of the people.

Thousands came to Hebron to observe the coronation of the new king. "More than eight thousand of the descendants of Aaron and of the Levites waited upon David. The change in the sentiments of the people was marked and decisive. The revolution was quiet and dignified, befitting the great work they were doing. Nearly half a million souls, the former subjects of Saul, thronged Hebron and its environs. The very hills and valleys were alive with the multitudes. The hour for the coronation was appointed; the man who had been expelled from the court of Saul, who had fled to the mountains and hills and to the caves of the earth to preserve his life, was about to receive the highest honor that can be conferred upon man by his fellow man. Priests and elders, clothed in the garments of their sacred office, officers and soldiers with glittering spear and helmet, and strangers from long distances, stood to witness the coronation of the chosen king. David was arrayed in the royal robe. The sacred oil was put upon his brow by the high priest, for the anointing by Samuel had been prophetic of what would take place at the inauguration of the king. The time had come, and David, by solemn rite, was consecrated to his office as God's vicegerent. The scepter was placed in his hands. The covenant of his righteous sovereignty was written, and the people gave their pledges of loyalty. The diadem was placed upon his brow, and the coronation ceremony was over."[1]

"Trust in the LORD with all thine heart; and lean not unto thine own understanding. In all thy ways acknowledge him, and he shall direct thy paths" (Proverbs 3:5, 6).

---

1. Ellen G. White, *Patriarchs and Prophets* (Mountain View, CA: Pacific Press®, 1943), 701, 702.

THE CITY OF DAVID

Nevertheless David took the strong hold of Zion:
the same is the city of David.

—2 Samuel 5:7

D avid realized a more centralized capital was needed, and Jerusalem seemed to be the best location. But Jerusalem was held by the Jebusites. "Joshua had slain and defeated the king of Jerusalem (Joshua 10:23–26; 12:10), and later the city had been taken and destroyed by Judah (see on Judges 1:7). But the Jebusites, who occupied Jerusalem, were not completely conquered, and either continued to hold at least a part of the city or retook it after being driven out (Joshua 15:63; Judges 1:21; 19:11, 12)."[1]

David laid siege, but the Jebusites scorned his ability to take their stronghold. They sent him a cryptic message: "Except thou take away the blind and the lame, thou shalt not come in hither" (2 Samuel 5:6). "This statement has puzzled commentators, and many interpretations of the passage have been given. The one that offers perhaps the most reasonable explanation has the Jebusites saying, 'You will not enter the city, but the blind and the lame will keep you out.' "[2] Seemingly secure in their stronghold, the inhabitants of Jebus [Jerusalem] shamelessly taunted David.

"The Jebusite stronghold was on Mt. Zion, south of Mt. Moriah, the elevation on which the Temple was later built. The mountain was flanked on two sides by deep valleys, and was admirably suited for defense."[3] But David was cunning, observing that water was brought into the city walls by a conduit chiseled from solid rock, running from the spring of Gihon to an underground reservoir within the walls, and then a vertical shaft dropped below to reach the water. By traversing the underground tunnel and climbing the shaft, David's men might enter the city and open the gates. The man who accomplished this would be rewarded as commander in chief of the army. "So Joab the son of Zeruiah went first up, and was chief" (1 Chronicles 11:6).

"Ultimate success in life comes not by human might or wisdom but by the Spirit of the Lord (see Zech. 4:6)."[4]

---

1. Francis D. Nichol, ed., *The Seventh-day Adventist Bible Commentary*, vol. 2 (Washington, DC: Review and Herald®, 1976), 620.
2. Nichol, 620.
3. Nichol, 620.
4. Nichol, 621.

THE PHILISTINES AGAIN

But when the Philistines heard that they had anointed David king over Israel, all the Philistines came up to seek David; and David heard of it, and went down to the hold.
—2 Samuel 5:17

During the early years of his reign David had had no difficulty with the Philistines. In the time of his exile from Saul the Philistines had befriended him, and when David became king of Judah they hoped for friendship from him in opposition to Saul's house. They felt confident that they could retain their power over a divided Hebrew nation. But when David became king over all Israel, and succeeded in capturing Jebus and effected an alliance with Hiram of Tyre, the Philistines, fearing David's growing strength, determined to make war against Israel and curb the power of its new king."[1] The alliance with Hiram of Tyre was beneficial to both kings. Trade was enhanced, and having an ally on Israel's northwestern border provided security from that quarter. This exchange did not go unnoticed by the Philistines. They were now confronted with armed forces to their north and east, with their backs to the Mediterranean Sea in the west.

Approaching Jerusalem from the southwest, they set up camp in the Valley of Rephaim—"the valley of the giants" (Joshua 15:8). David marshaled his forces within the city of Jerusalem and sought guidance from the Lord. "And David enquired of the LORD, saying, Shall I go up to the Philistines? wilt thou deliver them into mine hand? And the LORD said unto David, Go up: for I will doubtless deliver the Philistines into thine hand" (2 Samuel 5:19).

David's forces broke through the Philistine line of battle and overwhelmed the invaders. The victory happened so quickly that the Philistines abandoned their idols on the field and fled. They expected their wooden idols would guarantee a victory. Now the images were dumped as useless baggage. And David said, "The LORD hath broken forth upon mine enemies before me, as the breach of waters. Therefore he called the name of that place Baalperazim" (v. 20). Literally, *Baal-perazim* means " 'lord of the breaking through' or 'possessor of the burstings.' "[2]

"The beginning of strife is as when one letteth out water: therefore leave off contention, before it be meddled with" (Proverbs 17:14).

1. Francis D. Nichol, ed., *The Seventh-day Adventist Bible Commentary*, vol. 2 (Washington, DC: Review and Herald®, 1976), 622.
2. Nichol, 622.

A Sound in the Mulberry Trees

And when David enquired of the Lord, he said,
Thou shalt not go up; but fetch a compass behind them,
and come upon them over against the mulberry trees.
—2 Samuel 5:23

The Philistines were not deterred by their defeat in the Valley of Rephaim. Reinforced, they again came against David and camped in the same valley with a larger force than before. David inquired of the Lord whether he should again attack. This time the Lord gave a different answer. David was told to circle behind their forces and attack from the rear. "Sometimes those who have asked for divine aid are instructed simply to stand still and see the salvation of the Lord (see Ex. 14:13, 14; 2 Kings 19:7, 32, 35). At other times deliverance comes through God's directing and blessing human effort. There is no manifestation of a lack of faith in one who, after presenting a petition to God, does all in his power to bring about its fulfillment."[1]

David was to wait for a signal from God before attacking. There would be a rustling in the tops of the trees as the armies of heaven marched ahead of Israel into battle. "In the work of the Lord we must do our part. Those who sit idly by, expecting the Lord to act while they do nothing, unless the Lord has so directed, must expect defeat. God gave the word that David and his people were to bestir themselves, and promised that then He would go before them to smite the hosts of the Philistines. God's promises, then and now, are conditional. When we do our part God will do His.

". . . The secret of David's success was simple; he did precisely what God instructed him to do. When man puts his will above God's will he invites defeat. We will not always understand the reasons for God's commands, nor is this always necessary. All we are expected to do is to trust and obey."[2]

God once again used nature to turn the tide of battle. This time He used the sound of marching in the tops of the mulberry (balsam) trees to signal the Israelite army to advance to another victory!

Listen for the "sound in the balsams," then advance to victory!

---

1. Francis D. Nichol, ed., *The Seventh-day Adventist Bible Commentary*, vol. 2 (Washington, DC: Review and Herald®, 1976), 622.
2. Nichol, 622, 623.

Psalm 144, Part 1: God's Strength in War

Blessed be the LORD my strength which teacheth
my hands to war, and my fingers to fight.
—Psalm 144:1

D avid's early life was filled with war and strife. For years David sought refuge in the wilderness while hunted by Saul. Psalm 144 echoes Psalm 18, where he asserts, "I will love thee, O LORD, my strength. The LORD is my rock, and my fortress, and my deliverer; my God, my strength, in whom I will trust; my buckler, and the horn of my salvation, and my high tower" (vv. 1, 2). Note the similar phrases: God is "my goodness, and my fortress; my high tower, and my deliverer; my shield, and he in whom I trust; who subdueth my people under me" (Psalm 144:2).

"As a fugitive from Saul, David had often found the rocks of the mountains a refuge and strength. God was to him as the strength of the rocks, providing him protection and deliverance from his enemies. . . . He had lived so close to the eternal hills, the rocks had so long been his abode, they had come to form an intrinsic part of his life and existence. It became second nature for him to weave these figures from the natural world into the songs that poured from his heart.

". . . David had learned to place his faith and confidence in God. He knew that whatever man might do, God would never fail him. God was as sure as the rocks of the eternal hills. Man could place his complete trust in Him."[1] God is as a high tower or mountain stronghold. "In the wilds of the hills such a place was lofty, inaccessible, and safe from attack. . . . It provided warning of approaching danger and also was a point of vantage from which to repel attacks."[2]

"To anyone not a man of war the figure of a shield [v. 2] would have little value or meaning. To David the shield had frequently meant life itself. He knew from the most vivid of personal experiences its supreme importance in some of the critical moments of life. . . . God had repeatedly saved him from the enemy of his soul. The figure is characteristic of David. His songs live and breathe the spirit of the warlike life that was his as a soldier accustomed to battle."[3]

"A mighty fortress is our God, / A bulwark never failing."[4]

---

1. Francis D. Nichol, ed., *The Seventh-day Adventist Bible Commentary*, vol. 2 (Washington, DC: Review and Herald®, 1976), 700.
2. Nichol, 700.
3. Nichol, 700.
4. Martin Luther, "A Mighty Fortress" (1529), in *The Seventh-day Adventist Hymnal* (Hagerstown, MD: Review and Herald®, 1985), hymn 506.

Psalm 144, Part 2: God's Arsenal

Bow thy heavens, O Lord, and come down: touch
the mountains, and they shall smoke. Cast forth lightning,
and scatter them: shoot out thine arrows, and destroy them.
—Psalm 144:5, 6

In his psalms, David repeatedly acknowledges God's deliverance. "The depths of the earth are the Lord's arsenal. . . . Waters gushing from the earth united with the waters from heaven to accomplish the work of desolation. Since the Flood, fire as well as water has been God's agent to destroy very wicked cities. These judgments are sent that those who lightly regard God's law and trample upon His authority may be led to tremble before His power and to confess His just sovereignty. As men have beheld burning mountains pouring forth fire and flames and torrents of melted ore, drying up rivers, overwhelming populous cities, and everywhere spreading ruin and desolation, the stoutest heart has been filled with terror and infidels and blasphemers have been constrained to acknowledge the infinite power of God."[1]

God reigns supreme over His creation. "The Lord hath his way in the whirlwind and in the storm, and the clouds are the dust of his feet. He rebuketh the sea, and maketh it dry, and drieth up all the rivers" (Nahum 1:3, 4). David contrasts humanity's insignificance with God's omnipotence and marvels that God notices humankind (Psalm 144:3, 4). "How transitory is this life of ours! We scarcely have developed our physical and mental powers when we are taken by death." "When heaven's artillery is set in motion how puny is the strength of man to resist it."[2] The Lord is an ever-present help in times of trouble (see Psalm 46:1), but *we* must accept His assistance.

Ellen G. White quotes Psalm 144:5, 6 as a portrayal of the breaking up of the earth at the second coming of Christ.[3] Nahum 1:5, 6; Acts 2:19; and Revelation 16:18, 20, 21 lend additional descriptions. David routinely asked God for deliverance (Psalm 144:7). We also may obtain strength when facing seemingly insurmountable problems.

"A wonderful Savior is Jesus my Lord, / He taketh my burden away, / He holdeth me up, and I shall not be moved, / He giveth me strength as my day."[4]

1. Ellen G. White, *Patriarchs and Prophets* (Mountain View, CA: Pacific Press®, 1943), 109.
2. Francis D. Nichol, ed., *The Seventh-day Adventist Bible Commentary*, vol. 3 (Washington, DC: Review and Herald®, 1977), 933.
3. White, *Patriarchs and Prophets*, 109.
4. Fanny J. Crosby, "He Hideth My Soul," in *The Seventh-day Adventist Hymnal* (Hagerstown, MD: Review and Herald®, 1985), hymn 520.

PSALM 144, PART 3: POLISHED FOR GOD

That our sons may be as plants grown up in their youth; that our daughters may be as corner stones, polished after the similitude of a palace.
—Psalm 144:12

D avid closes Psalm 144 on a note of prosperity. He depicts a nation blessed by God and at peace (v. 12). There is plenty of food, flocks are increasing, and towns and herds are safe (vv. 13, 14). The people are content in the Lord (v. 15)! When His people allow it, God works for their good.

"By trial, by warnings, by admonitions, God seeks to prepare us to fulfil His purpose. If we co-operate with Him, our characters will be fashioned 'after the similitude of a palace.' It is the specified work of the Comforter to transform us. At times it is hard for us to submit to the purifying, refining process. But this we must do if we would be saved at last."[1]

Christians must submit themselves to be sanctified. "We are God's workmanship. The value of the human agent depends wholly upon the polishing he receives. When the rough stones are prepared for the building, they must be taken into the shop, and hewed and squared. The process is often sharp as the stone is pressed down upon the wheel, but the rough coarseness is being removed, and the luster begins to appear. . . . Every soul must not only submit to the work of the divine hand, but must put to the tax every [spiritual] sinew and muscle, that the character may become more pure, the words more helpful, the actions such as God can approve."[2]

"The divine Worker spends little time on worthless material. Only the precious jewels does he polish after the similitude of a palace, cutting away all the rough edges. This process is severe and trying. . . . [Christ] cuts away the surplus surface, and putting the stone to the polishing wheel, presses it close, that all roughness may be worn away. Then, holding the jewel up to the light, the Master sees in it a reflection of himself, and he pronounces it worthy of a place in his casket."[3]

"When He cometh, when He cometh / To make up His jewels, / All His jewels, precious jewels, / His loved and His own."[4]

---

1. Ellen G. White, Letter 139, 1903.
2. Ellen G. White, Letter 27, 1896.
3. Ellen G. White, "The Return of the Exiles—No. 7," *Review and Herald*, December 19, 1907, 9.
4. W. O. Cushing, "When He Cometh" (1866), in *The Seventh-day Adventist Hymnal* (Hagerstown, MD: Review and Herald®, 1985), hymn 218.

PSALM 48: JERUSALEM!

Great is the LORD, and greatly to be praised in the city of our God, in the mountain of his holiness. Beautiful for situation, the joy of the whole earth, is mount Zion, on the sides of the north, the city of the great King.
—Psalm 48:1, 2

Psalm 48 is one of David's most cheerful songs. "It celebrates Jehovah's care of Jerusalem and the deliverance of His people from the hand of the enemy."[1] Jerusalem held a special place in the hearts of David and the nation. It was the capital of Israel, but more than that, it would soon be the center of worship. Set upon the highest point of the surrounding countryside, it was the focus of pride and beauty. David described it as "the joy of the whole earth." The importance of Mount Zion could not be underestimated in the eyes of David. Perhaps David wrote this psalm while thinking of a location for the temple. Because he conquered it, occupied it, rebuilt it, resided within its walls, and governed from it, Jerusalem became known as the City of David.

No enemy would attempt to conquer it (vv. 4–6), for God was watching over it and would protect it from danger (vv. 7, 8). Because God had delivered Israel in the past, there was nothing to fear for the future (v. 8). David envisioned the temple as the dwelling place of God from which His majesty and love should extend to the entire world (vv. 9, 10). He encouraged all of Israel to come, see, and rejoice over what God had provided (vv. 9–13). It is possible David saw the New Jerusalem in vision, and this brought forth his prophetic psalm of praise for the city.

The temple Solomon built is gone. The city David and Christ knew is no more. But a *new* Jerusalem will be the capital of the universe and once again the dwelling place of God on this earth. "And I John saw the holy city, new Jerusalem, coming down from God out of heaven, prepared as a bride adorned for her husband. And I heard a great voice out of heaven saying, Behold, the tabernacle of God is with men, and he will dwell with them, and they shall be his people, and God himself shall be with them, and be their God" (Revelation 21:2, 3).

"Jerusalem, my happy home, / O how I long for thee! / When will my sorrows have an end, / Thy joys when shall I see?"[2]

---

1. Francis D. Nichol, ed., *The Seventh-day Adventist Bible Commentary*, vol. 3 (Washington, DC: Review and Herald®, 1977), 747.

2. Anonymous, "Jerusalem, My Happy Home," in *The Seventh-day Adventist Hymnal* (Hagerstown, MD: Review and Herald®, 1985), hymn 420.

THE ARK OF THE COVENANT MOVED

And David arose, and went with all the people that were with him from Baale of Judah, to bring up from thence the ark of God, whose name is called by the name of the LORD of hosts that dwelleth between the cherubims.
—2 Samuel 6:2

As we have seen, the ark of the covenant was taken in battle by the Philistines while Samuel was still an "intern." The Philistines kept it for seven months before returning it. Upon its return, it was taken to Kirjath-jearim and placed in the hillside home of Abinadab (1 Samuel 4:4–7:1).

David longed to bring the ark to Jerusalem. When the nation found itself temporarily at peace with its neighbors, the time seemed right. "It was fitting that the capital of the nation should be honored with the token of the divine Presence.

"David summoned thirty thousand of the leading men of Israel, for it was his purpose to make the occasion a scene of great rejoicing and imposing display. The people responded gladly to the call. The high priest, with his brethren in sacred office and the princes and leading men of the tribes, assembled at Kirjath-jearim. David was aglow with holy zeal. The ark was brought out from the house of Abinadab and placed upon a new cart drawn by oxen, while two of the sons of Abinadab attended it."[1]

"The law of Moses provided that the ark should be carried by the sons of Kohath (Num. 4:4–15; 7:9). David should have heeded this instruction, but he probably reasoned that the conveying of the ark on a new cart drawn by oxen would be a mark of special respect. He no doubt remembered that when the Philistines returned the ark to Israel they brought it on a new cart (1 Sam. 6:7–14). That was an entirely different situation, however, for they had acted according to the best of their knowledge. When the ark arrived in Israel it was taken from the cart by Levites (1 Sam. 6:15) in harmony with the divine directions to Moses."[2]

Even though God is long-suffering, it is a grave mistake to presume upon His mercy when disobeying His instructions.

---

1. Ellen G. White, *Patriarchs and Prophets* (Mountain View, CA: Pacific Press®, 1943), 704.
2. Francis D. Nichol, ed., *The Seventh-day Adventist Bible Commentary*, vol. 2 (Washington, DC: Review and Herald®, 1976), 625.

Uzzah

And the anger of the LORD was kindled against Uzzah; and God smote him there for his error; and there he died by the ark of God.
—2 Samuel 6:7

T he ark was brought out of Abinadab's house, and his two sons, Uzzah and Ahio, were elected to drive the oxen. "Since Uzzah and Ahio had exercised supervisory care of the ark while it was in their home, the responsibility of transferring it to Jerusalem was now placed in their charge. This, however, was definitely out of line with the Lord's explicit directions that the ark was to be borne upon the shoulders of Kohathite Levites (Num. 4:15; 7:9). There was no valid excuse for a disregard of the divine directions in this matter."[1]

Apparently, Ahio walked in front and Uzzah slightly to the rear to keep watch on the ark (2 Samuel 6:4, 6). Things were going well until the cart passed a threshing floor (1 Chronicles 13:9; 2 Samuel 6:6). Here the cart lurched, and Uzzah reached out his hand to steady the ark. He was instantly struck dead. "The ark was holy. None but the priests, descendants of Aaron, were to touch it. . . . God is strict regarding His requirements."[2]

"To those accompanying Uzzah it might have seemed as if Uzzah's intentions were perfectly honorable—he was only trying to assist when he stretched forth his hand to steady the ark. . . . His act of touching the ark was one of presumption. A sinful being should not have dared to touch that which symbolized the presence of God. The Lord could not permit to pass unnoticed this flagrant disregard of His express command. If Uzzah's sins had been allowed to go unpunished, his guilt might have involved many others. Those who knew of Uzzah's defections would have become greatly emboldened in sin if they had been allowed to conclude that faults like Uzzah's could go uncorrected and the offender be accepted of God. Uzzah's death served as a warning to many that the Lord is a righteous God, who requires strict obedience from all."[3]

"And the people said unto Joshua, The LORD our God will we serve, and his voice will we obey" (Joshua 24:24).

---

1. Francis D. Nichol, ed., *The Seventh-day Adventist Bible Commentary,* vol. 2 (Washington, DC: Review and Herald®, 1976), 625.
2. Nichol, 625.
3. Nichol, 625, 626.

A CHANGE OF PLAN

And the ark of the LORD continued in the house of Obededom the Gittite three months: and the LORD blessed Obededom, and all his household.
—2 Samuel 6:11

The throng accompanying the ark was stunned. The music stopped, and the procession came to a halt. David was shocked at the death of Uzzah, and fear of the ark gripped him. He now realized, as never before, the sacredness of God's law and the exactitude necessary to obey. "David's displeasure at the death of Uzzah was due largely to the fact that his own heart was not entirely right. If he had been fully at peace with God, he would have had no reason to fear and he would have accepted the will of the Lord. Whatever the Lord does is perfect, and whenever man becomes displeased with the works of God, it is an indication that there is something wrong with his own experience. It would have been well for David to humble himself and to search his heart for the evils that were lurking there rather than to find fault with God."[1]

It was decided to house the ark in the home of Obed-edom, who was a Gittite. It is possible Obed-edom was from the Levitical city of Gath-rimmon and, therefore, a member of the tribe that had been honored to serve as caretakers for the ark (Joshua 21:24–26). "But Obed-edom, though he rejoiced with trembling, welcomed the sacred symbol as the pledge of God's favor to the obedient. The attention of all Israel was now directed to the Gittite and his household; all watched to see how it would fare with them."[2]

"The presence of the ark in the home of Obed-edom brought a blessing, not a curse. Obed-edom knew how fearfully the Lord had punished irreverence when the ark had been dishonored. He had probably seen David and the thousands of Israel quivering with fear, afraid of the presence of the ark of God. Yet in spite of all this he welcomed the ark to his house."[3] Because Obed-edom took joy in the presence of the Lord, his entire household was blessed. Humility and obedience are requirements God insists upon in His presence.

Is your rapport with God based on fear or joy?

---

1. Francis D. Nichol, ed., *The Seventh-day Adventist Bible Commentary*, vol. 2 (Washington, DC: Review and Herald®, 1976), 626.
2. Ellen G. White, *Patriarchs and Prophets* (Mountain View, CA: Pacific Press®, 1943), 706.
3. Nichol, *The Seventh-day Adventist Bible Commentary*, 2:626.

Six Paces

And it was so, that when they that bare the ark of the
Lord had gone six paces, he sacrificed oxen and fatlings.
—2 Samuel 6:13

D avid had learned another valuable lesson concerning the exactness of obedience to the dictates of the Lord. That which was holy was not to be approached by sinful humanity in a casual manner. "At the end of three months he resolved to make another attempt to remove the ark, and he now gave earnest heed to carry out in every particular the directions of the Lord. Again the chief men of the nation were summoned, and a vast assemblage gathered about the dwelling place of the Gittite. With reverent care the ark was now placed upon the shoulders of men of divine appointment, the multitude fell into line, and with trembling hearts the vast procession again set forth. After advancing six paces the trumpet sounded a halt. By David's direction sacrifices of 'oxen and fatlings' were to be offered. Rejoicing now took the place of trembling and terror. The king had laid aside his royal robes and had attired himself in a plain linen ephod. . . . In this holy service he would take his place as, before God, on an equality with his subjects. Upon that day Jehovah was to be adored. He was to be the sole object of reverence."[1]

The six paces taken by the priests carrying the ark were a test of the methodology being used to transport the ark for a second time. When no sign of God's displeasure was shown, a thanksgiving sacrifice was offered. Those initial six steps were no doubt taken very slowly and with some trepidation by those who carried the ark. Coming into the presence of the Lord, who is holy and sinless, is not to be taken lightly.

Reverence before God is expected. Moses learned the lesson of reverence when he approached the burning bush. Realizing he was in God's presence, he covered his face. "And when the Lord saw that he turned aside to see, God called unto him out of the midst of the bush, and said, Moses, Moses. And he said, Here am I. And he said, Draw not nigh hither; put off thy shoes from off thy feet, for the place whereon thou standest is holy ground" (Exodus 3:4, 5).

How respectful and reverential are the worshipers in your church as they approach God?

---

1. Ellen G. White, *Patriarchs and Prophets* (Mountain View, CA: Pacific Press®, 1943), 706, 707.

DAVID DANCES BEFORE THE LORD

And David danced before the LORD with all his might;
and David was girded with a linen ephod.
—2 Samuel 6:14

Second Samuel 6:14 has been used to justify popular dancing. To use this verse for that purpose is without merit. "In our day dancing is associated with folly and midnight reveling. Health and morals are sacrificed to pleasure. . . . This test should be decisive. Amusements that have a tendency to weaken the love for sacred things and lessen our joy in the service of God are not to be sought by Christians. The music and dancing in joyful praise to God at the removal of the ark had not the faintest resemblance to the dissipation of modern dancing. The one tended to the remembrance of God and exalted His holy name. The other is a device of Satan to cause men to forget God and to dishonor Him."[1]

This principle seems straightforward. If Christians find themselves where they would not want angels to accompany them, it would be best to seek other surroundings. "David's dancing was an act of solemn and holy joy. To an [Israelite] . . . such an activity was a natural mode of expression, however strange it may seem to us today. By this means David expressed his grateful praise and thus gave honor and glory to God's holy name. There was nothing in the dancing of David that is comparable to or that will justify the modern dance. The popular dance draws no one nearer to God, nor does it inspire to purer thoughts or holier living. It degrades and corrupts. It unfits a man for prayer or study of the Word of God and turns him away from righteousness into ways of revelry. Morals are corrupted, time is worse than wasted, and often health is sacrificed."[2]

David could finally worship God in the city he called home! Years of wandering had deprived him of worshiping with like-minded brethren. His joy knew no bounds! King of Israel he might be, but on this day, his focus was on the King of kings.

Would you feel comfortable inviting angels to accompany you to your places of amusement?

---

1. Ellen G. White, *Patriarchs and Prophets* (Mountain View, CA: Pacific Press®, 1943), 707.
2. Francis D. Nichol, ed., *The Seventh-day Adventist Bible Commentary*, vol. 2 (Washington, DC: Review and Herald®, 1976), 627.

MICHAL RIDICULES DAVID'S BEHAVIOR

Then David returned to bless his household. And Michal the daughter of Saul came out to meet David, and said, How glorious was the king of Israel to day, who uncovered himself to day in the eyes of the handmaids of his servants, as one of the vain fellows shamelessly uncovereth himself!
—2 Samuel 6:20

When the ark passed through the gates of Jerusalem, it was placed in the tent prepared for it. "The service ended, the king himself pronounced a benediction upon his people. . . . "All the tribes had been represented in this service, the celebration of the most sacred event that had yet marked the reign of David. The Spirit of divine inspiration had rested upon the king, and now as the last beams of the setting sun bathed the tabernacle in a hallowed light, his heart was uplifted in gratitude to God that the blessed symbol of His presence was now so near the throne of Israel."[1]

David returned to the palace and was met by Michal, who, with dripping sarcasm and irony, upbraided him for lacking pride of office. "Michal, whose father had been ecstatic on more than one occasion (1 Sam. 10:10; 19:22–24), had no right to complain of David's exuberance. But the occasion may have provided the excuse for giving vent to her pent-up feelings of ill will. She had once fallen in love with David as a young hero, but her marriage to him had soon ended with his flight from Saul. Now some 20 years had passed, during which she had been married to another man, from whom she had been taken by force and handed over to her former husband as a political prize after a long war against her father's house. The proud daughter of Saul was full of resentment and ready to find fault with David, even with his zeal for honoring the Lord in what was then an acceptable mode of praise."[2]

"David reminded Michal of the fact that her father had been rejected by the Lord, but he had been chosen. . . . David's words were not pleasant, but they were justified [2 Samuel 6:21, 22]."[3] And Michal "had no child unto the day of her death" (v. 23).

Worship should make us happy, not bitter nor finding fault with one another.

---

1. Ellen G. White, *Patriarchs and Prophets* (Mountain View, CA: Pacific Press®, 1943), 708.
2. Francis D. Nichol, ed., *The Seventh-day Adventist Bible Commentary*, vol. 2 (Washington, DC: Review and Herald®, 1976), 627.
3. Nichol, 628.

Psalm 122: The Brotherhood of Worship

I was glad when they said unto me,
Let us go into the house of the Lord.

—Psalm 122:1

P salm 122 is another of David's songs expressing the joy he felt in being able to worship in the house of the Lord with like-minded brethren. Spiritual fellowship should be a blessing to all who come together to worship God. The Israelites assembled annually for three commemorative feasts that turned their thoughts and gratitude to the Lord.

Only men and boys were required to attend these festivals, but often entire families traveled to worship at Jerusalem. Passover was the most largely attended. "The Passover was followed by the seven days' feast of unleavened bread. On the second day of the feast, the first fruits of the year's harvest, a sheaf of barley, was presented before the Lord. All the ceremonies of the feast were types of the work of Christ. The deliverance of Israel from Egypt was an object lesson of redemption, which the Passover was intended to keep in memory. The slain lamb, the unleavened bread, the sheaf of first fruits, represented the Saviour."[1]

Fifty days after Passover, Pentecost celebrated a successful harvest. The third gathering was the Feast of Tabernacles or Ingathering. This festival followed the Day of Atonement. Being assured their sins were forgiven, the people felt at peace with God. The harvest was done, and they were grateful for God's mercy. "At these yearly assemblies the hearts of old and young would be encouraged in the service of God, while the association of the people from the different quarters of the land would strengthen the ties that bound them to God and to one another. Well would it be for the people of God at the present time to have a Feast of Tabernacles—a joyous commemoration of the blessings of God to them."[2] "Verses 8, 9 lay down two great principles that should actuate every Christian: (1) love for the brethren, (2) love for the church. Those who love God will love the brethren of whom God's church is composed."[3]

"We gather together to ask the Lord's blessing."[4]

1. Ellen G. White, *The Desire of Ages* (Nampa, ID: Pacific Press®, 2005), 77.
2. Ellen G. White, *Patriarchs and Prophets* (Mountain View, CA: Pacific Press®, 1943), 540, 541.
3. Francis D. Nichol, ed., *The Seventh-day Adventist Bible Commentary*, vol. 3 (Washington, DC: Review and Herald®, 1977), 909.
4. Anonymous, "We Gather Together," in *The Seventh-day Adventist Hymnal* (Hagerstown, MD: Review and Herald®, 1985), hymn 8.

Psalm 92: The Righteous Shall Flourish

The righteous shall flourish like the palm tree:
he shall grow like a cedar in Lebanon.
—Psalm 92:12

Psalm 92 celebrates "the destruction of evil and the triumph and happiness of God's faithful children. The psalm was inspired by the poet's communion with the Creator on the Sabbath day and his observation of God's power in nature. . . . On the Sabbath it is well that we turn our eyes from the perplexing questions of this world to the eternal world, where we shall be above all doubt and perplexity."[1] Those who take no time to contemplate the wonders of creation are foolish. They cannot grasp the designs of the Creator. The larger picture of the great controversy between Christ and Satan is lost upon them. It is good to praise the Lord. Morning and evening worship are wonderful times to come away and study God's Word. Worship in music is especially appropriate.

Often in the psalms, David asks the question, Why does it seem like sinners prosper and go unpunished? "The problem that disturbed Job (Job 21:7–21) and that appears so often in the Psalms (See Ps. 73:2–15) does not disturb the author of this psalm. It is stated and immediately solved in the realization that the destruction of the wicked follows their triumph (see Ps. 73:18–20). Destruction is the natural and inevitable result of wickedness [Psalm 92:7–9]."[2] David knows God will preserve him, and he will witness the destruction of his enemies at the hand of God.

"The palm tree (v. 12) well represents the life of a Christian. It stands upright amid the burning desert sand, and dies not; for it draws its sustenance from the springs of life beneath the surface."[3] Even in old age and retirement, Christians may continue to bear fruit (v. 14). They should be happy, energetic, fit, and useful because God keeps His promise to provide for their needs, for He is upright and righteous (v. 15).

"When peace, like a river, attendeth my way, / When sorrows like sea billows roll— / Whatever my lot, Thou hast taught me to say, / It is well, it is well with my soul."[4]

---

1. Francis D. Nichol, ed., *The Seventh-day Adventist Bible Commentary*, vol. 3 (Washington, DC: Review and Herald®, 1977), 845.

2. Nichol, 845.

3. Ellen G. White, "Christian Courtesy," *Review and Herald*, September 1, 1885, 1.

4. Horatio G. Spafford, "It Is Well With My Soul" (1876), in *The Seventh-day Adventist Hymnal* (Hagerstown, MD: Review and Herald®, 1985), hymn 530.

PSALM 24, PART 1:
CLEAN HANDS AND A PURE HEART

Who shall ascend into the hill of the LORD? or who shall stand in his holy place? He that hath clean hands, and a pure heart; who hath not lifted up his soul unto vanity, nor sworn deceitfully.

—Psalm 24:3, 4

P salm 24 expands Jesus' statement from the Sermon on the Mount: "Blessed are the pure in heart: for they shall see God" (Matthew 5:8). The foundational requirement for citizenship in God's kingdom is purity. Jesus "did not speak one word to flatter the men of the highest authority, the worldly dignitaries. But He presents before all the traits of character which must be possessed by the peculiar people who will compose the royal family in the kingdom of heaven. He specifies those who shall become heirs of God and joint-heirs with Himself. He proclaims publicly His choice of subjects, and assigns them their place in His service as united with Himself."[1] Vanity and deceit must not be found in the Christian who is pure in heart.

What does it mean to have a pure heart? "True religion does not consist in mere outward conformity to religious ceremonies; it controls the heart and produces purity of thought and sincerity of motive."[2] Thus, even our thoughts must be brought under control lest we sin by wishing to commit an act while refraining from taking overt action. "God's law reaches the feelings and motives, as well as the outward acts. It reveals the secrets of the heart, flashing light upon things before buried in darkness. God knows every thought, every purpose, every plan, every motive. The books of heaven record the sins that would have been committed had there been opportunity. God will bring every work into judgment, with every secret thing. By His law He measures the character of every man. . . . God has a perfect photograph of every man's character, and this photograph He compares with His law. He reveals to man the defects that mar his life, and calls upon him to repent and turn from sin."[3]

"I would be true, for there are those who trust me; / I would be pure, for there are those who care."[4]

---

1. Ellen G. White, "Diary / A Divine Saviour," MS 187, 1903.
2. Francis D. Nichol, ed., *The Seventh-day Adventist Bible Commentary*, vol. 3 (Washington, DC: Review and Herald®, 1977), 688, 689.
3. Ellen G. White, "A Perfect Law," *Signs of the Times®*, July 31, 1901.
4. Howard A. Walter, "I Would Be True" (1906).

Psalm 24, Part 2:
Who Is This King of Glory?

Lift up your heads, O ye gates; and be ye lifted up, ye everlasting doors; and the King of glory shall come in. Who is this King of glory? The Lord strong and mighty, the Lord mighty in battle.
—Psalm 24:7, 8

D avid's goal of bringing the ark from Kirjath-jearim to Jerusalem occasioned the composition of Psalm 24. It was to be sung by two choirs answering each other from afar. The same verses are "used in the Sabbath morning and afternoon services of the modern synagogue before the Torah is returned to the ark."[1]

Were David's words penned solely to welcome the ark to Jerusalem? Did he, perhaps, in vision, see the ascension of Christ following His mission to save lost humanity? Ellen White paints a vivid picture of Christ's triumphant return to His heavenly home: "All heaven was waiting the hour of triumph when Jesus should ascend to His Father. Angels came to receive the King of glory and to escort Him triumphantly to heaven. After Jesus had blessed His disciples, He was parted from them and taken up. And as He led the way upward, the multitude of captives who were raised at His resurrection followed. A multitude of the heavenly host were in attendance, while in heaven an innumerable company of angels awaited His coming. As they ascended to the Holy City, the angels who escorted Jesus cried out, 'Lift up your heads, O ye gates; and be ye lifted up, ye everlasting doors; and the King of glory shall come in.' The angels in the city cried out with rapture, 'Who is this King of glory?' The escorting angels answered in triumph, 'The Lord strong and mighty, the Lord mighty in battle! Lift up your heads, O ye gates; even lift them up, ye everlasting doors, and the King of glory shall come in!' Again the waiting angels asked, 'Who is this King of glory?' and the escorting angels answered in melodious strains, 'The Lord of hosts, He is the King of glory.' And the heavenly train passed into the city of God."[2]

"Lift up your heads, ye mighty gates! / Behold the King of glory waits"[3]

---

1. Francis D. Nichol, ed., *The Seventh-day Adventist Bible Commentary*, vol. 3 (Washington, DC: Review and Herald®, 1977), 688, 689.

2. Ellen G. White, *Early Writings* (Hagerstown, MD: Review and Herald®, 2000), 190, 191.

3. Georg Weissel, "Lift Up Your Heads" (1642), in *The Seventh-day Adventist Hymnal* (Hagerstown, MD: Review and Herald®, 1985), hymn 226.

PSALM 24, PART 3:
HE IS THE KING OF GLORY

Who is this King of glory? The Lord *of hosts, he is the King of glory.*
—Psalm 24:10

P salm 24 has encouraged and strengthened more than one believer to lead a godly life, but there is also a historical aspect referring to the establishment of Jerusalem as the City of David and the religious center of Israel. Perhaps the psalm was written to mark the arrival of the ark of the covenant. "The anthem has two parts. In its original use, the first part was doubtless sung at the foot of the hill on which Jerusalem stood, before the procession began to ascend the heights (vs. 1–6); and the second part was sung in front of the gates of the city immediately preceding the grand entry (vs. 7–10). The two stanzas of the first part may have been sung by alternating choirs; the summonses, challenges, and responses. . . . Verses 7–10 appear in the inspiring chorus, 'Lift Up Your Heads, O Ye Gates,' in Handel's oratorio *The Messiah.*"[1]

"At the first response of the bearers of the ark (Ps. 24:8), the gates appear to have remained closed before the waiting procession. At this second response, 'The Lord of hosts,' instead of 'The Lord strong and mighty, the Lord mighty in battle,' appears to be a sort of glorious password that unlocks the city."[2] In verses 8 and 10, note the different responses to the same question: "Who is this King of glory?" The first response is "Jehovah, strong and mighty, a God of power, Creator and Proprietor of the earth, who shows His power in overthrowing His enemies."[3] The second response is "the Lord of hosts." Why the difference? The second states God's *sovereignty* is universal. "The psalm closes in perfect accord with the opening thought: God alone is ruler of the universe; He alone should be universally recognized. The ceremony of installing the ark in the hill of the Lord provides a fitting occasion for this proclamation."[4]

"*The King of kings is drawing near, / The Savior of the world is here.*"[5]

---

1. Francis D. Nichol, ed., *The Seventh-day Adventist Bible Commentary*, vol. 3 (Washington, DC: Review and Herald®, 1977), 688, 689.
2. Nichol, 690.
3. Nichol, 690.
4. Nichol, 690.
5. Georg Weissel, "Lift Up Your Heads" (1642), in *The Seventh-day Adventist Hymnal* (Hagerstown, MD: Review and Herald®, 1985), hymn 226.

PSALM 15, PART 1: THE GOOD CITIZEN

LORD, who shall abide in thy tabernacle? who shall dwell in thy holy hill?
—Psalm 15:1

Psalm 15 is a description of an ideal person. "The Talmud says that the 613 commandments of the Pentateuch are all summarized in this psalm."[1] In five verses, David lists the attributes a Christian must have in order to enter into the kingdom of heaven. There are eleven answers to the question, "LORD, who shall abide in thy tabernacle? who shall dwell in thy holy hill?" The person who walks uprightly, works righteousness, and speaks the truth in his or her heart is pleasing to God (v. 2). But what does it mean to walk uprightly, work righteousness, and speak heart truth?

Micah 6:8 outlines the requirements of the Christian: "He hath shewed thee, O man, what is good; and what doth the LORD require of thee, but to do justly, and to love mercy, and to walk humbly with thy God." Psalm 15 and Micah 6 both deal with character development. "There will be no second probation in which to prepare for eternity. It is in this life that we are to put on the robe of Christ's righteousness. This is our only opportunity to form characters for the home which Christ has made ready for those who obey His commandments."[2]

"Purity of mind is the first requisite for a sinless life. It is out of the abundance of the heart (mind) that good or evil comes into our lives (Luke 6:45). Sin is the indulging of the desires of the sinful, deceitful human heart (Jer. 17:9), hence the need for diligence in keeping the mind surrendered to God, who alone can keep it pure (see Eph. 4:17, 23)."[3]

In summary, Psalm 15:2 requires us, first, to be honest in word and deed. Walking "upright" is being scrupulously honest in all our dealings. Second, we must receive the robe of Christ's righteousness by accepting Him as our personal Savior. And third, we should cultivate purity of thought by dwelling on God's Word. These three decisions are a good place to start building an acceptable character to enter heaven.

"Purer yet and purer / I would be in mind, / Dearer yet and dearer / Every duty find."[4]

---

1. Francis D. Nichol, ed., *The Seventh-day Adventist Bible Commentary*, vol. 3 (Washington, DC: Review and Herald®, 1977), 663.
2. Ellen G. White, "Our Preparation for the End," *Signs of the Times®*, November 22, 1905, 9.
3. Nichol, *The Seventh-day Adventist Bible Commentary*, 3:961.
4. Anonymous, "Purer Yet and Purer," in *The Church Hymnal: The Official Hymnal of the Seventh-day Adventist Church* (Washington, DC: Review and Herald®, 1941), hymn 388.

Psalm 15, Part 2: Immovable

He that doeth these things shall never be moved.
—Psalm 15:5

Y esterday we discovered that a good Christian walks uprightly; works righteousness through Christ, our Lord; and speaks the truth honestly with purity of mind. Today we consider the remaining verses of Psalm 15. "He that backbiteth not with his tongue, nor doeth evil to his neighbour, nor taketh up a reproach against his neighbour" (v. 3) is the next set of virtues a Christian must attain. This verse is a mirror of the golden rule found in Matthew 7:12. Do not slander your neighbor. Do not harm your neighbor. Do not spread rumors or gossip about your neighbor. Be slow to believe ill of your neighbor.

"In whose eyes a vile person is contemned; but he honoureth them that fear the LORD. He that sweareth to his own hurt, and changeth not" (Psalm 15:4). Assess associates with honesty for who they really are. Do not excuse evil. Do justice to all. Be not a respecter of persons, treating all evenhandedly and fairly. Once an agreement is made, even if it means personal loss, honor the deal. The Christian's word is his or her bond. "He that putteth not out his money to usury, nor taketh reward against the innocent" (v. 5). The Christian does not charge interest of the poor. It is unethical to take advantage of those who are destitute. The Christian does not take a bribe (Exodus 23:8; Deuteronomy 16:19; Proverbs 17:23).

"He that doeth these things shall never be moved" (Psalm 15:5). These character-building traits are summed up in Jesus' words to the lawyer who asked, "Master, which is the great commandment in the law? Jesus said unto him, Thou shalt love the Lord thy God with all thy heart, and with all thy soul, and with all thy mind. This is the first and great commandment. And the second is like unto it, Thou shalt love thy neighbour as thyself. On these two commandments hang all the law and the prophets" (Matthew 22:36–40). Sanctification is the work of a lifetime.

"Lord, my sins they are many, / Like the sands of the sea, / But Thy blood, O my Saviour, / Is sufficient for me; / For Thy promise is written / In bright letters that glow, / 'Though your sins be as scarlet, / I will make them like snow.' "[1]

---

1. Mary A. Kidder, "Lord, I Care Not for Riches," in *The Church Hymnal: The Official Hymnal of the Seventh-day Adventist Church* (Washington, DC: Review and Herald®, 1941), hymn 617.

PSALM 26: PREPARING FOR PUBLIC WORSHIP

Judge me, O LORD; for I have walked in mine integrity: I have trusted also in the LORD; therefore I shall not slide. Examine me, O LORD, and prove me; try my reins and my heart.
—Psalm 26:1, 2

It is perhaps appropriate to consider Psalm 26 at this point in David's life. David wants to maintain integrity, but he needs God to evaluate his conduct. He therefore asks God to examine his life and put it to the test (v. 2). This is not an arrogant request, based on the feeling he cannot fail. Rather, he realizes God's mercy has always been there to save him when he unintentionally committed errors (v. 1). David has done his best to observe the commandments of God and walk in truth (v. 3). He has not associated with vain men and vows to continue to remain pure and undefiled (v. 4). As far as possible, he has attempted to have nothing to do with evildoers (v. 5). This is a similar sentiment to the one he penned in Psalm 1:1: "Blessed is the man that walketh not in the counsel of the ungodly, nor standeth in the way of sinners, nor sitteth in the seat of the scornful." David wishes to remain pure so he may continue to worship in the temple (Psalm 26:6). More than that, he wants to spread the good news of salvation to others. He wants to speak "with the voice of thanksgiving, and tell of all" God's "wondrous works" (v. 7). "I will praise thee, O LORD, with my whole heart; I will shew forth all thy marvellous works" (Psalm 9:1).

"It is good to shun evil, but if religious activity ends there, the experience is negative; it is better to go to the place where God is—that is positive (see on Ps. 27:4)."[1] "LORD, I have loved the habitation of thy house, and the place where thine honour dwelleth" (Psalm 26:8). David does not want to be linked with murderers or dishonest or ill-behaved men (vv. 9, 10). "The psalmist is determined to continue to walk in the path he had hitherto trodden. This resolution is the ground for the prayer in the second part of the verse [v. 11]."[2] David asks for mercy and redemption. Claiming God's answer to his prayer, David proclaims salvation for he is standing "in an even place" (v. 12).

"Lord, lift me up, and I shall stand / By faith, on heaven's tableland; / A higher plane than I have found; / Lord, plant my feet on higher ground."[3]

---

1. Francis D. Nichol, ed., *The Seventh-day Adventist Bible Commentary*, vol. 3 (Washington, DC: Review and Herald®, 1977), 694.
2. Nichol, 694.
3. Johnson Oatman Jr., "Higher Ground," in *The Seventh-day Adventist Hymnal* (Hagerstown, MD: Review and Herald®, 1985), hymn 625.

A MAJOR DISAPPOINTMENT

And it came to pass the same night, that the word of God came to Nathan, saying, Go and tell David my servant, Thus saith the LORD, Thou shalt not build me an house to dwell in.
—1 Chronicles 17:3, 4

I t was David's dream to build a permanent structure to house the ark of the covenant. He therefore asked the prophet Nathan if this action would be acceptable to God. "This is the first mention of Nathan the prophet, but he was evidently already a confidential counselor of the king, to be consulted on important matters in which David desired specific directions from God."[1] The original tabernacle had been at Gibeon (1 Chronicles 21:29; 2 Chronicles 1:3–6). The ark was now in Jerusalem. David believed the central house of worship should be in the capital. Nathan was of the same mind and told David to move forward with his plan (2 Samuel 7:3). That night Nathan received definitive instruction, and God's answer was no! Nathan had to retract his previous support.

"The reason why David was not to build the temple was declared: 'Thou hast shed blood abundantly, and hast made great wars: thou shalt not build a house unto My name. . . . Behold, a son shall be born to thee, who shall be a man of rest; and I will give him rest from all his enemies: . . . his name shall be Solomon [peaceable], and I will give peace and quietness unto Israel in his days. He shall build a house for My name.' 1 Chronicles 22:8-10."[2] It had been about 450 years since the Exodus, and the tabernacle had moved when the Israelites moved. A few more years of temporary housing would make little difference. "David was a servant of God and had himself spoken by inspiration, as in the composition of his psalms. To him also applied the title 'prophet' (Acts 2:30). On this occasion the Lord chose to speak to him not directly, but through another prophet. God works through different individuals and divine light comes through various channels."[3] It is our responsibility to test prophetic messages for authenticity (Numbers 12:6).[4]

Could you, as did Nathan, retract a previous statement and admit you were wrong?

1. Francis D. Nichol, ed., *The Seventh-day Adventist Bible Commentary*, vol. 2 (Washington, DC: Review and Herald®, 1976), 630.
2. Ellen G. White, *Patriarchs and Prophets* (Mountain View, CA: Pacific Press®, 1943), 712.
3. Nichol, *The Seventh-day Adventist Bible Commentary*, 2:631.
4. To review the tests of a prophet, see February 11's entry.

An Eternal Throne

And it shall come to pass, when thy days be expired that thou must go to be with thy fathers, that I will raise up thy seed after thee, which shall be of thy sons; and I will establish his kingdom. He shall build me an house, and I will stablish his throne for ever.
—1 Chronicles 17:11, 12

With the disappointing word that he was not to build the temple, God promised David that He would sustain David's family on the throne of Israel forever, and "David was also shown that the Messiah was to come in his lineage (see Acts 2:30)."[1] David was so astonished by the idea that "his" throne would be established forever, he was speechless (1 Chronicles 17:18). "What could David say more to glorify God, in view of the unparalleled honor God had shown to His servant? David was overwhelmed by the high honor God had shown to him, and words failed him to express the feelings of gratefulness that welled up within his heart."[2] As David sat before the Lord, he finally found words to express his thankfulness (2 Samuel 7:18–29; 1 Chronicles 17:16–27).

"O Lord, there is none like thee" (1 Chronicles 17:20). God is unique in the entire universe. Jehovah is the Creator and Sustainer of all life. "It was a thought of constant comfort and cheer to the true Israelite to know that he belonged to God's people—a people chosen, protected, and redeemed by Him. However, the same knowledge lulled many into a false security by causing them to ignore two facts: (1) that this status of 'chosen people' was also conditional on obedience (Ex. 19:5, 6); and (2) that true Israel included not merely the Hebrews, but people gathered from the ends of the earth, 'every one that is called by my name' (Isa. 43:1–7, 21)."[3]

David closes his prayer by asking God, if it pleases Him, to honor His promise. "At the same time he was fully aware of the possibility of human failure. But as God wished it, so he desired it to be and so he prayed that it might be."[4]

Is your spirit in tune with God's will?

---

1. Francis D. Nichol, ed., *The Seventh-day Adventist Bible Commentary*, vol. 2 (Washington, DC: Review and Herald®, 1976), 631.
2. Francis D. Nichol, ed., *The Seventh-day Adventist Bible Commentary*, vol. 3 (Washington, DC: Review and Herald®, 1977), 175.
3. Nichol, 3:176.
4. Nichol, 175, 176.

WHO AM I, O LORD GOD?

Then went king David in, and sat before the LORD,
and he said, Who am I, O Lord GOD? and what is my
house, that thou hast brought me hitherto?
—2 Samuel 7:18

I f David had possessed pride of opinion, he might have become highly incensed at having his ideas crossed. Instead he accepted the divine rebuke, even though it was contrary to both his purpose and the prophet's judgment."[1] "Though the cherished purpose of his heart had been denied, David received the message with gratitude. . . . 'And this was yet a small thing in Thy sight, O Lord God; but Thou hast spoken also of Thy servant's house for a great while to come.' . . .

"David knew that it would be an honor to his name and would bring glory to his government to perform the work that he had purposed in his heart to do, but he was ready to submit his will to the will of God. The grateful resignation thus manifested is rarely seen, even among Christians. How often do those who have passed the strength of manhood cling to the hope of accomplishing some great work upon which their hearts are set. . . . [Instead,] it is theirs to prepare the way for another to accomplish it. But instead of gratefully submitting to the divine direction, many fall back as if slighted and rejected, feeling that if they cannot do the one thing which they desire to do, they will do nothing. Many cling with desperate energy to responsibilities which they are incapable of bearing, and vainly endeavor to accomplish a work for which they are insufficient, while that which they might do, lies neglected. And because of this lack of cooperation on their part the greater work is hindered or frustrated."[2]

"As David sat in meditation he probably reviewed the years that had gone, thinking first of himself as a humble shepherd lad wandering over the hills and becoming acquainted with the ways of God; then how he had been chosen for the kingdom, . . . little knowing one day what new trial and danger the next would bring forth. Now at length he enjoyed peace, and with it came the promise from God as to the future of his kingdom."[3]

Humility is often lacking in those blessed with power.

---

1. Francis D. Nichol, ed., *The Seventh-day Adventist Bible Commentary*, vol. 2 (Washington, DC: Review and Herald®, 1976), 631.
2. Ellen G. White, *Patriarchs and Prophets* (Mountain View, CA: Pacific Press®, 1943), 712, 713.
3. Nichol, *The Seventh-day Adventist Bible Commentary*, 2:632.

PSALM 110: A MESSIANIC PSALM

The LORD said unto my Lord, Sit thou at my right
hand, until I make thine enemies thy footstool.
—Psalm 110:1

D avid wrote Psalm 110 sometime after receiving a vision of the coming Messiah. In Christ, the promise of the everlasting covenant would be fulfilled. "The psalm takes its place among the most majestic songs of Hebrew literature. It has been styled 'the pearl of Messianic psalms.' Christ is presented not only as King and Ruler of this world, but also, by God's solemn oath, as eternal Priest."[1]

Christ made mention of this psalm during a discussion with the Pharisees of His day. "Jesus asked them, Saying, What think ye of Christ? whose son is he? They say unto him, The son of David. He saith unto them, How then doth David in spirit call him Lord, saying, The LORD said unto my Lord, Sit thou on my right hand, till I make thine enemies thy footstool? If David then call him Lord, how is he his son?" (Matthew 22:41–45). The point Jesus was making was that Christ was the Son of God the Father, not David's son! The Father placed Christ at His right hand—the highest position in the universe. Ultimately, every knee will bow to the King of kings, and Christ will triumph over all earthly sovereigns (Philippians 2:5–11).

Psalm 110 also ascribes priestly duties to the Son of God. "In Christ the priesthood and the kingship are united as they were in Melchizedek, king of Salem, priest of God (see Gen. 14:18; Heb. 5:6, 10; 6:20; 7:1–3, 11, 15, 17, 24, 28)."[2] Christ offered up His body for us, and by His blood, we are cleansed. "Now the God of peace, that brought again from the dead our Lord Jesus, that great shepherd of the sheep, through the blood of the everlasting covenant, make you perfect in every good work to do his will, working in you that which is wellpleasing in his sight, through Jesus Christ; to whom be glory for ever and ever. Amen" (Hebrews 13:20, 21).

"Where high the heavenly temple stands, / The house of God not made with hands, / A great High Priest our nature wears, / The Guardian of mankind appears."[3]

---

1. Francis D. Nichol, ed., *The Seventh-day Adventist Bible Commentary*, vol. 3 (Washington, DC: Review and Herald®, 1977), 880.

2. Nichol, 880.

3. Michael Bruce, "Where High the Heavenly Temple Stands," in *The Church Hymnal: The Official Hymnal of the Seventh-day Adventist Church* (Washington, DC: Review and Herald®, 1941), hymn 137.

PSALM 86: WHY PRAY?

In the day of my trouble I will call upon thee: for thou wilt answer me.
—Psalm 86:7

Psalm 86 is a collection of thoughts on prayer. David expects God to answer his prayers and places explicit trust in his heavenly Father's care. God is merciful and ever ready to forgive all who call upon Him for help in times of trouble (v. 5). David experienced joy in seeing God work out his seemingly insurmountable problems (v. 4). Thus, through past acts of deliverance, he gained confidence that the Lord would hear future cries for help (vv. 6, 7).

God is unlike false gods, for He alone can deliver the petitioner from distress (v. 8). Eventually, all nations will realize Jehovah is the true God and will give up false gods to worship Him alone (vv. 9, 10).

David longed to learn the way of the Lord. It "cannot be known intuitively; man must be taught as he sits at the feet of God and learns the lessons life has to offer." "Only when we are taught by God can we walk in His truth."[1] "For thy lovingkindness is before mine eyes: and I have walked in thy truth" (Psalm 26:3). David wanted his whole heart to align with the will of God (Psalm 86:11). "And thou shalt love the LORD thy God with all thine heart, and with all thy soul, and with all thy might" (Deuteronomy 6:5). This aim was paramount in his life. "For where your treasure is, there will your heart be also" (Matthew 6:21). God stands ready to place a longing to connect with Him in our hearts, but we must ask in order to receive. "And I will give them one heart, and one way, that they may fear [love] me for ever, for the good of them, and of their children after them" (Jeremiah 32:39).

Because God is merciful, David praises His intervention during difficult times. Wicked men sought to do David evil—men who did not respect God or allow Him access to their lives (Psalm 86:14). God's attributes of compassion, civility, patience, mercy, and truth give confidence to those who call upon Him for help in their times of trouble (v. 15). David ends this psalm by praying that even his enemies will eventually acknowledge God's intervention on his behalf (v. 17).

"I love to steal awhile away / From every cumbering care, / And spend the hours of setting day / In humble, grateful prayer."[2]

1. Francis D. Nichol, ed., *The Seventh-day Adventist Bible Commentary*, vol. 3 (Washington, DC: Review and Herald®, 1977), 832.
2. Phoebe H. Brown, "I Love to Steal Awhile Away" (1818), in *The Church Hymnal: The Official Hymnal of the Seventh-day Adventist Church* (Washington, DC: Review and Herald®, 1941), hymn 317.

PSALM 80: SAVE US!

Turn us again, O God, and cause thy
face to shine; and we shall be saved.

—Psalm 80:3

E llen White tells us Psalm 80 was written by David.[1] It is a psalm written during a time of national crisis. David asks God to once again show favor to Israel, just as He did when He delivered the Israelites from Egyptian bondage. God is the Shepherd, and the children of Israel are His flock (v. 1). David mentions three of the twelve tribes in this psalm—Ephraim, Benjamin, and Manasseh. These three tribes descended from the same mother—Rachel, the wife of Jacob (Genesis 46:19, 20; Numbers 2:18–24; 10:22–24). Benjamin and Joseph were Rachel's children. Ephraim and Manasseh were the children of Joseph and his Egyptian wife, Aseneth. These specific tribes are mentioned as representative of those brought out of Egyptian bondage (Psalm 80:2, 8).

It seemed God had turned His back on Israel and they on Him (v. 4). David's common refrain, in which he changes only the name of the Lord, is "Turn us again, O God" (v. 3); "Turn us again, O God of hosts" (v. 7); "Return, we beseech thee, O God of hosts" (v. 14); "Turn us again, O LORD God of hosts" (v. 19). Why was God measuring out their tears of sorrow as one would measure out a drink (v. 5)? Israel was once a vine brought out of Egypt, planted in the fertile land of Palestine (vv. 8, 9, 15). The nation had spread north to Lebanon (v. 10). It extended its boundaries from the Euphrates in the east (Joshua 1:4) to the Mediterranean in the west (Psalm 80:11). Now those borders were no longer secure, and enemies were raiding at will (v. 12). The land was being laid waste by marauders (v. 13).

The vine, representing Israel, was being cut down, piled up, and burned (v. 16). David prayed for strength and guidance to deal with this calamity (v. 17). The people needed a revival of faith. They needed to awaken from their stupor and praise God's name once more (v. 18). If God would look upon them again with favor, they would be saved (v. 19).

"O Thou in whose presence my soul takes delight, / On whom in affliction I call, / My comfort by day and my song in the night, / My hope, my salvation, my all!"[2]

---

1. Ellen G. White, *Christ's Object Lessons* (Washington, DC: Review and Herald®, 1969), 214.
2. Joseph Swain, "O Thou in Whose Presence," in *The Seventh-day Adventist Hymnal* (Hagerstown, MD: Review and Herald®, 1985), hymn 36.

PSALM 124: O GOD OUR HELP!

Our soul is escaped as a bird out of the snare of the fowlers:
the snare is broken, and we are escaped. Our help is
in the name of the LORD, who made heaven and earth.
—Psalm 124:7, 8

Time and time again, the nation of Israel was confronted by enemies bent upon its destruction. David realized God had delivered him from impossible situations and the nation as well. "Many times it seemed that the chosen people would be annihilated. However, the Lord provided a way of escape."[1] It is all too easy to forget a prayer that has been answered once the crisis passes. The story of the ten lepers illustrates this point. Jesus healed ten men of the hideous and fatal disease of leprosy. Of the ten, only one returned to thank his Savior (Luke 17:11–19).

As a recipient of God's mercy and grace, when confronted with an insurmountable problem, do you remember to thank Him? David was not one to take God's deliverance for granted. As long as God remained on the side of Israel, he knew they had nothing to fear. Had not God been for them, "when men rose up against us: Then they had swallowed us up quick, when their wrath was kindled against us: Then the waters had overwhelmed us, the stream had gone over our soul: Then the proud waters had gone over our soul" (Psalm 124:2–5).

Were it not for God's protection, the righteous on this earth would perish. Like "a bird out of the snare of the fowlers: the snare is broken, and we are escaped" (v. 7). David uses the same symbolism of a bird helplessly trapped in Psalm 25:15 when he writes, "Mine eyes are ever toward the LORD; for he shall pluck my feet out of the net." Where is the sinner to turn when caught in an evil net? Our only hope, like that of Israel, is to turn to the Lord for salvation.

The psalms repeatedly tell us that God is our only help in times of trouble: "Our help is in the name of the LORD, who made heaven and earth" (Psalm 124:8). "My help cometh from the LORD, which made heaven and earth" (Psalm 121:2). "Give us help from trouble: for vain is the help of man" (Psalm 108:12).

"Just when I need Him, Jesus is near, / Just when I falter, just when I fear; / Ready to help me, ready to cheer, / Just when I need Him most."[2]

---

1. Francis D. Nichol, ed., *The Seventh-day Adventist Bible Commentary*, vol. 3 (Washington, DC: Review and Herald®, 1977), 910.
2. William C. Poole, "Just When I Need Him Most" (1907), in *The Seventh-day Adventist Hymnal* (Hagerstown, MD: Review and Herald®, 1985), hymn 512.

PSALM 60: A PRAYER FOR NATIONAL DELIVERANCE

Give us help from trouble: for vain is the help of man. Through God we shall do valiantly: for he it is that shall tread down our enemies.
—Psalm 60:11, 12

Psalm 60 was written by David during his war with the Edomites. Initially, the forces of Israel must have struggled because the psalm opens with David pleading, "O God, thou hast cast us off, thou hast scattered us, thou hast been displeased; O turn thyself to us again" (v. 1). The nation had been shaken to its core by this defeat. "Thou hast made the earth to tremble; thou hast broken it: heal the breaches thereof; for it shaketh" (v. 2). Israel had defeated the Philistines, Amalekites, Aramaeans, and Moabites, but the Edomites were tougher than expected.

"Thou hast shewed thy people hard things: thou hast made us to drink the wine of astonishment" (v. 3). The nation was reeling from a military setback and wondering, *Why has God seemingly deserted His chosen nation?* "Thou hast given a banner to them that fear thee, that it may be displayed because of the truth." (v. 4). Despite this setback, David hoped Israel would rally under the banner of the Lord and advance to victory.

God had promised to defeat Israel's enemies. David now asked Him to keep that promise (vv. 4–8). "Who will bring me into the strong city? who will lead me into Edom?" (v. 9). The kingdom of Edom lay south of the Dead Sea. The strong city David was referring to was most likely Petra, the Edomite capital. Petra "could be approached only through a narrow gorge with rocky, sometimes vertical, walls. The city was rock hewn and practically inaccessible to the invader (see Obadiah 1, 3). David expresses eagerness to capture this stronghold."[1]

David ends his psalm with a request: "Wilt not thou, O God, which hadst cast us off? and thou, O God, which didst not go out with our armies? Give us help from trouble: for vain is the help of man" (Psalm 60:10, 11). With God fighting alongside Israel's armies, victory would come.

With God as a force multiplier, Joab gained victory over the Edomites (1 Kings 11:15, 16).

"God is the refuge of His saints; / . . . Ere we can offer our complaints."[2]

---

1. Francis D. Nichol, ed., *The Seventh-day Adventist Bible Commentary*, vol. 3 (Washington, DC: Review and Herald®, 1977), 775.
2. Isaac Watts, "God Is the Refuge," in *The Church Hymnal: The Official Hymnal of the Seventh-day Adventist Church* (Washington, DC: Review and Herald®, 1941), hymn 89.

PSALM 66, PART 1:
THANK GOD FOR DELIVERANCE

Make a joyful noise unto God, all ye lands.
—Psalm 66:1

Psalm 66 is a song of thanksgiving for deliverance from some difficulty. It is difficult to place in the chronology of David's life as it might fit almost anywhere. The first half of Psalm 66 was written to be sung by a gathering of persons expressing joy at being saved from affliction (vv. 1–12). The second half is a more personal song of salvation (vv. 13–20).

God's deliverance of Israel is recounted; while other nations cringed before the power of God (v. 3), the Israelites rejoiced in His deliverance (v. 1). The crossing of the Red Sea and the Jordan River (v. 6) are mentioned: "He turned the sea into dry land: they went through the flood on foot: there did we rejoice in him." God watches the nations (Psalm 11:4) and takes care of His own. The rebellious (v. 7) are "those who are impatient under God's restraint, or who defy God. These should not be lifted up with pride, for they must eventually submit to God's power."[1]

Psalm 66:8–12 is a call for the people of the nation to praise God for His deliverance. Their trial has been long and severe. "For thou, O God, hast proved us: thou hast tried us, as silver is tried. Thou broughtest us into the net; thou laidst affliction upon our loins. Thou hast caused men to ride over our heads; we went through fire and through water: but thou broughtest us out into a wealthy place" (vv. 10–12). "Anciently the refining of silver was a slow process. Israel had suffered long."[2] The years of Egyptian oppression still resonated with Israel centuries later.

Going "through fire and through water" is now a part of our lexicon. It signifies passing through intense danger or peril and surviving the experience.[3] Surely it must have felt like that to Israel. The people had passed through long trials to reach the Promised Land. God's loving watch care over His chosen nation brought them at last to Canaan. Then it was time to rejoice and make a joyful noise in gratitude.

"Praise God, from whom all blessings flow."[4]

---

1. Francis D. Nichol, ed., *The Seventh-day Adventist Bible Commentary*, vol. 3 (Washington, DC: Review and Herald®, 1977), 785.

2. Nichol, 785.

3. Nichol, 785.

4. Thomas Ken, "Praise God, From Whom All Blessings Flow" (1695), in *The Seventh-day Adventist Hymnal* (Hagerstown, MD: Review and Herald®, 1985), hymns 694, 695.

Psalm 66, Part 2: God Heard Me!

But verily God hath heard me; he hath
attended to the voice of my prayer.

—Psalm 66:19

P salm 66 turns from congregational praise to personal gratitude. David promises to keep the vows made to God while mired in trouble (vv. 13–15). Christians who find themselves in difficulty will often promise God anything if He will just get them out of their predicament. Once the situation is resolved, they conveniently forget their promise. One should be extremely careful to keep resolutions made to God!

David invites all to hear his story of redemption (v. 16). God had heard his plea and answered his prayer (v. 19). But David notes that his heart had to be right with God for God to answer his request (v. 18). "In order for prayer to be acceptable to God, it must be coupled with a purpose to forsake all known sin (see Prov. 28:9; Isa. 1:15; 58:3–5)."[1] "When it is in the heart to obey God, when efforts are put forth to this end, Jesus accepts this disposition and effort as man's best service, and he makes up for the deficiency with his own divine merit."[2]

Some Christians believe God should answer their exact prayers. Instead, "when we come to Him we should pray . . . that our desires and interests may be lost in His. We should acknowledge our acceptance of His will, not praying Him to concede to ours. It is better for us that God does not always answer our prayers just when we desire, and in just the manner we wish. He will do more and better for us than to accomplish all our wishes, for our wisdom is folly."[3]

Why is it important to forsake all known sin if we want God to hear our prayers? Were God to grant the requests of a petitioner concealing evil in his or her heart, He would be endorsing sinful behavior. To be right with God is to accept our own sinfulness, put away those things that separate us from His presence, and pray His will be done in our lives.

"Praise ye the Father for His lovingkindness, / Tenderly cares He for His erring children; / Praise Him, ye angels, praise Him in the heavens; / Praise ye Jehovah!"[4]

---

1. Francis D. Nichol, ed., *The Seventh-day Adventist Bible Commentary*, vol. 3 (Washington, DC: Review and Herald®, 1977), 786.

2. Ellen G. White, "Faith and Works," *Signs of the Times*®, June 16, 1890.

3. Ellen G. White, *Testimonies for the Church* (Mountain View, CA: Pacific Press®, 1948), 2:148.

4. Elizabeth Rundle Charles, "Praise Ye the Father!" (1859), in *The Seventh-day Adventist Hymnal* (Hagerstown, MD: Review and Herald®, 1985), hymn 70.

DAVID STRENGTHENS THE BORDERS

And David reigned over all Israel; and David
executed judgment and justice unto all his people.
—2 Samuel 8:15

D avid now sought to secure Israel's borders. Hostile nations still surrounded Israel, and these had to be conquered if lasting peace was to be won. The aggressive Philistines in the west were defeated, and their capital of Gath was annexed (1 Chronicles 18:1). Next, David turned east to Moab. His parents had been given asylum in Moab when David was a fugitive (1 Samuel 22:3, 4). We are not told what caused David's change of attitude toward Moab, but he "measured" and then killed two-thirds of their fighting men (2 Samuel 8:2). Perhaps the Moabites attacked Israel while David's armies were occupied with conquering the Philistines. In any case, the remaining Moabites became servants of Israel (v. 2). David next turned northeast and destroyed Hadadezer (also called Hadarezer), the king of a small Aramaean kingdom located just west of the Euphrates River (v. 3). Though a small kingdom, David took a thousand chariots, seven hundred horsemen, and twenty thousand Aramaean footmen as spoils of battle (v. 4; 1 Chronicles 18:3, 4). The Syrians of Damascus came to the aid of the Aramaeans at Zobah, and David's forces destroyed twenty-two thousand Syrian opponents (2 Samuel 8:5). David occupied all of Syria, extending to the Euphrates River, and had it garrisoned.

When Toi, king of Hamath, heard David had destroyed Hadadezer, he sent his son Joram to thank David for removing a common enemy (v. 10). By sending his own son, Toi showed the esteem in which he held David. All the defeated nations brought tribute to David in the form of brass, gold, silver vessels, and plated shields. David dedicated these gifts of tribute to the Lord.

David lastly looked south, where Amalekite tribes still raided settlements. Saul had battled these desert nomads (1 Samuel 15), as had David (1 Samuel 30). David successfully pushed back these persistent enemies once again. To the southeast, the nation of Edom was conquered, and eighteen thousand men were killed by Abishai, brother of Joab, in the Valley of Salt (1 Chronicles 18:12). The borders of Israel were extended and secured. In every battle, David was victorious. "And the LORD preserved David whithersoever he went" (2 Samuel 8:14).

"Both riches and honour come of thee, and thou reignest over all; and in thine hand is power and might; and in thine hand it is to make great, and to give strength unto all" (1 Chronicles 29:12).

MEPHIBOSHETH

And the king said, Is there not yet any of the house of Saul, that I may shew the kindness of God unto him? And Ziba said unto the king, Jonathan hath yet a son, which is lame on his feet.
—2 Samuel 9:3

David had made a covenant with Jonathan that once his enemies were conquered, he would show kindness to the house of Saul. Now, with the borders secure, David remembered his promise, and "he was told of a son of Jonathan, Mephibosheth, who had been lame from childhood. At the time of Saul's defeat by the Philistines at Jezreel, the nurse of this child, attempting to flee with him, had let him fall, thus making him a lifelong cripple."[1] Mephibosheth had been in hiding these many years for fear David would have him killed as a rival for the throne. Very few were privy to his location. It was a closely guarded secret that he even existed, but a palace servant named Ziba knew of the existence of Jonathan's son. When summoned, Ziba disclosed to David the location of Mephibosheth: "Behold, he is . . . in Lodebar" (2 Samuel 9:4).

The residence, east of the Jordan River, had been a place of safety for the son of Jonathan. David sent for the lad at once, commanding him to appear. "Mephibosheth realized that his life was at the mercy of the king. If David had so desired, he could have given orders for his execution in order that the seed of Saul might be completely wiped out of existence, and that there would be no possibility for a rival to arise from that source who might claim the throne."[2]

Mephibosheth bowed before David and pledged his loyalty. What a shock when David treated him kindly! All of Saul's property was restored to Mephibosheth. He was given a life pension and was treated as one of David's own sons (v. 11). "Through reports from the enemies of David, Mephibosheth had been led to cherish a strong prejudice against him as a usurper; but the monarch's generous and courteous reception of him and his continued kindness won the heart of the young man; he became strongly attached to David, and, like his father Jonathan, he felt that his interest was one with that of the king whom God had chosen."[3]

"Love your enemies, do good to them which hate you" (Luke 6:27).

---

1. Ellen G. White, *Patriarchs and Prophets* (Mountain View, CA: Pacific Press®, 1943), 713.
2. Francis D. Nichol, ed., *The Seventh-day Adventist Bible Commentary*, vol. 2 (Washington, DC: Review and Herald®, 1976), 639.
3. White, *Patriarchs and Prophets*, 713.

ENVOYS ABUSED

*And it came to pass after this, that the king of the children
of Ammon died, and Hanun his son reigned in his stead.*
—2 Samuel 10:1

Nahash "had shown kindness to David when he was a fugitive from the rage of Saul."[1] But Nahash never forgave Saul for coming to the aid of Jabesh-gilead (1 Samuel 11:1–11). As Saul was the enemy of David, it stood to reason that the enemy of Nahash's enemy was his friend. Thinking that Hanun, Nahash's son, must be grieving the loss of his father, David sent ambassadors to express condolences. Apparently, Nahash had never really embraced David as a friend, and his scornful attitude toward all of Israel colored his son's attitude toward David.

The Ammonite princes convinced the young king that David's emissaries were spying on their defenses and suggested a radical insult be administered to these "spies." So Hanun ordered half of each ambassador's beard cut off and their long robes shortened to a ridiculous length. It was, and still is, customary among nations to treat ambassadors with respect, so these actions essentially constituted a declaration of war. When informed of the treatment his ambassadors had received, David ordered them to tarry in Jericho until their beards grew back. As a full beard was a sign of dignity, shaving off any remaining portion so as to be clean-shaven was not an option.[2]

"It was by the advice of his counselors that Nahash, half a century before, had been led to make the cruel condition required of the people of Jabesh-gilead, when, besieged by the Ammonites, they sued for a covenant of peace. Nahash had demanded the privilege of thrusting out all their right eyes. The Ammonites still vividly remembered how the king of Israel had foiled their cruel design, and had rescued the people whom they would have humbled and mutilated. The same hatred of Israel still prompted them. They could have no conception of the generous spirit that had inspired David's message. When Satan controls the minds of men he will excite envy and suspicion which will misconstrue the very best intentions."[3]

Consider this: had the ambassadors succeeded in making peace, Israel would have formed an alliance with treacherous heathen people. Man's ways are not God's ways.

---

1. Ellen G. White, *Patriarchs and Prophets* (Mountain View, CA: Pacific Press®, 1943), 714.
2. Francis D. Nichol, ed., *The Seventh-day Adventist Bible Commentary*, vol. 2 (Washington, DC: Review and Herald®, 1976), 642.
3. White, *Patriarchs and Prophets*, 714.

PSALM 20: GOD SAVE THE KING

Now know I that the LORD saveth his anointed; he will hear him
from his holy heaven with the saving strength of his right hand.
—Psalm 20:6

Psalm 20 is a three-part song to be sung by choirs of people. Verses 1–5 were to be sung by all the people, verses 6–8 by the king alone, and the last verse again by the people in response. It is a prayer of intervention, asking the Lord to accompany the king as he goes into battle. It is the wish of the congregation that God hear David's plea for help and that the Lord will defend their king against his enemies. They want all his battle plans to be successful and victory to be theirs. "Grant thee according to thine own heart, and fulfil all thy counsel. We will rejoice in thy salvation, and in the name of our God we will set up our banners" (vv. 4, 5).

David responds to his people's wish for success with confidence because the Lord will indeed grant him victory. "Now know I that the LORD saveth his anointed; he will hear him from his holy heaven with the saving strength of his right hand" (v. 6). His confidence has been built by God's deliverance from myriad past difficulties and trials. God will accomplish great things through us and for us if we trust Him.

Verses 7 and 8 may interest students of warfare: "Some trust in chariots, and some in horses: but we will remember the name of the LORD our God. They are brought down and fallen: but we are risen, and stand upright." Remember that "Pharaoh trusted in chariots (Ex. 14:7). David's northern enemies, the Syrians, were especially formidable because of their use of chariots and horsemen (see 1 Chron. 18:4; 19:18); his own troops seem to have consisted entirely of infantry. . . . It was never God's plan that His people should have to rely upon brute force for victory (see Deut. 17:16). This verse is a wonderful confession of faith in the right as against confidence in might."[1] The last verse of the psalm was to be sung by the congregation in response to the king's solo. "Save, LORD: let the king hear us when we call" (Psalm 20:9).

"God save our gracious king, / Long live our noble king, / God save the king. / Send him victorious, / Happy and glorious, / Long to reign over us, / God save the king."[2]

---

1. Francis D. Nichol, ed., *The Seventh-day Adventist Bible Commentary*, vol. 3 (Washington, DC: Review and Herald®, 1977), 679.

2. Anonymous, "God Save Our Gracious King," in *The Church Hymnal: The Official Hymnal of the Seventh-day Adventist Church* (Washington, DC: Review and Herald®, 1941), hymn 506.

THE AMMONITE-SYRIAN ALLIANCE

And when the children of Ammon saw that the Syrians were fled, then fled they also before Abishai, and entered into the city. So Joab returned from the children of Ammon, and came to Jerusalem.
—2 Samuel 10:14

Israel's military power alarmed the countries bordering Canaan. Victory after victory increased the fear that they would eventually be swallowed up by David's forces. Realizing war was inevitable, Hanun, king of Ammon, hired Syrian mercenaries (1 Chronicles 19:6, 7). Together, they hoped to overwhelm Israel and gain victory. "It was indeed a formidable alliance. The inhabitants of the region lying between the river Euphrates and the Mediterranean Sea had leagued with the Ammonites. The north and east of Canaan was encircled with armed foes, banded together to crush the kingdom of Israel.

"The Hebrews did not wait for the invasion of their country. Their forces, under Joab, crossed the Jordan and advanced toward the Ammonite capital."[1]

Joab found himself between two forces. If he advanced on one, the other would fall upon his rear guard. Joab's only advantage lay in the fact he had a consolidated force. Dividing his army, he had one-half attack one way while the other half attacked in the opposite direction simultaneously. "The best of the Israelite troops were chosen for the attack on the Syrians, since with their chariots and cavalry they formed the strongest part of the enemy forces. Joab himself took charge of these troops."[2] The fate of Israel rested upon the outcome of this battle. Joab's forces and his brother Abishai's forces were fighting back to back. Each trusted the other to come to his aid if needed. Had the Syrians resisted Israel's attack, the Ammonites would have advanced to encircle the embattled Israelite army, but the Syrians fled. When the Ammonites saw their allies leaving, they lost heart and retreated into their city. Joab could not pursue the rapidly fleeing Syrian chariots, and he was not prepared to lay siege to the Ammonite capital. Instead, he led the victorious Hebrew army home to Jerusalem.

Just because we resist the occasional temptation does not mean our war against sin is over!

---

1. Ellen G. White, *Patriarchs and Prophets* (Mountain View, CA: Pacific Press®, 1943), 715.
2. Francis D. Nichol, ed., *The Seventh-day Adventist Bible Commentary*, vol. 2 (Washington, DC: Review and Herald®, 1976), 643.

Syria Defeated

And when the Syrians saw that they were smitten before Israel, they gathered themselves together.
—2 Samuel 10:15

Hadarezer, the Syrian king of Zobah, was embarrassed by the cowardly behavior of his troops against the Israelites. Surely the Syrian army was stronger than that of Israel. To be driven from the field of battle in disorder was unacceptable. "Previously the Syrians had entered the conflict only as hired auxiliaries, but now they determined to fight to restore their lost prestige. Hadarezer's influence extended beyond the Euphrates, into territory that later was distinctly Assyrian, and thence he drew additional forces to bolster his strength."[1] David now faced the most solemn crisis of his reign. A call went out to muster the entire nation to arms, and David took the field himself. Shobach, the commander of the Syrian host, gathered his army east of the Jordan River. David crossed the Jordan and opposed the Syrian host.

David's forces destroyed "seven hundred chariots of the Syrians, and forty thousand horsemen" (2 Samuel 10:18). The book of 2 Samuel emphasizes the cavalry, while the book of 1 Chronicles stresses the infantry (1 Chronicles 19:18). Both accounts tell of a humiliating Syrian defeat. Through the blessing of God, David defeated the Syrians, and they became tributary to Israel. While the Ammonites had joined Syria in an alliance for strength, David had relied on strength from God, and that made all the difference.

The "vassal kings who had been tributary to Hadarezer now transferred their allegiance to David and paid tribute to him. God had predicted through Abraham (Gen. 15:18) and Moses (Deut. 11:24) that the dominion of Israel would extend to the Euphrates, and these prophecies were now fulfilled. Israel had become a mighty power that was to be reckoned with by the nations about. The countries that had arrayed themselves against Israel had been laid low, and the efforts to crush David served only to enhance his power and prestige. No weapon directed against God or the people of God can prosper."[2]

"There may be periods of trial and difficulty, but from every trial the cause of God will emerge victorious."[3]

---

1. Francis D. Nichol, ed., *The Seventh-day Adventist Bible Commentary*, vol. 2 (Washington, DC: Review and Herald®, 1976), 644.
2. Nichol, 644.
3. Nichol, 644.

DAVID'S SONG OF DELIVERANCE

And he said, The LORD is my rock, and my fortress,
and my deliverer; The God of my rock; in him will I trust:
he is my shield, and the horn of my salvation, my high tower,
and my refuge, my saviour; thou savest me from violence.
—2 Samuel 22:2, 3

D avid wrote Psalm 18 in recognition of the marvelous deliverance he received from the Lord. (The psalm is repeated in 2 Samuel 22 with variations.) In God, David finds a refuge as solid and steadfast as the mountains, which served as sanctuaries for him in the past. When surrounded by rocks and crags, David is comforted by their fastness and strength. God likewise never fails him, for He is as solid and trustworthy as the rocks and as eternal as the hills.

God is David's shield against the powerful blows of his enemies. Second Samuel 22:2, 3 vividly pictures a warrior in a fierce struggle against an enemy. The shield wards off the blows of the wicked and protects the innocent. Like the horns of a bull, God provides both protection and defensive strength. While Psalm 18 does not include the phrase "my refuge, my saviour," the word *saviour* sums up the entirety of those adjectives that have gone before.

David praises the power and vigilance of God. For the Lord constantly looks down upon David's distress and, with great wrath, executes vengeance upon his enemies. God is surrounded by lightning and thunder, and at His approach, the earth shakes. David's enemies are pelted with "hail stones and coals of fire" (Psalm 18:13). Thus, David is saved from a host of enemies. God gives him the swiftness, bravery, and supremacy needed to crush his enemies. Though David's path has been steep and rocky, God leads him with the surefootedness of a mountain goat. With God at his side, no foe can stand before him. "God was more than a theory or a mere abstraction to David—he had learned to know Him as a personal Friend and Saviour, and he now expresses his grateful praise to Him for His wonderful deliverance and care."[1]

"I have found a friend in Jesus, / He's ev'rything to me, / He's the fairest of ten thousand to my soul. . . . / A wall of fire about me, I've nothing now to fear— / With His manna He my hungry soul shall fill."[2]

---

1. Francis D. Nichol, ed., *The Seventh-day Adventist Bible Commentary*, vol. 2 (Washington, DC: Review and Herald®, 1976), 703.
2. Charles W. Fry, "The Lily of the Valley" (1881).

PSALM 18: GOD IS MY STRENGTH

The LORD is my rock, and my fortress, and my deliverer;
my God, my strength, in whom I will trust; my buckler,
and the horn of my salvation, and my high tower.
—Psalm 18:2

G od providentially delivered, and David expressed his gratitude:
"The LORD liveth; and blessed be my rock; and let the God of my
salvation be exalted. It is God that avengeth me, and subdueth
the people under me. He delivereth me from mine enemies: yea, thou
liftest me up above those that rise up against me: thou hast delivered
me from the violent man. Therefore will I give thanks unto thee, O LORD,
among the heathen, and sing praises unto thy name" (Psalm 18:46–49).

This psalm covers the entirety of David's struggle with his enemies.
From each one, David emerged victorious. "This commemorative Song
of Triumph is heart history, the story of a human heart ever devoted to
God and sincere in its integrity in the things of God."[1] God's intervention on behalf of His servant David is depicted as the forces of nature in
all their magnificent power—Jehovah is in them all (vv. 7–15)!

Verses 16–19 relate that "God intervened because David did not deserve the treatment he was receiving at the hands of Saul and his other
enemies. God rewards and recompenses according to His eternal law.
Verses 20–30 enlarge on the reason for God's delivering David."[2] This
psalm was written prior to David's sin with Bathsheba; after that event,
he could not write, "I was also upright before him, and I kept myself
from mine iniquity. Therefore hath the LORD recompensed me according
to my righteousness, according to the cleanness of my hands in his eyesight" (vv. 23, 24).

David writes, God is the "God of my salvation" (Psalms 25:5; 27:9;
38:22; 51:14; 88:1). He saw "the importance of the union of human and
divine effort. God arms His servant with material means of protection
and then gives him support as he employs these means."[3]

"God moves in a mysterious way / His wonders to perform; / He plants His
footsteps in the sea, / And rides upon the storm."[4]

---

1. Francis D. Nichol, ed., *The Seventh-day Adventist Bible Commentary*, vol. 3 (Washington,
DC: Review and Herald®, 1977), 669.
2. Nichol, 672, 673.
3. Nichol, 673.
4. William Cowper, "God Moves in a Mysterious Way," in *The Seventh-day Adventist Hymnal*
(Hagerstown, MD: Review and Herald®, 1985), hymn 107.

PSALM 21: VICTORY!

The king shall joy in thy strength, O LORD;
and in thy salvation how greatly shall he rejoice!
—Psalm 21:1

P salm 21 was written for public worship. "It is a psalm of thanksgiving on the success of the campaign for which the preceding
psalm was the supplication. It has three parts: direct thanksgiving
to God on behalf of the king (vs. 1–7), an address to the king (vs. 8–12),
and a final ejaculation of praise (v. 13)."[1] Part of verse 2 has entered the
English vernacular: "Thou hast given him his heart's desire, and hast not
withholden the request of his lips." We speak of obtaining our "heart's
desire" as having our fondest wish realized.

God gave King David and his army victory over the Syrians. The enemy was daunting, yet their chariots and horses had no success. It had
been anticipated God would give Israel victory (Psalm 20:5, 6, 9). That
victory had been achieved in a miraculous fashion. The congregation
recognized God had worked through their king. "For the king trusteth
in the LORD, and through the mercy of the most High he shall not be
moved" (Psalm 21:7). God had blessed David repeatedly during his lifetime, and the expectation was He would continue to bless the king with
long life and joy (vv. 4–6). The people recognized God had caused His
face to shine upon David. "For thou hast made him most blessed for
ever: thou hast made him exceeding glad with thy countenance" (v. 6).
The congregation thus thanked God for blessing their king.

The second part of Psalm 21 is addressed to King David. Following
this victory, there is confidence that all the king's enemies will be vanquished (v. 8). Enemy plans will fail (v. 11). David's forces will encircle
and destroy the fleeing enemy (v. 12). Psalm 21 closes with a final shout
of praise to the Lord. "Be thou exalted, LORD, in thine own strength: so
will we sing and praise thy power" (v. 13). David also asks God to lend
His strength to His people. "Here is a final picture of universal praise
(see Rev. 7:10–12; 12:10; 19:1–3)."[2]

"Praise God, from whom all blessings flow; / Praise Him, all creatures here be-
low; / Praise Him above, ye heavenly host; / Praise Father, Son, and Holy Ghost."[3]

1. Francis D. Nichol, ed., *The Seventh-day Adventist Bible Commentary*, vol. 3 (Washington,
DC: Review and Herald®, 1977), 680.
2. Nichol, 681.
3. Thomas Ken, "Praise God, From Whom All Blessings Flow" (1695), in *The Seventh-day
Adventist Hymnal* (Hagerstown, MD: Review and Herald®, 1985), hymns 694, 695.

Psalm 46: A Place of Safety

God is our refuge and strength, a very present help in
trouble. Therefore will not we fear, though the earth be
removed, and though the mountains be carried into the midst
of the sea; Though the waters thereof roar and be troubled,
though the mountains shake with the swelling thereof.

—Psalm 46:1–3

P salm 46 has been a source of strength and solace to Christians through the ages. It has been called Luther's Psalm because it is said that Martin Luther sang it during times of trouble, and this is reflected in his amazing song "A Mighty Fortress." "It may well be the hymn of God's people during the increasing perils of the last days."[1] God reigns supreme over all earthly powers, and He provides His people a place of refuge (vv. 1–3). "The convulsions of nature, the earthquake that throws the mountains into the sea, the roaring of the waves, the cataclysm of the tidal wave—these phenomena as well as any commotions and revolutions in the political world need not shake the one who trusts in God. Whatever may happen, God is a proved refuge."[2]

The psalm depicts the world in turmoil (vv. 1–3) and then shows the calm and serenity God gives His followers during mayhem (vv. 4–7). God's city sits placidly amid the chaos of the kingdoms of the earth. Nations rise and fall, but God's city shall not be moved. "The Lord of hosts is with us; the God of Jacob is our refuge" (v. 7). This is the crux of the entire psalm. "We have nothing to fear for the future, except as we shall forget the way the Lord has led us, and His teaching in our past history."[3]

God will ultimately cause war to cease, and all nations will bow in submission to His power. The picture painted is one of a battlefield in ruin—broken bows, burned chariots, and severed spears litter the ground. God reigns supreme, and all is serene. "Be still, and know that I am God: I will be exalted among the heathen, I will be exalted in the earth" (v. 10).

"When storms of sharp distress invade; . . . Behold Him present with His
aid!"[4]

---

1. Francis D. Nichol, ed., *The Seventh-day Adventist Bible Commentary*, vol. 3 (Washington, DC: Review and Herald®, 1977), 744.
2. Nichol, 744.
3. Ellen G. White, *Life Sketches of Ellen G. White* (Mountain View, CA: Pacific Press®, 1943), 196.
4. Isaac Watts, "God Is the Refuge of His Saints," in *The Church Hymnal: The Official Hymnal of the Seventh-day Adventist Church* (Washington, DC: Review and Herald®, 1941), hymn 89.

DAVID AND BATH-SHEBA

And it came to pass in an eveningtide, that David arose from off his bed, and walked upon the roof of the king's house: and from the roof he saw a woman washing herself; and the woman was very beautiful to look upon.
—2 Samuel 11:2

When spring arrived, David sent Joab and the army back to besiege Rabbah and finish the task of subduing the Ammonites while he remained in Jerusalem (2 Samuel 11:1). David was now triumphant at home and abroad. "But in the midst of prosperity lurked danger. In the time of his greatest outward triumph David was in the greatest peril, and met his most humiliating defeat."[1] "Feeling himself strong and secure against his earthly enemies, intoxicated by his prosperity and success, while receiving the plaudits of men, Israel's honored hero and saint was thrown off his guard. Imperceptibly the inner defenses of his soul had weakened, until he yielded to a temptation that transformed him into a shameless sinner."[2]

David walked onto the roof of the palace and saw a beautiful woman bathing. He learned she "was the wife of Uriah the Hittite, one of David's bravest and most faithful officers."[3] David sent for her. "There is no indication that David's messengers took Bath-sheba by force. Bath-sheba was beautiful, and she was not beyond temptation. Possibly she was flattered by the overtures made to her by the king, and yielded herself to David without resistance."[4]

A pregnancy resulted from this encounter. Under God's law, the penalty for adultery was death for both parties (Leviticus 20:10). Bath-sheba made her pregnancy known to David and sought his help. The injured party in a case of adultery might avenge him or herself by slaying both parties that had engaged in prohibited sex. Uriah would have been within his rights to kill both David and Bath-sheba regardless of the fact one guilty party was the king. The pregnancy could not be long hidden. Their sin would soon become public knowledge.

Avoid lust! It often results in numerous bad decisions and ends in sorrow and regret.

1. Ellen G. White, *Patriarchs and Prophets* (Mountain View, CA: Pacific Press®, 1943), 716.
2. Francis D. Nichol, ed., *The Seventh-day Adventist Bible Commentary*, vol. 2 (Washington, DC: Review and Herald®, 1976), 646.
3. White, *Patriarchs and Prophets*, 718.
4. Nichol, *The Seventh-day Adventist Commentary*, 2:647.

FAITHFUL URIAH

*But Uriah slept at the door of the king's house with all
the servants of his lord, and went not down to his house.*
—2 Samuel 11:9

U riah was a Hittite. "The Hittites as a people were warlike and brave. David's offense was particularly grievous since Bath-sheba was a married woman and her husband was one of David's most noble and trusted officers, a man of an alien race who had been brought in contact with the religion of the true God."[1] David devised a plan. If he could get Uriah to sleep with Bath-sheba, he might conceal the identity of the child's father. David ordered Joab to send Uriah to Jerusalem with dispatches. This would not seem odd as Uriah was familiar with all aspects of the siege at Rabbah and could further report on Joab's management of the siege.

Once Uriah's report was delivered, David instructed him to go home to his wife and relax. However, Uriah slept in the palace guardroom. When told Uriah had not gone home, David asked, "Why then didst thou not go down unto thine house?" (2 Samuel 11:10). Uriah's reply showed his desire to share the trials and undergo the privations his men were experiencing in the field. Why should he enjoy benefits they could not? He swore he would not break faith with his men (v. 11). "It seems strange that he would make an issue of such a point in opposition to the king. It was either pervfervid loyalty and patriotism or a suspicion of the truth."[2]

David tried another tactic—he got Uriah intoxicated, hoping this would get him to go home to his wife. But Uriah spent a second night with the troops in the guardhouse (vv. 12, 13). In desperation, David decided to murder him. David ordered Joab to place Uriah at the front of the next assault, then the men around him were to fall back, leaving him exposed. This was done, and Uriah fell at the gates of Rabbah with his men. Joab, whose allegiance was to David rather than God, became an accomplice to murder simply because his king told him to do so.

"So low had David sunk that he made his trusted officer the bearer of his own death warrant. The valor of Uriah was to pay the price for the king's transgression."[3]

---

1. Francis D. Nichol, ed., *The Seventh-day Adventist Bible Commentary*, vol. 2 (Washington, DC: Review and Herald®, 1976), 647.
2. Nichol, 648.
3. Nichol, 648.

THE AFTERMATH

And the shooters shot from off the wall upon thy
servants; and some of the king's servants be dead,
and thy servant Uriah the Hittite is dead also.
—2 Samuel 11:24

I t was murder, pure and simple, chargeable first to the king and next to Joab, who carried out David's orders. Implicit obedience to the orders of superiors is not a virtue when it leads to disobedience of the laws of God. If Joab had been a truly upright man, willing to give a word of honest remonstrance . . . , Uriah and his men need not have been sent to their untimely deaths. But David had as his commander in chief a man with apparently few conscientious scruples, a man willing to become a party to foul murder to please his king."[1]

Joab sent word to David: the deed is done. Joab knew David would question sending a detachment of men against the most strongly defended portion of the enemy's wall. He wanted David to know his orders had been followed, even though they had no basis for success. "Then David said unto the messenger, Thus shalt thou say unto Joab, Let not this thing displease thee, for the sword devoureth one as well as another: make thy battle more strong against the city, and overthrow it: and encourage thou him" (2 Samuel 11:25).

When Bath-sheba was told her husband was dead, she mourned his death for the prescribed seven days (Genesis 50:10; 1 Samuel 31:13). As soon as the mourning period was over, David sent for Bath-sheba to make her his wife. At this time, David was already married to Michal (daughter of Saul), Abigail (former wife of Nabal), Ahinoam of Jezreel, Maacah (daughter of King Talmai of Geshur), Haggith, Abital, and Eglah (2 Samuel 2–6). The result of David's sins of adultery, deceit, and murder would plague his family for decades. Satan makes sin appear attractive. "But the Lord in His kindness allows men to see that the results of sin are not increased prosperity and happiness, but misery, woe, and death."[2]

"There is a way which seemeth right unto a man, but the end thereof are the ways of death" (Proverbs 14:12).

---

1. Francis D. Nichol, ed., *The Seventh-day Adventist Bible Commentary*, vol. 2 (Washington, DC: Review and Herald®, 1976), 649.
2. Nichol, 649.

NATHAN REBUKES DAVID

And Nathan said to David, Thou art the man.
—2 Samuel 12:7

A s time passed, it became common knowledge that David was the father of Bathsheba's unborn child. It was rumored he had also orchestrated Uriah's death. David was God's anointed and, as such, both the civic and religious leader of the people. He who was to enforce God's law appeared guilty of breaking it with impunity. God sent the prophet Nathan to rebuke the king and show him the enormity of his transgression. "To few sovereigns could such a reproof be given but at the price of certain death to the reprover. Nathan delivered the divine sentence unflinchingly, yet with such heaven-born wisdom as to engage the sympathies of the king, to arouse his conscience, and to call from his lips the sentence of death upon himself. Appealing to David as the divinely appointed guardian of his people's rights, the prophet repeated a story of wrong and oppression that demanded redress."[1]

"There were two men in one city; the one rich, and the other poor. The rich man had exceeding many flocks and herds: But the poor man had nothing, save one little ewe lamb, which he had bought and nourished up: and it grew up together with him, and with his children; it did eat of his own meat, and drank of his own cup, and lay in his bosom, and was unto him as a daughter. And there came a traveller unto the rich man, and he spared to take of his own flock and of his own herd, to dress for the wayfaring man that was come unto him; but took the poor man's lamb, and dressed it for the man that was come to him" (2 Samuel 12:1–4).

David was incensed by this injustice. "As the LORD liveth, the man that hath done this thing shall surely die: And he shall restore the lamb fourfold, because he did this thing, and because he had no pity" (vv. 5, 6). Nathan, staring directly at the king, raised his right hand to heaven and gravely declared, "Thou art the man" (v. 7). David realized he had just passed judgment upon himself. David had tried to hide his secret, "but all things are naked and opened unto the eyes of him with whom we have to do" (Hebrews 4:13).

David's fall is a warning to all Christians to guard the portals of the heart and mind.

---

1. Ellen G. White, *Patriarchs and Prophets* (Mountain View, CA: Pacific Press®, 1943), 720, 721.

"A MAN AFTER GOD'S OWN HEART"?

And David said unto Nathan, I have sinned against the LORD. And Nathan said unto David, The LORD also hath put away thy sin; thou shalt not die.
—2 Samuel 12:13

D avid listened as Nathan pronounced the judgment of the Lord. The sword would never depart from the descendants of David (see 2 Samuel 12:10). David's sin would jeopardize his ability to command the respect of his family. His influence over the people would be damaged. Where David had sinned in secret and tried to cover up his actions, God now stated his punishment would be open for all to see (v. 12). With eyes now open, David recoiled with horror from his selfish actions. God had blessed him and placed him on the throne of Israel. He had promised David's seed would reign forever. In return, David abused God's blessings and used his position as king to do evil in the sight of God. As the nation's religious ideal, David had failed to set a positive example.

In slaying Uriah and then taking his wife, "David committed an offense that throughout the ages has given enemies of the Lord the opportunity to blaspheme and reproach God's holy name."[1] Scoffing, they say, "A man after his [God's] own heart" (1 Samuel 13:14; see also Acts 13:22)? He committed these horrific deeds and sinned appallingly, but God just ignored his acts and did not require his death, as required by law (2 Samuel 12:13). Did God, therefore, sanction David's behavior?

"Few have been guilty of any baser sin, any greater ingratitude, any more intense or brutal selfishness than was David in his murder of Uriah. Yet when he sincerely acknowledged his sin the Lord readily granted forgiveness and restored him to divine favor. At the same time a course such as David pursued is fraught with extreme danger. Repentance involves a change in the basic attitude of the sinner toward his sin. Men generally sin because they love to. This makes it difficult for them to be sorry for a sin they deliberately planned and purposely executed. . . . Any man interested only in receiving forgiveness for past transgression while planning to repeat his sin, is insincere and seeks forgiveness in vain."[2]

True repentance requires a change in behavior and an honest endeavor to never repeat the offense.

---

1. Francis D. Nichol, ed., *The Seventh-day Adventist Bible Commentary*, vol. 2 (Washington, DC: Review and Herald®, 1976), 652.
2. Nichol, 652, 653.

THE WAGES OF SIN

But when David saw that his servants whispered, David perceived that the child was dead: therefore David said unto his servants, Is the child dead? And they said, He is dead.
—2 Samuel 12:19

David had pronounced the death sentence upon himself (2 Samuel 12:5), but God said Bath-sheba's child would die (v. 14). "To David the death of the child would be a far greater punishment than his own death. As a result of the bitter experience he would pass through, David would be brought to a full measure of repentance and conversion.

". . . Even after He has pronounced judgment God has sometimes seen fit to turn aside the penalty in response to sincere repentance and earnest petitions to Him (Ex. 32:9–14; cf. Jonah 3:4–10). David knew that God was 'merciful and gracious, longsuffering, and abundant in goodness and truth' (Ex. 34:6). He therefore pleaded earnestly for forgiveness and for the life of the child. However, this does not imply that he refused submission to the divine will. He simply hoped that God's mercy might spare the child."[1]

It was not to be. David, learning of the infant's death, cleansed himself and went to the house of the Lord to worship. The servants were amazed by his reaction. "And he said, While the child was yet alive, I fasted and wept: for I said, Who can tell whether GOD will be gracious to me, that the child may live? But now he is dead, wherefore should I fast? can I bring him back again? I shall go to him, but he shall not return to me" (2 Samuel 12:22, 23).

"These words portray David's resignation to the will of God, and his understanding of the state of the dead. After the child had died, there was nothing further he could do about the matter, and he humbly accepted the inevitable."[2] The people of Israel understood one who died went into the grave to sleep with his fathers (2 Samuel 7:12; 1 Kings 1:21; 2:10; 2 Kings 22:20). David was saying he would eventually join his son in death, but his son would not be returning from the grave. There was nothing he could do to change these facts (Ecclesiastes 9:5, 6).

"The judgments upon him [David] and upon his house testify to God's abhorrence of the sin."[3]

---

1. Francis D. Nichol, ed., *The Seventh-day Adventist Bible Commentary*, vol. 2 (Washington, DC: Review and Herald®, 1976), 653.
2. Nichol, 653.
3. Ellen G. White, *Patriarchs and Prophets* (Mountain View, CA: Pacific Press®, 1943), 723.

PSALM 32: A PRAYER OF CONFESSION

I acknowledge my sin unto thee, and mine iniquity have
I not hid. I said, I will confess my transgressions unto
the LORD; and thou forgavest the iniquity of my sin.
—Psalm 32:5

D avid composed Psalms 32 and 51 following his sin with Bath-sheba. As with many of the psalms David wrote, Psalm 32 contains personal facts as well as guidance for those who are experiencing similar problems. Verses 1–5 review with the ordeal David was going through following the realization of his grievous sins against Bath-sheba, Uriah, Joab, and God. Verses 6–11 provide counsel for those who wish to confess their own sins.

"Confession (1 John 1:9) is of value only when accompanied by repentance. Some Christians confuse the two processes and claim forgiveness on the ground of acknowledgment of guilt alone. But God is interested in the practical aspects of the case. Besides sorrow for sin, repentance includes the expulsion of sin from the life. . . .

"Many Christians seem to be more concerned with obtaining forgiveness for their sins than with ridding the soul of all known sin. . . .

" 'The righteousness of Christ will not cover one cherished sin.'. . . Before this precious gift can be imputed, the old, tattered garments of inherited and cultivated wrongdoing must be laid aside. This was the experience of David. It was on this basis that he obtained forgiveness for his great sin. His repentance was genuine. He loathed the sin of which he had been guilty."[1]

For a whole year after sinning against Uriah and Bathsheba, David's conscience troubled him (Psalm 32:3, 4).[2] Only when he acknowledged and confessed his sin (v. 5) was he relieved of guilt. God stands ever ready to forgive the sins of those who are sincere in seeking pardon (vv. 6, 7). Concern for the consequences of one's actions is not enough to secure His forgiveness. Those who would follow the Lord in all things must pray and read the Bible daily. Only thus may we intelligently know what is required of us in every situation (v. 8). Animals must sometimes be forced onto the right path, but we have been given the intelligence to choose our own paths (v. 9). Those who have been forgiven will not be able to keep silent (vv. 7, 10, 11).

"I've wandered far away from God, / Now I'm coming home."[3]

1. Francis D. Nichol, ed., *The Seventh-day Adventist Bible Commentary*, vol. 3 (Washington, DC: Review and Herald®, 1977), 706.
2. Nichol, 707.
3. William J. Kirkpatrick, "Lord, I'm Coming Home" (1902), in *The Seventh-day Adventist Hymnal* (Hagerstown, MD: Review and Herald®, 1985), hymn 296.

PSALM 51, PART 1: THE PENITENT'S PSALM

Create in me a clean heart, O God; and renew a right spirit within me.
—Psalm 51:10

Psalm 51 "is a penitential psalm. . . . It was composed by David 'after his great sin [with Bath-sheba], in the anguish of remorse and self-abhorrence.'. . . It is an expression of his 'repentance, when the message of reproof came to him from God,' intended 'to be sung in the public assemblies of his people, . . . that others might be instructed by the sad history of his fall.'. . . It is a prayer for forgiveness and for sanctification through the Holy Spirit."[1]

David realized the depths to which he had sunk. He was inconsolable in the anguish he felt because he had sinned against God and his fellow man. He, therefore, sought to blame no one but himself. The language of his psalm is beautiful! "Have mercy upon me, O God, according to thy lovingkindness: according unto the multitude of thy tender mercies blot out my transgressions. Wash me throughly from mine iniquity, and cleanse me from my sin. For I acknowledge my transgressions: and my sin is ever before me. Against thee, thee only, have I sinned, and done this evil in thy sight: that thou mightest be justified when thou speakest, and be clear when thou judgest" (Psalm 51:1–4). While acknowledging he had sinned against Uriah and Bath-sheba, David also recognized all sin is really sin against God. David realized he shared the sinful propensities all members of the human race possess (v. 5), but he was confident God would forgive him and cleanse his sinful heart (Ezekiel 36:26). But asking for forgiveness with the intention of repeating the same sin is insincerity in its most scandalous form.

David realized he had grieved the Holy Spirit, and so he pleaded for the Spirit's return (Psalm 51:11). He wanted his burden of guilt lifted so he might feel the joy he once felt (v. 12). Recognizing salvation comes only from God (v. 14), David requests deliverance from the burden of sin weighing him down. Verse 17 sums up all David can offer the Lord in the way of an acceptable sacrifice—"a broken spirit: a broken and a contrite heart."

"Trusting only in Thy merit, / Would I seek Thy face; / Heal my wounded, broken spirit, / Save me by Thy grace."[2]

---

1. Francis D. Nichol, ed., *The Seventh-day Adventist Bible Commentary*, vol. 3 (Washington, DC: Review and Herald®, 1977), 755.

2. Fanny J. Crosby, "Pass Me Not, O Gentle Savior" (1868), in *The Seventh-day Adventist Hymnal* (Hagerstown, MD: Review and Herald®, 1985), hymn 569.

PSALM 51, PART 2:
FORGIVENESS REQUIRES REPENTANCE

Wash me throughly from mine iniquity, and cleanse me from my sin.
For I acknowledge my transgressions: and my sin is ever before me.
—Psalm 51:2, 3

avid's repentance was sincere and deep. . . . He saw the enormity of his transgression against God; . . . he loathed his sin. It was not for pardon only that he prayed, but for purity of heart. . . . In the promises of God to repentant sinners he saw the evidence of his pardon and acceptance. . . .

"Though David had fallen, the Lord lifted him up. He was now more fully in harmony with God and in sympathy with his fellow men than before he fell. . . .

"Many have murmured at what they called God's injustice in sparing David, whose guilt was so great, after having rejected Saul for what appear to them to be far less flagrant sins. But David humbled himself and confessed his sin, while Saul despised reproof and hardened his heart in impenitence.

"This passage in David's history is full of significance to the repenting sinner. It is one of the most forcible illustrations given us of the struggles and temptations of humanity, and of genuine repentance toward God and faith in our Lord Jesus Christ. Through all the ages it has proved a source of encouragement to souls that, having fallen into sin, were struggling under the burden of their guilt. Thousands of the children of God, who have been betrayed into sin, when ready to give up to despair have remembered how David's sincere repentance and confession were accepted by God, notwithstanding he suffered for his transgression; and they also have taken courage to repent and try again to walk in the way of God's commandments.

"Whoever under the reproof of God will humble the soul with confession and repentance, as did David, may be sure that there is hope for him. Whoever will in faith accept God's promises, will find pardon. The Lord will never cast away one truly repentant soul. He has given this promise: 'Let him take hold of My strength, that he may make peace with Me; and he shall make peace with Me.' Isaiah 27.5."[1]

"Show pity, Lord; O Lord, forgive! / Let a repenting sinner live; / Are not Thy mercies large and free? / May not the guilty trust in Thee?"[2]

---

1. Ellen G. White, *Patriarchs and Prophets* (Mountain View, CA: Pacific Press®, 1943), 725, 726.
2. Isaac Watts, "Show Pity, Lord," *The Church Hymnal: The Official Hymnal of the Seventh-day Adventist Church* (Washington, DC: Review and Herald®, 1941), hymn 240.

PSALM 77: WILL GOD CAST ME OFF?

Will the Lord cast off for ever? and will he be favourable no more?
Is his mercy clean gone for ever? doth his promise fail for evermore?
—Psalm 77:7, 8

The psalmist David in his experience had many changes of mind. At times, as he obtained views of God's will and ways, he was highly exalted. Then as he caught sight of the reverse of God's mercy and changeless love, everything seemed to be shrouded in a cloud of darkness. But through the darkness he obtained a view of the attributes of God, which gave him confidence and strengthened his faith. But when he meditated upon the difficulties and danger of life, they looked so forbidding that he thought himself abandoned by God because of his sins. He viewed his sin in such a strong light that he exclaimed, 'Will the Lord cast off for ever? [and] will he be favorable no more?' [Psalm 77:7.]

"But as he wept and prayed, he obtained a clearer view of the character and attributes of God, being educated by heavenly agencies, and he decided that his ideas of God's justice and severity were exaggerated. He rejected his impressions as being the result of his weakness, ignorance, and physical infirmities, and as dishonoring to God, and with renewed faith he exclaimed, 'This is my infirmity; but I will remember the years of the right hand of the Most High.' [Verse 10.] Most earnestly he studied the ways of God, expressed by Christ when enshrouded in the pillar of cloud, and given to Moses to be faithfully repeated to all Israel. He called to mind what God had wrought to secure for Himself a people to whom He could entrust sacred and vital truth for future ages.

"God wrought most wondrously to free more than a million people; and as David considered His pledges and promises to them, knowing they were for all who need them as much as for Israel, he appropriated them to himself, saying, 'I will remember the works of the Lord: surely I will remember thy wonders of old. I will meditate also of all thy work, and talk of thy doings.' [Verses 11, 12.]"[1] David testified that God cares for all with love, tender mercy, and patience.

"Blessed Lord, how much I need Thee! / Weak and sinful, poor and blind; / Take my trembling hand and lead me; / Strength and sight in Thee I find."[2]

---

1. Ellen G. White, "Rightly Dividing the Word," in *Letters and Manuscripts,* vol. 11 (Silver Spring, MD: Ellen G. White Estate, n.d.), MS 4, 1896 (February 4, 1896).
2. F. E. Belden, "Blessed Lord, How Much I Need Thee!," in *The Church Hymnal: The Official Hymnal of the Seventh-day Adventist Church* (Washington, DC: Review and Herald®, 1941), hymn 578.

DAVID TAKES RABBAH

And David gathered all the people together,
and went to Rabbah, and fought against it, and took it.
—2 Samuel 12:29

T he story of Bath-sheba and the killing of Uriah interrupted the biblical narrative of the war against the Ammonites. Now the focus shifts back to the siege of Rabbah. The city was on a lower level than the walled citadel, which stood apart at the top of a cliff. Once the lower city with its water source fell, the upper city could not hold out. Joab sent word to David that he should come down immediately and direct the final assault (2 Samuel 12:27, 28).

"The siege of Rabbah was practically over. The most important part of the city had already fallen, and it was evident that the rest of the city would soon be in Israelite hands. Joab graciously extended the invitation to David to bring the rest of the forces of Israel, that the king might take the city in person and have the glory of its capture.

". . . When David took Jerusalem, it was given the name 'city of David' (ch. 5:7, 9). It seems that Joab planned that Rabbah, after its capture, should receive, not his name, but David's."[1] David mustered the people and went down to Rabbah. The city did not last long before Israel triumphed.

"And he [David] took their king's crown from off his head, the weight whereof was a talent of gold with the precious stones: and it was set on David's head. And he brought forth the spoil of the city in great abundance" (v. 30). As a talent weighed around seventy-five pounds, it is doubtful David, or any other king, wore it for long. "The same Hebrew consonants that here form the words 'their king' also form the name Malcham (or Milcom), the national god of the Ammonites (Zeph. 1:5). Some thus believe that the crown taken by David was that of the idol rather than of the king, since the crown would seem to be too heavy to be worn by a man."[2] David put the Ammonites to work as laborers (2 Samuel 12:31). The war was over.

"Let the wicked forsake his way, and the unrighteous man his thoughts: and let him return unto the LORD, *and he will have mercy upon him; and to our God, for he will abundantly pardon" (Isaiah 55:7).*

---

1. Francis D. Nichol, ed., *The Seventh-day Adventist Bible Commentary*, vol. 2 (Washington, DC: Review and Herald®, 1976), 654.
2. Nichol, 654.

PSALM 103: PRAISE OUR FORGIVING GOD!

The LORD is merciful and gracious, slow to anger, and
plenteous in mercy. He will not always chide: neither will
he keep his anger for ever. He hath not dealt with us after
our sins; nor rewarded us according to our iniquities.

—Psalm 103:8–10

P salm 103 is enthusiastic in its praise of God for His mercy and kindness. "In it David praises God for blessings in his own life (vs. 1–5), tells of the loving-kindness God exercises toward His children generally (vs. 6–14), shows man's dependence upon the mercy [of] God (vs. 15–18), and invites the whole creation to worship God (vs. 19–22)."[1] "Bless the LORD, O my soul, and forget not all his benefits: Who forgiveth all thine iniquities; who healeth all thy diseases; Who redeemeth thy life from destruction; who crowneth thee with lovingkindness and tender mercies; Who satisfieth thy mouth with good things; so that thy youth is renewed like the eagle's" (vv. 2–5).

From the time of Moses, God had shown mercy to Israel. "As far as the east is from the west, so far hath he removed our transgressions from us. Like as a father pitieth his children, so the LORD pitieth them that fear him" (vv. 12, 13). Israel had not been treated as their sins required but rather with mercy and forgiveness (vv. 8–10). Although humankind is weak and our time on this earth is short, God "knoweth our frame; he remembereth that we are dust. As for man, his days are as grass: as a flower of the field, so he flourisheth. For the wind passeth over it, and it is gone; and the place thereof shall know it no more" (vv. 14–16). The fact we are frail, helpless beings brings forth all-encompassing compassion from our Creator.

David ends his psalm by calling on all of creation to bless the Lord. "Bless the LORD, ye his angels, that excel in strength, that do his commandments, hearkening unto the voice of his word" (v. 20). David ends the psalm exactly as he started it: "Bless the LORD, O my soul" (v. 22). Knowing the entire universe is singing the praises of God, David adds his voice to the song!

"From all that dwell below the skies / Let the Creator's praise arise; / Let His almighty name be sung / Through every land, by every tongue."[2]

---

1. Francis D. Nichol, ed., *The Seventh-day Adventist Bible Commentary*, vol. 3 (Washington, DC: Review and Herald®, 1977), 861.

2. Isaac Watts, "From All That Dwell Below the Skies," in *The Church Hymnal: The Official Hymnal of the Seventh-day Adventist Church* (Washington, DC: Review and Herald®, 1941), hymn 2.

AMNON AND TAMAR

And it came to pass after this, that Absalom the son of David had a fair sister, whose name was Tamar; and Amnon the son of David loved her.
—2 Samuel 13:1

The result of David's sin with Bath-sheba slowly took root. "His own sons refused to obey him and no longer respected his counsel. Where before he had been strong and courageous, he now became weak and hesitant. A sense of shame constantly hung over him."[1] The defects found in David's character had found a place in the characters of his sons. Absalom's sister was Tamar. Both were the children of Maacah, the daughter of the king of Geshur. Amnon was the son of "Ahinoam the Jezreelitess" (2 Samuel 3:2) and was David's firstborn son. Amnon lusted after his half-sister Tamar, for she was a beautiful virgin. When Amnon explained the problem to his cousin Jonadab, Jonadab suggested Amnon act ill. When the king would check on Amnon, he should request Tamar bring him food, then take her.

The plot played out as planned. In ordering Tamar to serve her brother, David set in motion a string of events that would end in the death of his son, shame to his daughter, and ultimately threaten the very throne.

Amnon ordered his court cleared. He then ordered Tamar to bring the food into his bedchamber. Alone with his half sister, he took hold of her and said, "Come lie with me, my sister" (v. 11). Tamar refused his advances, saying if he persisted in his demands, he would look the fool and she would be disgraced (vv. 12, 13).

"Amnon was utterly selfish, lustful, and determined to have his own way regardless of consequences. He could not be reasoned with. The requirements of God, the virtue of his sister, and the honor of his own name meant nothing to him. For these characteristics David was in part to blame. He avoided bringing his children to account when they did wrong, and permitted them to have their own way. Now they were beyond reason and restraint."[2] Amnon raped Tamar, and then he ordered his servants to remove her from his presence and bolt the door behind her.

How could David punish his son for doing what he himself had once done? Even confessed sins must sometimes run their course, bringing additional pain and sorrow.

---

1. Francis D. Nichol, ed., *The Seventh-day Adventist Bible Commentary*, vol. 2 (Washington, DC: Review and Herald®, 1976), 655, 656.
2. Nichol, 657.

ABSALOM AVENGES TAMAR

Now Absalom had commanded his servants, saying, Mark ye
now when Amnon's heart is merry with wine, and when I say
unto you, Smite Amnon; then kill him, fear not: have
not I commanded you? be courageous, and be valiant.
—2 Samuel 13:28

Tamar made no attempt to hide her shame. She tore her colorful robes and left Amnon's presence in tears. "Thus she prevented Amnon from inventing the tale that she had been guilty of misconduct toward him and for this reason had been expelled from his presence. Tamar was evidently entirely sincere, her actions betokening the keen indignation and grief that were hers. Had she kept quiet she might have been considered a party to the crime."[1] Absalom immediately knew something was wrong. Instead of taking direct legal action as was his right, Absalom delayed. Amnon's crime angered David, but he failed in his duty to execute justice for Tamar.

" 'He shall restore fourfold,' had been David's unwitting sentence upon himself, on listening to the prophet Nathan's parable; and according to his own sentence he was to be judged. Four of his sons must fall, and the loss of each would be a result of the father's sin.

"The shameful crime of Amnon, the first-born, was permitted by David to pass unpunished and unrebuked. The law pronounced death upon the adulterer, and the unnatural crime of Amnon made him doubly guilty. But David, self-condemned for his own sin, failed to bring the offender to justice. For two full years Absalom, the natural protector of the sister so foully wronged, concealed his purpose of revenge, but only to strike more surely at the last."[2]

The opportunity arose at the annual sheepshearing festival. Absalom skillfully obtained the king's blessing to hold a feast attended by all of David's sons. David declined to attend, and Amnon was appointed to represent his father as heir apparent and eldest son. David may have been suspicious when he asked, "Why should he go with thee?" (2 Samuel 13:26). In the end, Amnon attended. Absalom had his servants get him drunk and then execute him.

Consider: David's sons had now acted out the exact sins he had committed in taking Bath-sheba and slaying Uriah.

---

1. Francis D. Nichol, ed., *The Seventh-day Adventist Bible Commentary*, vol. 2 (Washington, DC: Review and Herald®, 1976), 657.
2. Ellen G. White, *Patriarchs and Prophets* (Mountain View, CA: Pacific Press®, 1943), 727.

ABSALOM FLEES

So Absalom fled, and went to Geshur, and was there three years.
—2 Samuel 13:38

The brothers of Absalom fled in terror. They were not entirely sure Absalom was not killing all heirs to the throne to secure his own position as heir apparent. News reached David that Absalom had killed all the princes. David tore his clothes and fell to the ground in grief. His servants tore their clothes in sympathy with the agony of the king at such a horrendous loss of life. What must have gone through David's mind as he recalled the reservations he had about allowing all his sons to congregate in one place at one time? "Exaggerated as the report was, David accepted it as true. His very hesitancy in agreeing to have his sons attend the feast suggests that he had some misgivings. In fact he consented only after urgings (see vs. 26, 27), and then probably against his better judgment. Now he believed that his worst fears had been realized and that a general massacre of all the royal princes had taken place."[1]

Jonadab's evil suggestion to Amnon had started this disastrous chain of events. Now, seeking to ingratiate himself with the king, he said, "Let not my lord suppose that they have slain all the young men the king's sons; for Amnon only is dead: for by the appointment of Absalom this hath been determined from the day that he forced his sister Tamar. Now therefore let not my lord the king take the thing to his heart, to think that all the king's sons are dead: for Amnon only is dead" (2 Samuel 13:32, 33). Jonadab knew a day of reckoning was eventually coming for Amnon. He no doubt feared Absalom would also seek him out for retribution for his part in the rape.

David's surviving sons made their way to Jerusalem, bearing shocking news. They had witnessed the murder of their eldest brother. Jonadab was not slow in pointing out he had been right concerning the death of Amnon. Absalom fled north to Geshur, knowing he would not be safe in Israel. Here, east of the Sea of Galilee, he found sanctuary with Talmai, king of Geshur, his mother's father.

God corrected what David neglected. Events sometimes take their natural course, and God does not intervene to restrain the evil of sin punishing sin.

1. Francis D. Nichol, ed., *The Seventh-day Adventist Bible Commentary*, vol. 2 (Washington, DC: Review and Herald®, 1976), 658, 659.

A WISE WOMAN'S TALE

*And thy handmaid had two sons, and they two strove
together in the field, and there was none to part them,
but the one smote the other, and slew him.*

—2 Samuel 14:6

J oab knew Absalom felt betrayed by David. Forced into exile, Absalom
was cut off from the affairs of the state and his immediate family. He had
only avenged the dishonor of his sister, which his father should have
adjudicated in the first place. The longer their estrangement lasted, the
more bitter Absalom became toward his father's refusal to allow him to
come home. Joab felt the time had come to attempt a reconciliation between the two. Seeking out a woman he knew from the town of Tekoah,
just south of Bethlehem, Joab invented a parable he felt sure would bring
forth from David a judgment applicable to the situation existing between
himself and Absalom. The woman would have to be subtle in the presen-
tation of her case so David would not suspect it also pertained to him.

Claiming to be a widow, she said her two sons had quarreled in the field
one day, and one brother had killed the other. The entire family demanded
the woman surrender her remaining son so they might kill him to avenge the
death of the murdered son. This would leave no family heir. Their lineage and
her dead husband's name would cease to exist. David promised her remaining son would be protected, even though the law clearly required death for
the crime of murder. The woman asked that any guilt for this pardon be on
her head and not the king's. David reassured the woman he would also protect her from harm. Pressing him for more assurance, she got David to swear
an oath before God that the life of her remaining son would be protected.

David had just mercifully pardoned a fictitious murderer for killing his fictitious brother. Why was he not treating his own son, guilty of the same crime,
with equal justice? The woman called his attention to the similarity. Amnon
was dead. Nothing could change that fact. Why not restore Absalom to his
family? God forgives the sinner. Why not David? David now saw clearly that
the people of Israel wished Absalom to be forgiven and returned home. If
God forgave David's sins, why could David not forgive his son's? Surely the
Lord would honor the king for doing what was right and merciful.

*"It is of the Lord's mercies that we are not consumed, because his compas-
sions fail not" (Lamentations 3:22).*

ABSALOM BROUGHT HOME

And the king said unto Joab, Behold now, I have done this thing: go therefore, bring the young man Absalom again.
—2 Samuel 14:21

David thought he saw the hand of Joab in the story the woman had told regarding her two sons. Joab had probably spoken to him of the unfairness he perceived in banishing Absalom. As Joab had persisted in his attempts to get David to pardon Absalom, this parable was likely just another bid to get him to reconsider his stance on the matter. David now asked the woman a very pointed question: "Hide not from me, I pray thee, the thing that I shall ask thee. . . . Is not the hand of Joab with thee in all this?" (2 Samuel 14:18, 19). And she answered David, "Thy servant Joab, he bade me, and he put all these words in the mouth of thine handmaid: To fetch about this form of speech hath thy servant Joab done this thing: and my lord is wise, according to the wisdom of an angel of God, to know all things that are in the earth" (vv. 19, 20).

Joab had finally convinced David that bringing Absalom home was the right thing to do. David commissioned his general to bring the young man home. Joab was grateful that David had reconsidered, because had he not agreed, Joab might have been held responsible for attempting to influence the king by going behind his back to trick him. "And Joab fell to the ground on his face, and bowed himself, and thanked the king: and Joab said, To day thy servant knoweth that I have found grace in thy sight, my lord, O king, in that the king hath fulfilled the request of his servant" (v. 22).

The fact Absalom was back in no way changed David's mind as to the murderer of his firstborn son. Absalom was still banished from court, and David refused to see him. All this did was embitter Absalom further and cause the populace to feel he was still being wronged. After all, Absalom had only administered justice that David failed to sanction. The people sympathized with Absalom and believed he was a hero.

"Absalom lived two years in his own house, but banished from the court. His sister dwelt with him, and her presence kept alive the memory of the irreparable wrong she had suffered."[1]

Why did David not consult with God regarding the decision to bring Absalom home?

---

1. Ellen G. White, *Patriarchs and Prophets* (Mountain View, CA: Pacific Press®, 1943), 729.

235

ABSALOM REINSTATED

So Joab came to the king, and told him: and when he had called for Absalom, he came to the king, and bowed himself on his face to the ground before the king: and the king kissed Absalom.

—2 Samuel 14:33

E ssentially, Absalom had upheld the law by seeking justice for his sister. He had returned home but was still banished from seeing his father. "Absalom was selfish and unscrupulous, ambitious and impulsive. He was admired by the people and was gradually winning their sympathies. It was hardly the part of wisdom for David to allow such a situation to continue."[1]

Joab had been successful in persuading David to allow Absalom to return to Jerusalem. Now Absalom sought to have him intercede once again on his behalf. Joab refused to answer Absalom's summons. Absalom sent for him a second time, and again Joab refused to answer. Perhaps Joab realized he had pushed David to his limit, and no further movement on the topic was to be gained. Pushing further might anger David and result in penalties.

Absalom called his servants and said, "See, Joab's field is near mine, and he hath barley there; go and set it on fire. And Absalom's servants set the field on fire" (2 Samuel 14:30). This was sure to bring Joab to Absalom's house to inquire as to why such a deed had been done. When Joab came to complain, Absalom made no excuse for his arson. Instead, he said, "Behold, I sent unto thee, saying, Come hither, that I may send thee to the king, to say, Wherefore am I come from Geshur? it had been good for me to have been there still: now therefore let me see the king's face; and if there be any iniquity in me, let him kill me" (v. 32).

"Absalom treated Joab as his servant, giving to him his orders and expecting them to be carried out. His conduct reveals how far he had already gone in his course of rebellion and his determination to secure a redress of his supposed grievances and a restoration to privileges he believed to be rightfully his."[2] Joab gained the audience with David that Absalom sought. David rose and kissed his son, showing at least a superficial reunion.

"Be not hasty in thy spirit to be angry: for anger resteth in the bosom of fools" (Ecclesiastes 7:9).

---

1. Francis D. Nichol, ed., *The Seventh-day Adventist Bible Commentary*, vol. 2 (Washington, DC: Review and Herald®, 1976), 664, 665.
2. Nichol, 665.

ABSALOM'S TREACHERY

And on this manner did Absalom to all Israel that came to the king
for judgment: so Absalom stole the hearts of the men of Israel.
—2 Samuel 15:6

A bsalom sought to impress the people by appointing a personal bodyguard to accompany him whenever he rode in his chariot. This display showed he considered himself to be the next king. Daily he sat at the city gate and questioned those coming to seek redress from David. Being a skilled politician, Absalom gained their gratitude and loyalty. "Absalom assumed an air of benignity and righteous indignation at the sad state of affairs. If only he were judge, the people would not be deprived of their rights, for he would see that the situation was quickly remedied. Every cause for dissatisfaction he turned to his own advantage and against the king. At every opportunity he expressed his sympathies and regrets at the inefficiencies of administration, and his earnest wish to set things right."[1]

It was not long before the people were openly advocating the abdication of David in favor of his son. Absalom now moved to the next phase of his plan. He told David he had sworn a sacred oath that if the Lord allowed him to return to Jerusalem, he would serve the Lord faithfully. He, therefore, asked permission to go to Hebron to fulfill that vow. David bade him go in peace. Hebron was the birthplace of Absalom (2 Samuel 3:2, 3) and was the site of David's first capital. Many in Hebron were still unhappy that David had moved the capital and its commerce to Jerusalem. Absalom fooled his father into thinking he was a dutiful son. He now sent spies throughout the land, telling his followers to say he had been crowned king at Hebron.

In Ahithophel the Gilonite, David's counselor, Absalom had a valuable ally who furthered the conspiracy. Ahithophel "was estranged from David by personal resentment over David's misconduct against Bathsheba, Ahithophel's granddaughter. . . . His son Eliam ([2 Sam.] 23:34) was the father of Bath-sheba (ch.11:3)."[2]

Absalom thought he had foreseen every detail in his plot to be made king, but
he failed to see his ambition would lead to his own demise.

---

1. Francis D. Nichol, ed., *The Seventh-day Adventist Bible Commentary*, vol. 2 (Washington, DC: Review and Herald®, 1976), 666, 667.
2. Nichol, 668.

DAVID FLEES JERUSALEM

*And David said unto all his servants that were with him at Jerusalem,
Arise, and let us flee; for we shall not else escape from Absalom:
make speed to depart, lest he overtake us suddenly, and bring
evil upon us, and smite the city with the edge of the sword.*
—2 Samuel 15:14

News of the rebellion reached David in Jerusalem. As if awakening
from a long sleep, David shook off his lethargy and regained his
fighting spirit. The son he had trusted had plotted against him,
and some of those he had relied on most had gone over to the enemy.
David knew the public was not on his side in this struggle. Looking out
over his beloved Jerusalem, David trembled to think what would become
of the beautiful city should war occur. David would leave the city rather
than see it destroyed. From afar, he would seek to rally loyal followers. He
would trust in God, who had placed him on the throne in the first place.

Absalom had issued a call for those supporting him to come to Hebron, which was only twenty miles from Jerusalem. David, who was not
prepared to face this crisis, chose to retire and fight another day. This decision proved "to have been the correct course of action. Both Ahithophel
([2 Sam.] 17:1, 2) and Hushai (ch. 17:7–13) recognized that delay would
be fatal, and that Absalom's greatest hope for success would be to take
immediate steps against David. By his flight David gave himself time to
make ready a defense, and the people time to ponder their course. The
horrors of a long civil war were thus averted."[1]

"David was never more worthy of admiration than in his hour of adversity. Never was this cedar of God truly greater than when wrestling
with the storm and tempest. He was a man of the keenest temperament,
which might have been raised to the strongest feelings of resentment. . . .
But there was nothing of this which would naturally be expected of a man
with his stamp of character. With spirits broken and in tearful emotion,
but without one expression of repining, he turns his back upon the scenes
of his glory and also of his crime, and pursues his flight for his life."[2]

The Christian life is a constant battle to shape a worthy character.

---

1. Francis D. Nichol, ed., *The Seventh-day Adventist Bible Commentary*, vol. 2 (Washington,
DC: Review and Herald®, 1976), 668.
2. Ellen G. White, *Letters and Manuscripts*, vol. 3 (Silver Spring, MD: Ellen G. White Estate,
n.d.), Letter 6, 1880 (September 28, 1880).

ITTAI THE GITTITE

Then said the king to Ittai the Gittite, Wherefore goest thou also with us? return to thy place, and abide with the king: for thou art a stranger, and also an exile.
—2 Samuel 15:19

In humility and sorrow David passed out of the gate of Jerusalem—driven from his throne, from his palace, from the ark of God, by the insurrection of his cherished son. The people followed in long, sad procession, like a funeral train. David's bodyguard of Cherethites, Pelethites, and six hundred Gittites from Gath, under the command of Ittai, accompanied the king. But David, with characteristic unselfishness, could not consent that these strangers who had sought his protection should be involved in his calamity. He expressed surprise that they should be ready to make this sacrifice for him."[1]

David ordered Ittai to return to Jerusalem, but Ittai gave a stirring response: "As the LORD liveth, and as my lord the king liveth, surely in what place my lord the king shall be, whether in death or life, even there also will thy servant be" (2 Samuel 15:21). "These men had been converted from paganism to the worship of Jehovah, and nobly they now proved their fidelity to their God and their king. David, with grateful heart, accepted their devotion to his apparently sinking cause, and all passed over the brook Kidron on the way toward the wilderness."[2]

"It was essential now that he [David] have with him only those in whom he could place the fullest dependence. Thus far these men had proved themselves true. But now that David was engaged in a civil war, he may not have been certain that they would continue loyal.

". . . David's concern for these strangers was well repaid. Treating these men kindly, he found them ready to throw in their lot fully with him.

". . . David could ask for nothing more."[3] It must have warmed David's heart to hear these men pledge to defend him with their lives. The future might look bleak, yet David's spirits were lifted by knowing that the Lord was with him still.

"The LORD is my light and my salvation; whom shall I fear? the LORD is the strength of my life; of whom shall I be afraid?" (Psalm 27:1).

1. Ellen G. White, *Patriarchs and Prophets* (Mountain View, CA: Pacific Press®, 1943), 731.
2. White, 732.
3. Francis D. Nichol, ed., *The Seventh-day Adventist Bible Commentary*, vol. 2 (Washington, DC: Review and Herald®, 1976), 669.

ZADOK AND THE LEVITES

*And lo Zadok also, and all the Levites were
with him, bearing the ark of the covenant of God.*
—2 Samuel 15:24

When David fled Jerusalem, the priests Zadok and Abiathar planned to accompany him and bring with them the ark of the covenant. The priests met the procession clad in holy robes, with Levites shouldering the ark. David's followers believed the arrival of the ark was a good sign. With the ark accompanying them, ultimate victory was assured. Surely Absalom's followers would lament the loss of such a sacred item. The arrival of the ark was therefore greeted with great joy and thanksgiving.

"Not personal interests, but the glory of God and the good of his people, were to be uppermost in the mind of Israel's king. God, who dwelt between the cherubim, had said of Jerusalem, 'This is My rest' (Psalm 132:14); and without divine authority neither priest nor king had a right to remove therefrom the symbol of His presence. And David knew that his heart and life must be in harmony with the divine precepts, else the ark would be the means of disaster rather than of success. His great sin was ever before him. He recognized in this conspiracy the just judgment of God. The sword that was not to depart from his house had been unsheathed. He knew not what the result of the struggle might be. It was not for him to remove from the capital of the nation the sacred statutes which embodied the will of their divine Sovereign, which were the constitution of the realm and the foundation of its prosperity."[1]

"And the king said unto Zadok, Carry back the ark of God into the city: if I shall find favour in the eyes of the LORD, he will bring me again, and shew me both it, and his habitation" (2 Samuel 15:25). David placed his future in the hands of the Lord. He was content to let God determine the outcome of this battle. Knowing the priests were positioned to know everything going on in Jerusalem, David sought to keep them in place as his eyes and ears in the capital. Ahimaaz, son of Zadok, and Jonathan, son of Abiathar, would serve as messengers, carrying vital information from the priests to David.

"Wait on the LORD: be of good courage, and he shall strengthen thine heart: wait, I say, on the LORD" (Psalm 27:14).

---

1. Ellen G. White, *Patriarchs and Prophets* (Mountain View, CA: Pacific Press®, 1943), 732.

MEETING ON THE MOUNT OF OLIVES

And it came to pass, that when David was come to the top of the mount, where he worshipped God, behold, Hushai the Archite came to meet him with his coat rent, and earth upon his head.
—2 Samuel 15:32

As David left the priests, he turned his feet toward the Mount of Olives. Those who followed him had left their homes and belongings. Families had been torn apart by politics. David's followers were fleeing for their lives. At this moment, someone came to him, confirming more disturbing news. "Ahithophel is among the conspirators with Absalom. And David said, O LORD, I pray thee, turn the counsel of Ahithophel into foolishness" (2 Samuel 15:31).

"Again David was forced to recognize in his calamities the results of his own sin. The defection of Ahithophel, the ablest and most wily of political leaders, was prompted by revenge for the family disgrace involved in the wrong to Bathsheba, who was his granddaughter."[1] Upon reaching the top of the mount, David bowed his head in prayer. Everything seemed to be coming apart, and he knew not which way to turn. In deep humility, he asked the Lord for mercy. It seemed as if his prayer was instantly answered.

Who should appear at just this moment but Hushai, the king's loyal and faithful counselor (1 Chronicles 27:33). Hushai had come to throw his lot in with his friend David and share exile with his king. David must have been extremely grateful to receive some good news for a change. Hushai appeared with his coat torn and earth upon his head, signifying he was in mourning. David's greeting to his friend must have puzzled him at first. "If thou passest on with me, then thou shalt be a burden unto me: But if thou return to the city, and say unto Absalom, I will be thy servant, O king; as I have been thy father's servant hitherto, so will I now also be thy servant: then mayest thou for me defeat the counsel of Ahithophel" (vv. 33, 34).

David took Hushai into his confidence by revealing that he should coordinate the passing of information with the priests Zadok and Abiathar. The priests would then task their sons, Ahimaaz and Jonathan, to carry word to David. This spy system might yield valuable information and possibly even defeat the cunning counsel of Ahithophel.

When things look their worst, God often sends help that brightens our attitude.

---

1. Ellen G. White, *Patriarchs and Prophets* (Mountain View, CA: Pacific Press®, 1943), 735.

DAVID AND ZIBA

And when David was a little past the top of the hill, behold, Ziba the servant of Mephibosheth met him, with a couple of asses saddled, and upon them two hundred loaves of bread, and an hundred bunches of raisins, and an hundred of summer fruits, and a bottle of wine.

—2 Samuel 16:1

Just over the crest of the hill, David met Ziba, the servant of Saul, whom he had appointed to care for Mephibosheth. David had some questions. Noticing the supplies being brought, he asked two questions: "What meanest thou by these? . . . And where is thy master's son [Mephibosheth]?" (2 Samuel 16:2, 3). Ziba's answer to the first question seemed logical enough. "The asses be for the king's household to ride on; and the bread and summer fruit for the young men to eat; and the wine, that such as be faint in the wilderness may drink" (v. 2). Cunningly, Ziba sought this moment to curry favor with David, and it cost him little to bestow on David the property of Mephibosheth.

The answer to David's second question was so implausible that David should have recognized the lie. "Behold, he abideth at Jerusalem: for he said, To day shall the house of Israel restore me the kingdom of my father" (v. 3). "Mephibosheth was a cripple and had little to gain from Absalom's revolt. Even if that revolt had proved successful, it would not have given the throne to the seed of Saul, for Absalom wanted the throne for himself. Ziba had probably invented the tale in order to secure certain concessions from David."[1]

Rashly, David believed the slander Ziba had perpetrated upon his master. As a reward for his loyalty, "then said the king to Ziba, Behold, thine are all that pertained unto Mephibosheth. And Ziba said, I humbly beseech thee that I may find grace in thy sight, my lord, O king" (v. 4). David had based his decision on only one side of an unsubstantiated story. It was clearly unfair to Mephibosheth to have his property given away in such a hasty and impulsive manner. Ziba had obtained his master's inheritance through deceit. He had proven himself to be a grasping individual who would stoop so low as to deprive a cripple of every comfort. David had fallen for the lie, believing even Mephibosheth had turned against him.

Beware the schemer bearing gifts and promising friendship.

---

1. Francis D. Nichol, ed., *The Seventh-day Adventist Bible Commentary*, vol. 2 (Washington, DC: Review and Herald®, 1976), 671.

SHIMEI CURSES DAVID

And when king David came to Bahurim, behold, thence came out a man of the family of the house of Saul, whose name was Shimei, the son of Gera: he came forth, and cursed still as he came. And he cast stones at David, and at all the servants of king David.
—2 Samuel 16:5, 6

With sorrow, David turned his back on the capital he loved and made his way down the eastern slope of the Mount of Olives. His followers trudged down steep, rocky paths, passing through natural ravines and bleak wastelands toward the distant river Jordan. It was here that David once again encountered fierce opposition and scorn.

Shimei, a Benjamite and a member of Saul's family, cursed David and threw stones at him from a distance. "Shimei had not previously given any indication that he was disloyal to David. But as soon as adversity struck he showed his true colors. Where previously he had honored David, now he reviled and cursed him. Such a spirit is inspired by Satan, who delights to bring misery upon those who are already suffering misfortune."[1]

Shimei shouted for David to get out of the country (2 Samuel 16:7). He accused him of having the blood of Saul's family on his hands (v. 8). "Shimei's accusations against David were utterly false—a baseless and malignant slander. David had not been guilty of wrong toward Saul or his house. When Saul was wholly in his power, and he could have slain him, he merely cut the skirt of his robe, and he reproached himself for showing even this disrespect for the Lord's anointed."[2] The Lord had rejected Saul and chosen David to lead the nation. Shimei's charge was really against God!

David's nephew Abishai asked for authorization to lop off the head of the contemptible heckler. David refused. Perhaps God told this man to curse David. If so, why question God's motives? Put into that perspective, this man was no threat. The real threat was Absalom, who wanted to kill his own father (vv. 11, 12). This rude behavior could be expected from a member of Saul's family. David humbly accepted it as yet another trial he must endure.

Christians should sympathize with others who are experiencing tough times.

1. Francis D. Nichol, ed., *The Seventh-day Adventist Bible Commentary*, vol. 2 (Washington, DC: Review and Herald®, 1976), 671.
2. Ellen G. White, *Patriarchs and Prophets* (Mountain View, CA: Pacific Press®, 1943), 736.

Psalm 25: God Will Guide the Humble Spirit

The meek will he guide in judgment: and the meek will he teach his way.
—Psalm 25:9

When difficulties arose, David resorted to prayer. It is the privilege of all Christians to pray for clarification to understand the ways of the Lord (Psalm 25:4). Sometimes it is difficult to understand God's leading. Frequently what we perceive as truth is not God's truth (v. 5). As God only wants the best for us, we would do well to humbly pray He might light our path forward. Remembering how God has led us in the past brings peace when present difficulties arise.

Looking back on the sins of youth, we often regret our foolish adolescent acts. So it was with David (v. 7). In retrospect, God always uses these stumbling youthful escapades as means to teach us His way (v. 8). God may correct and admonish us, but He never forsakes us. If we are humble and teachable, He will guide us into better ways (v. 10). "Humility is the first rung of the ladder of Christian growth (see Matt. 18:3)."[1] For those who honor God, He will do great things (Psalm 25:12). "God will so teach him that he will choose the right way. Man is not an automaton. He has the power of choice. But when a man fears God, his power of choice is exercised in the right direction: he chooses God's way."[2] Though the path may be difficult, we are never alone (v. 13). We have a Friend in Jesus!

"God does not keep us out of the snare, if we willfully seek to become entangled, but He promises to deliver and save us."[3] But it is difficult for the proud and arrogant to ask for help. "Blessed are the meek [humble]: for they shall inherit the earth" (Matthew 5:5). David's enemies were many, and they hated him (Psalm 25:19). David prayed that the Lord would not allow his enemies to triumph. He had no problem asking for help (v. 20). David closed this song with a prayer for all of Israel because his subjects were struggling through the same issues he was facing (v. 22).

"Lead, kindly Light, amid the encircling gloom, / Lead Thou me on; / The night is dark, and I am far from home; / Lead Thou me on."[4]

---

1. Francis D. Nichol, ed., *The Seventh-day Adventist Bible Commentary*, vol. 3 (Washington, DC: Review and Herald®, 1977), 692.
2. Nichol, 692.
3. Nichol, 692.
4. John H. Newman, "Lead Kindly Light" (1833), in *The Church Hymnal: The Official Hymnal of the Seventh-day Adventist Church* (Washington, DC: Review and Herald®, 1941), hymn 403.

PSALM 61: A PRAYER IN EXILE

Lead me to the rock that is higher than I.
—Psalm 61:2

I t is believed that David wrote Psalm 61 while in exile at the time of Absalom's rebellion. David had been forced from the city he loved and the sanctuary where he worshiped. He felt so far removed from those beloved locations that it seemed to him as if he were at the ends of the earth (v. 2). How he longed for a high place from which things might look brighter. "It is well to pray not so much for deliverance as for endurance and elevation. Troubles tend to decrease when they are surveyed from a height."[1]

God had protected David and been a refuge when he was beset with past difficulties. This trial was perhaps the most difficult event of his life thus far. But now, all seemed lost. It seemed impossible that God could reward such treachery as Absalom had committed against his father, yet David was the one in exile. It appeared he had lost his throne. The country and many of his subjects had turned on him. His top counselor was a traitor. He no longer lived in the city he loved. Worse still, he could no longer worship God in the sanctuary (v. 4). This was his most bitter disappointment. Still, he never doubted God would protect and shelter him under cover of His wings (v. 4).

Apparently, David had made certain vows to the Lord, and these emboldened him to make daring prayer requests. David was sure God's character would not allow Him to ignore the prayers of an honest supplicant (v. 5). He, therefore, prayed God would extend his life (v. 6). This is "a beautiful prayer for a long and useful life in God's presence, a life controlled by mercy and truth."[2] David closed his prayer by promising to keep the vows made in verse 5. His strongest desire was to worship the Lord once again in the sanctuary of the people (v. 8).

"O sometimes the shadows are deep, / And rough seems the path to the goal; / And sorrows, how often they sweep / Like tempests down over the soul! / O, then to the Rock let me fly, let me fly— / To the Rock that is higher than I."[3]

1. Francis D. Nichol, ed., *The Seventh-day Adventist Bible Commentary*, vol. 3 (Washington, DC: Review and Herald®, 1977), 776.
2. Nichol, 777.
3. Erastus Johnson, "O Sometimes the Shadows Are Deep," in *The Church Hymnal: The Official Hymnal of the Seventh-day Adventist Church* (Washington, DC: Review and Herald®, 1941), hymn 633.

PSALM 64: PROTECT ME
FROM SECRET PLOTS

*Hear my voice, O God, in my prayer: preserve my life from
fear of the enemy. Hide me from the secret counsel of the
wicked; from the insurrection of the workers of iniquity.*
—Psalm 64:1, 2

Psalm 64 is a prayer for deliverance from David's enemies (v. 1). It seemed even those he trusted most had turned against him. Absalom's rebellion had been planned in great secrecy. His accusations had hit the mark, just as arrows fired at a target (v. 3). But David was innocent of the things of which he was being accused (v. 4). The perpetrators of the falsehoods did not fear God's wrath for lying. "They encourage themselves in an evil matter: they commune of laying snares privily; they say, Who shall see them?" (v. 5). They imagined that God could not see what they were plotting.

"They search out iniquities; they accomplish a diligent search: both the inward thought of every one of them, and the heart, is deep" (v. 6). The wicked spent an inordinate amount of time planning their evil deeds. "It would be well for the righteous to be as diligent in the practice of righteousness. Too often godliness becomes an entirely passive matter. No growth in grace is discernible, no new exploits for God are planned. The words of Christ are pertinent, 'The children of this world are in their generation wiser than the children of light' (Luke 16:8)."[1]

Ultimately, God will not allow evil men to triumph (Psalm 64:7). By their own words, they will stand judged and be destroyed. "So they shall make their own tongue to fall upon themselves: all that see them shall flee away" (v. 8). It will come to pass that wise men eventually will come to acknowledge God's deliverance of the righteous (v. 9). "The righteous shall be glad in the LORD, and shall trust in him; and all the upright in heart shall glory" (v. 10). "All God's people, whether involved in the danger that is the subject of the psalm or not, will rejoice in the triumph of the psalmist."[2] And evil will be no more (Revelation 21:27).

"Ne'er think the victory won, / Nor lay thine armor down; / Thy arduous task will not be done / Till thou obtain the crown."[3]

---

1. Francis D. Nichol, ed., *The Seventh-day Adventist Bible Commentary*, vol. 3 (Washington, DC: Review and Herald®, 1977), 781.
2. Nichol, 781.
3. George Heath, "My Soul, Be on Thy Guard" (1781), in *The Seventh-day Adventist Hymnal* (Hagerstown, MD: Review and Herald®, 1985), hymn 605.

PSALM 35: A PRAYER FOR JUSTICE

Plead my cause, O LORD, with them that strive with me:
fight against them that fight against me. Take hold of
shield and buckler, and stand up for mine help.
—Psalm 35:1, 2

Psalm 35 is a clarion cry for help. David implores the Lord to defend him against his accusers. David wants God to fight on his side against those who have turned on him (v. 1). He urges God to take up the large "shield" as well as the smaller "buckler" and act in his defense (v. 2). And not just a passive defense—an active defense is needed. David asks God to draw His spear against those who are persecuting him (v. 3).

David would have the Lord baffle and confuse his enemies (v. 4). He wants to have the angel of the Lord chase and persecute those who wish him harm (vv. 5, 6). He desires that they might fall into the very trap they have set for him (vv. 7, 8). If God will answer this prayer and save David, he will rejoice with his whole being (v. 10). The first ten verses of this psalm contain David's prayer for justice, and the middle verses detail his enemies' actions (vv. 11–18).

False witnesses have testified of untruths about David and his actions (v. 11). David has treated all with kindness and generosity, but these men have vilified him and secretly despised his acts as weakness. Their actions have left David feeling quite alone (see Psalm 38), puzzled, and saddened (Psalm 35:12). David had mourned with these men as if they were his own family (v. 14), but when adversity struck, these same men celebrated and banded together to mock him and stop his return to power (vv. 15, 16). David promises to praise the Lord if He delivers him from these lions who seek his destruction (vv. 17, 18).

The last division of this psalm is a request for divine involvement (vv. 19–28). David knows God has seen the truth and can make known to all that these liars have spread deceit (vv. 19–23). David pleads with God as the Righteous Judge to judge him innocent of those things ascribed to him (v. 24). Evil men think they have won (v. 25), but those who believe in righteousness will praise God for judging David innocent (vv. 27, 28).

"When Thou, my righteous Judge, shalt come, / To call Thy ransomed people home, / Shall I among them stand?"[1]

---

1. Attributed to Selina Hastings, Countess of Huntingdon, "When Thou, My Righteous Judge," in *The Church Hymnal: The Official Hymnal of the Seventh-day Adventist Church* (Washington, DC: Review and Herald®, 1941), hymn 190.

PSALM 62: GOD IS OUR REFUGE

Truly my soul waiteth upon God: from him cometh
my salvation. He only is my rock and my salvation;
he is my defence; I shall not be greatly moved.

—Psalm 62:1, 2

P salm 62 is a short twelve-verse song. The chorus, found in verses 1 and 2, is repeated almost verbatim in verses 5 and 6. The Hebrew word *'ak* (translated as *truly*, *only*, and *surely*) is found six times in this psalm (vv. 1, 2, 4, 5, 6, 9) and emphasize the fact David relies on God and no one else for deliverance. No human being can help him out of the troubles into which he has fallen. David's faith in God never wavers, even when confronted with seemingly impossible odds. He recognized many dire events in his past had flowed from the times he wandered away from the path of righteousness.

"The psalmist observes that not only does his salvation come from God (v. 1); God *is* his salvation."[1] David has been deeply wounded by those supposed friends who spread false rumors about him and attacked his character. How long will the Lord allow these liars to go unpunished? Like a weakened wall or "a tottering fence," they will eventually fall under the weight of their own falsehoods (v. 3), but when? These men gathered secretly to devise plans to bring about the downfall of their "friend." To his face, they acted one way, but behind his back, they acted another (v. 4). Their one goal was to see the downfall of David.

In this psalm, David expresses confidence that God will intervene. Victory is assured. Righteousness will prevail for all who put their trust in the Lord (vv. 5–7). Do not trust riches or other men (vv. 9, 10). The only safe Rock to cling to in times of trouble is Christ! He alone has the power and mercy to deliver justice according to the works of man (vv. 11, 12). "For we must all appear before the judgment seat of Christ; that every one may receive the things done in his body, according to that he hath done, whether it be good or bad" (2 Corinthians 5:10). "When a man is rewarded for well-doing, it is of God's mercy, for no man of himself deserves a reward."[2]

"*Yes, it is so; the judgment hour / Is swiftly hastening to its close; / Then will the Judge, in mighty power, / Descend in vengeance on His foes.*[3]

---

1. Francis D. Nichol, ed., *The Seventh-day Adventist Bible Commentary*, vol. 3 (Washington, DC: Review and Herald®, 1977), 778; emphasis in the original.

2. Nichol, 779.

3. R. F. Cottrell, "O, Solemn Thought" (1886), in *The Seventh-day Adventist Hymnal* (Hagerstown, MD: Review and Herald®, 1985), hymn 417.

PSALM 38: DO NOT FORSAKE ME!

Forsake me not, O LORD: O my God, be not far from me.
Make haste to help me, O Lord my salvation.
—Psalm 38:21, 22

D
avid felt his suffering was the direct result of his sin, and his anguish was made even worse because those who should have been his friends had deserted him in his hour of need. "God does not work a miracle to preserve men from suffering the consequences of violating nature's laws. . . . If men were shielded from the disastrous results of their wrongdoing, sinners would become greatly emboldened in their iniquity.

"However, not all suffering is the direct result of personal sin on the part of the sufferer. Many of the ancients regarded every affliction as the penalty of some wrongdoing either in the sufferer or in his parents (see John 9:2). Conversely they judged the degree of man's guilt by the amount of suffering. 'Satan, the author of sin and all its results, had led men to look upon disease and death as proceeding from God,—as punishment arbitrarily inflicted on account of sin.'. . . Because of this misconception they regarded the heavenly Father as a stern and exacting executor of justice.

"Many Christians are under the same misapprehension. In spite of the lessons of the book of Job, and the lessons taught by Jesus (see Luke 13:16; Acts 10:38; . . .), these Christians look at God as the one who brings disease.

"Here is the true philosophy of suffering: 'Suffering is inflicted by Satan, and is overruled by God for purposes of mercy.'. . . The reason God does not always shield His children from disease and suffering is that if He did, Satan would bring the same charges against God as he did in the case of Job, that God was unfairly placing a hedge about His servant (Job 1:10). God must allow Satan the opportunity to afflict the righteous, so that all charges of unfairness will ultimately be shown to be groundless."[1]

David knew that God was aware of his suffering (Psalm 38:9). He asked for forgiveness and healing. God looks upon the heart of the supplicant and answers according to the devotion found there.

"Come, every soul by sin oppressed, / There's mercy with the Lord, / And He will surely give you rest, / By trusting in His word."[2]

1. Francis D. Nichol, ed., *The Seventh-day Adventist Bible Commentary*, vol. 3 (Washington, DC: Review and Herald®, 1977), 726.
2. J. H. Stockton, "Only Trust Him," in *The Seventh-day Adventist Hymnal* (Hagerstown, MD: Review and Herald®, 1985), hymn 279.

249

PSALM 41: A PSALM OF COMPASSION

Blessed is he that considereth the poor:
the LORD will deliver him in time of trouble.

—Psalm 41:1

P salm 41 "deals with a time of heavy sickness in the life of the psalmist. The suffering is made all the harder to bear by the psalmist's realization that those who formerly were friends are now traitors. The psalm begins with a blessing on those who lovingly help the needy, continues with a description of the treachery of his former friends, and closes with a prayer of hope for restoration. The psalm resembles [Psalm] 38".[1] David believed his illness was the result of some sin he had committed (v. 4). His enemies could not wait for him to die and even wanted to erase his name from history (v. 5). The most poignant verse is verse 6, wherein David laments a false well-wisher's visit to his sickroom. This man "speaks hypocritical words, gathers material for doing him wrong, and carries slanderous tales out of the sickroom. This is a graphic picture of one who poses as a friend, but is the worst of enemies."[2] This false friend then meets with others who share his hatred for the sick man, and collectively they wish him a speedy demise (v. 7).

"In the book of Job the friends of Job actually came to the place where they accused Job of the grossest sins (see Job 22:5–10)."[3] The accusation intensified his suffering because it was not valid (Psalm 41:8). Some believe this psalm was written during the rebellion of Absalom, and David was speaking of Ahithophel, his former friend and counselor (2 Samuel 15:31). How callous must a person be to return evil for kindness? Psalm 41:9 has also been applied to Judas (John 13:18), who shared a table with his Master and then betrayed Him. David is sure God will act counter to the wishes of his enemies and raise him up from his bed of sickness (Psalm 41:10, 11). God imparts blessings on both the righteous and the wicked (Matthew 5:45); therefore, blessings cannot automatically be taken as evidence of God's approval. Yet friends do not betray one another!

"I would be true, for there are those who trust me; / I would be pure, for there are those who care."[4]

---

1. Francis D. Nichol, ed., *The Seventh-day Adventist Bible Commentary*, vol. 3 (Washington, DC: Review and Herald®, 1976), 732, 733.

2. Nichol, 733.

3. Nichol, 733.

4. Howard A. Walter, "I Would Be True" (1906).

PSALM 84: COMMUNAL WORSHIP

For a day in thy courts is better than a thousand.

—Psalm 84:10

D avid misses the fellowship of worship. He misses the connectivity found on sacred grounds. Psalm 84 portrays "the deepest sentiments of every child of God who, deprived of the privilege of communion with fellow Christians, has ever longed for fellowship with his brethren in the corporate worship of God."[1] It is significant that David uses the term "living God" to describe Jehovah (v. 2). He longs to worship the one and only true God, the Lord of hosts, the Living God!

Note this amazing imagery: "Yea, the sparrow hath found an house, and the swallow a nest for herself, where she may lay her young, even thine altars, O LORD of hosts, my King, and my God" (v. 3). "The general meaning of the verse, whose conclusion the poet only implies, is that even the birds have free access to the sacred precincts of the sanctuary, they make their homes there undisturbed, while the psalmist is exiled from the source of his joy, is denied the privilege of worshiping within the sacred enclosure. The nostalgic appeal of this verse is one of the most delicately beautiful expressions of homesickness in the whole realm of literature."[2]

Pilgrims, coming to worship in Jerusalem, often rejoiced to see familiar landmarks and grew increasingly glad as they approached their destination (vv. 5–7). "Here is a lovely illustration of the life of Christians journeying together to the New Jerusalem—by their praise, prayer, and mutual comfort, cheering one another along the way, strengthening their faith in God, and making the way less difficult as they approach the city."[3] David's desire to spend time in the sanctuary is even more poignant when we realize he wrote these words while in exile. He would rather spend one day in the house of the Lord than enjoy a thousand elsewhere (v. 11). We may always worship in spirit and truth (see John 4:20–24) by trusting God completely (Psalm 84:12).

"How pleasant, how divinely fair, / O Lord of hosts, Thy dwellings are! / With longing desire my spirit faints / To meet th' assemblies of Thy saints."[4]

---

1. Francis D. Nichol, ed., *The Seventh-day Adventist Bible Commentary*, vol. 3 (Washington, DC: Review and Herald®, 1977), 828.

2. Nichol, 828.

3. Nichol, 829.

4. Isaac Watts, "How Pleasant, How Divinely Fair," in *The Church Hymnal: The Official Hymnal of the Seventh-day Adventist Church* (Washington, DC: Review and Herald®, 1941), hymn 24.

PSALM 7: A PRAYER FOR EXONERATION

God judgeth the righteous, and God is angry with the wicked every day.
—Psalm 7:11

Psalm 7 is a prayer for vindication and affirmation that God protects the righteous and punishes the wicked according to His law. This psalm may have been written during the time David was in exile. It might also have been written during the time he was hunted by Saul. Either way, it is a plea for justice. The enemy is like a savage lion, seeking to destroy body and soul (v. 2). David is not aware of any wrongdoing on his part. In fact, he had done just the opposite; he had saved his enemy's life during battle (v. 4). David would rather die than live under false criticism (v. 5).

The psalmist asks God to sit in judgment upon those who spitefully use him (v. 6). "David asks God to vindicate the principles of His moral government (see Gen. 18:25)."[1] The people watching David's predicament will rejoice when they see God intervene on his righteous behalf (Psalm 7:7). David is confident that he is not guilty of the crimes of which he is accused. He calls on God to judge him according to his honesty (v. 8). "Although we should continually feel unworthy of salvation, it is proper, when we are unjustly accused, to pray that according to His will God will vindicate us in a particular case, and declare us innocent of false charges."[2]

Because God will never countenance sin, David trusts Him to eventually defend the innocent and punish the wicked (vv. 9–11). "The law that punishment inevitably falls upon the unrepentant sinner is made clear by representing God as a mighty warrior preparing His weapons for the punishment of the wicked (see Deut. 32:41–43)."[3] David describes the sinner as a man digging a hole in loose soil. The deeper he digs, the more dirt caves in on him (Psalm 7:15). The evil he seeks to work upon others becomes his own (Esther 3–7; Proverbs 26:27; Ecclesiastes 10:8). David closes by praising God as the worthy Judge of all humankind (Psalm 7:17).

"The judgment has set, the books have been opened; / How shall we stand in that great day / When every thought, and word, and action; / God, the righteous Judge, shall weigh?"[4]

1. Francis D. Nichol, ed., *The Seventh-day Adventist Bible Commentary*, vol. 3 (Washington, DC: Review and Herald®, 1977), 646.
2. Nichol, 646.
3. Nichol, 647.
4. F. E. Belden, "The Judgment Has Set" (1886), in *The Seventh-day Adventist Hymnal* (Hagerstown, MD: Review and Herald®, 1985), hymn 416.

PSALMS 14 AND 53: A GODLESS SOCIETY

The fool hath said in his heart, There is no God. They are corrupt, they have done abominable works, there is none that doeth good.
—Psalm 14:1

Psalms 14 and 53 are nearly identical. Both describe the moral corruption of our world. "The fool may profess God for social and business purposes, but 'in his heart' there is no room for a belief in God (see Rom. 1:20, 21)."[1] Paul uses portions of this psalm to prove all are sinners. "As it is written, There is none righteous, no, not one" (Romans 3:10). Here is "a picture of God, contrary to the fool's claims (v. 1), bending over the ramparts of heaven to scrutinize the activities of mortals (see Ps. 102:19). The world seems ripe for judgment, as in Noah's time."[2]

David questions why sinners foolishly think God does not see their actions (Psalm 14:4). Paul amplified this text to show that many in his day denied the existence of Jehovah. "How then shall they call on him in whom they have not believed? and how shall they believe in him of whom they have not heard? and how shall they hear without a preacher?" (Romans 10:14).

God will protect the believer, but terror will seize the wicked when He rises up in indignation and judges them (Psalm 14:5). These haughty men, who mocked those who believed in God, will finally recognize their mistake and tremble in fear (vv. 5, 6). The ungodly who have profited without acknowledging God are the first to claim He does not exist. "And they say, How doth God know? and is there knowledge in the most High?" (Psalm 73:11). David knows firsthand that God does exist. He hopes Israel will eventually agree and achieve community salvation (Psalm 14:7). Unfortunately, Israel will lose its moral and ethical compass repeatedly, suffer exile, and ultimately fail as a nation under God. Today's nations are rapidly approaching the same point. Lawlessness is rampant. The family unit has disintegrated, and with it, a sense of responsibility to anyone other than self. The nation that fails to recognize and uphold God's laws will fall!

"O joyful day, when He appears / With all His saints, to end their fears! / Our Lord will then His right obtain, / And in His kingdom ever reign."[3]

---

1. Francis D. Nichol, ed., *The Seventh-day Adventist Bible Commentary*, vol. 3 (Washington, DC: Review and Herald®, 1977), 661.

2. Nichol, 662.

3. Anonymous, "Star of Our Hope," in *The Church Hymnal: The Official Hymnal of the Seventh-day Adventist Church* (Washington, DC: Review and Herald®, 1941), hymn 188.

Psalm 55: The Lord Will Sustain

Cast thy burden upon the Lord, and he shall sustain thee:
he shall never suffer the righteous to be moved.

—Psalm 55:22

D avid was brought into great distress by this rebellion. . . . His wisdom from God, his energy and war-like skill, had enabled him to successfully resist the assaults of his enemies. But this unnatural warfare, arising in his own house, and the rebel being his own son, seemed to confuse and weaken his calm judgment. And knowing that this evil had been predicted by the prophet, and that he had brought it upon himself, by his transgressing the commandments of God, destroyed his skill and former unequaled courage."[1]

David has four pleas: "Give ear to my prayer, O God; and hide not thyself from my supplication. Attend unto me, and hear me" (Psalm 55:1, 2). He is beset by guilt and the fear of death (vv. 1–5). He longs to fly from trouble with dove's wings and escape strife (vv. 6–8). "We need to beware of following the instinct that prompts us to escape from circumstances. . . . Our work, our home, our relationships, our responsibilities, are a discipline essential to the development of Christian character. Rather than 'fly away,' we should 'call upon God' (v. 16)."[2]

David could have handled the duplicity of strangers (vv. 9–12), but he finds the treachery and betrayal of a close friend devastating (vv. 13, 14). This confidant had worshiped with David (vv. 13, 14)! Morning, noon, and night, David calls upon God to punish these turncoats (vv. 15–17). The traitor, who had been his close friend, is once again in his thoughts in verse 20. This man, professing friendship, was cunning (v. 21). His betrayal is difficult to bear. Only God can support David and see him triumph over this painful personal loss (v. 22). Evil will be punished, for David trusts God to carry the burden of justice (v. 23).

"Cast thy burden upon the Lord, / And He shall sustain thee; / He never will suffer the righteous to fall."[3]

1. Ellen G. White, *Spiritual Gifts*, vol. 4 (Washington, DC: Review and Herald®, 1945), 89, 90.
2. Francis D. Nichol, ed., *The Seventh-day Adventist Bible Commentary*, vol. 3 (Washington, DC: Review and Herald®, 1977), 764.
3. Psalms 55:22; 16:8, "Cast Thy Burden Upon the Lord," in *The Seventh-day Adventist Hymnal* (Hagerstown, MD: Review and Herald®, 1985), hymn 666.

PSALM 28: DELIVER ME FROM TEMPTATION

The LORD *is my strength and my shield; my heart trusted*
in him, and I am helped: therefore my heart greatly
rejoiceth; and with my song will I praise him.
—Psalm 28:7

D avid faced the prospect of fighting his own kinsmen. Such a
battle would split the nation apart and destroy any hope of
ruling by popular acclaim. David was puzzled because he had
repeatedly prayed, but God had not responded to his plea for guidance
(Psalm 28:1, 2).

Not wishing to be grouped with evildoers, David prays God will not
number him among those who will ultimately receive just punishment
(vv. 3, 4). Many psalms request God to punish David's enemies. This
seems contrary to Christ's statement given during the Sermon on the
Mount: "But I say unto you, Love your enemies, bless them that curse
you, do good to them that hate you, and pray for them which despitefully use you, and persecute you; That ye may be the children of your
Father which is in heaven" (Matthew 5:44, 45). But David understood
the final judgment of the wicked would come as a result of their choice to
follow a course of evil. He likewise knew God would not follow momentary wishes but rather would deal justly with those who did not walk in
the paths of righteousness. During Old Testament times, people equated
sin and the sinner as one entity. As such, calling for the destruction of the
sinner was synonymous with calling for the destruction of evil.

David had been anointed of God. The Hebrew nation was chosen to
represent God on Earth. An attack against either was an attack against
God. Wherever sin is found, David feels justified in calling it by its right
name and asking God to eradicate it (Psalm 28:5). David therefore thanks
God for saving His anointed people (see 1 Peter 2:5, 9). "The wicked
will be destroyed, not because of their malice toward the psalmist, but
because of their malice toward God."[1]

"Anywhere with Jesus I can safely go, / Anywhere He leads me in this world
below; / Anywhere without Him, dearest joys would fade; / Anywhere with
Jesus I am not afraid."[2]

1. Francis D. Nichol, ed., *The Seventh-day Adventist Bible Commentary*, vol. 3 (Washington,
DC: Review and Herald®, 1977), 698.
2. Jessie H. Brown, "Anywhere With Jesus" (1886), in *The Seventh-day Adventist Hymnal*
(Hagerstown, MD: Review and Herald®, 1985), hymn 508.

PSALM 69, PART 1: A PRAYER FOR DELIVERANCE

Hear me, O LORD; for thy lovingkindness is good: turn unto me according to the multitude of thy tender mercies. And hide not thy face from thy servant; for I am in trouble: hear me speedily. Draw nigh unto my soul, and redeem it: deliver me because of mine enemies.
—Psalm 69:16–18

P salm 69 is yet another plea for deliverance. David compares his difficulties here to drowning in deep water with no footing. He is bowed down with anguish and plagued by hostile enemies. David admits he is a sinner, and his sins are known to God (v. 5), yet he can find no specific reason for his enemies to hate him. He has done nothing to cause such virulent hatred (v. 4).

David pleads with God that his situation should not impede others or cause them shame (vv. 6–8). He has done his best to be a sincere follower of God. He donned sackcloth and ashes and fasted, feeling the depth of his separation from God and his need to repent of his sins. These actions had been ridiculed by his enemies. They had reproached his efforts to repent as merely a sham. They had made up stories ridiculing him, making him the target of their jokes (vv. 9–12).

Then David returns to the metaphor of sinking into the deep waters of depression. He pleads for a speedy response (vv. 13–15). He is reliant upon the goodness and mercy of the Lord for redemption (vv. 16–18). God alone knows the pain, shame, dishonor, and lack of pity David is experiencing (vv. 19–21). David therefore requests the sinners defaming him be treated as they deserve and that their names be blotted out of the book of life (vv. 22–28).

David wants justice to prevail and righteousness to triumph. He wants his cause and that of all followers of God to be vindicated. Even though he is currently "poor and sorrowful," he knows God has the power to reverse his situation (v. 29). When he is ultimately rescued, he promises to praise God in song and with thank offerings (vv. 30–33). The people will see his salvation and praise God too. "The psalmist's assurance of deliverance is based on the principle stated in this verse [v. 33]: God cares for the afflicted . . . , 'the poor in spirit' (see Matt. 5:3)."[1]

"I know my heavenly Father knows / The storms that would my way oppose; / But He can drive the clouds away, / And turn my darkness into day."[2]

---

1. Francis D. Nichol, ed., *The Seventh-day Adventist Bible Commentary*, vol. 3 (Washington, DC: Review and Herald®, 1977), 796.

2. S. M. I. Henry, "I Know My Heavenly Father," in *The Church Hymnal: The Official Hymnal of the Seventh-day Adventist Church* (Washington, DC: Review and Herald®, 1941), hymn 591.

PSALM 109: BEWARE OF EVIL MEN

For my love they are my adversaries: but I give myself unto prayer.
And they have rewarded me evil for good, and hatred for my love.
—Psalm 109:4, 5

P salm 109 is yet another appeal for help (vv. 1–5). David asks that his enemies be punished for their evil actions (vv. 6–20). He has endured without retaliating (Matthew 5:11), and he asks God to intervene on his behalf. He ends by thanking God for the deliverance he is sure will occur (Psalm 109:21–31). "The kindness of the psalmist to his enemies was requited by more severe hatred on their part. The greatest demonstration of love toward enemies was seen in Christ, the Son of God (see Rom. 5:7–10). There never was love manifested like His. Despite the manifestation of this love He was betrayed and crucified. Yet in His dying agony His love for His enemies lost none of its ardor as He prayed, 'Father, forgive them; for they know not what they do' (Luke 23:34)."[1]

Apparently, one instigator is leading those spreading vicious lies about David. David calls upon God to ignore the prayers of this individual because he believes him to be truly unrepentant and only seeks to escape punishment (Psalm 109:7). Surely God cannot accept such a prayer (Proverbs 28:9; Isaiah 1:15)! Children often cannot escape their parents' bad example and follow their footsteps into sin (Psalm 109:10). David would punish this man's children, but he wants additional justice. He wants this scoundrel to lack offspring (v. 13). As the Israelites placed great value on family cohesion and the continuance of the family unit, childlessness would be catastrophic for this individual. Inevitably, this man's evil actions will rebound upon his own family.

Feeling helpless (vv. 22–25), David places his entire faith in the merciful Lord he serves (vv. 26, 27). "The psalm closes with the joyous prospect that after the suffering will come the glory, after the cross, the crown." "What matters whether we are cursed by wicked men as long as we know that the blessing of Heaven is resting upon us?"[2]

"Once to every man and nation / Comes the moment to decide, / In the strife of truth with falsehood, / For the good or evil side."[3]

1. Francis D. Nichol, ed., *The Seventh-day Adventist Bible Commentary*, vol. 3 (Washington, DC: Review and Herald®, 1977), 879.
2. Nichol, 879.
3. James Russell Lowell, "Once to Every Man and Nation" (1845), in *The Seventh-day Adventist Hymnal* (Hagerstown, MD: Review and Herald®, 1985), hymn 606.

PSALM 58: HUMAN JUDGES ARE UNJUST

So that a man shall say, Verily there is a reward for the
righteous: verily he is a God that judgeth in the earth.
—Psalm 58:11

Psalm 58 contrasts duplicitous human judges with God, the righteous Judge. David sarcastically asks earthly judges, "Do ye indeed speak righteousness, O congregation? do ye judge uprightly, O ye sons of men?" (v. 1). He answers, "Yea, in heart ye work wickedness; ye weigh the violence of your hands in the earth" (v. 2).

Like adders, they pretend to be deaf to the song of charmers. They stubbornly refuse to follow truth (vv. 4, 5). They have always been this way, and it is doubtful they will ever change (v. 3). The psalmist uses multiple metaphors asking God to destroy these ministers of injustice.

David likens corrupt judges to young lions wreaking havoc upon the innocent (v. 6). He asks God to break their teeth so they might no longer harm the innocent (Psalm 3:7). He wants them to melt away like water soaking into the desert sand or see them evaporate under a hot summer sun (Psalm 58:7). David wants them destroyed like a snail trapped under a hot sun (v. 8). It matters not how God destroys them, just that He does it quickly. Verse 9 is an interesting metaphor: "Before your pots can feel the thorns, he shall take them away as with a whirlwind." "The picture is not entirely clear. Some think it is that of desert nomads building a fire in the open air; a gust of wind puts out the fire before the cooking vessels are warmed."[1]

The righteous shall rejoice in the destruction of the wicked (v. 10), and a reward awaits those who overcome (Isaiah 3:10; John 14:3; 1 Timothy 4:8). "Although it may at times seem that God permits the wrong and injustice of earth to continue unhindered, the fact remains that His eye is upon all the misdeeds of sinful men, that He is keeping a strict account, and that in due time He will interpose."[2]

"When Jesus shall gather the nations, | Before Him at last to appear, | Then how shall we stand in the judgment, | When summoned our sentence to hear?"[3]

---

1. Francis D. Nichol, ed., *The Seventh-day Adventist Bible Commentary*, vol. 3 (Washington, DC: Review and Herald®, 1977), 770.

2. Nichol, 770.

3. Harriet B. M'Keever, "When Jesus Shall Gather the Nations," in *The Church Hymnal: The Official Hymnal of the Seventh-day Adventist Church* (Washington, DC: Review and Herald®, 1941), hymn 538.

PSALM 69, PART 2: CHRIST'S MISSION FORETOLD

*For the zeal of thine house hath eaten me up; and the
reproaches of them that reproached thee are fallen upon me.*
—Psalm 69:9

Paul, writing in Romans 11:9, attributes Psalm 69 to David: "And David saith, Let their table be made a snare, and a trap, and a stumblingblock, and a recompense unto them." David and Paul both refer to hardened sinners who refuse to repent. Prophetic phrases found in Psalm 69 are applicable to the life of Christ. Jesus described His reception at the hands of Israel's priests and rulers: "They hated me without a cause" (John 15:25). "In the language of [verses 8, 9, 20] . . . , Christ foretold, through David, the treatment that He was to receive from men."[1] "I am become a stranger unto my brethren, and an alien unto my mother's children" (Psalm 69:8).

David wanted, above all things, to build a temple for God in Jerusalem. He wanted the ark to be given a permanent resting place where all believers might come to worship in peace. By the time of Christ's advent, the temple had ceased to be a place of quiet meditation and had become a bustling marketplace, filled with shouting merchants. Jesus wanted His Father's house to once again be called a house of prayer and not a raucous marketplace. He subsequently drove out the merchants and money changers with righteous zeal, thereby incurring their wrath and hatred. John uses Psalm 69:9 to describe the cleansing of the temple by Christ and the ensuing hatred it generated toward Him (John 2:13–17). Paul uses the same verse to describe Christ's reception by Israel: "For even Christ pleased not himself; but, as it is written, The reproaches of them that reproached thee fell on me" (Romans 15:3).

Psalm 69:20, 21 describe Christ's future agony in Gethsemane and on Calvary: "Reproach hath broken my heart; and I am full of heaviness: and I looked for some to take pity, but there was none; and for comforters, but I found none. They gave me also gall for my meat; and in my thirst they gave me vinegar to drink."

"Go to dark Gethsemane, / Ye that feel the tempter's power; / Your Redeemer's conflict see; / Watch with Him one bitter hour."[2]

1. Francis D. Nichol, ed., *The Seventh-day Adventist Bible Commentary*, vol. 3 (Washington, DC: Review and Herald®, 1977), 794.

2. James Montgomery, "Go to Dark Gethsemane" (1820), in *The Seventh-day Adventist Hymnal* (Hagerstown, MD: Review and Herald®, 1985), hymn 157.

WHY ME?

And the king, and all the people that were with him,
came weary, and refreshed themselves [beside the Jordan].
—2 Samuel 16:14

C onscience was uttering bitter and humiliating truths to David. While his faithful subjects wondered at his sudden reverse of fortune, it was no mystery to the king. He had often had forebodings of an hour like this. He had wondered that God had so long borne with his sins, and had delayed the merited retribution. And now in his hurried and sorrowful flight, . . . he thought of his loved capital— of the place which had been the scene of his sin—and as he remembered the goodness and long-suffering of God, he was not altogether without hope. He felt that the Lord would still deal with him in mercy.

"Many a wrongdoer has excused his own sin by pointing to David's fall, but how few there are who manifest David's penitence and humility. . . . He had confessed his sin, and for years had sought to do his duty as a faithful servant of God; he had labored for the upbuilding of his kingdom, and under his rule it had attained to strength and prosperity never reached before. . . . Must the results of years of consecrated toil, . . . pass into the hands of his reckless and traitorous son, who regarded not the honor of God nor the prosperity of Israel? How natural it would have seemed for David to murmur against God in this great affliction!"[1]

The agony of spirit embedded in David's penitential psalms is evident. His pleading for forgiveness and deliverance is an example for us. He does not hide his sins but makes them public so that others might learn from his mistakes. "And the Lord did not forsake David. This chapter in his experience, when, under cruelest wrong and insult, he shows himself to be humble, unselfish, generous, and submissive, is one of the noblest in his whole experience."[2]

"When the righteous turn from their righteousness and do evil, their past righteousness will not save them from the wrath of a just and holy God."[3] Yet He is merciful and still ready to forgive the truly repentant.

---

1. Ellen G. White, *Patriarchs and Prophets* (Mountain View, CA: Pacific Press®, 1943), 737, 738.
2. White, 738.
3. Ellen G. White, *Spiritual Gifts*, vol. 4 (Washington, DC: Review and Herald®, 1945), 87.

TRAITORS AND BAD COUNSELORS

And Absalom, and all the people the men of Israel,
came to Jerusalem, and Ahithophel with him.
—2 Samuel 16:15

S oon after David left Jerusalem, Absalom and his army entered, and without a struggle took possession of the stronghold of Israel. Hushai was among the first to greet the new-crowned monarch, and the prince was surprised and gratified at the accession of his father's old friend and counselor. Absalom was confident of success. Thus far his schemes had prospered, and eager to strengthen his throne and secure the confidence of the nation, he welcomed Hushai to his court."[1]

"Hushai was known to be a great friend of David, and his appearance at the court of Absalom was totally unexpected. Why he too should have forsaken his friend and master appeared strange indeed. Absalom had looked for David to retain his hold on many of the people, and certainly on such a stalwart follower of his as Hushai. To have Hushai also forsake David seemed too good a fortune to be true. Absalom was both surprised and flattered, and no doubt felt more certain than ever of the success of his cause."[2] To all appearances, Hushai was a traitor. Even his reason for switching allegiances seemed to be rational and heartfelt (2 Samuel 16:16–19). Hushai claimed that by serving Absalom, he was honorably serving the house of David.

"Absalom was now surrounded by a large force, but it was mostly composed of men untrained for war. . . . Ahithophel well knew that David's situation was far from hopeless. . . . He was surrounded by tried warriors, who were faithful to their king, and his army was commanded by able and experienced generals. Ahithophel knew that after the first burst of enthusiasm in favor of the new king, a reaction would come. Should the rebellion fail, Absalom might be able to secure a reconciliation with his father; then Ahithophel, as his chief counselor, would be held most guilty for the rebellion; upon him the heaviest punishment would fall. To prevent Absalom from retracing his steps, Ahithophel counseled him to an act that in the eyes of the whole nation would make reconciliation impossible."[3]

Susceptibility to flattery and conceit often blind a person to the true objectives of false friends.

1. Ellen G. White, *Patriarchs and Prophets* (Mountain View, CA: Pacific Press®, 1943), 738.
2. Francis D. Nichol, ed., *The Seventh-day Adventist Bible Commentary*, vol. 2 (Washington, DC: Review and Herald®, 1976), 673.
3. White, *Patriarchs and Prophets*, 738, 739.

Ahithophel's Counsel

Then said Absalom to Ahithophel,
Give counsel among you what we shall do.
—2 Samuel 16:20

Ahithophel knew something was required that would completely remove Absalom from his father's mercy. Should David's anger be focused upon Absalom, there was a slim chance that Ahithophel might escape responsibility and evade the repercussions for his traitorous behavior. When David left Jerusalem, he was forced to leave ten concubines behind in his harem (2 Samuel 15:16). Ahithophel counseled Absalom to have sexual relations with these concubines. This act would show utter disdain for his father and establish his own claim to the throne.

"With hellish cunning this wily and unprincipled statesman urged Absalom to add the crime of incest to that of rebellion. In the sight of all Israel he was to take to himself his father's concubines, according to the custom of oriental nations, thus declaring that he succeeded to his father's throne. And Absalom carried out the vile suggestion. Thus was fulfilled the word of God to David by the prophet, 'Behold, I will raise up evil against thee out of thine own house, and I will take thy wives before thine eyes, and give them unto thy neighbor. . . . For thou didst it secretly: but I will do this thing before all Israel, and before the sun.' 2 Samuel 12:11, 12. Not that God prompted these acts of wickedness, but because of David's sin He did not exercise His power to prevent them."[1]

Was this particular counsel given because Ahithophel was Bathsheba's grandfather, and he sought revenge? Was it possible Ahithophel wanted to give David a taste of the same medicine David had given Uriah? Is it possible Ahithophel wanted these concubines to understand his granddaughter's adulterous situation firsthand? Ahithophel additionally urged immediate action against David's forces while they were still weak. He suggested choosing twelve thousand men to pursue David, forcing David's warriors to retreat, leaving the king alone to be slaughtered (2 Samuel 17:1, 2). "This plan was approved by the king's counselors. Had it been followed, David would surely have been slain, unless the Lord had directly interposed to save him."[2]

God controls multiple outcomes beyond our limited means to visualize even one.

1. Ellen G. White, *Patriarchs and Prophets* (Mountain View, CA: Pacific Press®, 1943), 739.
2. White, 740.

HUSHAI'S COUNSEL

Then said Absalom, Call now Hushai the Archite
also, and let us hear likewise what he saith.
—2 Samuel 17:5

By this time David would barely have had time to reach the Jordan, and with his followers not yet completely organized, he would have been an easy victim for the forces of Absalom. If Ahithophel's proposal had been followed, the men with David would doubtless have been utterly routed, and David killed. Thus Absalom would have been made secure on his throne."[1] Absalom now called on Hushai for his advice. Hushai, realizing David's cause would be lost if Ahithophel's plan was enacted, urged prudence. While not wanting to directly contradict Ahithophel's advice as unwise, Hushai suggested an alternative might be better suited at this time.

Hushai advised caution rather than rashly rushing into battle against proven men of war. He pointed out David was a mighty warrior, and he certainly would not be found among his men but would have set up a command post in some secluded area. If Absalom sent his untested men against trained warriors, it was highly unlikely they would prevail. If routed, all Israel would see success must follow David, and their allegiance might shift to him. Rather, they should gather an invincible host from all of Israel and proceed when there was little chance of David's forces being able to resist such an overwhelming army. Furthermore, Absalom should be at the head of this large force so that he might claim personal triumph. Victory would strengthen his claim to the throne in the eyes of the people. This seemed like sound counsel to Absalom and certainly played upon his vanity—leading an invincible army into battle seemed like the better option.

"In his conspiracy against David, Absalom failed to reckon with God. He had able counselors and powerful supporters, and the hearts of many of the people were with him. But the nation of Israel, after all, belonged to the Lord, and it was David who had been divinely anointed as king. If he were to be deposed, God would have to be taken into the reckoning. Wise as the counsel of Ahithophel was, from a human point of view, the Lord decreed that it be brought to nought.

". . . A wisdom higher than that of men was directing in the affairs of Israel."[2]

God still directs the affairs of nations.

---

1. Francis D. Nichol, ed., *The Seventh-day Adventist Bible Commentary*, vol. 2 (Washington, DC: Review and Herald®, 1976), 675.
2. Nichol, 677.

COVERT OPERATIONS

Now therefore send quickly, and tell David, saying, Lodge not this night in the plains of the wilderness, but speedily pass over; lest the king be swallowed up, and all the people that are with him.

—2 Samuel 17:16

Hushai knew Absalom might change his mind at any moment. If he were to launch an immediate attack on David's forces, whose backs were to the Jordan River, escape would be impossible. He therefore hastened to Zadok and Abiathar and informed them of Ahithophel's dangerous counsel. He urged them to get word to David, warning him to cross the Jordan and escape into the eastern wilderness. The sons of Zadok and Abiathar had set up a watch at the well of En-rogel. They did not want to be seen suspiciously coming and going from Jerusalem. Women frequented the well to draw water, and it would not be hard for them to pass messages from the priests to their sons. A maidservant was immediately sent to the young men, telling them to relay Hushai's urgent warning to David. But the covert operation had developed a problem.

The suspicious actions of the sons of the priests were reported to Absalom. Jonathan and Ahimaaz knew they had been compromised, so they hid in a well in the courtyard of friends sympathetic to David. The woman of the house covered the top of the well with a tarp and placed grain on it to dry. When Absalom's servants tracked the men to her house, she did not deny they had been there but said they had moved on. The servants looked in the direction she indicated but could not find the pair. Frustrated, they returned to Jerusalem and reported failure.

When the coast was clear, the messengers climbed out of the well and made their way to David. Here they delivered the message of Hushai: "Arise, and pass quickly over the water: for thus hath Ahithophel counselled against you" (2 Samuel 17:21). "David, spent with toil and grief after that first day of flight, received the message that he must cross the Jordan that night, for his son was seeking his life.

"What were the feelings of the father and king, so cruelly wronged, in this terrible peril?"[1] His words are found in Psalm 3.

"Iron sharpeneth iron; so a man sharpeneth the countenance of his friend" (Proverbs 27:17). Mutual help is a force multiplier.

---

1. Ellen G. White, *Patriarchs and Prophets* (Mountain View, CA: Pacific Press®, 1943), 741.

CROSSING JORDAN

*Then David arose, and all the people that were with him,
and they passed over Jordan: by the morning light there
lacked not one of them that was not gone over Jordan.*
—2 Samuel 17:22

David knew he was in no position to withstand an assault while he had women and children to consider. His personal bodyguards were elite fighters, but against the numbers they would face, the outcome would be in doubt. He lacked supplies and arms with which to conduct a battle. The best option—in fact, the only option—was to stage a skillful retreat and live to fight another day.

Crossing a rapid river in the dead of night was no small undertaking. We are not told whether barges were at their crossing point. If not, swimming in the darkness would be their only option. Crossing with any baggage during the dead of night would be problematic. Yet David did not hesitate to act! He immediately ordered the company to cross the Jordan. Once on the eastern shore, he had to move quickly into a defensive position. With that location reached and barricaded, only then could he and his party rest until dawn, but they must keep moving. "That very night they were again on their way, crossing the Jordan and placing a barrier of water between themselves and the forces of Absalom."[1] David's implicit trust in the Lord for deliverance during this ordeal is found in Psalm 3.

"David and all his company—warriors and statesmen, old men and youth, the women and the little children—in the darkness of night crossed the deep and swift-flowing river. 'By the morning light there lacked not one of them that was not gone over Jordan.'

"David and his forces fell back to Mahanaim. . . . This was a strongly fortified city, surrounded by a mountainous district favorable for retreat in case of war. The country was well-provisioned, and the people were friendly to the cause of David. Here many adherents joined him, while wealthy tribesmen brought abundant gifts of provision, and other needed supplies.

"Hushai's counsel had achieved its object, gaining for David opportunity for escape; but the rash and impetuous prince could not be long restrained, and he soon set out in pursuit of his father."[2]

Man's difficulties are God's opportunities!

1. Francis D. Nichol, ed., *The Seventh-day Adventist Bible Commentary*, vol. 2 (Washington, DC: Review and Herald®, 1976), 678.
2. Ellen G. White, *Patriarchs and Prophets* (Mountain View, CA: Pacific Press®, 1943), 742.

Psalm 3: A Morning Prayer

*Many there be which say of my soul, There is no help
for him in God. Selah. But thou, O Lord, art a shield
for me; my glory, and the lifter up of mine head.*

—Psalm 3:2, 3

Psalm 3 "was composed by David when he fled from Absalom his son. 'Spent with grief and the weariness of his flight, he with his company had tarried beside the Jordan for a few hours' rest. He was awakened by the summons to immediate flight. In the darkness the passage of the deep and swift-flowing stream must be made by that whole company of men, women, and little children; for hard after them were the forces of the traitor-son.'. . . In the hours of darkest trial, David sang this sublime hymn of trust in God in the face of the enemy. . . . The psalm has been termed A Morning Prayer. It is the cry of the soul in the presence of danger; of trouble relieved by the passing of the night. It is closely related to [Psalm] 4, An Evening Prayer, which may be considered its sequel."[1]

Nearly all of Israel had revolted against David (2 Samuel 15:6, 13). "Lord, how are they increased that trouble me! many are they that rise up against me. Many there be which say of my soul, There is no help for him in God. Selah. But thou, O Lord, art a shield for me; my glory, and the lifter up of mine head. I cried unto the Lord with my voice, and he heard me out of his holy hill" (Psalm 3:1–4). David could hold his head up, confident that God would deliver him.

Trusting God's protection, David lay down and slept peacefully. His faith in God allowed him to rest prior to facing the trials of the coming day. "I laid me down and slept; I awaked; for the Lord sustained me. I will not be afraid of ten thousands of people, that have set themselves against me round about" (vv. 5, 6). His night of sadness was changed to courage! The number of enemies no longer mattered. David was confident God would crush them all (v. 7). "Salvation belongeth unto the Lord: thy blessing is upon thy people" (v. 8). Selflessly, David considered the welfare of all his subjects—both those who remained loyal and those in rebellion. He prayed that God would bless all of Israel!

"Whisper a prayer in the morning, / Whisper a prayer at noon; / Whisper a prayer in the evening, / To keep your heart in tune."[2]

---

1. Francis D. Nichol, ed., *The Seventh-day Adventist Bible Commentary*, vol. 3 (Washington, DC: Review and Herald®, 1977), 635–637.

2. Unknown, "Whisper a Prayer."

PSALM 4: AN EVENING PRAYER

I will both lay me down in peace, and sleep:
for thou, LORD, only makest me dwell in safety.
—Psalm 4:8

At the end of the day, David is satisfied with the progress of his little band. God has been with him during the trying day, and He will abide with him during the night. "It has been suggested that [Psalm] 5 also should be read together with [Psalm] 4, for [Psalm] 4 is a prayer appropriate to evening devotions and [Psalm] 5 is a petition appropriate to the period of morning worship."[1]

No longer hemmed in by enemies, David has gained freedom of movement (Psalm 4:1). His condition is that of an exile having no dignity or riches, but his persecutors, who believe they have succeeded because they now have his riches and power, will find their success empty (v. 2). God has ordained David to a special work, and because of that blessing, men trying to undo His purposes will fail (v. 3). "If the Christian is faithfully carrying out God's plan for him, he may expect God to uphold him until he has completed the work that Heaven designs for him to do."[2]

When all is still and silent, a Christian should consider his own plans and consult his better judgment (v. 4). "The true child of God finds durable satisfaction, not in the material things and sensual delights of the world, but in the consciousness that he has heaven's approval as he enjoys fellowship with God [vv. 6, 7]. . . .

". . . Confidence in God gives assurance of sleep. . . . This condition is the counterpart of the experience described in [Psalm] 3:5, in which the psalmist, in the morning, reflected that God had permitted him to sleep, although fearful enemies surrounded him; now, in the evening, he goes a step further and lies down serenely in the consciousness that, although he is still surrounded by his enemies, God will give him the gift of quiet and restful sleep."[3]

"The Christian who shares the confidence of the psalmist need have no fear during either the slumbers of the night or the duties of the day."[4]

---

1. Francis D. Nichol, ed., *The Seventh-day Adventist Bible Commentary*, vol. 3 (Washington, DC: Review and Herald®, 1977), 638.
2. Nichol, 639.
3. Nichol, 639, 640.
4. Nichol, 640.

Psalm 5: A Morning Prayer

*My voice shalt thou hear in the morning, O LORD; in the
morning will I direct my prayer unto thee, and will look up.*

—Psalm 5:3

The rising sun finds David again in prayer. In the midst of trials and perplexities, he asks for guidance and mercy. He recognizes God hears not only the spoken word but also the meditation of the heart (v. 1). " 'Prayer is the soul's sincere desire, unuttered or expressed.' "[1] David appreciates morning worship as a time to start the day right by sharing his innermost thoughts with God. Humbly, he calls God his King (vv. 2, 3). He knows that evil people—the proud, the insolent, the boaster, the liar, the murderer, and the defrauder—cannot exist in the presence of God. David, on the other hand, feels at peace in the presence of God (vv. 4–7). Because the men opposing David are evil, he can boldly approach God, asking for mercy and relief (v. 8).

Absalom's rebellion has been characterized by disloyalty and deceit. Lies have been told about David's motives and character. Flattery has gained Absalom allies (v. 9). The psalmist petitions God to "treat his enemies as guilty, which they undoubtedly are. He asks that they may 'fall by their own counsels,' that is, that their own plans may be the means of their destruction. . . . This idea is frequent in the OT [Old Testament]. Sin eventually consumes itself [v. 10]."[2]

In contrast, the Christian finds joy in the Lord. God will shield all who place their trust in Him. Thus protected, David is ready to face the challenges of a new day.

" 'Devotion should be both the morning star and the evening star.' If we start the day right, we shall be more aware of God's presence through its hours, and surer of coming to our beds at night with quietness and confidence in our hearts."[3] Morning and evening worship are the bookends between which a Christian navigates life's perplexities.

"Joyful, joyful, we adore Thee, / God of glory, Lord of love; / Hearts unfold like flow'rs before Thee, / Hail Thee as the sun above."[4]

---

1. James Montgomery, "Prayer Is the Soul's Sincere Desire," quoted in Francis D. Nichol, ed., *The Seventh-day Adventist Bible Commentary*, vol. 3 (Washington, DC: Review and Herald®, 1957), 641.

2. Nichol, 642.

3. Charles Spurgeon, *Psalm I to XXVI*, vol. 1 of *The Treasury of David* (London: Robert Culley, 1870), 50, quoted in Nichol, 642.

4. Henry van Dyke, "Joyful, Joyful, We Adore Thee" (1907), in *The Seventh-day Adventist Hymnal* (Hagerstown, MD: Review and Herald®, 1985), hymn 12.

HUMILIATED

And when Ahithophel saw that his counsel was not followed,
he saddled his ass, and arose, and gat him home to his house,
to his city, and put his household in order, and hanged himself,
and died, and was buried in the sepulchre of his father.
—2 Samuel 17:23

We leave David briefly on the far side of the Jordan River while we concentrate on Ahithophel. A shrewd counselor, Ahithophel knew Absalom had made a fatal error and "the cause of the rebels was lost. And he knew . . . there was no hope for the counselor who had instigated his greatest crimes. Ahithophel had encouraged Absalom in rebellion; he had counseled him to the most abominable wickedness, to the dishonor of his father; he had advised the slaying of David and had planned its accomplishment; he had cut off the last possibility of his own reconciliation with the king; and now another was preferred before him, even by Absalom. Jealous, angry, and desperate, Ahithophel 'gat him home to his house, to his city, and put his household in order, and hanged himself, and died.' Such was the result of the wisdom of one, who, with all his high endowments, did not make God his counselor. Satan allures men with flattering promises, but in the end it will be found by every soul, that the 'wages of sin is death.' Romans 6:23."[1]

But there is more to the story. Ahithophel had asked to command the men who would pursue David (2 Samuel 17:1). His request had been emphatically denied. This had humiliated him more than having his counsel ignored. Had he been able to bring about the death of David, he might have remained close to the seat of power. Now David had a chance to gather forces and strike back. Ahithophel had all but handed the crown to Absalom, and this was how he was shamefully repaid! "Ahithophel felt certain that his doom was only a question of time. When David regained his throne Ahithophel would certainly be held responsible as a ringleader of the revolt and would be put to an ignominious death. But it was more than fear of swift reprisal that caused Ahithophel to take his life. He could not bear to see his counsel ignored and consequently took the cowardly way out."[2]

"Pride goeth before destruction, and an haughty spirit before a fall" (*Proverbs 16:18*).

---

1. Ellen G. White, *Patriarchs and Prophets* (Mountain View, CA: Pacific Press®, 1943), 741.
2. Francis D. Nichol, ed., *The Seventh-day Adventist Bible Commentary*, vol. 2 (Washington, DC: Review and Herald®, 1976), 678.

PSALM 10: AVENGE US!

Why standest thou afar off, O LORD?
why hidest thou thyself in times of trouble?

—Psalm 10:1

Psalm 10 describes the enemies of God and asks Him to punish those troubling the faithful (vv. 1–11). Who has not asked a similar question when beset with difficulties and attacks from enemies? Proud enemies have surrounded the psalmist and have hatched covetous plans to cause his downfall (vv. 2, 3). They do not consider God in their plans. It is as if He does not exist; even if God does exist, He is too far away to intervene or even take notice of what is going on (vv. 4–6, 11). "Because of his success in evildoing, the wicked imagines that his success will continue so, and that he may carry on his nefarious work with impunity. Too often those who observe him think the same (see Job 12:6; Jer. 12:1). This is one of the great problems discussed by OT [Old Testament] writers."[1]

These men and women are sly and deceitful (v. 7). They tell falsehoods with impunity just to see how much trouble they can cause. They hide their true motives. They spread vicious gossip after calculating when it will do the utmost damage. They delight in harming innocents (v. 8). They often pick the weakest of the flock to attack, knowing these cannot or will not defend themselves (vv. 9, 10). David had seen these behaviors acted out time and time again—as have those who have had dealings with unconverted professed believers.

In verses 12–18, David shifts from describing evildoers to asking God to destroy them and their works. The wicked think God has forgotten the upright (v. 11), but He has *not* forgotten His children (v. 12). Justice will be served in the final Judgment Day reckoning (v. 13). "The arrogant belief of the wicked man, who denies God's observation of man's evil ways, is stoutly denied by the psalmist [v. 14]."[2] David would have God establish justice and free the humble from oppression (vv. 15–18). "Faith counts the thing as done."[3]

"O Thou God of all, / Hear us when we call, / Help us, one and all, / By Thy grace."[4]

1. Francis D. Nichol, ed., *The Seventh-day Adventist Bible Commentary*, vol. 3 (Washington, DC: Review and Herald®, 1977), 655.
2. Nichol, 655.
3. Nichol, 655.
4. William F. Sherwin, "Sound the Battle Cry" (1869), in *The Seventh-day Adventist Hymnal* (Hagerstown, MD: Review and Herald®, 1985), hymn 614.

Psalm 9: A Song of Thanksgiving

I will praise thee, O Lord, with my whole heart; I will shew forth all thy marvellous works. I will be glad and rejoice in thee: I will sing praise to thy name, O thou most High.

—Psalm 9:1, 2

P salm 9 is filled with thanksgiving for deliverance from oppressors (vv. 1, 2). When God appears, evildoers are defeated by His power (v. 3). God's judgment is accurate, and His righteousness is vindicated (v. 4). The enemies of righteousness will eventually be destroyed forever. Nothing will mark their prior existence (vv. 5, 6). God, who changes not, is immortal (v. 7). His judgments are pure, and He will judge the whole world during the final judgment (v. 8).

The righteous have no need to fear God's verdicts. He is a refuge for those who are oppressed (v. 9). He can be trusted to protect His children in the latter days. He will not forsake them (v. 10). "God's wondrous ways to Israel are to be proclaimed to all nations, that these nations too may acknowledge God and enjoy His protection. God's mercy was not meant for Israel alone (see Ps. 105:1). This sentiment occurs throughout the psalms. If Israel had learned this lesson, the rigid exclusiveness practiced by the Pharisees would never have existed."[1]

God will avenge the taking of innocent life (v. 12). David would have God be merciful and consider the difficulties he is currently experiencing (v. 13). "Since the dead cannot praise God (Ps. 88:10–12; 115:17), the psalmist calls on God to save him so that he may praise Him among the living [vv. 13, 14]."[2] God allows the nations that plot evil to fall by their own hand. In the final judgment, wicked people will receive their just reward. God will not forget the poor and needy on that great Judgment Day (vv. 15–18). David asks God to arise and judge the world (v. 19). "For the Lord will not cast off his people, neither will he forsake his inheritance. But judgment shall return unto righteousness: and all the upright in heart shall follow it" (Psalm 94:14, 15). Humankind cannot prevaricate in the sight of this eternal Judge [v. 20].

"How long, O Lord our God, / Holy and true and good, / Wilt Thou not judge Thy suffering church, / Her sighs and tears and blood?"[3]

---

1. Francis D. Nichol, ed., *The Seventh-day Adventist Bible Commentary*, vol. 3 (Washington, DC: Review and Herald®, 1977), 652.

2. Nichol, 652.

3. Horatius Bonar, "The Church Has Waited Long," in *The Seventh-day Adventist Hymnal* (Hagerstown, MD: Review and Herald®, 1985), hymn 217.

PSALM 94: THE ROCK OF MY REFUGE

But the LORD is my defense; and my God is the rock of my refuge.
—Psalm 94:22

Psalm 94 asks God to explain why it seems the wicked prosper (vv. –7). Why do unjust leaders boast of their wickedness, maintaining God is detached and not interested in the affairs of men (vv. 8–11)? In truth, justice will prevail, and right will eventually triumph. David repeatedly asks the Lord, "to whom vengeance belongeth" (v. 1), to rise up and judge the wicked, for they defy Him openly (vv. 2, 7). How long will the Lord remain silent? The wicked boast of immunity to punishment and seem to sin without penalty (vv. 3, 4). The evildoers are preying on the most vulnerable members of society with seeming impunity (v. 6). "Weary with the apparent supremacy of evil, the psalmist wonders why God is so slow in manifesting Himself."[1]

How foolish to think the Creator will not require evildoers to ultimately account for their sins. Thinking they are immune from prosecution is arrogance (vv. 8–11). The Son of man will judge humanity in the final judgment, declaring them either righteous or unrighteous (Matthew 25:31–46). Those who have heeded the Lord's chastisement and accepted His discipline will be known by obedience to His Word. "If the Christian accepts discipline, he is happy! One of the chief values of chastening is that it gives the afflicted fuller sympathy with others."[2] The Christian has nothing to fear, resting peacefully in the arms of the Savior (vv. 12–15).

David now personally appeals for relief from those who have risen up against him. The knowledge that the Lord has been merciful in the past sustains him. The knowledge that God is always near brings comfort to an otherwise stressed mind. David's enemies have supplanted justice, misapplying the law to justify their evil actions. Despite these injustices, David finds solace in the Rock of Ages. He trusts God will make all things right, and justice will prevail (vv. 16–23).

"Rock of Ages, cleft for me, / Let me hide myself in Thee; / Let the water and the blood, / From Thy riven side which flowed, / Be of sin the double cure, / Cleanse me from its guilt and power."[3]

---

1. Francis D. Nichol, ed., *The Seventh-day Adventist Bible Commentary*, vol. 3 (Washington, DC: Review and Herald®, 1977), 847.

2. Nichol, 848.

3. Augustus M. Toplady, "Rock of Ages" (1776), in *The Seventh-day Adventist Hymnal* (Hagerstown, MD: Review and Herald®, 1985), hymn 300.

PSALM 40: PRESERVE ME, O LORD!

I delight to do thy will, O my God: yea, thy law is within my heart.
—Psalm 40:8

David's psalms often present either a prayer for forgiveness or a prayer requesting deliverance. Psalm 40 sees him remembering past instances when God has intervened to protect His servant (vv. 1–10). David is in need of deliverance once again from his current crisis (vv. 10–17). While waiting "patiently for the LORD" to hear him (v. 1), it seems God is not listening. But God does hear the psalmist's prayer and lifts David up, setting his feet on solid ground again. David is thus given a new song of personal deliverance and victory to sing (vv. 1–3). Those who place their trust in the Lord will not be disappointed (v. 4)!

Recalling the many times God has blessed the psalmist in the past is the inspiration for this particular psalm. No one can number the blessings given to humankind by our benevolent heavenly Father. David wonders how he can thank God adequately. Sacrifices and offerings do not seem to be enough. God wants a higher service (vv. 5–8). "Obedience is superior to mere sacrifice (see Ps. 51:16, 17)."[1]

"It was Christ's joy to obey His Father; His was a joyful obedience. When the law is inscribed in the heart, obedience becomes a pleasure."[2] Psalm 40:6–8 "point out one of the primary objectives of the teachings of the Messiah. To the Jews the externals were the sum total of religion. Jesus taught that these were only a means to an end and that the end itself was harmony with the will of God. The basic function of the plan of salvation is to restore in man the image of God . . . , and any system of religion that subordinates this function to adherence to ceremony and tradition thereby obscures the primary purpose of true religion."[3]

Those who have experienced the love of Christ will want to share it with others (vv. 8–10).

David once again brings to God's attention his current problems and asks for deliverance, and then David ends his song by asking God not to tarry or delay in sending help (vv. 12–17).

"Come, we that love the Lord, / And let our joys be known."[4]

1. Francis D. Nichol, ed., *The Seventh-day Adventist Bible Commentary*, vol. 3 (Washington, DC: Review and Herald®, 1977), 731.

2. Nichol, 731.

3. Nichol, 731.

4. Isaac Watts, "Marching to Zion" (1707), in *The Seventh-day Adventist Hymnal* (Hagerstown, MD: Review and Herald®, 1985), hymn 422.

PSALM 70: DELIVER ME, O LORD!

Make haste, O God, to deliver me; make haste to help me, O LORD.
—Psalm 70:1

Psalm 70 "is the cry of a soul in deep distress, perhaps representative of the nation of Israel in its realization of its utter need of God. It has two contrasting stanzas: vs. 1–3 are concerned with the enemies of God; vs. 4, 5, with those who seek Him. It has been suggested that these verses may have been taken from Ps. 40 to form a separate psalm for use in Temple worship."[1] The wording of Psalm 40:14 is taken almost verbatim and used in Psalm 70:2.

The events of David's life were an unending sequence of turmoil: Initially hailed as a national hero, he was later chased from home and family into the wilderness, hunted like a wild animal. King Saul first treated David like a son, but later, in fits of jealous rage, the king twice tried to impale David with a javelin. Once acclaimed as a great warrior by the women of Israel, he was later declared an outlaw and traitor. David was twice betrayed by the Ziphites, whom he thought to be his protectors. Hounded from one hiding place to another, he knew the depths of danger and despair. Finally, David found refuge with Israel's enemies. Yet even they distrusted him. The Philistines would not fight with David in their ranks. The village of Ziklag was raided, and his family and possessions were carted off into the desert. His best friend, Jonathan, was slain in battle. Although David was anointed as king by Judah, the nation was still divided, and he did not have the full allegiance of Israel. Joab killed Abner, who was under the protection of the king. The transport of the ark to Jerusalem had resulted in the death of Uzzah. David had been denied his wish to build the temple.

Falling into the trap of lust, he had committed adultery, deceit, and murder. Even though he repented of those sins, his child with Bathsheba had died. His daughter Tamar was raped by her brother. Absalom killed Amnon and fled. Now Absalom, his oldest remaining son, had risen against him and forced him into exile with just the clothes on his back. All seemed lost. Was it any wonder that David described himself as "poor and needy" (v. 5)?

"I need Thee, precious Jesus, / For I am very poor; / A stranger and a pilgrim, / I have no earthly store."[2]

---

1. Francis D. Nichol, ed., *The Seventh-day Adventist Bible Commentary*, vol. 3 (Washington, DC: Review and Herald®, 1977), 796.

2. Frederick Whitfield, "I Need Thee, Precious Jesus" (1855), in *The Seventh-day Adventist Hymnal* (Hagerstown, MD: Review and Herald®, 1985), hymn 484.

PSALM 89, PART 1:
PRAISE GOD FOR HIS PROMISES

I will sing of the mercies of the LORD for ever: with my mouth will I make known thy faithfulness to all generations.
—Psalm 89:1

Psalm 89 deals with the covenant between God and David and therefore has been called the "Psalm of the Covenant."[1] God had promised to establish David's throne forever (v. 4). Now it seemed God had broken His promise (v. 38). Yet God reigns supreme above all humankind. Even the angels in heaven cannot compare to His power (vv. 5–7). God commands the seas (Job 38:8–11; Psalms 65:7; 107:23–30; Matthew 8:26, 27). He broke the power of Egypt and scattered her forces. He created all things in heaven and on earth (Psalm 89:9–12). God's character is defined by justice, mercy, and truth. Those who bask in the presence of God are blessed because they know the joy of salvation (vv. 14, 15). Their strength is increased, and their defense is solid. Therefore, David praises God; "the Holy One of Israel is our king" (v. 18).

Thus far, David has extolled the wonders of God—His strength, His justice and judgment, His mercy and truth, and His righteousness. Now David reminds God of their covenant and wonders why God has seemingly broken it. He recalls how he was chosen from among common men of Israel (v. 19) and given strength and power to do God's will (v. 21). God had promised to defeat David's enemies while showing him tender mercy (vv. 23, 24). David had called God "my father, my God, and the rock of my salvation" (v. 26). The feeling had been reciprocated, for God had called David his "firstborn" son (v. 27). "David was the first from whom a line of royal descendants was to extend to the Messiah."[2]

God had promised to make David higher than the kings of the earth (v. 27). His throne would endure forever, even "as the days of heaven" (v. 29). David's children might forsake God and break His law, thus requiring God to punish them, but God would remain faithful and keep their covenant intact. David acknowledges that once God has sworn something, He does not go back on His word (vv. 30–35)! God is faithful, loving, and kind (vv. 1, 2, 5, 8, 14, 24, 28, 33, 49).

"Now thank we all our God / With heart and hands and voices."[3]

1. Francis D. Nichol, ed., *The Seventh-day Adventist Bible Commentary*, vol. 3 (Washington, DC: Review and Herald®, 1977), 837.
2. Nichol, 838.
3. Martin Rinkart, "Now Thank We All Our God" (1636), in *The Seventh-day Adventist Hymnal* (Hagerstown, MD: Review and Herald®, 1985), hymn 559.

PSALM 89, PART 2:
WILL GOD KEEP HIS PROMISES?

But thou hast cast off and abhorred,
thou hast been wroth with thine anointed.

—Psalm 89:38

Yesterday we saw David extol the honor of God. In the middle of Psalm 89, the theme changes and asks the question, Will God keep His promises? "Despite the surety of God's promises and the pledge of His faithfulness, it seems that the covenant has been broken and that not good, but only evil, has come upon Israel and the Lord's anointed. How is this? the psalmist inquires. What will be the outcome? Is God's faithfulness failing?"[1] It seems God has abandoned David (v. 38). The crown has been lost to Absalom (v. 39). David's defenses have been destroyed (v. 40). His subjects blame him (v. 41). Israel's enemies are rejoicing at his apparent downfall (v. 42). The royal line is an embarrassment, and the kingdom's success appears to be at an end (vv. 43–45). God seems displeased with His servant David, and the covenant between them appears broken. Here is a simple recitation of facts as David saw them. Things could get no worse.

He knows he is but a weak human being and all things are under the power of the Almighty, but things are going desperately wrong. David does not have a clue as to why or how long this state of affairs is going to last. Perhaps this is the new reality, and Absalom is to be the descendant through which the covenant will be fulfilled. How can this be? This disturbing situation is so wrong. David argues, "Surely, God, You cannot have ordained things to happen the way they have turned out. Please, Lord, right these wrongs while there is yet time."

David is growing old, and the life span of man is short (v. 47); therefore, if God is to intervene, He must do so quickly. David has little time left to see things set right. All men die, and no one can cheat death (v. 48). Where is the promised loving-kindness (v. 49)? Will God permit the enemies of Israel to rejoice over the turmoil now occurring (v. 49)? "Like Moses . . . , the psalmist felt that the burdens of all his people rested upon him, and that he was no longer able to bear their weight."[2]

"Like as a father, constant is He, / God in compassion regardeth our plea."[3]

---

1. Francis D. Nichol, ed., *The Seventh-day Adventist Bible Commentary*, vol. 3 (Washington, DC: Review and Herald®, 1977), 839.

2. Nichol, 840.

3. F. E. Belden, "Like as a Father," in *The Church Hymnal: The Official Hymnal of the Seventh-day Adventist Church* (Washington, DC: Review and Herald®, 1941), hymn 66.

THE BATTLE IN THE WOODS

*So the people went out into the field against Israel:
and the battle was in the wood of Ephraim.*
—2 Samuel 18:6

David realized Absalom would attack as soon as possible. Marshaling his forces, he divided them into three divisions, placing each under one of his best commanders. Joab retained command of the entire army. Abishai, who had sought to defend David's honor against Shimei (2 Samuel 16:9), was given command of the second division. Ittai the Gittite, who had professed his undying support for David (2 Samuel 15:19–21), was given the third division. It was David's intention to join his forces in the field, but "if the opposing army learned that David was with his men, every effort would be made against his person. If he could be slain, Absalom would have attained his purpose. So David was urged not to be present in the battle."[1] At his soldiers' request, David remained in the city of Mahanaim with the reserve forces.

"From the walls of the city the long lines of the rebel army were in full view. The usurper was accompanied by a vast host, in comparison with which David's force seemed but a handful. But as the king looked upon the opposing forces, the thought uppermost in his mind was not of the crown and the kingdom, nor of his own life, that depended upon the wage of battle. The father's heart was filled with love and pity for his rebellious son. As the army filed out from the city gates David encouraged his faithful soldiers, bidding them go forth trusting that the God of Israel would give them the victory. But even here he could not repress his love for Absalom. As Joab, leading the first column, passed his king, the conqueror of a hundred battlefields stooped his proud head to hear the monarch's last message, as with trembling voice he said, 'Deal gently for my sake with the young man, even with Absalom.' "[2]

The battle took place in a wooded area covered with dense foliage and rocky undergrowth interspersed with a marsh. In such terrain, Absalom's vast army lost its advantage. The veteran forces of David maintained discipline and delivered a stunning defeat to the rebel army. Twenty thousand of Absalom's followers were slain (2 Samuel 18:7), and Absalom was put to flight.

How should you—and do you—treat those who oppose you?

---

1. Francis D. Nichol, ed., *The Seventh-day Adventist Bible Commentary*, vol. 2 (Washington, DC: Review and Herald®, 1976), 680, 681.
2. Ellen G. White, *Patriarchs and Prophets* (Mountain View, CA: Pacific Press®, 1943), 743.

Entangled

And Absalom met the servants of David. And Absalom rode upon a mule, and the mule went under the thick boughs of a great oak, and his head caught hold of the oak, and he was taken up between the heaven and the earth; and the mule that was under him went away.
—2 Samuel 18:9

In retreating from the battlefield, Absalom's long hair was caught in the branches of a large oak tree. His mule kept going, leaving him dangling from the tree, unable to touch the ground. In this helpless state, he was surrounded by enemies. A soldier, fearing to anger David by disobeying an explicit order, left Absalom and reported his finding to Joab, who would have rewarded him if he had killed Absalom. He replied, "Though I should receive a thousand shekels of silver in mine hand, yet would I not put forth mine hand against the king's son" (2 Samuel 18:12). He knows that the life of the one who kills Absalom in violation of orders will be forfeit.

"Joab was restrained by no scruples. He had befriended Absalom, having twice secured his reconciliation with David, and the trust had been shamelessly betrayed. But for the advantages gained by Absalom through Joab's intercession, this rebellion, with all its horrors, could never have occurred. Now it was in Joab's power at one blow to destroy the instigator of all this evil."[1] "Then said Joab, I may not tarry thus with thee. And he took three darts [javelins] in his hand, and thrust them through the heart of Absalom" (v. 14).

Joab's bodyguards took down the dead prince's body and threw it into a pit in the woods to deny him burial in his family's vault. Over the body, they piled stones so he might not be found. "During his lifetime Absalom had reared for himself a costly monument in the king's dale, but the only memorial which marked his grave was that heap of stones in the wilderness."[2] Such "was the end of the proud and handsome prince who placed his own interests before the interests of his people, his father, and his God."[3] The trumpet sounded, recalling David's men from their pursuit of the enemy. With the usurper killed, there was no need for further bloodshed.

What, if any, memorial do you desire?

1. Ellen G. White, *Patriarchs and Prophets* (Mountain View, CA: Pacific Press®, 1943), 743, 744.
2. White, 744.
3. Francis D. Nichol, ed., *The Seventh-day Adventist Bible Commentary*, vol. 2 (Washington, DC: Review and Herald®, 1976), 682.

A FOOTRACE

Then Ahimaaz ran by the way of the plain, and overran Cushi.
—2 Samuel 18:23

Messengers were chosen to carry the news of the battle to David. Ahimaaz, the son of the priest Zadok, requested the honor. He and Jonathan had been chosen to carry clandestine messages from their fathers to David (2 Samuel 17:17–21). Apparently, he was also a swift runner (2 Samuel 18:27). Joab denied his request, knowing that news of Absalom's status would be the only thing David wanted to hear. Delivery of such a dire message would forever link Ahimaaz with bad news in David's mind. This might adversely affect the way David looked upon the young man in the future. Instead, Joab selected a non-Israelite to carry the bad news. He called upon a Cushite to take word to David. Ahimaaz would not take Joab's refusal as final. After the Cushite left, he again petitioned Joab to be allowed to run. Joab remonstrated with him, "Wherefore wilt thou run, my son, seeing that thou hast no tidings ready?" (v. 22). The message was already on its way. There was no reason to send it twice. But Ahimaaz was resolute; he wanted to run. Joab relented.

While the Cushite took the more direct route through woods and over hills to Mahanaim, Ahimaaz chose the longer but more level route up the Jordan River valley. Being swifter than the Cushite, Ahimaaz outran him and came within sight of Mahanaim first. The watchman on the wall saw a runner approach. He called down to alert David, who was sitting by the gate. David wondered whether it was a single runner. If many, it might have signaled a retreat. The answer was one runner who looked like Ahimaaz. David knew him to be a good man. Suddenly, a second runner appeared. This complicated the issue.

Ahimaaz reached David first and divulged that David's enemies had lost the battle. As Joab expected, David only wanted to know about Absalom. Ahimaaz skillfully evaded David's question (v. 29). The Cushite arrived and repeated that victory had been won. David asked, "Is the young man Absalom safe?" (v. 32). The answer leaves no doubt in David's mind as to his son's status: "All that rise against thee to do thee hurt, [should] be as that young man is" (v. 32).

How often do our actions bring about the very things we dread most?

DAVID MOURNS ABSALOM

And the king was much moved, and went up to the chamber over the gate, and wept: and as he went, thus he said, O my son Absalom, my son, my son Absalom! would God I had died for thee, O Absalom, my son, my son!
—2 Samuel 18:33

D avid had now lost four sons. David's sin with Bath-sheba resulted in the death of the infant they had conceived (2 Samuel 12:18). Absalom had caused his older brother Amnon's death (2 Samuel 13:29). Chileab, second in line for the throne (2 Samuel 3:3), had probably died as no mention of him is found in the genealogical records. With Amnon and Chileab dead, Absalom had become the heir apparent. Now he was dead (2 Samuel 18:15). David had received the very punishment for his sin with Bath-sheba that he had prescribed: "As the LORD liveth, the man that hath done this thing shall surely die: And he shall restore the lamb fourfold, because he did this thing, and because he had no pity. And Nathan said to David, Thou art the man" (2 Samuel 12:5–7).

Every judgment of the Lord, as expressed by the prophet Nathan, had come true. The sword had not departed from his house (v. 10). His concubines had been raped in public by Absalom (vv. 11, 12). The child of David and Bath-sheba had died (v. 18). The penalty he himself had voiced had come true—four of his sons had died.

"There are few places in the Bible that picture more poignant grief. David's sorrow was not merely that of a father for his departed son, although for the tenderhearted king such a sorrow would be heavy enough. What made the situation more difficult for David was that he himself was responsible for the course of events that had had its climax in this terrible tragedy. Absalom had slain his brother after Amnon had violated his sister, Tamar, and now he in turn was slain in battle against his own father. All this followed in natural consequence of David's heinous sin."[1]

God did not directly cause these deaths, but often "His restraining power will be in a measure removed from the agencies of evil, so that a train of circumstances will arise which will punish sin with sin."[2]

One can only imagine the remorse David must have felt in seeing the end result of his sin.

---

1. Francis D. Nichol, ed., *The Seventh-day Adventist Bible Commentary*, vol. 2 (Washington, DC: Review and Herald®, 1976), 683, 684.
2. Ellen G. White, *Patriarchs and Prophets* (Mountain View, CA: Pacific Press®, 1943), 728.

JOAB CRITICIZES DAVID

And Joab came into the house to the king, and said, Thou
hast shamed this day the faces of all thy servants, which this day
have saved thy life, and the lives of thy sons and of thy daughters,
and the lives of thy wives, and the lives of thy concubines.

—2 Samuel 19:5

A s the victorious hosts approached the city, the king, who should have been on hand to greet them, was not there. Instead of offering words of thanks and cheer for the troops who that day had risked their lives for him, David sat above the gate, loudly wailing for the loss of his son. Instead of marching proudly in triumph the men now broke their ranks, slinking into the city, downcast and ashamed. It seemed that all their effort had been in vain, and what they had thought of as a glorious victory was only a mistake and, in the eyes of the king, a sad defeat. They entered the city with the air of men defeated in battle."[1]

Joab confronted David about his response. "The gruff old commander in chief took the king severely to task for his conduct before his returning soldiers. These men had fought valiantly and well. They had risked their all for the king, and for the members of his family, but he had no word of thanks for them. He could think only of his personal loss. That others too that day were sad and mourned the loss of brothers, husbands, and fathers who had given their lives in order that David might retain his throne, meant nothing to the king. It was a cutting and bitter rebuke from the old general, but he was simply telling the harsh truth."[2]

Absalom had commanded a large part of Israel's sympathies, and David was now in danger of alienating even those who still remained loyal. Joab said, "For I swear by the Lord, if thou go not forth, there will not tarry one with thee this night: and that will be worse unto thee than all the evil that befell thee from thy youth until now" (2 Samuel 19:7). David realized Joab spoke the truth. His grief for a rebel son would cost him his throne. He needed to be seen by his troops and thank them for their loyalty and courage. He removed himself to the city gate, where he mingled with and offered words of thanks and comfort to those returning from battle.

Always remember to thank those who support you.

---

1. Francis D. Nichol, ed., *The Seventh-day Adventist Bible Commentary*, vol. 2 (Washington, DC: Review and Herald®, 1976), 685, 686.

2. Nichol, 686.

DAVID REGAINS THE THRONE

So the king returned, and came to Jordan. And Judah came to
Gilgal, to go to meet the king, to conduct the king over Jordan.
—2 Samuel 19:15

The overthrow of Absalom did not at once bring peace to the kingdom. So large a part of the nation had joined in revolt that David would not return to his capital and resume his authority without an invitation from the tribes. In the confusion that followed Absalom's defeat there was no prompt and decided action to recall the king, and when at last Judah undertook to bring back David, the jealousy of the other tribes was roused, and a counter-revolution followed."[1]

The tribes were divided in their support for David. Many vocal opponents objected to his return. Those supporting the return of David could not understand what was taking their leaders so long to invite him back from exile. They pointed out the many times David had saved their country from its enemies. Why was he not again welcome in his own land? David was wondering the same thing. Why was his own tribe of Judah taking so long to recall him (2 Samuel 19:11)? Finally, Judah sent a message to David, saying, "Return thou, and all thy servants" (v. 14). This formal invitation to reclaim the throne was not the consent of all the tribes, but at least it was a start. David moved from Mahanaim to the Jordan, where he was met by an official delegation. He then went on to Gilgal, where all the people of Judah and half the people of Israel welcomed him back to the kingdom (v. 40).

David now made a startling change to his army command. David chose his nephew Amasa to replace Joab (1 Chronicles 2:13–17). Amasa had been Absalom's commander in chief. It was a shrewd political move. Amasa could influence the warriors who had followed Absalom, and he would be prevented from continuing to foment dissent by having to swear allegiance to David. It was a bold stroke for another reason. Even though Joab had been with David from the beginning, David was tired of Joab's familiarity and domineering influence. It was Joab who petitioned for Absalom's return from exile. It was Joab who killed Absalom in direct contravention of David's order. It was Joab who rebuked David for mourning his son and told him to stop acting selfishly.

Popularity, being changeable, is a tenuous asset.

---

1. Ellen G. White, *Patriarchs and Prophets* (Mountain View, CA: Pacific Press®, 1943), 746.

SHIMEI FORGIVEN

Therefore the king said unto Shimei,
Thou shalt not die. And the king sware unto him.
—2 Samuel 19:23

Shimei and one thousand Benjamites crossed over the Jordan to ferry David and his household across. They wanted David to know they harbored no ill will, but Shimei was at the ford because he feared David's return! He realized it was better to apologize for his behavior, lest he be put to death. "Let not my lord impute iniquity unto me, neither do thou remember that which thy servant did perversely the day that my lord the king went out of Jerusalem, that the king should take it to his heart. For thy servant doth know that I have sinned: therefore, behold, I am come the first this day of all the house of Joseph to go down to meet my lord the king" (2 Samuel 19:19, 20). Basically, he was saying, "I did not really mean what I said. Do not take it seriously. I was just kidding." He confessed his guilt and threw himself on the mercy of David, but Abishai insisted, "Shall not Shimei be put to death for this, because he cursed the LORD's anointed?" (v. 21).

"According to the customs of the time Shimei's cruel cursing of David at the time of David's flight would normally merit death, but Shimei had cast himself on David's mercy and asked for forgiveness. David was willing to be lenient, whereas Abishai could think only of stern justice."[1] David "not only spared the life of Shimei, but mercifully forgave him. Had David possessed a revengeful spirit, he could readily have gratified it, by putting the offender to death."[2] "This was a time for mercy, not hard, cold justice. The occasion called for reconciliation, not a meting out of punishment upon all who had previously turned their backs upon David. The greatness and magnanimity of David was displayed on this occasion. The king attempted to win the nation back to himself by kindness and mercy. He indicated that all would be forgiven who wished to make their peace with him."[3]

"Forgive, and ye shall be forgiven" (Luke 6:37).

1. Francis D. Nichol, ed., *The Seventh-day Adventist Bible Commentary*, vol. 2 (Washington, DC: Review and Herald®, 1976), 687, 688.
2. Ellen G. White, *The Spirit of Prophecy*, vol. 1 (Battle Creek, MI: Seventh-day Adventist Pub. Assn., 1870), 384.
3. Nichol, *The Seventh-day Adventist Bible Commentary*, 2:688.

WHERE WERE YOU, MEPHIBOSHETH?

*And Mephibosheth the son of Saul came down to
meet the king, and had neither dressed his feet, nor
trimmed his beard, nor washed his clothes, from the day
the king departed until the day he came again in peace.*
—2 Samuel 19:24

Ziba came to the Jordan to welcome David back home as well. Mephibosheth also arrived in a state of mourning, showing his grief over David's exile and his loyalty to his king. Upon seeing Mephibosheth, David asked, "Wherefore wentest not thou with me, Mephibosheth?" (2 Samuel 19:25). "Mephibosheth claimed that for purposes of personal gain, Ziba had told David a base falsehood, thus causing David to regard as ungrateful and disloyal his erstwhile faithful servant. . . . According to the new version of the incident the two asses Ziba brought to David had actually been prepared at Mephibosheth's orders, so that he could take his flight with David. Instead they had been stolen by Ziba, who left Mephibosheth at home, helpless in his lameness."[1]

Mephibosheth left justice in the hands of David, for the king had dealt mercifully with him in the past. David could have had all descendants of Saul put to death so there would never be a challenge to his throne. Instead, David had treated the son of Jonathan with graciousness. "David had done Mephibosheth an injustice in accepting Ziba's story without verification and in bestowing on him all his master's possessions before hearing the other side of the case ([2 Samuel] 16:4). David now realized that an injustice had been done and endeavored to undo it by returning to Mephibosheth half his property. This would hardly seem sufficient, however, to satisfy justice. If Ziba told the truth, he should have kept all; if not, he should have been deprived of all his gains and been punished besides. David's compromise was both weak and unjust."[2]

Mephibosheth did not complain about this unfair judgment. He wanted David to know he had not come down to see him in order to get his property back. He offered to let Ziba have everything: "Yea, let him take all, forasmuch as my lord the king is come again in peace unto his own house" (2 Samuel 19:30). It was enough. David was back.

Would you, as a Christian, be content with such an injustice?

---

1. Francis D. Nichol, ed., *The Seventh-day Adventist Bible Commentary,* vol. 2 (Washington, DC: Review and Herald®, 1976), 688.
2. Nichol, 688.

Barzillai

Now Barzillai was a very aged man, even fourscore years old: and he had provided the king of sustenance while he lay at Mahanaim; for he was a very great man.
—2 Samuel 19:32

When David fled Jerusalem and crossed over the Jordan to the east, he had been met by three men who welcomed him and provided his entourage with supplies. "And it came to pass, when David was come to Mahanaim, that Shobi the son of Nahash of Rabbah of the children of Ammon, and Machir the son of Ammiel of Lodebar, and Barzillai the Gileadite of Rogelim, brought beds, and basons, and earthen vessels, and wheat, and barley, and flour, and parched corn, and beans, and lentiles, and parched pulse, and honey, and butter, and sheep, and cheese of kine [cows], for David, and for the people that were with him, to eat: for they said, The people is hungry, and weary, and thirsty, in the wilderness" (2 Samuel 17:27–29).

The supplies were a welcome relief after the rapid flight from Jerusalem. Little is known about these three men aside from their kindness. Shobi may have been the son of Nahash, the king of Ammon, who helped David when Saul was hunting him (2 Samuel 10:2). Machir was "the man who had been the guardian of Mephibosheth, the lame son of Jonathan. . . . As Machir once had shown kindness to the house of Saul, so now he showed kindness to David."[1]

Barzillai "was the ancestor, through a daughter, of a family of priests who were called the children of Barzillai (Ezra 2:61–63)."[2] Barzillai, following the courteous Middle Eastern custom of a host, accompanied his guest partway on his return journey. The Bible mentions Barzillai as "a very aged man" at eighty years old (2 Samuel 19:32). David offered to feed Barzillai if he would accompany him to Jerusalem, but Barzillai respectfully declined. He "sought nothing for himself. God had been kind to him. There was nothing further to seek in the pleasures of this world. Life for David during his exile beyond the Jordan had been happier because of the kindness of Barzillai."[3] This gracious host bade him goodbye after seeing him safely to the west bank.

Giving, without thought of reward, is the mark of a true Christian (Luke 6:35).

---

1. Francis D. Nichol, ed., *The Seventh-day Adventist Bible Commentary*, vol. 2 (Washington, DC: Review and Herald®, 1976), 679.
2. Nichol, 679.
3. Nichol, 689.

WE WERE MORE LOYAL THAN YOU!

*And, behold, all the men of Israel came to the king,
and said unto the king, Why have our brethren the men
of Judah stolen thee away, and have brought the king, and
his household, and all David's men with him, over Jordan?*
—2 Samuel 19:41

A dispute arose among the tribes as to who had been most loyal. How quickly the tribes had changed their minds from seeking to depose David to welcoming him back. The tide of public opinion had turned in David's favor. Elders on both sides were quick to sense this sentiment and, like true politicians, sought to align themselves with the returning king. The majority of those waiting to welcome David home were from his own tribe of Judah. This was to be expected as the tribes of Israel were further west and north of the Jordan River's border. Additionally, word of David's return had not yet reached all the tribes to the north, so it was expected their turnout would be lower (2 Samuel 19:41). Yet division had always existed between the people of Israel in the north and Judah in the south. These tribes always seemed to be engaged in some sort of resentment or another (Judges 8:1; 12:1). David's reign had begun with only the tribe of Judah anointing him king (2 Samuel 2:4). Attempts to get all the tribes of Israel to recognize David's right to the throne met with little success until he had sat on the throne in Hebron for seven years (2 Samuel 3:10; 5:1–5). Now David was back, and so was the loathing.

Judah had every right to claim David as their own, for he was kin. Yet they wanted it made clear that they had not received special treatment from the king (2 Samuel 19:42). "And the men of Israel answered the men of Judah, and said, We have ten parts in the king, and we have also more right in David than ye: why then did ye despise us, that our advice should not be first had in bringing back our king? And the words of the men of Judah were fiercer than the words of the men of Israel" (v. 43). "The dispute was happily arrested after a time, but the fact of its occurrence did not augur well for the future. The present differences between north and south foreshadowed greater troubles to come. Sectional jealousies and rivalries were constantly sowing the seeds of disaster."[1]

Church jealousies and rivalries still lead to disaster!

---

1. Francis D. Nichol, ed., *The Seventh-day Adventist Bible Commentary*, vol. 2 (Washington, DC: Review and Herald®, 1976), 689.

SHEBA'S REVOLT

And there happened to be there a man of Belial, whose
name was Sheba, the son of Bichri, a Benjamite: and he blew
a trumpet, and said, We have no part in David, neither have we
inheritance in the son of Jesse: every man to his tents, O Israel.
—2 Samuel 20:1

The return of David was not smooth. Israel and Judah had recently disputed over who was most loyal. This spirit of rivalry had existed throughout Israel's history, and the tribes had fought incessantly among themselves—as far back as their disagreement concerning the fate of their brother Joseph. "Under the judges God had made each tribe virtually independent. Taxes were extremely low. Although the tribes worked together as allies, 'there was no king in Israel: every man did that which was right in his own eyes' (Judges 21:25)."[1]

Now a Benjamite named Sheba took advantage of these differences to fan the flames of controversy against David. He issued a call for each man to return to his own tribe and revolt against having one king over all. This was especially attractive to the northern tribes, who had little stake in giving allegiance to a man not of their tribe. His message was calculated to create a divide between Judah and the rest of the tribes. Why should they swear allegiance to a king who was not a relative? "Only a short time before the men of Israel were loud in their protestations that they had a greater claim upon David than had the men of Judah. . . . Human nature is fickle indeed. David's throne was still far from secure in spite of all the loud words of welcome."[2]

If David was to regain control over the entire kingdom, he would have to fight a civil war to do so. "The rebellion of Absalom had originated in Judah, and it was Judah that had been tardy in returning to the standard of David ([2 Samuel] 19:11), but now Judah clave to him. It was well for David that he had wooed rather than alienated the affections of Judah, for it was to these men who were so slow to welcome him that he now owed his throne."[3] Could one man rule over these contentious people and get them to agree on anything?

Consider: covetousness of an exalted position was the original sin in heaven.

---

1. Francis D. Nichol, ed., *The Seventh-day Adventist Bible Commentary*, vol. 2 (Washington, DC: Review and Herald®, 1976), 486.
2. Nichol, 691.
3. Nichol, 691.

AMASA SLAIN

And Joab said to Amasa, Art thou in health, my brother? And
Joab took Amasa by the beard with the right hand to kiss him.
—2 Samuel 20:9

D avid had promised Amasa he would take the place of Joab as
commander of the army (2 Samuel 19:13). Now that a crisis had
come up, Amasa was put to the test. As a new commander, he
had his hands full with trying to come to grips with his new command.
David ordered him to gather the troops and prepare to march in three
days. It took him longer than the three days allotted to complete the
muster. It is safe to assume Joab, the former commander, did not do
much to help Amasa meet the deadline.

At this point, David turned to Joab's brother Abishai and ordered him
to take the field before Sheba had time to consolidate his forces within
fortified cities. Speed was essential if the revolt was to be crushed. Giving
Sheba time to organize meant his rebellion might become established and
would be harder to stamp out. In reaching out to Abishai, David strategically bypassed Joab, who had become too powerful and had disagreed
with David's actions on too many recent occasions. His disobedience,
coupled with the loyalty of the army, was a matter to be taken seriously.

David's own bodyguard of Cherethites and Pelethites were called
upon to undertake this hurried mission. This threat was serious enough
for David to strip himself of personal protection in order to rapidly destroy Sheba's forces. David's men were handpicked for their bravery and
loyalty. In the town of Gibeon, nearly six miles northwest of Jerusalem,
Amasa caught up with the vanguard under Abishai.

As Amasa approached at the head of his troops, Joab came forward
to greet him. He had a dagger thrust into his belt. The blade fell out as
he came near Amasa. Some believe he stooped to pick it up with his left
hand. Others believe he had secreted a second knife on his person. In
any event, it appeared he was unarmed. Grasping Amasa's beard with
his right hand, he kissed his cousin. As he did so, he plunged the blade
into Amasa's stomach. It happened so fast that Amasa had no time to
suspect deceit or defend himself against such treachery. With Amasa
removed, Joab simply resumed his previous position as commander in
chief of the army and continued the pursuit of Sheba.

"Deceit is in the heart of them that imagine evil" (Proverbs 12:20).

THE REVOLT CRUSHED

When he [Amasa] was removed out of the highway, all the people
went on after Joab, to pursue after Sheba the son of Bichri.
—2 Samuel 20:13

Amasa's body lay in the middle of the road. Those following behind him recognized his body and questioned his death. Joab, therefore, placed one of his most loyal men beside the body to make it known that Amasa had been killed because he was guilty of treachery against David. The army knew Amasa had led the forces of Absalom, and it was not difficult to suspect him of continued disloyalty. They were equally glad to welcome Joab back as their commander. Amasa's body was moved off the road and covered so no further disturbance would arise from the following ranks.

Forces were flocking to Sheba's banner, and it would not be long before he would amass a formidable army. He retreated to Abel-beth-maachah, located in the territory allotted to the tribe of Naphtali (1 Kings 15:20; 2 Kings 15:29). The city had been fortified with a wall and moat, forcing Joab to lay siege to it. Fresh earth was piled into the ditch surrounding the town. Once the earthen ramp was high enough, attacking forces would be brought forward to breach the wall and gain entrance to the city.

At this point in the siege, a wise woman called out from the city wall, seeking an audience with the commander of David's army. Her city was about to become the scene of a slaughter of innocents. It did not seem right that many should die for the sake of one agitator. Joab came forward and identified himself to the woman. She asked, Why it is "thou seekest to destroy a city and a mother in Israel: why wilt thou swallow up the inheritance of the LORD?" (2 Samuel 20:19). Joab stated he only wanted Sheba and would spare the city if the traitor were turned over to him. The woman replied, "Behold, his head shall be thrown to thee over the wall" (v. 21).

The woman told her neighbors that if they would surrender Sheba, their town and the lives of its inhabitants would be spared. The citizens wasted no time in cutting off the head of the troublemaker and throwing it over the wall. Joab kept his end of the bargain. He recalled the troops, and they dispersed.

"For by wise counsel thou shalt make thy war: and in multitude of counsellors there is safety" (Proverbs 24:6).

289

JOAB GETS AWAY WITH MURDER

Now Joab was over all the host of Israel.

—2 Samuel 20:23

F ollowing the suppression of Sheba's revolt, David reorganized his staff. Most of the positions remained the same, but there were some notable changes. Benaiah, son of Jehoiada, remained in command of the Cherethites and Pelethites, who were David's bodyguard. He had distinguished himself by killing two fierce warriors during the battle with Moab (2 Samuel 23:20). Adoram (or Adoniram) was made overseer of the labor crew. These workers were conscripted to work on national projects, such as building the temple (1 Kings 5:13, 14). Jehoshaphat, son of Ahilud, was appointed recorder (2 Samuel 8:16), and Sheva was appointed scribe or secretary of state (2 Samuel 20:25). Zadok and Abiathar retained their places as priests.

Perhaps the most interesting appointment to office was that of Joab, who again became the leader of David's army. Let us take a moment to review his checkered past: First, Joab was family. He was the son of David's sister Zeruiah. Joab's relationship with his uncle was complicated. We first see him in the battle against the forces of Saul's son Ish-bosheth at Gibeon. While fleeing the battle, Abner, leader of Ish-bosheth's defeated forces, kills Joab's younger brother Asahel (2 Samuel 2:12–32). After Abner defects to David, Joab and his brother Abishai assassinate Abner (2 Samuel 3:12, 20–30). Abner's death was not simply an act of revenge. Joab feared David would appoint Abner to replace him as army commander. David did little to punish Joab and Abishai for this murder (vv. 31–39).

Jerusalem was taken as a result of Joab's bravery, and he was rewarded by being made chief of David's army (1 Chronicles 11:6). There then followed victorious wars against the Edomites, Syrians, and Ammonites (1 Kings 11:16; 2 Samuel 10:6–14; 1 Chronicles 19:6–15). At the siege of Rabbah, Joab followed David's instructions and made possible Uriah's death (2 Samuel 11:1–17). Joab was instrumental in influencing David to recall Absalom from his banishment. Feeling betrayed, he went against David's wishes and personally had his cousin killed (2 Samuel 18:14–17). He then rebuked David for excessive grief (2 Samuel 19:5–8). He killed Amasa to retain his position as the army's leader and then efficiently put down Sheba's revolt. Joab was brave, unscrupulous, insubordinate, ruthless, vindictive, and a threat to the throne!

Was David blind to these faults or fearful of the army's loyalty to Joab?

REPARATIONS

Then there was a famine in the days of David three years, year after year; and David enquired of the LORD. And the LORD answered, It is for Saul, and for his bloody house, because he slew the Gibeonites.
—2 Samuel 21:1

At some unknown time during the course of David's reign, the events of 2 Samuel 21:1 took place. "At the time of the conquest of Canaan the Gibeonites had succeeded through guile in making a league with Joshua. According to the terms of this league they were to be allowed to live with Israel in a state of servitude (Joshua 9:3–27)."[1] The leaders of Israel had sworn a solemn oath before God. Saul had broken that pact and sought to exterminate their race, and the people of Israel supported him in his effort. All Israel was, therefore, guilty of breaking their word to both the Gibeonites and God. God's punishment accordingly fell upon the entire nation.

Knowing the reason for the famine, David asked the remaining Gibeonites what they would have him do to atone for Israel's breach of trust. They did not want reparations for their confiscated property. Instead, they believed the main guilt should fall upon the house of Saul, for he was primarily responsible for inflicting their pain. The request seemed generous and proportional. "Let seven men of his sons be delivered unto us, and we will hang them up unto the LORD in Gibeah [the home] of Saul, whom the LORD did choose. And the king said, I will give them" (2 Samuel 21:6). But God was not consulted regarding the acceptability of their request!

David had given his own solemn word to Jonathan that he would protect Jonathan's children. He therefore exempted Mephibosheth from the list of sons to be surrendered, lest he be guilty of breaking his own vow. Were these seven sons of Saul guilty of following their father in his zeal to exterminate the Gibeonites? We are not told whether they were culpable in crimes against humanity. Rizpah, the mother of two of the executed sons, made a rough shelter of sackcloth near their exposed bodies and kept an estimated six-month-long vigil over them, keeping away birds of prey and wild animals that might desecrate the bodies of her sons.

David was so impressed by this mother's loving devotion that he showed increased respect for the remaining members of Saul's family.

---

1. Francis D. Nichol, ed., *The Seventh-day Adventist Bible Commentary*, vol. 2 (Washington, DC: Review and Herald®, 1976), 695.

CLOSING THE BOOK ON SAUL

And the bones of Saul and Jonathan his son buried they in the country of Benjamin in Zelah, in the sepulchre of Kish his father.
—2 Samuel 21:14

With the famine at an end, things, at last, returned to normal in Israel. David had been impressed by Rizpah's devotion as she stood vigil over the bodies of her two dead sons, preventing birds and wild beasts from devouring their remains. "Rizpah was one of the concubines of Saul, with whom Abner had been charged with committing adultery ([2 Samuel] 3:7).[1] As a result of this mother's watchfulness and steadfast endurance in the face of such a heartbreaking task, David decided to return the remains of Saul and Jonathan to their ancestral home.

It was time to tie up loose ends. The Philistines had fastened the bodies of Saul and his sons to a wall facing the public square in their town of Beth-shan (1 Samuel 31:10–12). It was from this place, in the dead of night, the brave men of Jabesh-gilead had recovered them (vv. 11–13). The bones, plucked from their foes, had been kept in Jabesh-gilead ever since that night raid. "Wishing to show that he cherished no enmity against the former king, David brought the bones of Saul and Jonathan from Jabesh-gilead and gave them an honorable burial in the ancient family sepulcher."[2] David had them returned to Zelah, a town in Benjamin (Joshua 18:28) that must have been near Gibeah, for that was the family home of Saul.

"And after that God was intreated for the land" (2 Samuel 21:14). This verse does not suggest "that David had followed God's plan for atoning for Saul's evil deed. The Lord might measure an act by the sincerity of heart that prompted it, even though He condemned the act itself."[3] David surrendered the seven sons of Saul to the Gibeonites, knowing they would be put to death. He sincerely desired to administer justice and ruled that it would be served by offering up the men.

"The eyes of the LORD are in every place, beholding the evil and the good" (Proverbs 15:3).

---

1. Francis D. Nichol, ed., *The Seventh-day Adventist Bible Commentary*, vol. 2 (Washington, DC: Review and Herald®, 1976), 696.
2. Nichol, 697.
3. Nichol, 697.

Psalm 65: The Farmer's Psalm

Thou visitest the earth, and waterest it: thou greatly enrichest it with the river of God, which is full of water: thou preparest them corn, when thou hast so provided for it.

—Psalm 65:9

I t seems appropriate to place Psalm 65, "a glorious harvest hymn," at this time in the chronology of David's reign.[1] It might have been penned following the three-year famine mentioned in 2 Samuel 21:1. This awe-inspiring psalm praises "God for (1) His moral qualities (vs. 1–4), (2) His power and majesty in nature (vs. 5–8), and (3) the abundant harvest (vs. 9–13)."[2]

"Praise waiteth for thee, O God" (v. 1). "When every other voice is hushed, and in quietness we wait before Him, the silence of the soul makes more distinct the voice of God."[3] God cares for those who recognize their need for mercy and forgiveness. The Father has created a way for all to receive salvation (John 3:16). All humanity may place confidence in the Divine Creator (Psalm 65:5). His power raised majestic mountains (v. 6). His power calms the turbulent sea (v. 7). Humans stand awestruck by His power as expressed through the forces of nature (v. 8). The beauty of a sunrise and the serenity of a sunset inspire reflection on God's wondrous creation (v. 8).

"The psalmist adores God for His bountiful providence in the harvest, tracing the various steps in the processes of nature, until the glorious culmination is reached. The verses are a graphic description of the hills and valleys of Palestine, terraced tier on tier, and covered with olives, vines, and expanses of wheat, barley, and millet. Especially because of this section of the poem, [Psalm] 65 has been called The Farmer's Psalm."[4] "The meadows in the valleys, rich with undulating grain, shout and sing for the very joy of being. All nature rejoices in God."[5]

"Lo, the scene of verdure brightening! | See the rising grain appear; | Look again! the fields are whitening, | For the harvesttime is near."[6]

---

1. Francis D. Nichol, ed., *The Seventh-day Adventist Bible Commentary*, vol. 3 (Washington, DC: Review and Herald®, 1977), 782.

2. Nichol, 782.

3. Ellen G. White, *The Desire of Ages* (Mountain View, CA: Pacific Press®, 1940), 363.

4. Nichol, *The Seventh-day Adventist Bible Commentary*, 3:783.

5. Nichol, 784.

6. T. Hastings, "He That Goeth Forth," in *The Church Hymnal: The Official Hymnal of the Seventh-day Adventist Church* (Washington, DC: Review and Herald®, 1941), hymn 627.

PSALM 36: GOD'S LOVING-KINDNESS

*Thy mercy, O LORD, is in the heavens; and thy faithfulness reacheth
unto the clouds. Thy righteousness is like the great mountains; thy
judgments are a great deep: O LORD, thou preservest man and beast.*

—Psalm 36:5, 6

David could not understand the depravity of the wicked. Their actions puzzled him. This psalm describes the steps taken by one who turns his back on the Lord and walks in his own shadow. A man first pays no heed to his conscience (v. 1). He cherishes a sin in his heart and thinks longingly upon it. He then speaks of how it might be accomplished. His conscience becomes numb to sin and no longer condemns it (v. 2). Once the conscience has become corrupted (vv. 3, 4), the man yields to impulse and commits the act. "For out of the heart proceed evil thoughts, murders, adulteries, fornications, thefts, false witness, blasphemies" (Matthew 15:19).

The psalmist next speaks of God's mercy and faithfulness (v. 5). God is just. His judgments are limitless and profound (v. 6). He cares for all creation and provides merciful safety under His wings for those oppressed by evil men (v. 7). In God may be found all that is necessary for a believer to live in trust and plenty. David compares God's blessings to drinking one's fill (v. 8; see also John 4:10–14). This is an especially powerful image for those who have lived in areas where water is precious. Believing in God gives meaning to life (John 1:4; 5:26).

God's commandments set boundaries for one's conscience. Only by walking in the Light can we see to adjust our course in this dark world of sin (v. 9). David therefore asks God to continue to reveal Himself (v. 10), so knowledge of Him might deliver a fountain of joy (John 17:3). David prays for deliverance from proud sinners and for protection from those who would harm and separate him from God (v. 11). Those who love the Lord will ultimately be triumphant while the wicked will be permanently destroyed (v. 12). "And, behold, I come quickly; and my reward is with me, to give every man according as his work shall be" (Revelation 22:12).

"Live out Thy life within me, / O Jesus, King of kings! / Be Thou Thyself the answer / To all my questionings; / Live out Thy life within me, / In all things have Thy way! / I, the transparent medium / Thy glory to display."[1]

---

1. Frances Ridley Havergal, "Live Out Thy Life Within Me," in *The Seventh-day Adventist Hymnal* (Hagerstown, MD: Review and Herald®, 1985), hymn 316.

PSALM 50: GOD IS JUDGE HIMSELF

Our God shall come, and shall not keep silence: a fire shall devour before him, and it shall be very tempestuous round about him.
—Psalm 50:3

Psalm 50 was written by David for Asaph—his Levite choir leader. "Against a magnificent background description of a judgment, which may be applied to the last judgment (vs. 1–6; . . .), the psalm unfolds its message as a rebuke to the worshiper who follows religious ceremony but lacks sincerity of heart and purity of conduct. The body of the psalm has two parts: condemnation of the evils of mere formalism in worship (vs. 7–15), and condemnation of hypocrisy (vs. 16–21)."[1]

Verse 1 will be fulfilled at the second coming of Christ (Matthew 24:30). Angels will gather the redeemed (Psalm 50:5), and God Himself will pronounce judgment upon all humankind (vv. 4, 6). Justice will be swift and accurate. The standard is obedience to God's commandments and faith in Jesus (Revelation 14:12). Israel will not be judged remiss for following their ceremonies and rites of religion (Psalm 50:7–15). Yet religious formalism is of no value. "Only lives full of penitence, love, gratitude, obedience, and devotion can be acceptable in the sight of God."[2]

The psalm now turns to man's hypocrisy (vv. 16–21). The wicked claim to obey God but are quick to do evil when an opportunity presents itself (v. 18). They slander relatives and tell falsehoods about their brethren (vv. 19, 20). God remains silent but not because He is unaware of their actions. He will deal with them at the final judgment (v. 21). External piety can hide a sinful nature from fellow believers, but God reads the heart, and phony Christians will finally understand their guilt at the judgment. "We may participate in all the ordinances of the church, be constant attendants at divine service, give freely to help the poor, engage in much missionary activity, and yet be reprobate if we fail to serve God in spirit, or if we cherish sin in our hearts."[3]

"Forever firm Thy justice stands, / As mountains their foundations keep; / Wise are the wonders of Thy hands; / Thy judgments are a mighty deep."[4]

---

1. Francis D. Nichol, ed., *The Seventh-day Adventist Bible Commentary*, vol. 3 (Washington, DC: Review and Herald®, 1977), 752.

2. Nichol, 753.

3. Nichol, 754.

4. Isaac Watts, "High in the Heavens," in *The Church Hymnal: The Official Hymnal of the Seventh-day Adventist Church* (Washington, DC: Review and Herald®, 1941), hymn 69.

PSALM 73: WHY DO THE WICKED PROSPER?

Behold, these are the ungodly, who prosper in the
world; they increase in riches. Verily I have cleansed
my heart in vain, and washed my hands in innocency.
—Psalm 73:12, 13

Why does it seem the wicked prosper in life while the righteous suffer? This question distresses David. He confesses he has almost lost faith in God over the issue (Psalm 73:2). He has become skeptical of trying to lead a good and decent life and begun to envy those with more material wealth and peace (v. 3). They seem to thrive in spite of their wicked ways. His life has been one of hardship, while others, who profess no belief in God, seemingly cruise through life with little or no difficulty. They even appear to die peacefully with little suffering (v. 4).

Evil men seem to escape the difficulties most of humanity suffers (v. 6). They have whatever they wish for and seemingly live very well with little effort (v. 7). They even boast of their corruption and how wily and clever they are (v. 8). They are confident God does not exist (v. 11). If He did, would He not cause their evil tactics to fail? Surely, reflects David, there is no benefit in being chaste before God (v. 13). This problem of the obvious unfairness in God's rule is too deep to understand (v. 16).

But with the new morning comes enlightenment (Job 7:18). David decides to keep his doubts to himself, lest he be a stumbling block for others (Psalm 73:15). Instead, he goes to the house of the Lord to find an answer in silent communion with God. Here he finally puts things into perspective (v. 17). He is placing too much emphasis on this present life. The wicked may prosper for a time during their short life spans, but they will have no part in eternity. Everything they gain in this life will ultimately be lost in an instant when their lives are over (vv. 18–20). A relationship with God is worth much more than any material wealth (vv. 23–28)! "To be with God is life; to be far from Him is death. The psalmist's realization of this fact solved the problem of God's dealings with men."[1]

"Jesus, to Thee I now can fly, / On whom my help is laid; / Oppressed by sins,
I lift mine eye, / And see the shadows fade."[2]

---

1. Francis D. Nichol, ed., *The Seventh-day Adventist Bible Commentary*, vol. 3 (Washington, DC: Review and Herald®, 1977), 804, 805.

2. Charles Wesley, "Jesus, to Thee I Now Can Fly," in *The Church Hymnal: The Official Hymnal of the Seventh-day Adventist Church* (Washington, DC: Review and Herald®, 1941), hymn 233.

PSALM 37: RIGHT WILL TRIUMPH

*Fret not thyself because of evildoers, neither be thou
envious against the workers of iniquity. For they shall soon
be cut down like the grass, and wither as the green herb.*
—Psalm 37:1, 2

Psalm 37 was written when David was old (v. 25), and like Psalm 73, it counsels us not to fret over the visible success of the wicked (v. 1). "As Christians we should conquer fretting, for in fretting we lose perspective and clarity of vision. Moreover, when we are angry with the sinner, we are unable to help him, and also put ourselves in the wrong."[1] A sinner's gains will be short lived (v. 2). One should not envy the wicked or their prosperity. Instead, we should (1) trust in God, (2) keep active in doing good, (3) quietly dwell where God places us, and (4) watch for God's faithfulness (v. 3). "Commit thy way unto the LORD; trust also in him; and he shall bring it to pass" (v. 5). Let Jesus carry your burdens. Place your confidence in God, and He will cause others to see the rightness of your course (v. 6). He will calm your soul when troubles arise (v. 7).

Above all, do not cherish anger against evildoers (v. 8). God holds their destiny in His hands (v. 9). Meekly follow your Lord and Savior, and in time, you will inherit the earth (vv. 10, 11; see also Matthew 5:5). The wicked take advantage of the poor and weak and laugh at the Christian trying to do right (vv. 12–14), but all their evil will eventually return upon their own heads (v. 15). The righteous will emerge victorious with an eternal inheritance (vv. 16–18).

Those who are a blessing to their fellow man in this life will inherit the earth made new. Those who abuse and steal from their fellow man will be destroyed (vv. 21, 22). We may make mistakes, but the righteous repent of their sins and do their best to make things right (vv. 23, 24). The crux of the entire psalm is found in verse 27: "Depart from evil, and do good; and dwell for evermore." Eventually, right *will* triumph, and truth *will* be vindicated (vv. 28–40)! "In studying this psalm, it is well to bear in mind that this life is a school preparing us for the life hereafter, the prelude to the drama of life eternal. Ultimately it will be well with the righteous."[2]

"I'm but a stranger here, / Heaven is my home; / . . . I shall be glorified."[3]

---

1. Francis D. Nichol, ed., *The Seventh-day Adventist Bible Commentary*, vol. 3 (Washington, DC: Review and Herald®, 1977), 721, 722.
2. Nichol, 724.
3. Thomas R. Taylor, "I'm but a Stranger Here" (1835), in *The Seventh-day Adventist Hymnal* (Hagerstown, MD: Review and Herald®, 1985), hymn 445.

DAVID FAINTS IN BATTLE

Moreover the Philistines had yet war again with Israel; and David went down, and his servants with him, and fought against the Philistines: and David waxed faint.

—2 Samuel 21:15

I t is hard to place the timing of 2 Samuel 21:15–22 into the chronology of other events in the life of David. It probably took place after David had been on the throne for some time. It was customary for a king to take the field of battle with his men. For example, David did not go up against the city of Rabbah until the last moment when victory was assured and he was summoned by Joab to be present during the surrender (2 Samuel 12:26–31). Sometime later, at the urging of his men, David did not expose himself during the battle with Absalom's men. They feared for his safety. If David were killed, their cause would be lost (2 Samuel 18:3).

During this era, personal combat was expected of a king. Kings did not send men into places they themselves would not go. Saul had fallen in combat against the Philistines. But in the war with the Philistines in 2 Samuel 21:15–22, David was putting himself needlessly in harm's way. He had nothing to prove when it came to valor. He was a warrior-king. As a strategist, he was second to none. The men surrounding him were handpicked for their courage and valor. His captains possessed vast military experience. The rank and file willingly followed these leaders into battle, confident of victory. With God on the side of Israel, surely they could not fail. There was no reason then for David to continue placing his life in jeopardy. Nor was there any reason to face the tallest and fiercest warrior on the opposing side in hand-to-hand combat.

Here, however, we see David once again taking the field against the Philistines. The Philistine giant Ishbi-benob, wielding a spear weighing seven pounds and a new sword, appeared to have defeated David in personal combat. Seeing this, Abishai came to David's aid. Standing over his prostrate king, he killed the giant in mortal combat. Such a close call was clearly one too many for the men of David's army. "Then the men of David sware unto him, saying, Thou shalt go no more out with us to battle, that thou quench not the light of Israel" (2 Samuel 21:17).

Wisdom is often the better part of valor.

PSALM 44: JEHOVAH IS OUR DELIVERER

For I will not trust in my bow, neither shall my sword save me. But thou hast saved us from our enemies, and hast put them to shame that hated us.
—Psalm 44:6, 7

Psalm 44 "is an earnest prayer to God to interpose and deliver His people from their enemies. The psalm has four sections: vs. 1–8, God's goodness to Israel in days of old; vs. 9–16, the present sad plight of Israel; vs. 17–22, the psalmist's contention that Israel has remained true to God; and vs. 23–26, the psalmist's appeal to God to deliver Israel."[1] The Israelites were proud of their heritage. Father passed to his son the verbal history of God's provident care of His people (v. 1). The tribes of Canaan had been cast out, and the Promised Land had been settled because God had gone before His people in battle (vv. 2, 3). God had always been with Israel, and the nation took great pride in this fact (vv. 4–8). Now Israel was again in dire straits (vv. 9–12). The people were being slaughtered like sheep (vv. 11, 22). It seemed God had sold Israel out (v. 12). The surrounding nations mocked and derided them (vv. 13, 14). Why was this happening (v. 15)? It was shameful that God's enemies could blaspheme Him and Israel could do nothing (vv. 15, 16).

David here argues that Israel does not deserve to be rejected (vv. 17–19). "It is difficult to understand how the psalmist could maintain that Israel had remained faithful, in the light of her continued defection. Perhaps he means that although individuals—even a majority of them—had broken the covenant, still, as a nation, she had not formally disavowed God."[2] Yet the country had been laid to waste and was fit only for wild animals (v. 19). God knows what David is saying is true (v. 21). The Israelites have not broken the covenant; they are suffering simply because they are God's people (v. 22). David pleads with God to awaken to the affliction of His people and come to their aid (vv. 23, 25). "Arise for our help, and redeem us for thy mercies' sake" (v. 26). David believes God still loves Israel, but he just cannot comprehend God's ways.

"Jesus, the very thought of Thee, / With sweetness fills my breast; / But sweeter far Thy face to see, / And in Thy presence rest."[3]

---

1. Francis D. Nichol, ed., *The Seventh-day Adventist Bible Commentary*, vol. 3 (Washington, DC: Review and Herald®, 1977), 738.
2. Nichol, 739, 740.
3. Attributed to Bernard of Clairvaux, "Jesus, the Very Thought of Thee," in *The Seventh-day Adventist Hymnal* (Hagerstown, MD: Review and Herald®, 1985), hymn 241.

WHAT GIANTS DO YOU FIGHT?

These four were born to the giant in Gath, and fell by
the hand of David, and by the hand of his servants.

—2 Samuel 21:22

The land of Canaan spawned Philistine giants. When spies from Israel were first sent into the land, they returned after forty days with tales of giants. "The land . . . is a land that eateth up the inhabitants thereof; and all the people that we saw in it are men of a great stature. And there we saw the giants, the sons of Anak, which come of the giants: and we were in our own sight as grasshoppers, and so we were in their sight" (Numbers 13:32, 33). David had met Goliath on the field of battle and slain him. During a subsequent battle with the Philistines, Sibbechai the Hushathite killed Saph, also the son of a giant (2 Samuel 21:18). Facing them must have been intimidating. Their towering height gave them an advantage, and the longer reach of their arms also favored them during hand-to-hand combat. They were also stronger than the average warrior. These were truly intimidating warriors, wielding massive weaponry.

Now another battle took place between the Israelites and the Philistines. This one likely occurred near Gezer, "a strongly fortified bastion overlooking the Philistine plain about 7 mi. (11.2 km.) northeast of Ekron, near the Valley of Aijalon."[1] The account given in 2 Samuel 21 states the battle took place near Gob, but that town had probably already been eclipsed by the larger nearby town of Gezer when the same battle was recorded in 1 Chronicles 20:4. In this battle, Lahmi, the brother of Goliath, was slain by Elhanan of Bethlehem, the son of Jaare-oregim (v. 5). Another giant from Gath was also present in this battle. He possessed six fingers on each hand and six toes on each foot—a total of twenty-four digits. David's nephew Jonathan (v. 7; 1 Samuel 16:9), son of Shimeah, killed this warrior (2 Samuel 21:21).

In four separate battles, four giants from Gath fell before David or his kinsmen. While we may not fight physical giants, we are nevertheless in a giant struggle against evil.

"Put on the whole armour of God, that ye may be able to stand against the wiles of the devil" (Ephesians 6:11).

---

1. Francis D. Nichol, ed., *The Seventh-day Adventist Bible Commentary*, vol. 2 (Washington, DC: Review and Herald®, 1976), 697, 698.

David's Trustworthy Fighters

These be the names of the mighty men whom David had.
—2 Samuel 23:8

D avid owed much to the cadre of brave fighters who rallied to him. The hand of God was certainly seen in the gathering of these gifted warriors. Time and time again, these men stood beside David as he faced down enemies. Many flocked to him while he was evading Saul. Others came to him once he became king. All pledged their loyalty, honor, and very lives to his service. The list of these men is long, and while many have little or nothing noted after their names, all were mighty men of valor. Lists of these men are found in 2 Samuel 23:8–39 and again in 1 Chronicles 11:10–47; 12:1–28.

Originally, David singled out thirty men as heroes and grouped them by threes. The list was later expanded. The first of three to gain honorable mention is Adino the Eznite, commander of David's first division. In one battle, he single-handedly dispatched eight hundred enemies. Eleazer, son of Dodo the Ahohite, fought the Philistines at Pas-dammim (1 Chronicles 11:13). He fought with such sustained bravery for so long, that his hand had to be pried from the hilt of his sword. Shammah, son of Agee the Hararite, single-handedly defended a field against Philistines who were foraging during a harvest raid.

The second list of three includes Abishai, brother of Joab and son of Zeruiah. He broke through the Philistine lines to draw water from the well at the gate of Bethlehem. Although Abishai killed three hundred during this foray, he is still not listed among the top three. Benaiah, commander of David's third division (1 Chronicles 27:5, 6), accompanied Abishai to retrieve the well water for David. Benaiah commanded David's bodyguard of Cherethites and Pelethites (2 Samuel 8:18; 20:23). The third warrior who took part in the water mission is not listed in the second group of three.

Second Samuel 23:26–39 is a list of David's men of valor—sort of a Hall of Fame for warriors. Asahel, commander of the fourth division, who was slain by Abner (2 Samuel 2:22, 23), is mentioned. The last name on the list in 2 Samuel 23 is Uriah the Hittite, and his name also appears on the list in 1 Chronicles 11 (v. 41).

"Most men will proclaim every one his own goodness: but a faithful man who can find?" (Proverbs 20:6).

THE PROUD MONARCH

And Joab gave up the sum of the number of the people unto the king: and there were in Israel eight hundred thousand valiant men that drew the sword; and the men of Judah were five hundred thousand men.

—2 Samuel 24:9

D avid, in his prosperity, did not preserve that humility of character and trust in God which characterized the earlier part of his life. He looked upon the accessions to the kingdom with pride, and contrasted their then prosperous condition with their few numbers and little strength when he ascended the throne, taking glory to himself. He gratified his ambitious feelings in yielding to the temptations of the Devil to number Israel [1 Chronicles 21:1], that he might compare their former weakness to their then prosperous state under his rule. This was displeasing to God, and contrary to his express command. It would lead Israel to rely upon their strength of numbers, instead of the living God."[1]

Joab was selected to take the count since this was a military census and he commanded the army. He objected strenuously but was overruled by David (2 Samuel 24:3, 4). The figures in 2 Samuel 24 probably numbered just the standing army (Israel: 800,000 + Judah: 500,000 = 1.3 million), while the figures in 1 Chronicles 21 (Israel: 1.1 million + Judah: 470,000 = 1.57 million) must have included the reserves. The tribes of Levi and Benjamin were omitted (1 Chronicles 21:6). "Benjamin was probably omitted because that may have been the center of opposition to David's plans for a greater army; and Joab, fearful of results if a forced census were taken, may have regarded discretion as the better part of valor."[2]

Too late, David realizes pride and ambition had caused him to sin. "He sees his error, and humbles himself before God, confessing his great sin in foolishly numbering the people. But his repentance came too late. The word had already gone forth from the Lord to his faithful prophet, to carry a message to David, and offer him his choice of punishments for his transgression."[3]

"A man's pride shall bring him low" (Proverbs 29:23).

---

1. Ellen G. White, *Spiritual Gifts*, vol. 4 (Washington, DC: Review and Herald®, 1945), 92.
2. Francis D. Nichol, ed., *The Seventh-day Adventist Bible Commentary*, vol. 3 (Washington, DC: Review and Herald®, 1977), 185.
3. White, *Spiritual Gifts*, 3:92.

A CHOICE OF PUNISHMENTS

Go and say unto David, Thus saith the LORD, I offer thee three things; choose thee one of them, that I may do it unto thee.
—2 Samuel 24:12

The prophet Gad said David must choose a punishment: (1) seven years of famine, (2) his enemies triumphing and causing him to flee before them for three months, or (3) three days of pestilence raining down on the people. David knew cruel human foes would have no mercy, but he trusted God. Either famine or pestilence might be the Lord's instrument of punishment. "Both judgments would fall upon the nation as much as upon the king, but inasmuch as the people cherished the same sins as those that prompted David's action, the Lord through David's error punished the sins of Israel."[1]

"Swift destruction followed. Seventy thousand were destroyed by pestilence. David and the elders of Israel were in the deepest humiliation, mourning before the Lord. As the angel of the Lord was on his way to destroy Jerusalem, God bids him to stay his work of death. A pitiful God loves his people still, notwithstanding their rebellion. The angel clad in warlike garments, with a drawn sword in his hand, stretched out over Jerusalem, is revealed to David, and to those who were with him. David is terribly afraid, yet he cries out in his distress, and his compassion for Israel. He begs of God to save the sheep. In anguish he confesses, 'I have sinned, and I have done wickedly. Let thine hand be against me, and against my father's house, and not upon the people.' God speaks to David by his prophet, and bids him make atonement for his sin."[2]

David knew he was responsible for numbering his warriors, dreaming of greater personal glory. He shouldered full blame for his failure to give credit to God for Israel's status. "Ambition for worldly greatness and a desire to be like the nations round about had arisen, and with it had come a decreasing sense of the solemn destiny to which the nation had been called."[3]

"Only by pride cometh contention: but with the well advised is wisdom" (Proverbs 13:10).

---

1. Francis D. Nichol, ed., *The Seventh-day Adventist Bible Commentary*, vol. 2 (Washington, DC: Review and Herald®, 1976), 711.
2. Ellen G. White, *Spiritual Gifts*, vol. 4 (Washington, DC: Review and Herald®, 1945), 92, 93.
3. Nichol, *The Seventh-day Adventist Bible Commentary*, 2:710.

THE THRESHING FLOOR OF ARAUNAH

And David built there an altar unto the Lord, and offered burnt offerings and peace offerings. So the Lord was intreated for the land, and the plague was stayed from Israel.

—2 Samuel 24:25

David and those with him were given a glimpse beyond the veil separating seen from unseen. Just as Balaam had seen an angel with a drawn sword blocking his way (Numbers 22:31), David now saw an angel with an outstretched hand, ready to deliver justice to those living in Jerusalem. While David had expressed sincere repentance for his actions, the punishment of Israel for prideful failure to credit God for their blessings was in the hands of the Lord. Would God, in His mercy, spare Jerusalem? The prophet Gad came just then with another message for David. "Go up, rear an altar unto the Lord in the threshingfloor of Araunah the Jebusite" (2 Samuel 24:18).

Even though the Jebusites were a conquered people (2 Samuel 5:6, 7), Jerusalem was still home to many of these early inhabitants. As soon as Araunah (or Ornan; 1 Chronicles 21:18) knew David's reason for wanting his threshing floor, he offered the land willingly, along with anything necessary to stop the dreadful plague (2 Samuel 24:21, 22). "But David tells him who would make this generous offering, that the Lord will accept the sacrifice which he is willing to make, but that he would not come before the Lord with an offering which cost him nothing. He would buy it of him for full price. He offered there burnt-offerings and peace-offerings. God accepted the offering by answering David in sending fire from Heaven to consume the sacrifice. The angel of God was commanded to put his sword into his sheath, and cease his work of destruction."[1]

"The spot where the angel halted was on Mt. Moriah, the mountain where Abraham had erected an altar for the offering of Isaac and where God had appeared unto him (Gen. 22:1–14; 2 Chron. 3:1), and it was here that Solomon later erected his temple. The place where death had been stayed by mercy was holy ground and was henceforth recognized as such by God's people. . . .

". . . With this account of David's repentance and reconciliation to God the book of Samuel closes."[2]

"Blessed is he whose transgression is forgiven, whose sin is covered" (Psalm 32:1).

---

1. Ellen G. White, *Spiritual Gifts*, vol. 4 (Washington, DC: Review and Herald®, 1945), 93.
2. Francis D. Nichol, ed., *The Seventh-day Adventist Bible Commentary*, vol. 2 (Washington, DC: Review and Herald®, 1976), 711, 712.

PSALM 30: PRAISING GOD IN ADVERSITY AND PROSPERITY

I will extol thee, O LORD; for thou hast lifted
me up, and hast not made my foes to rejoice over me.
O LORD my God, I cried unto thee, and thou hast healed me.
—Psalm 30:1, 2

I t is difficult to assign Psalm 30 to a specific time during the life of David. It may have been written following a serious illness. It might have taken place at the dedication of the altar on the future temple site in Jerusalem. It could easily be applied to the time following the end of the pestilence outbreak, recorded in 2 Samuel 24:25, when David's repentance, confession, and offerings on the threshing floor of Araunah the Jebusite brought the pestilence to an end.

Psalm 30 is intensely private. It expresses thanks to God for saving the psalmist from danger or illness. Verse 2 specifically mentions the Lord healing David. Verse 3 speaks of a personal illness so severe that the sufferer is looking into the abyss of death.

Verse 5 suggests while God is angry, He expresses mercy and cuts short His justice. "God's anger is very short in the case of one who sins, repents, confesses, and prays for mercy (vs. 8–10).

". . . Unlike His wrath, His favor is enduring; it lasts throughout men's lives (see Ps. 16:11)."[1] The contrasting words used in verse 5 are powerful: *anger* turns into *favor*, a *moment* turns into *life*, *night* turns into *morning*, and *weeping* turns into *joy*.

It seems David had lost sight of the fact that God's favor had created his success (vv. 6, 7). Upon falling ill, David realized he had separated from God (v. 7). Should he die, how would that profit God (v. 9)? Suffering finally causes him to realize help comes only from the Lord (v. 10). The contrasting words found in verse 11 shadow those found in verse 5: *mourning* turns into *dancing*, and *sackcloth* turns into *gladness*. David has learned an important lesson. During the remainder of his life, he "purposes in his heart to thank God in all the activities of his life. He has learned the lesson of adversity that will fit him to survive prosperity."[2]

"When all my labors and trials are o'er, / And I am safe on that beautiful shore, / Just to be near the dear Lord I adore, / Will through the ages be glory for me."[3]

---

1. Francis D. Nichol, ed., *The Seventh-day Adventist Bible Commentary*, vol. 3 (Washington, DC: Review and Herald®, 1977), 702.

2. Nichol, 703.

3. Charles H. Gabriel, "The Glory Song" (1900), in *The Seventh-day Adventist Hymnal* (Hagerstown, MD: Review and Herald®, 1985), hymn 435.

PSALM 138: A PSALM OF GRATITUDE

Though the LORD be high, yet hath he respect unto
the lowly: but the proud he knoweth afar off.
—Psalm 138:6

We should cherish gratitude of heart all the days of our life because the Lord has put on record these words: 'For thus saith the high and lofty One that inhabiteth eternity, whose name is Holy; I dwell in the high and holy place, with him also that is of a contrite and humble spirit, to revive the spirit of the humble, and to revive the heart of the contrite ones.' The reconciliation of God to man, and man to God, is sure when certain conditions are met. The Lord says, 'The sacrifices of God are a broken spirit: a broken and a contrite heart, O God, Thou wilt not despise.' Again He says, 'The Lord is nigh unto them that are of a broken heart; and saveth such as be of a contrite spirit.' 'Though the Lord be high, yet hath He respect unto the lowly: but the proud He knoweth afar off.' "[1] "Although God is exalted high above heaven, He stoops low to touch the humble of earth. He looks graciously upon the poor in spirit and has promised to dwell with them."[2]

" 'Thus saith the Lord, The heaven is My throne, and the earth is My footstool: where is the house that ye build unto Me? and where is the place of My rest? For all those things hath Mine hand made, and all those things have been, saith the Lord: but to this man will I look, even to him that is poor and of a contrite spirit, and trembleth at My word.'. . . The psalmist writes, 'He healeth the broken in heart, and bindeth up their wounds.' Though He is the restorer of fallen humanity, yet 'He telleth the number of the stars; He calleth them all by their names. Great is our Lord, and of great power: His understanding is infinite. The Lord lifteth up the meek: He casteth the wicked down to the ground. Sing unto the Lord with thanksgiving; sing praise upon the harp unto our God.' "[3]

Pride was Lucifer's sin (Isaiah 14:12–14). Humility was Christ's virtue (Philippians 2:8).

"Before Jehovah's awful throne, / Ye nations, bow with sacred joy; / Know that the Lord is God alone; / He can create, and He destroy."[4]

---

1. Ellen G. White, *Fundamentals of Christian Education* (Nashville, TN: Southern Pub. Assn., 1923), 370, 371.

2. Francis D. Nichol, ed., *The Seventh-day Adventist Bible Commentary*, vol. 3 (Washington, DC: Review and Herald®, 1977), 924.

3. White, *Fundamentals of Christian Education*, 371.

4. Isaac Watts, "Before Jehovah's Awful Throne" (1719), in *The Seventh-day Adventist Hymnal* (Hagerstown, MD: Review and Herald®, 1985), hymn 82.

Psalm 139: God Is Omnipotent and Omnipresent

O Lord, thou hast searched me, and known me.
—Psalm 139:1

The theme of Ps. 139 is God's omniscience and omnipresence. The psalmist recognizes God as present everywhere, One who is not only all-powerful, but also all-knowing. . . . The first section (vs. 1–6) dwells upon the omniscience of God; the second (vs. 7–12), on His omnipresence. The third (vs. 13–18) gives the reason for the profound conviction of these truths of which the poet's heart is full. In the last strophe [stanza] (vs. 19–24) the psalmist changes his theme and expresses his dislike for wicked men. He then closes with a prayer that his own heart may be right with God, and that he may be led by Him in the way everlasting."[1]

God searches each heart and knows the soul's condition (Jeremiah 17:10). He understands hidden motives and deep-seated emotions better than we know ourselves (Psalm 139:1–3). Even before words are formed to express thoughts, God knows what we will say (v. 4). He reads our very minds. It is impossible to escape His presence (v. 5). How He does this is beyond our understanding (v. 6). David does not want to escape God's presence but rather wants to express the idea that His spirit is felt everywhere in His vast creation (v. 7). No matter how high or low we might go, God is there (v. 8). The deepest sea cannot hide us from God's presence (v. 9). Darkness may hide the acts of men, but God's sight pierces the darkness. For Him, all is seen, even in the darkest night, as if it were a bright day (vv. 11, 12). Man cannot hide from God.

God knew us before we were born (vv. 13–16). "As an architect draws out his plan and prepares his specifications for a new dwelling, so God plans what each individual will be, even before that soul is born into the world. It is for the individual to decide whether he will follow the divine blueprint or not. . . .

". . . Only God, who knows our inmost thoughts, can lead us safely. We all need an infallible Guide."[2]

"Creatures that borrow life from Thee / Are subject to Thy care; / There's not a place where we can flee / But God is present there."[3]

---

1. Francis D. Nichol, ed., *The Seventh-day Adventist Bible Commentary*, vol. 3 (Washington, DC: Review and Herald®, 1977), 925.

2. Nichol, 926.

3. Isaac Watts, "I Sing the Mighty Power of God," in *The Seventh-day Adventist Hymnal* (Hagerstown, MD: Review and Herald®, 1985), hymn 88.

DAVID BATTLES OLD AGE

Now king David was old and stricken in years; and
they covered him with clothes, but he gat no heat.

—1 Kings 1:1

S till another shadow was to gather over the last years of David. He had reached the age of threescore and ten. The hardships and exposures of his early wanderings, his many wars, the cares and afflictions of his later years, had sapped the fountain of life. Though his mind retained its clearness and strength, feebleness and age, with their desire for seclusion, prevented a quick apprehension of what was passing in the kingdom, and again rebellion sprang up in the very shadow of the throne."[1] We shall address that threat, but first, we consider David's old age.

The book of 1 Kings opens with a description of David's health prior to moving on to cover the reign of Solomon. At the age of seventy, David was "older at the time of death than any other Hebrew king of whom the record has been preserved. His life had been difficult and trying. Hardship, suffering, exposure, and sorrow had worn down a constitution once robust, and now the king found himself robbed of his strength and greatly enfeebled."[2] The fact David had led an active outdoor life no doubt benefited him. And his reliance upon God removed much stress from both mind and body. Yet old age comes to us all unless sudden death or terminal illness intervenes. While David did not suffer from dementia or any decline in mental acuity, a strenuous life had taken a toll on bone and muscle.

David's circulation could not produce enough heat to warm his body. His physicians suggested he seek a young girl as his nurse. There was nothing sexual in this suggestion. Perhaps a shared bed might ease his pain. "The maiden selected was not merely to assist in providing life and vitality to the ailing monarch but also to act as nurse and attendant, to stand before him for the performance of such duties as would serve the comfort and health of the king."[3]

"To every thing there is a season, and a time to every purpose under the heaven" (Ecclesiastes 3:1).

---

1. Ellen G. White, *Patriarchs and Prophets* (Mountain View, CA: Pacific Press®, 1943), 749.
2. Francis D. Nichol, ed., *The Seventh-day Adventist Bible Commentary*, vol. 2 (Washington, DC: Review and Herald®, 1976), 723, 724.
3. Nichol, 725.

PSALM 39, PART 1: WHY AM I SUFFERING?

LORD, make me to know mine end, and the measure of my
days, what it is: that I may know how frail I am. Behold, thou
hast made my days as an handbreadth; and mine age is as nothing
before thee: verily every man at his best state is altogether vanity.
—Psalm 39:4, 5

As David neared the end of his life, he was suffering physical, emotional, and spiritual pain. "Incapable of repressing his emotions forever, the psalmist finally pours out his heart to God. There is in this psalm only one gleam of light, the profession of faith, 'my hope is in thee' (v. 7). Like Job, the psalmist is concerned with the problem of suffering under the rule of a good God."[1] David resolved not to sin by giving voice to his doubts, thereby strengthening those who were already angry with God (Psalm 39:1). The more he holds his tongue, the more his repressed feelings boil. He finally expresses his feelings with heated words (vv. 2, 3).

David does not understand why God created man and then gave him such a short life span. Life seems uncertain and the human body frail (v. 4). Compared with eternity, the life of a man is simply a blink in time. What is it man can accomplish in such a short period of time? Everything we do passes away and is not remembered (v. 5). Why try? Life, after all, is but a vapor (see James 4:13, 14). "Life is so short and we accomplish so little during our brief lives that it is natural for all of us at times to inquire why God made us so."[2] "The psalmist sees the phantoms called men spending most of their energy amassing wealth, at the same time recognizing that they have no control over their wealth after death [v. 6]."[3]

The only thing David can see that makes life worthwhile is hope in the Lord (v. 7). He believes if God does not deliver him from his sins, the wicked will point to him as proof God does not protect even a righteous man (v. 8). This will further embolden them in godlessness.

"I'm a pilgrim, and I'm a stranger; / I can tarry, I can tarry but a night; / Do not detain me, for I am going / To where the fountains are ever flowing."[4]

---

1. Francis D. Nichol, ed., *The Seventh-day Adventist Bible Commentary*, vol. 3 (Washington, DC: Review and Herald®, 1977), 728.
2. Nichol, 728.
3. Nichol, 728.
4. Mary S. B. Dana, "I'm a Pilgrim" (1841), in *The Seventh-day Adventist Hymnal* (Hagerstown, MD: Review and Herald®, 1985), hymn 444.

Psalm 39, Part 2: Remove Thy Stroke

I was dumb, I opened not my mouth; because thou didst it. Remove thy stroke away from me: I am consumed by the blow of thine hand.

—Psalm 39:9, 10

The psalmist attempted to solve his problem by a blind submission to the will of God. Many attempt to solve the problem of suffering in the same way. They try to convince themselves that if God sends the punishment, it must be right and good. Like the psalmist, they do not understand the true philosophy of suffering (see on Ps. 38:3). Instead of recognizing Satan as the true author of disease and affliction, and God as the one who is working out the devices of the enemy for the good of the sufferer . . . , they see disease and death as proceeding from God, as punishment arbitrarily inflicted on account of transgression.

". . . It is proper to pray that the stroke of the enemy be removed (see 2 Cor. 12:8), but the petitioner should fully submit to the divine will (see Luke 22:42). God alone can judge the case in the light of all the issues involved in the great controversy. It is our part to remove any hindrances to what Heaven would like to accomplish for us, then to leave the results with God. If the stroke is not removed, we should say with Paul, 'Most gladly therefore will I rather glory in my infirmities, that the power of Christ may rest upon me' (2 Cor. 12:9)."[1]

David asks God to remove his affliction, for there is no hope found in earthly cures. If he has some unconfessed transgression, he wants God to forgive him and lift His curse. He does not see that Satan is the author of pain and suffering. God is not the author of David's troubles. God might ease them, eliminate them, or permit them, but He does not initiate them!

"In contrast with the usual prayer for God to look toward him and help, the psalmist now prays that God may turn away from him what to the psalmist is His punishing gaze."[2] The thirty-ninth psalm is a sad dirge that ends with David pleading for strength before he dies (v. 13).

"Thy way, not mine, O Lord, / However dark it be; / Lead me by Thine own hand, / Choose out the path for me."[3]

1. Francis D. Nichol, ed., *The Seventh-day Adventist Bible Commentary*, vol. 3 (Washington, DC: Review and Herald®, 1977), 728, 729.

2. Nichol, 729.

3. Horatius Bonar, "Thy Way, Not Mine" (1857), in *The Church Hymnal: The Official Hymnal of the Seventh-day Adventist Church* (Washington, DC: Review and Herald®, 1941), hymn 396.

Psalm 6: A Prayer for Mercy

I am weary with my groaning; all the night make I my bed to swim; I water my couch with my tears. Mine eye is consumed because of grief; it waxeth old because of all mine enemies.

—Psalm 6:6, 7

P salm 6 is a penitential prayer. David is suffering physically, and his enemies are taunting him. Surely he must be a sinner for God to be punishing him with such pain (v. 1, 2). "In his anguish the psalmist assumes that God is displeased with him and therefore chastises him. The psalmist pleads that his well-deserved rebuke may be in mercy, not in anger (see Jer. 10:24)."[1]

David pleads with God to be merciful, for he is extremely weak. The pain reaches his very bones (v. 2). Even more painful than physical suffering is mental distress. Is God displeased with him? How long must he endure the Lord's anger (v. 3)? It appears God has forsaken him. Christ asked the same question from the cross: "My God, my God, why hast thou forsaken me?" (Matthew 27:46). David begs for mercy (v. 4). He reminds God that in death, there is no consciousness (v. 5). "This verse constitutes evidence against the doctrine of a conscious intermediate state between death and the resurrection (see Ps. 88:10; 146:4; Isa. 38:18)."[2]

All night David weeps in physical and mental pain (v. 6). His enemies say he is finally getting what he deserves (v. 7). Verse 8 sees a sudden transition in David's mood. "Light breaks suddenly on the darkness as if the sun had burst forth in the blackness of a moonless midnight. Faith triumphs; and by faith, seeing his enemies scattered, the psalmist commands them to leave. This is faith in action."[3] David is at peace, knowing that his troublers will be brought to justice (v. 9). Psalm 6 "should bring special comfort to the one who is afflicted with intense, seemingly incurable, physical or mental distress. 'Prayer changes things.' "[4]

"When all my labors and trials are o'er, / And I am safe on that beautiful shore, / Just to be near the dear Lord I adore, / Will through the ages be glory for me."[5]

---

1. Francis D. Nichol, ed., *The Seventh-day Adventist Bible Commentary*, vol. 3 (Washington, DC: Review and Herald®, 1977), 643.
2. Nichol, 644.
3. Nichol, 644.
4. Nichol, 644.
5. Charles H. Gabriel, "The Glory Song" (1900), in *The Seventh-day Adventist Hymnal* (Hagerstown, MD: Review and Herald®, 1985), hymn 435.

PSALM 22: THE PSALM OF THE CROSS

My God, my God, why hast thou forsaken me? why art thou
so far from helping me, and from the words of my roaring?
—Psalm 22:1

Psalm 22 "has been called a prophetic and Messianic psalm of the greatest pathos, and has sometimes been termed The Psalm of the Cross, because of references in it that NT [New Testament] writers apply to the sufferings of the sinless Son of God during His passion, when, despite His trust in God, it appeared that God had forsaken Him. There is in the entire psalm no confession of sin or trace of bitterness. The imagery is that of David, and the psalm abounds in expressions which appear in psalms that are generally attributed to David. Though the psalmist appears to be relating his own experience, frequent references in the NT attest the Messianic character of at least portions of this psalm (Matt. 27:35, 39, 43, 46; Mark 15:24, 34; Luke 23:34, 35; John 19:24, 28)."[1]

This psalm asks the eternal question: Why? (v. 1). God the Father heard every word spoken by His Son. Jesus, however, had no evidence of His Father's presence. David also felt abandoned, yet God was near (v. 2). David wanted to know why he must pass through such trials (vv. 3–5). Why had God helped others and not him (vv. 4, 5)? Had he been foolish to place his trust in the Lord (vv. 6–8)? No! He would not go that far (vv. 9–11). Yet he is encompassed by enemies (vv. 12, 13). He has lost strength and courage (v. 14). His body has become fragile. He is thirsty and near death (v. 15). He is so emaciated that his skin delineates his bones (v. 17).

The psalm now takes a decided turn: "Thou hast heard me" (v. 21). The last part of the psalm praises God for deliverance (vv. 22–31). David vows to praise Him as a witness in the congregation (vv. 22, 25). Many also will turn to God because of the gospel of Jesus Christ, and generations to come will hear and rejoice at the good news of salvation (vv. 30, 31)!

"*O sacred Head, now wounded, / With grief and shame weighed down, / Now scornfully surrounded / With thorns, Thine only crown; / How pale Thou art with anguish, / With sore abuse and scorn! / How does that visage languish / Which once was bright as morn!*"[2]

---

1. Francis D. Nichol, ed., *The Seventh-day Adventist Bible Commentary*, vol. 3 (Washington, DC: Review and Herald®, 1977), 682.

2. Attributed to Bernard of Clairvaux, "O Sacred Head Now Wounded," in *The Church Hymnal: The Official Hymnal of the Seventh-day Adventist Church* (Washington, DC: Review and Herald®, 1941), hymn 130.

Psalm 88: The Darkest Psalm

O Lord God of my salvation, I have cried day and night before thee:
Let my prayer come before thee: incline thine ear unto my cry; For
my soul is full of troubles: and my life draweth nigh unto the grave.
—Psalm 88:1–3

Psalm 88 "has been called the most mournful and despondent of the psalms. This psalm, attributed to David . . . , was probably composed at a time of most grievous physical and mental suffering. There is in it not a single ray of hope (except in the trustful address: 'O Lord God of my salvation'). It is one long wail of undiluted sorrow, concluding with the word 'darkness.' David suffers, fears death, prays for relief, but shows no expectation of receiving the answer to his prayer. Nevertheless, he holds serenely on to God and continues to pray in simple faith that God will hear (vs. 1, 2, 9, 13)."[1] David never despairs, even in the face of seemingly insurmountable odds. Though beset with troubles, his faith in God is solid (v. 1).

David knows that many believe him as good as dead (v. 4). He mistakenly believes God forgets those who sleep in death (v. 5). He is in deep despair (v. 6). He believes his suffering is caused by God's anger (v. 7). David has been isolated (v. 8). He wonders why God has left him to die since the dead cannot praise God (vv. 10, 11).

David does not give up hope (v. 13). He is perplexed, however, why God is not answering him (v. 14). Why is he being left to suffer alone? As far back as memory will allow, he can remember no time he has not had to deal with this worsening affliction (v. 15). David is like a drowning man. He fears the future (vv. 15–17). In verse 18, like verse 8, he says that he has no friends to support him. "It is well to note, despite the hopelessness of the psalm, that David confesses God as his Saviour (v. 1); acknowledges His loving-kindness, faithfulness, strength, and righteousness (vs. 10–12); and continues to pray (v. 13)."[2]

"Not now, but in the coming years, / It may be in the better land, / We'll read the meaning of our tears, / And there, sometime, we'll understand."[3]

---

1. Francis D. Nichol, ed., *The Seventh-day Adventist Bible Commentary*, vol. 3 (Washington, DC: Review and Herald®, 1957), 834.
2. Nichol, 835.
3. Maxwell N. Cornelius, "Not Now, but in the Coming Years," in *The Church Hymnal: The Official Hymnal of the Seventh-day Adventist Church* (Washington, DC: Review and Herald®, 1941), hymn 495.

PSALM 71: COUNSEL FOR THE AGED

*In thee, O LORD, do I put my trust: let me never be put
to confusion. Deliver me in thy righteousness, and cause
me to escape: incline thine ear unto me, and save me.*
—Psalm 71:1, 2

David entreated the Lord not to forsake him in old age. And why did he thus pray? He saw that most of the aged around him were unhappy, because of the unfortunate traits of their character being increased with their age. If they had been naturally close and covetous, they were most disagreeably so in mature years. If they had been jealous, fretful, and impatient, they were especially so when aged.

"David was distressed as he saw those who once seemed to have the fear of God before them, now in old age seemingly forsaken of God and exposed to ridicule by the enemies of the Lord. And why were they thus situated? As age crept on they seemed to lose their former powers of discernment, and were ready to listen to the deceptive advice of strangers in regard to those whom they should confide in. Their jealousy unrestrained sometimes burned into a flame, because all did not agree with their failing judgment. . . .

"David was strongly moved. He was distressed. He looked . . . to the time when he should be aged, and feared that God would leave him and he would be as unhappy as other aged persons whose course he had noticed, and that he should be left to the reproach of the enemies of the Lord. . . . David felt the necessity of guarding against the evils which attend old age."[1]

God had ever been a fortress for David. Now David needed God's support even more as his strength began to fail (vv. 9, 16, 18). David's positive outlook was grounded in his past experience (v. 20). He was sure God would not desert him in his old age and would see him triumphant at last. David's future was securely held in the hands of His Lord and Savior, and with that realization came comfort and peace from the stress of growing old. God would hold his hand, even in death, for He had redeemed him (v. 23).

"Will your anchor hold in the storm of life, / When the clouds unfold their wings of strife?"[2]

---

1. Francis D. Nichol, ed., *The Seventh-day Adventist Bible Commentary*, vol. 3 (Washington, DC: Review and Herald®, 1977), 1148.
2. Priscilla J. Owens, "Will Your Anchor Hold?" in *The Seventh-day Adventist Hymnal* (Hagerstown, MD: Review and Herald®, 1985), hymn 534.

No Primogeniture

Then Adonijah the son of Haggith exalted himself,
saying, I will be king: and he prepared him chariots
and horsemen, and fifty men to run before him.

—1 Kings 1:5

David, seeking seclusion in old age, was unaware that another revolt was brewing in his household. "The one who now aspired to the throne was Adonijah, 'a very goodly man' in person and bearing, but unprincipled and reckless. In his youth he had been subjected to but little restraint.... He now rebelled against the authority of God, who had appointed Solomon to the throne. Both by natural endowments and religious character Solomon was better qualified than his elder brother to become ruler of Israel; yet although the choice of God had been clearly indicated, Adonijah did not fail to find sympathizers. Joab, though guilty of many crimes, had heretofore been loyal to the throne; but he now joined the conspiracy against Solomon, as did also Abiathar the priest."[1]

With Joab's and Abiathar's support, Adonijah believed he could win over both the army and the priesthood. "Abiathar was the son of Ahimelech, who suffered death in David's cause. Abiathar had been one of David's firmest friends.... The reason for his defection at this time is not clear, but it might be that he did not view Adonijah's conduct as an actual rebellion. David's designation of Solomon for the throne might have been looked upon as springing from excessive fondness, and the assumption of the crown by the eldest son might have seemed only right and justifiable. On his part, Joab may have given support to Adonijah because of a grudge against the king for demoting him (2 Sam. 19:13)."[2]

Adonijah publicly announced his ascension at En-rogel. Only conspirators were invited. Nathan, the prophet; Zadok, the priest; Benaiah, the captain of David's bodyguards; and Solomon, Adonijah's brother and contender were not on the list of invitees. As David's bodyguards did not answer to Joab, they were also not in attendance.

"Many a life has been ruined by an excess of paternal affection."[3]

---

1. Ellen G. White, *Patriarchs and Prophets* (Mountain View, CA: Pacific Press®, 1943), 749.

2. Francis D. Nichol, ed., *The Seventh-day Adventist Bible Commentary*, vol. 2 (Washington, DC: Review and Herald®, 1976), 725.

3. Nichol, 725.

BATH-SHEBA AND NATHAN

Go and get thee in unto king David, and say unto him,
Didst not thou, my lord, O king, swear unto thine handmaid,
saying, Assuredly Solomon thy son shall reign after me, and
he shall sit upon my throne? why then doth Adonijah reign?
—1 Kings 1:13

Nathan heard of the conspiracy unfolding and immediately informed Bath-sheba. "The mother of Solomon had the freedom of the palace and quickly made her way into the king's presence, ill as he was. As she bowed low with the humble prostration of a suppliant, David recognized immediately that something of unusual import had prompted the call and he asked for details. . . . Bath-sheba began by reminding her husband of his promise to her that her son Solomon would succeed to the throne, and then abruptly informed him that in spite of this promise Adonijah was already king. Adonijah had presumed to take the kingdom while David himself was still on the throne. In such a situation the eyes of all Israel were on David to see what his move would be. Bath-sheba reminded him of his responsibility to the nation at this hour of crisis, and of the fact that if he did not act he would bear the blame for whatever fate would befall her and her son.

". . . At the climactic moment, Nathan entered and interrupted the queen with his urgent report. Bath-sheba adroitly withdrew (see v. 28), allowing Nathan the opportunity to make the same startling announcement, that Adonijah reigned. Surely this could not be without the command of the king! But how could David have given such orders as these? Why had he done it without a word to his trusted counselor and friend? Each question was an implied rebuke, a thrust at the king for having had part in a procedure so uncalled for, an outrage aimed directly at Solomon, Benaiah, and Zadok. How could David have turned his back on these men who had been so close to him? The questions were asked, of course, merely to draw a vehement denial from the king."[1]

"Seest thou a man wise in his own conceit? there is more hope of a fool than of him" (Proverbs 26:12).

---

1. Francis D. Nichol, ed., *The Seventh-day Adventist Bible Commentary*, vol. 2 (Washington, DC: Review and Herald®, 1976), 726, 727.

SOLOMON ANOINTED

*And Zadok the priest took an horn of oil out of the
tabernacle, and anointed Solomon. And they blew the
trumpet; and all the people said, God save king Solomon.*
—1 Kings 1:39

David took immediate steps to thwart Adonijah. He summoned Zadok, the high priest; Nathan, the prophet; and Benaiah, the captain of his bodyguard. He gave the following instructions: "Take with you the servants of your lord, and cause Solomon my son to ride upon mine own mule, and bring him down to Gihon: And let Zadok the priest and Nathan the prophet anoint him there king over Israel: and blow ye with the trumpet, and say, God save king Solomon. Then ye shall come up after him, that he may come and sit upon my throne; for he shall be king in my stead: and I have appointed him to be ruler over Israel and over Judah" (1 Kings 1:33–35).

The people would recognize David's mule and know their king was publicly abdicating in favor of Solomon. As reigning king, David had the absolute right to name his successor, and he did so at this time. His instructions were explicit. David had been anointed by Samuel, who was both prophet and priest (1 Samuel 16:13). Now Solomon would be anointed by both a prophet and a priest to his duties as king of Israel and Judah.

This would be no covert ceremony. Gihon, the location selected for Solomon's anointing, was just east of Jerusalem, about half a mile north of En-rogel, where Adonijah's sham coronation was taking place. Upon reaching Gihon, Zadok anointed Solomon with oil from the tabernacle, the trumpet was blown, and those present rejoiced greatly. Joab, being a military man, first took notice of the sound of the trumpet. "And Adonijah and all the guests that were with him heard it as they had made an end of eating. And when Joab heard the sound of the trumpet, he said, Wherefore is this noise of the city being in an uproar?" (1 Kings 1:41).

Jonathan, son of Abiathar, once loyal (2 Samuel 15:27, 36; 17:17–21) but now a coconspirator, arrived at Adonijah's ceremony with news. He had probably been left behind in Jerusalem to spy on the palace. He informed the gathering that Solomon had been anointed king with David's blessing and that he sat upon the throne (1 Kings 1:42–48).

"The righteous shall never be removed: but the wicked shall not inhabit the earth" (Proverbs 10:30).

THE COUP TERMINATED

*And all the guests that were with Adonijah were afraid, and rose up,
and went every man his way. And Adonijah feared because of Solomon,
and arose, and went, and caught hold on the horns of the altar.*
—1 Kings 1:49, 50

F acts were facts, unwelcome though they might be to the conspirators. The significant fact was that Solomon, not Adonijah, sat on
the royal throne. He had been formally chosen by David as his successor; he had been caused to ride to the place of his coronation on the
royal mule; he had been solemnly anointed; the royal guard was with him;
Zadok, Nathan, and Benaiah were all at his side; the hearts of the people
were his; everything had been done properly and in order, in accord with
the will of David and with the evident approval of God; the utmost pub-
licity had been given to the whole transaction; and the only thing for the
rebels now to do was to acknowledge that Solomon indeed was king."[1]

David "bowed himself upon the bed" (1 Kings 1:47). "The fact that
David knew that his end had come and that the royal scepter must now
fall into the hands of another is not without a note of sadness. But David
quietly accepted his fate, prostrating himself upon his bed in humble
acknowledgment of the fact that his successor sat upon the throne."[2]

Adonijah, terrified Solomon would have him killed for attempting
a coup d'état and realizing the hopelessness of the situation, sought
sanctuary at the altar. News came to Solomon that his brother wanted
assurances he would not be executed. "David had shown his wisdom
in dealing with the matter by setting up Solomon as king and allowing
events to take their natural course rather than by sending troops to put
down the usurper. Solomon took the course of wisdom and mercy by
extending pardon, yet at the same time making it clear that clemency
had been extended only upon condition of consequent good behavior."[3]

*"When a man's ways please the LORD, he maketh even his enemies to be at
peace with him" (Proverbs 16:7).*

---

1. Francis D. Nichol, ed., *The Seventh-day Adventist Bible Commentary*, vol. 2 (Washington,
DC: Review and Herald®, 1976), 728.
2. Nichol, 728.
3. Nichol, 729.

Organizing the Temple Service

And he gathered together all the princes
of Israel, with the priests and the Levites.
—1 Chronicles 23:2

The transition from David's reign to Solomon's was eased because David still lived. David had reigned for forty years (1 Chronicles 26:31) and realized it was time to hand over the reins to a new leader. Part of that turnover involved getting a permanent temple built for the Lord and assigning the Levites their sacred duties. Those associated with this tribe were not called to be warriors but priests. The age of Levites called to minister before the Lord had been set down during the time of Moses. Those aged thirty to fifty were to perform the sacred duties of the priesthood and minister within the temple (Numbers 4:47). Those between the ages of twenty-five and fifty were called "to wait upon the service of the tabernacle" (Numbers 8:24, 25), probably meaning they did the requisite tasks associated with the sacred services.

Twenty-four thousand Levites were therefore set apart to serve the Lord. Six thousand were called to be judges and officers. Only four thousand porters were assigned. As the mobile tabernacle used in the wilderness was being replaced by a permanent temple, there was no need to transport the articles of tabernacle furniture any longer. The Levites tasked with the job of carrying these items were no longer needed (1 Chronicles 23:26). "The priests were divided into twenty-four courses, and a full and accurate record was made regarding this division. Each course was thoroughly organized under its chief, and each was to come to Jerusalem twice a year, to attend for one week to the ministry of the sanctuary."[1]

Four thousand musicians, divided into twenty-four courses (1 Chronicles 25), were led by men who were especially skillful. First Chronicles 23:5 states, "Four thousand praised the LORD with the instruments which I made, said David, to praise therewith." We know David was a skilled composer who sang and played his own music. Apparently, he also designed distinctive musical instruments as well (Amos 6:5; Nehemiah 12:36). Praising God in song is an important worship component. Heaven's courts ring with angelic songs praising our Savior and King.

"Praise the LORD; for the LORD is good: sing praises unto his name; for it is pleasant" (Psalm 135:3).

---

1. Ellen G. White, "Lessons From the Life of Solomon—No. 4," *Review and Herald,* October 5, 1905, 7.

THE TEMPLE PROJECT

But God said unto me, Thou shalt not build an house for my name,
because thou hast been a man of war, and hast shed blood.
—1 Chronicles 28:3

D avid called the chiefs and princes of Israel together for an official coronation for Solomon. Solomon had been anointed swiftly to prevent Adonijah's attempted usurpation of the throne. Now David wanted to publicly acknowledge his choice of Solomon as his successor (1 Chronicles 28:5) and, at the same time, place before the leaders his plan to have Solomon build the temple (v. 6). Many did not expect David to be well enough to address the assembly in person. But he "stood up upon his feet, and said, Hear me, my brethren, and my people: As for me, I had in mine heart to build an house of rest for the ark of the covenant of the LORD, and for the footstool of our God, and had made ready for the building" (v. 2).

"To build a house for the Lord was a worthy purpose, but God had reasons why it would be better for someone other than David to build the Temple.

". . . It was hardly appropriate that a man of war should build the world's great temple of peace. The wars of David were perhaps necessary and justifiable wars, but they were wars nevertheless, and they resulted in the shedding of much blood. It seemed inappropriate that such a ruler should build the Temple [1 Chronicles 22:8]."[1] David's dream of building a dwelling place for the Lord was not to be fulfilled. Heartbroken though he was, David did not question God's command. The Lord had blessed Israel with a good land (Exodus 3:8). If Israel remained faithful and kept the commandments of the Lord, they would leave a rich inheritance to their children (1 Chronicles 28:8).

The promise to David that his throne would be established forever was also contingent upon obedience to God's commandments (vv. 7, 8). "By his own bitter experience he had learned that the pathway of transgression is hard. He knew by experience what it meant to be condemned before God and to reap the fruits of transgression. Therefore with all the earnestness of his soul he urged the people to be true to God."[2]

"There is no such thing as forced Christianity."[3]

---

1. Francis D. Nichol, ed., *The Seventh-day Adventist Bible Commentary*, vol. 3 (Washington, DC: Review and Herald®, 1977), 203.
2. Nichol, 203, 204.
3. Nichol, 204.

PSALM 132: REMEMBER YOUR PROMISE!

For the LORD *hath chosen Zion; he hath desired it for his habitation.*
—Psalm 132:13

P salm 132 memorializes David's desire to build a house for the Lord (2 Samuel 7:1–13) and rejoices in God's promise to establish David's line upon an everlasting throne. David asks the Lord to remember the afflictions he has dealt with during his life (Psalm 132:1). Through it all, David's fondest wish had been to find a permanent resting place for the ark (vv. 3–5). He wanted to bring the ark to Jerusalem from Kirjath-jearim, where it had rested for twenty years (1 Samuel 7:2; 1 Chronicles 13:5, 6). He wanted the Lord to inhabit a temple prepared specifically for the ark (Psalm 132:8). Jerusalem—Zion—was to be God's earthly capitol (vv. 13–16). "Had Israel as a nation preserved her allegiance to Heaven, Jerusalem would have stood forever, the elect of God."[1] "Temporal prosperity would have been the lot of Israel if she had followed the divine plan (see Deut. 18:1–14).

". . . Israel tragically failed in her mission."[2]

David also wanted God to remember the promise He made years before: "And when thy days be fulfilled, and thou shalt sleep with thy fathers, I will set up thy seed after thee, which shall proceed out of thy bowels, and I will establish his kingdom. He shall build an house for my name, and I will stablish the throne of his kingdom for ever" (2 Samuel 7:12, 13). The promise of an eternal throne was contingent upon David's descendants keeping God's covenant and testimonies (Psalm 132:12). While the history of Israel's rulers is sad indeed, a "Branch" would arise out of the house of David to fulfill God's promise (Zechariah 3:8; 6:12; Jeremiah 33:15, 16). "Behold, the days come, saith the LORD, that I will raise unto David a righteous Branch, and a King shall reign and prosper, and shall execute judgment and justice in the earth. In his days Judah shall be saved, and Israel shall dwell safely: and this is his name whereby he shall be called, THE LORD OUR RIGHTEOUSNESS" (Jeremiah 23:5, 6).

"The Lord in Zion reigneth, / These hours to Him belong; / O enter now His temple gates, / And fill His courts with song; / Beneath His royal banner / Let every creature fall, / Exalt the King of heaven and earth, / And crown Him Lord of all."[3]

---

1. Ellen G. White, *The Great Controversy* (Mountain View, CA: Pacific Press®, 1950), 19.

2. Francis D. Nichol, ed., *The Seventh-day Adventist Bible Commentary*, vol. 3 (Washington, DC: Review and Herald®, 1977), 918.

3. Fanny J. Crosby, "The Lord in Zion Reigneth," in *The Seventh-day Adventist Hymnal* (Hagerstown, MD: Review and Herald®, 1985), hymn 7.

OFFERINGS FOR THE TEMPLE

Then the people rejoiced, for that they offered willingly,
because with perfect heart they offered willingly to the
LORD: and David the king also rejoiced with great joy.

—1 Chronicles 29:9

From the very opening of David's reign one of his most cherished plans had been that of erecting a temple to the Lord. Though he had not been permitted to execute this design, he had manifested no less zeal and earnestness in its behalf. He had provided an abundance of the most costly material—gold, silver, onyx stones, and stones of divers colors; marble, and the most precious woods. And now these valuable treasures that he had collected must be committed to others; for other hands must build the house for the ark, the symbol of God's presence."[1]

David told the assembly he had gathered 3,000 talents of gold and 7,000 talents of refined silver to cover the walls of the temple (1 Chronicles 29:3–5). Estimating a talent to weigh roughly 75 pounds, he had collected 113 tons of gold and 263 tons of silver! He now challenged the wealthy men of Israel to match his devotion by giving liberally to the cause. After all, this was to be a house for the Lord. "David had willingly consecrated himself and his service to the Lord, and he could now call upon his people to do likewise. He identified the project of building the Temple with the service of God. By their faithfulness in this matter the people would reveal the extent of their faithfulness to God. Acceptable service to God is willing, cheerful, and immediate service."[2]

"Because of David's love and devotion to God he was willing to give liberally of his own treasure that the Temple might be built. He had set an example in liberality, and now he could call for liberality."[3] In answer to David's request, the chiefs and princes of Israel pledged 5,000 talents and 10,000 drams of gold as well as 10,000 talents of silver, 18,000 talents of brass, and 100,000 talents of iron. "Then the people rejoiced, for that they offered willingly, because with perfect heart they offered willingly to the LORD" (v. 9).

"*A liberal Christian should be a joyous Christian.*"[4]

---

1. Ellen G. White, *Patriarchs and Prophets* (Mountain View, CA: Pacific Press®, 1943), 750.
2. Francis D. Nichol, ed., *The Seventh-day Adventist Bible Commentary*, vol. 3 (Washington, DC: Review and Herald®, 1977), 207.
3. Nichol, 207.
4. Nichol, 207.

PSALM 145: A SONG OF PRAISE

*The LORD is nigh unto all them that call upon
him, to all that call upon him in truth.*
—Psalm 145:18

Psalm 145 is an acrostic psalm, with each verse starting with a letter of the Hebrew alphabet. The letters are in order, with the exception of *nun*, which is omitted. This is the first of six "triumphant" psalms that complete the book of Psalms. All six were written by David to be sung during religious services. He asks how a person can possibly measure God. Humans cannot comprehend the depths of His mercy, glory, power, and righteousness (v. 3). How does one measure eternity? History is replete with stories of His marvelous works, which are handed down from one generation to the next (v. 4). How can one define the attributes of God (v. 5)?

God's power is immeasurable (v. 6). Every Christian should sing God's praises (vv. 2, 7). God is compassionate and patient (Numbers 14:18; Exodus 34:6; Nehemiah 9:16, 17; Ezekiel 33:11; Hosea 11:8). He is "not willing that any should perish, but that all should come to repentance" (2 Peter 3:9). God is impartial, causing rain to fall on the just and the unjust alike (Psalm 145:9; see also Matthew 5:45). All nature sings His praise, and the saints speak of His power (Psalm 145:2, 6–12). "The Lord never abdicates His throne. Earthly kings and rulers may change, but the Ruler of the universe changeth not. The perpetuity of the kingdom of God stands out in contrast to the transitory nature of the kingdoms of this world (Dan. 2:44)."[1] God stands eternally ready to sustain humankind, and He provides for all creatures (Psalm 145:13–16).

God hears the cries of the holy (v. 19). "Holy hearts will desire only what is holy, so God has no problem in fulfilling such desires. He does not promise to grant the desire of the sinner. It would not be wise or kind to do so.

". . . As the tender mother's love is drawn out toward the cry of her child, so the Lord's ear is ever attuned to hear the cries of His children [v. 19]."[2] God preserves and ultimately will save His children. The wicked will be destroyed (v. 20). Jesus is patiently calling His lost sheep home. All humanity should praise His holy name (v. 21).

"Softly and tenderly Jesus is calling, / Calling for you and for me; / At the heart's portal He's waiting and watching, / Watching for you and for me."[3]

---

1. Francis D. Nichol, ed., *The Seventh-day Adventist Bible Commentary*, vol. 3 (Washington, DC: Review and Herald®, 1977), 935.

2. Nichol, 935.

3. Will L. Thompson, "Softly and Tenderly," in *The Seventh-day Adventist Hymnal* (Hagerstown, MD: Review and Herald®, 1985), hymn 287.

DAVID'S PRAYER

Wherefore David blessed the LORD before all the
congregation: and David said, Blessed be thou,
LORD God of Israel our father, for ever and ever.
—1 Chronicles 29:10

The gifts we give to God are only a part of what He has provided. Everything comes from the hand of God. Thus David "recognized his own unworthiness, and the utter inability of either himself or his people to give unto God unless God Himself had put into their hearts the spirit of giving and into their hands the wherewithal to give."[1]

"This subject of the use of the means entrusted to us should be carefully considered; for the Lord will require his own with usury. While in poverty, many regard systematic giving as a Bible requirement; but when they come into possession of money or property, they do not acknowledge God's claim upon them. They look upon their means as their own. But not so did King David regard his possessions. He understood that God is the great proprietor of all things, and that he himself was highly honored in that he had been taken into partnership with God. His heart was filled with gratitude for the favor and mercy of God, and in his prayer when presenting offerings for the building of the temple, he said, 'Of thine own have we given thee.' "[2]

God takes pleasure in a religion of the heart. "God's interest is in righteousness and mercy, not in religious formalism and outward conformity to law. Uprightness within results in kindness, justice, honesty, and goodness without. God calls for a religion of the heart that produces the fruits of upright living."[3] "He hath shewed thee, O man, what is good; and what doth the LORD require of thee, but to do justly, and to love mercy, and to walk humbly with thy God?" (Micah 6:8). But how does God judge a person as walking uprightly? He tests the impulses that control one's actions (Psalm 7:9; 11:4; 26:2; 139:1; Jeremiah 11:20; Revelation 2:23). "I know also, my God, that thou triest the heart, and hast pleasure in uprightness" (1 Chronicles 29:17). David closed his prayer by requesting that his people remain generous toward God.

When God searches your heart, what motives will He see defining your actions?

---

1. Francis D. Nichol, ed., *The Seventh-day Adventist Bible Commentary*, vol. 3 (Washington, DC: Review and Herald®, 1977), 208.
2. Ellen G. White, "God's Claim Upon Us," *Review and Herald*, December 8, 1896, 1.
3. Nichol, *The Seventh-day Adventist Bible Commentary*, 3:208.

PSALM 1: THE THRESHOLD PSALM

*Blessed is the man that walketh not in the counsel of the
ungodly, nor standeth in the way of sinners, nor sitteth
in the seat of the scornful. But his delight is in the law of
the LORD; and in his law doth he meditate day and night.*
—Psalm 1:1, 2

P salm 1 may also be called the "Two Ways."[1] Here is found the
theme repeated over and over in the psalms of David: the righteous will succeed and the unrighteous fail. The contrast between
the "two ways" is comparable to Christ's parable of the two houses
(Matthew 7:24–27).

"Verses 1–3 [of Psalm 1] describe the happiness of the good man, deliberately avoiding evil and as deliberately avowing his delight in God's law;
and vividly portray the results of the good life by comparing the good
man to a tree, producing the fruits of righteousness. Verses 4–6 describe
the unhappiness of the evil man under the figure of the chaff, state the outcome of such a life, and conclude that God is concerned with the ultimate
success of the good man, whereas the end of the bad man is destruction."[2]

There exists a progression for those who follow a life of evil—walking,
standing, and sitting. Evildoers first *walk* away from God to follow the
customs of the world. They then *stand* with those who are sinning and
yield to temptation. Finally, they *sit* at the table of the wicked and join
those who have chosen evil (v. 1). The righteous man, in contrast, delights
in the regular study of God's Word. David certainly studied the Word and
delighted in the law of God (Psalm 119:15, 16, 35, 47, 148). He did not
simply read the Word—he meditated upon it day and night (Psalm 1:2).

"There are three blessings vouchsafed the godly man as a result of his
devotion to God's Word: (1) he lives a useful life, producing the fruits of
the Spirit (see Gal. 5:22, 23; Heb. 12:11); (2) he is perennially fresh and
vigorous (Ps. 92:12, 13); (3) he ultimately succeeds in his endeavors."[3]
The true Christian is deeply rooted in the Word (v. 3). The wicked have
no such foundation and are blown about by the winds of the world (v. 4).

*The last judgment (vv. 5, 6) will separate the sheep from the goats (Matthew
25:31–46).*

---

1. Francis D. Nichol, ed., *The Seventh-day Adventist Bible Commentary*, vol. 3 (Washington,
DC: Review and Herald®, 1977), 630.
2. Nichol, 630.
3. Nichol, 631.

Psalm 2: Song of the Lord's Anointed

Serve the LORD with fear, and rejoice with trembling.

—Psalm 2:11

P salm 2 "shows the futility of universal rebellion against the Lord and the blessedness of peoples that put their trust in the Son of God. . . . That Ps. 2 has Messianic import is attested in Acts 4:25–27. . . .

"Structurally, the psalm falls into four portions, each stanza containing almost the same number of words. The first stanza (vs. 1–3) presents a picture of the high and mighty of earth defying the Ruler of the universe and His Messiah; the second stanza (vs. 4–6), in a contrasting picture, shows the Lord's disdain for their taunts and establishes Messiah as King in Zion. The third stanza (vs. 7–9) represents the Son of God contemplating the decree that made Him the legal owner of the world; the fourth stanza (vs. 10–12) advises submission to the Lord's Anointed. A blessing concludes the psalm (v. 12)."[1]

The kings and rulers of the earth have boldly set themselves against God (Psalm 2:2, 3), but eventually, He will stem their rebellion (vv. 4, 5). "Jesus, the Anointed One, the Word, God's spokesman, speaks in turn, interpreting God's great declaration of His Sonship. He is no usurper; He holds His office as Messiah by His Father's decree. This decree implies (1) that Jesus is to be acknowledged as the Son of God, and (2) that His reign is to be universal (vs. 8–9)."[2]

David counsels earthly rulers to obey God, for disobedience only leads to destruction. They cannot win against God's purposes. There is joy in loving God and following His commandments. All should pay homage to Christ and reverence His name (vv. 10–12). "All men, of all ages, climes, and nations, have sinned and need a Saviour. Blessed are they who recognize their need and put their trust in the Messiah."[3]

"The Lord in Zion reigneth, / Let all the world rejoice, / And come before His throne of grace / With tuneful heart and voice; / The Lord in Zion reigneth, / And there His praise shall ring, / To Him shall princes bend the knee / And kings their glory bring."[4]

---

1. Francis D. Nichol, ed., *The Seventh-day Adventist Bible Commentary*, vol. 3 (Washington, DC: Review and Herald®, 1977), 633.

2. Nichol, 634.

3. Nichol, 635.

4. Fanny J. Crosby, "The Lord in Zion Reigneth," in *The Seventh-day Adventist Hymnal* (Hagerstown, MD: Review and Herald®, 1985), hymn 7.

ALEPH: WALKING IN THE WORD

Blessed are the undefiled in the way, who walk in the law of the LORD.
—Psalm 119:1

D avid divided Psalm 119 into twenty-two sections, each containing eight verses. Each section corresponds to one of the twenty-two letters in the Hebrew alphabet. All the verses in the first section begin with the Hebrew letter *aleph*. All the verses in the second section begin with the Hebrew letter *beth*, and so forth until the twenty-second letter, *tau*. The psalm speaks of the joy found in following the law of God, using its precepts to guide one's life. David refers to the law of the Lord using various descriptive words to avoid repetition. He starts with "law" (v. 1), then "testimonies" (v. 2), "ways" (v. 3), "precepts" (v. 4), "statutes" (v. 5), "commandments" (v. 6), "judgments" (v. 7), and ends by repeating "statutes" (v. 8). Aligning one's life with the ways of the Lord leads to happiness. "God's law is a transcript of His character. It was given to man in the beginning as the standard of obedience."[1]

In his longest psalm, David expounds on his love for the law of God. David truly valued the Word of the Lord. "The mind that is earthly finds no pleasure in contemplating the word of God; but for the mind renewed by the Holy Spirit, divine beauty and celestial light shine from the sacred page. That which to the earthly mind was a desolate wilderness, to the spiritual mind becomes a land of living streams."[2]

"Let the student take the Bible as his guide and stand like a rock for principle, and he may aspire to any height of attainment. All the philosophies of human nature have led to confusion and shame when God has not been recognized as all in all. But the precious faith inspired of God imparts strength and nobility of character. As His goodness, His mercy, and His love are dwelt upon, clearer and still clearer will be the perception of truth; higher, holier, the desire for purity of heart and clearness of thought."[3]

"When we walk with the Lord / In the light of His word, / What a glory He sheds on our way! / While we do His good will, / He abides with us still, / And with all who will trust and obey."[4]

---

1. Ellen G. White, *Testimonies for the Church* (Mountain View, CA: Pacific Press®, 1948), 8:207.
2. White, 319, 320.
3. White, 322.
4. J. H. Sammis, "Trust and Obey," in *The Seventh-day Adventist Hymnal* (Hagerstown, MD: Review and Herald®, 1985), hymn 590.

BETH: HEARKEN TO THE
WORD WHEN YOUNG

Thy word have I hid in mine heart, that I might not sin against thee.
—Psalm 119:11

From his youth, David studied the Word of God. Additionally, he came to appreciate his Creator on a personal level as his Good Shepherd. If a person wants to develop a character pleasing to the Lord, he or she must study the Word. Paul advised young Timothy: "Study to shew thyself approved unto God, a workman that needeth not to be ashamed, rightly dividing the word of truth" (2 Timothy 2:15). We are told to spend time contemplating the deeper meanings of God's Word by comparing scripture with scripture.

"Victory in temptation comes to those who effectively employ the 'sword of the Spirit, which is the word of God' (Eph. 6:17). 'It is written' was the way the Master met Satan's subtle allurements (see Matt. 4:4, 7, 10). The youth of today must employ the same spiritual weapons. The mind must constantly feed upon the Word, else the defenses of [the] soul will break down, and Satan will gain the advantage. A neglect to study and to meditate upon the Word for even one day results in serious loss."[1]

With so many worldly attractions vying for attention, it requires a decision on our part to read the Word. The world beckons us to spend time considering these enticements to the neglect of God's Word. Few Christians value the Bible as they should. God cannot assist us if we do not cooperate with Him by first opening our Bibles. "We are so prone to wander. Like the sheep on the mountainside, how often we go astray (see Isa. 53:6)."[2] As a youth, David hid God's words deep in his heart. Psalm 119:11 "contains the secret of true Christian living. A mere knowledge of the Word will not keep us from sin, but when the Word is treasured up in the heart we have the weapons with which to meet and conquer the wily foe (see Job 23:12; Prov. 2:1, 9; Jer. 31:33)."[3]

"Lord, bless Thy word to every heart / In this Thy house today, / And help us each as now we part, / Its precepts to obey. / Amen, Amen."[4]

---

1. Francis D. Nichol, ed., *The Seventh-day Adventist Bible Commentary*, vol. 3 (Washington, DC: Review and Herald®, 1977), 897.
2. Nichol, 897.
3. Nichol, 897.
4. Pearl Waggoner Howard, "Lord, Bless Thy Word to Every Heart," in *The Seventh-day Adventist Hymnal* (Hagerstown, MD: Review and Herald®, 1985), hymn 667.

GIMEL: I DELIGHT IN THE LAW

Open thou mine eyes, that I may behold wondrous things out of thy law.
—Psalm 119:18

D avid's prayer found in this section is a request for help in fathoming the depths of God's law (Psalm 119:17, 18). He needs the Holy Spirit to illuminate his mind to things beyond his understanding, to open the doors of wisdom, and to shed light on the paths of righteousness. "Such prayers as this the Lord's servants should be continually offering to him. This prayer reveals a consecration to God of heart and mind; it is the consecration that God is asking us to make."[1]

"The Bible should be studied with prayer. We should pray as did David, 'Open thou mine eyes, that I may behold wondrous things out of thy law.' No man can have insight into the word of God without the illumination of the Holy Spirit. If we will but come into the right position before God, his light will shine upon us in rich, clear rays. This was the experience of the early disciples. . . .

"The Lord did not lock the reservoir of heaven after pouring his Spirit upon the early disciples. We, also, may receive of the fullness of his blessing. Heaven is full of the treasures of his grace, and those who come to God in faith may claim all that he has promised. If we do not have his power, it is because of our spiritual lethargy, our indifference, our indolence. Let us come out of this formality and deadness."[2]

"We cannot penetrate the deep things of God with our natural perceptive powers. 'The natural man receiveth not the things of the Spirit of God' (1 Cor. 2:14). We need to pray that the Lord will take the dimness away from our soul, and that He will grant to us the Holy Spirit, who alone can reveal the things of God to us (1 Cor. 2:10)."[3] We are but strangers here on Earth. Heaven is our home (Hebrews 11:13, 14). On this earth, we need a chart to guide us. God's commandments are that map. But a map is of no use if it is not consulted. David meditated on God's statutes and delighted in His testimonies. God's Word was his counselor (Psalm 119:19, 23, 24).

"Open my eyes, that I may see / Glimpses of truth Thou hast for me."[4]

---

1. Ellen G. White, "Lamps Without Oil," *Review and Herald*, September 17, 1908, 7.
2. Ellen G. White, "Constant Attainment Essential to Christian Life," *Review and Herald*, June 4, 1889, 1.
3. Francis D. Nichol, ed., *The Seventh-day Adventist Bible Commentary*, vol. 3 (Washington, DC: Review and Herald®, 1977), 898.
4. Clara H. Scott, "Open My Eyes That I May See" (1895), in *The Seventh-day Adventist Hymnal* (Hagerstown, MD: Review and Herald®, 1985), hymn 326.

NUN: FAITHFUL TO THE LAST

Thy word is a lamp unto my feet, and a light unto my path.
—Psalm 119:105

Many walk our world in darkness. They drift along, content to take things as they come, with no thought for their future and no anchor for their soul. They might have a vague understanding of the plan of salvation and perhaps some idea of heaven and how to attain it but are too busy to care much about such things. "The Word of God illuminates the way so that men may walk safely in the spiritual darkness of this world [Psalm 119:105]. He who has this light to guide him need not stumble even though his path is beset with evil."[1] "We have also a more sure word of prophecy; whereunto ye do well that ye take heed, as unto a light that shineth in a dark place, until the day dawn, and the day star arise in your hearts" (2 Peter 1:19).

The Bible shows us Jesus Christ, the Light of the world. His shining words and example light our way. That is not to say a Christian will never have difficulties or trials (Psalm 119:107). "Service to God does not guarantee freedom from difficulties or sufferings (['For unto you it is given in the behalf of Christ, not only to believe on him, but also to suffer for his sake'] Phil. 1:29). Trials develop noble characters."[2]

The path of the wicked is broad and often enticing. David understood both affliction and enticement. He realized his future depended on his daily decisions, and in this, he vowed to keep God's law (Psalm 119:109). Evil men tried to lead him astray, but he promised to persevere in following the Lord's precepts (v. 110). David resolved to follow the Lord in all things, even if it cost him his life (v. 112). "When it is in the heart to obey God, when efforts are put forth to this end, Jesus accepts this disposition and effort as man's best service, and he makes up for the deficiency with his own divine merit."[3] This is the key to acceptable prayer. One must walk in obedience.

"*O Master, let me walk with Thee / In lowly paths of service free; / Tell me Thy secret; help me bear / The strain of toil, the fret of care.*"[4]

---

1. Francis D. Nichol, ed., *The Seventh-day Adventist Bible Commentary*, vol. 3 (Washington, DC: Review and Herald®, 1977), 902.
2. Nichol, 902.
3. Ellen G. White, "Faith and Works," *Signs of the Times®*, June 16, 1890.
4. Washington Gladden, "O Master, Let Me Walk With Thee" (1879), in *The Seventh-day Adventist Hymnal* (Hagerstown, MD: Review and Herald®, 1985), hymn 574.

SAMEKH: PICK GOOD COMPANIONS

Depart from me, ye evildoers: for I will keep the commandments of my God.
—Psalm 119:115

To the obedient child of God, the commandments are a delight. . . . "Did the contempt shown to the law of God extinguish David's loyalty? Hear his words. He calls upon God to interfere and vindicate his honor, to show that there is a God, that there are limits to His forbearance, that it is possible to so presume upon the mercy of God as to exhaust it. 'It is time, O Lord, for thee to work,' he says; 'for they have made void thy law.'

". . . Did the scorn and contempt cast upon the law lead him to cowardly refrain from making an effort to vindicate the law? On the contrary his reverence for the law of Jehovah increased as he saw the disregard and contempt shown for it by others."[1]

David did not want to associate with those who would adversely affect his religious growth (Psalm 119:115). If we surround ourselves with evil associations, their influence will cause us to seek their approval by lowering our personal standards of conduct. When evil influences seek to entice us, our only refuge is in God. "When the darts of the enemy are being hurled at us, we can turn them aside by the 'shield of faith' (Eph. 6:16). When we are afflicted by gloom and discouragement, we can always find hope in God's Word."[2]

David was unashamed of his hope (Psalm 119:116). "And hope maketh not ashamed; because the love of God is shed abroad in our hearts by the Holy Ghost which is given unto us" (Romans 5:5). Others might ridicule David; therefore, he asked God to give him the courage to persevere (Psalm 119:117). David trusts the Righteous Judge to deal fairly with him, for he has done his best. "The dross and the precious metal are together now, but soon there will come a day of separation, when the Refiner will accomplish His work of purification (Mal. 3:3; cf. Matt. 13:30)."[3]

"Take the world, but give me Jesus; / All its joys are but a name, / But His love abideth ever, / Through eternal years the same."[4]

---

1. Ellen G. White, "The Great Standard of Righteousness," in *Letters and Manuscripts*, vol. 14 (Silver Spring, MD: Ellen G. White Estate, n.d.), MS 27, 1899 (March 19, 1899).

2. Francis D. Nichol, ed., *The Seventh-day Adventist Bible Commentary*, vol. 3 (Washington, DC: Review and Herald®, 1977), 902.

3. Nichol, 902, 903.

4. Fanny J. Crosby, "Take the World, but Give Me Jesus," in *The Seventh-day Adventist Hymnal* (Hagerstown, MD: Review and Herald®, 1985), hymn 329.

AYIN: CONTEMPT FOR THY LAW

It is time for thee, LORD, to work: for they have made void thy law.
Therefore I love thy commandments above gold: yea, above fine gold.
—Psalm 119:126, 127

D avid had been falsely accused, and his character maligned by his best friends. His own family sought to undermine his authority and usurp his throne. His closest counselor deceived and betrayed him. David began to question whether he was, in fact, guilty of what these men were saying. If so, he feared God's judgment in the matter (Psalm 119:120). But his conscience was clear as far as he could tell (v. 121). "He had endeavored to be just in his dealings with his fellow men. He had done the best he could, and confidently expected that the Lord would answer his prayer. He appealed to the great Judge to be delivered from the injustice of his oppressors."[1]

David longed to hear God's verdict regarding his case; he was sure he would get a fair hearing from God (v. 123). David knew God would deal mercifully with him (v. 124). He was not ashamed to be called the servant of God (v. 125). In fact, "the wicked have gone to such depths in disobedience that David feels the Lord should interpose and bring swift judgment upon them. However, God is long-suffering and slow to destroy anyone. He longs for all to repent and turn from their evil way (see Eze. 33:11; 2 Peter 3:9)."[2]

"What position will the church take? Will those who in the past have had respect for the law of God be drawn into the current of evil? Will the almost universal transgression and contempt of the law of God darken the spiritual atmosphere of the souls of all alike? . . . Because it is made void by the great majority of those living on the earth, shall the few loyal ones become like all the disloyal and act as the wicked act? Shall they not rather offer up the prayer of David, 'It is time for Thee, LORD, to work; for they have made void Thy law'?"[3]

"Jesus, keep me near the cross; / There a precious fountain / Free to all, a healing stream, / Flows from Calvary's mountain."[4]

---

1. Francis D. Nichol, ed., *The Seventh-day Adventist Bible Commentary*, vol. 3 (Washington, DC: Review and Herald®, 1977), 903.

2. Nichol, 903.

3. Ellen G. White, "It Is Time for Thee, Lord, to Work," in *Letters and Manuscripts*, vol. 21 (Silver Spring, MD: Ellen G. White Estate, n.d.), MS 15, 1906 (January 18, 1904).

4. Fanny J. Crosby, "Near the Cross" (1869), in *The Seventh-day Adventist Hymnal* (Hagerstown, MD: Review and Herald®, 1985), hymn 312.

QOPH: MEDITATING ON THE LAW

I cried with my whole heart; hear me, O LORD: I will keep thy statutes.
—Psalm 119:145

D avid's prayer was not an attempt to placate his Lord with words; rather, David was sincere when he prayed (Psalm 119:145). Even before the sun arose in the morning, he could be found on his knees in prayer. "I prevented the dawning of the morning, and cried: I hoped in thy word" (v. 147). In this, he was no different than Jesus Christ, our Divine Example. "And in the morning, rising up a great while before day, he [Jesus] went out, and departed into a solitary place, and there prayed" (Mark 1:35). "Mine eyes prevent the night watches, that I might meditate in thy word" (Psalm 119:148). "The psalmist likens himself to one listed for duty during these night watches. Before the time of his appointment he is awake and meditating upon God's Word."[1]

Often our prayers are not worded in such a way that God can or should grant them. Sometimes, in human wisdom, we ask for things that would not be beneficial if granted. At times, we ask for the healing of a friend or family member when, in God's mercy, such should not be the case. We, like David, should ask God to grant us our prayer requests according to His will and not ours. "We should ask God to answer our prayers not according to our desires but in the light of His all-wise providence."[2] Christ taught His disciples to pray thus, "Thy will be done, as in heaven, so in earth" (Luke 11:2).

David contrasts the wicked with the faithful. "They draw nigh that follow after mischief: they are far from thy law. Thou art near, O LORD; and all thy commandments are truth" (Psalm 119:150, 151). The faithful trust that God is only a prayer away. "No child of God in affliction ever cries to the Lord in vain. God may not grant the desired deliverance, but He will provide courage and faith to endure the test."[3]

"Come, Thou almighty King, / Help us Thy name to sing, / Help us to praise! / Father all glorious, / O'er all victorious, / Come, and reign over us, / Ancient of Days."[4]

1. Francis D. Nichol, ed., *The Seventh-day Adventist Bible Commentary*, vol. 3 (Washington, DC: Review and Herald®, 1977), 904.
2. Nichol, 904.
3. Nichol, 904.
4. Anonymous, "Come, Thou Almighty King," in *The Seventh-day Adventist Hymnal* (Hagerstown, MD: Review and Herald®, 1985), hymn 71.

Shin: The Law Brings Peace

Great peace have they which love thy law: and nothing shall offend them.
—Psalm 119:165

D avid did not rely on feelings when considering whether to praise God. Whether discouraged or joyful, sad or elated, sorrowful or jubilant, he praised God, no matter what the feeling. Circumstances did not alter his relationship with God. Nothing could shake his faith. There were times when he felt lonely and forsaken. There were times when he felt God had abandoned him and his prayers were ascending no higher than the ceiling of his room, but at no time did he cease to pray. At no time did he turn his back on the Lord and walk away.

David understood trials come to all who would lead godly lives. Satan does not give up tempting those who have taken a stand for the right. In fact, he redoubles his efforts to win them back to his side. Sometimes it seems things become even worse when a person is trying his hardest to do what is right. The one who loves the commandments of the Lord will be at peace with himself. "There is no peace in unrighteousness; the wicked are at war with God. But he who receives the righteousness of the law in Christ is in harmony with heaven."[1]

David wrote concerning those who love the law that "nothing shall offend them." There is a clear demarcation between what is right and what is wrong. Nothing is a stumbling block to a Christian. "They walk with firm and steady step along the straight path of God's law and do not turn aside to the bypaths of sin."[2] "To those who love God it will be the highest delight to keep His commandments and to do those things that are pleasing in His sight. . . .

"There is no mystery in the law of God. All can comprehend the great truths which it embodies. The feeblest intellect can grasp these rules. . . .

"Obedience to the law is essential, not only to our salvation, but to our own happiness and the happiness of all with whom we are connected."[3]

"Perfect submission, all is at rest, / I in my Savior am happy and blest, / Watching and waiting, looking above, / Filled with His goodness, lost in His love."[4]

---

1. Ellen G. White, *Selected Messages*, bk. 1 (Washington, DC: Review and Herald®, 1958), 235.
2. Francis D. Nichol, ed., *The Seventh-day Adventist Bible Commentary*, vol. 3 (Washington, DC: Review and Herald®, 1977), 904.
3. Ellen G. White, *My Life Today* (Washington, DC: Review and Herald®, 1952), 163.
4. Fanny J. Crosby, "Blessed Assurance, Jesus Is Mine!" (1873), in *The Seventh-day Adventist Hymnal* (Hagerstown, MD: Review and Herald®, 1985), hymn 462.

TAU: THE LAW IS A DELIGHT

I have gone astray like a lost sheep; seek thy
servant; for I do not forget thy commandments.
—Psalm 119:176

D avid ends Psalm 119 by reaffirming the righteousness of God's commandments (Psalm 119:172; Romans 7:12). The "law is a transcript of the holy and righteous character of God. We should pattern our lives after its instruction.

". . . To man has been given freedom of choice (see Deut. 30:19). Happy are they who, like David, choose the precepts of God as their guide."[1]

"When a sheep strays from the fold it seldom finds its way back without help. Like all the rest of us, the psalmist had wandered into forbidden paths, but the Lord sought him and brought him home again.

". . . The good shepherd does not return from his search empty-handed. The way may be long and arduous, the path rough and thorny, but the shepherd perseveres and does not give up until he finds his lost sheep (Matt. 18:12–14; Luke 15:4–7)."[2] David wanted his life extended so he might continue to share his religious experience with others (Psalm 119:175). He wanted all to recognize the devotion the Good Shepherd has for His sheep.

How does a sheep become lost? It makes a conscious choice to no longer follow the Shepherd and keep His commandments (Exodus 20:6; John 14:15; 15:10; 1 John 3:22–24; 5:3; Revelation 14:12; 22:14). The only path of safety lies in obedience to the law of God. "Let us hear the conclusion of the whole matter: Fear [love] God, and keep his commandments: for this is the whole duty of man" (Ecclesiastes 12:13). Christ Himself emphasized the eternal and binding nature of God's law (Matthew 5:17–20). In dedicating his longest psalm to the subject, David recognized that obedience to God's law is supremely important. The apostle John agreed and wrote, "Blessed are they that do his commandments, that they may have right to the tree of life, and may enter in through the gates into the city" (Revelation 22:14). The redeemed will keep the commandments of God and have faith in Jesus Christ (Revelation 14:12)!

"Hark! 'tis the Shepherd's voice I hear, / Out in the desert dark and drear, /
Calling the sheep who've gone astray, / Far from the Shepherd's fold away."[3]

---

1. Francis D. Nichol, ed., *The Seventh-day Adventist Bible Commentary*, vol. 3 (Washington, DC: Review and Herald®, 1977), 904.

2. Nichol, 904, 905.

3. Alexcenah Thomas, "Hark! 'Tis the Shepherd's Voice I Hear," in *The Seventh-day Adventist Hymnal* (Hagerstown, MD: Review and Herald®, 1985), hymn 361.

DAVID'S CHARGE TO SOLOMON

*Now the days of David drew nigh that he should die;
and he charged Solomon his son, saying, I go the way of all
the earth: be thou strong therefore, and shew thyself a man.*

—1 Kings 2:1, 2

D avid knew he would soon die, and even though Solomon was still young, he was now king. "He was to be a man in full control of himself and of his people, fearless, above bribery and corruption. He was to seek first, not his own interests, but those of the people whom he had been appointed to serve and of the God whose representative he was."[1]

David charged Solomon first to always be true to God. Solomon "sat on the throne of the LORD" (1 Chronicles 29:23), and he represented the true Ruler of Israel—the Lord of hosts. Second, set an example for the people by obeying the commandments of the Lord. Third, keep God's statutes, judgments, and testimonies. Fourth, remember God's promise to establish the house and kingdom of David forever is contingent upon obeying God's law (Psalm 132:12). Fifth, do not forget the crimes committed by Joab. David could not prosecute him at the time, but justice was long overdue because Joab had murdered Abner and Amasa (2 Samuel 3:27–30; 19:13; 20:8–10). "The death of these two was to be avenged. . . . Joab was guilty also of acts that David does not here expressly mention, such as the slaying of Absalom against David's express command (2 Sam. 18:14, 15), and his recent treason in the support of Adonijah (1 Kings 1:7)."[2] Sixth, treat benevolently the sons of Barzillai who had shown such kindness during David's flight from Absalom (2 Samuel 19:31–39). Seventh and last, David wanted Solomon to remember Shimei had cursed David during his flight from Jerusalem (2 Samuel 16:5–13). "David, in arranging his business, sets a good example to all who are advanced in years, to settle their matters while they are capable of doing so."[3]

"Hear counsel, and receive instruction, that thou mayest be wise in thy latter end" (Proverbs 19:20).

---

1. Francis D. Nichol, ed., *The Seventh-day Adventist Bible Commentary*, vol. 2 (Washington, DC: Review and Herald®, 1976), 730, 731.

2. Nichol, 732.

3. Ellen G. White, *Spiritual Gifts*, vol. 4 (Washington, DC: Review and Herald®, 1945), 96.

PSALM 72: A PSALM FOR SOLOMON

Give the king thy judgments, O God, and
thy righteousness unto the king's son.

—Psalm 72:1

P salm 72 is a psalm we may safely place at the beginning of Solomon's reign and the end of David's life. It "was probably composed by David for his son Solomon on his accession to the throne, as an incentive to consecrated rulership. It breathes the spirit of David's last words, as recorded in 2 Sam. 23:1–5."[1] Psalm 72 depicts a king whose decisions accord with the will of the Lord. He judges the people justly and impartially. As a result, there is peace in the land (vv. 1–3).

Verses 3–6 are applicable to the Messiah, the King of Righteousness, the Prince of Peace (Isaiah 9:6; Hebrews 7:2). "He shall judge the poor of the people, he shall save the children of the needy, and shall break in pieces the oppressor. They shall fear thee as long as the sun and moon endure, throughout all generations. He shall come down like rain upon the mown grass: as showers that water the earth" (Psalm 72:4–6). "Glorious are the promises made to David and his house, promises that look forward to the eternal ages, and find their complete fulfillment in Christ."[2] The King of kings shall rule over the entire earth (vv. 8–10), and all kings shall bow down before Him (v. 11). All will bow before Him for He is merciful and just (vv. 11, 12). He will protect the needy and poor (vv. 12, 13). He will not let the blood of the innocent go without punishment. "Never is the tempest-tried soul more dearly loved by his Saviour than when he is suffering reproach for the truth's sake."[3]

Prosperity will abound within the kingdom (vv. 15, 16). "His name shall endure for ever: his name shall be continued as long as the sun: and men shall be blessed in him: all nations shall call him blessed" (v. 17). Here is a description of the Messiah as King of kings (Matthew 25:31). Psalm 72:18, 19 is a doxology that closes this section of the Psalms.

"Deep are His counsels, and unknown, / But grace and truth support His throne; / Though gloomy clouds His way surround, / Justice is their eternal ground."[4]

---

1. Francis D. Nichol, ed., *The Seventh-day Adventist Bible Commentary*, vol. 3 (Washington, DC: Review and Herald®, 1977), 800.
2. Ellen G. White, *Patriarchs and Prophets* (Mountain View, CA: Pacific Press®, 1943), 754.
3. Ellen G. White, *The Acts of the Apostles* (Mountain View, CA: Pacific Press®, 1960), 85.
4. Isaac Watts, "He Reigns! The Lord, the Saviour, Reigns" (1707), in *The Church Hymnal: The Official Hymnal of the Seventh-day Adventist Church* (Washington, DC: Review and Herald®, 1941), hymn 179.

Psalm 68: God Has Watched Over Israel

*Ascribe ye strength unto God: his excellency
is over Israel, and his strength is in the clouds.*

—Psalm 68:34

P salm 68 "depicts in striking details Israel's journey through the desert, the conquest of Canaan, the flight of hostile kings, and the final establishment of Jerusalem as the religious center of the nation."[1] God's enemies scatter before His power. The righteous, on the other hand, have nothing to fear from the Lord. God is truly to be exalted by those who follow Him. He is a Father to the fatherless and brings justice to the widow. He provides for the bachelor who cannot afford a bride and sees that his heritage continues. He releases the captives from their chains (vv. 1–6).

The psalm records the history of God's marvelous leadership during Israel's sojourn from Egypt to Canaan. The awesome presence of God atop Mount Sinai is depicted as well as His provision of manna. The kings of Canaan flee before the power of the Lord (vv. 7–14) and the armies of Israel (Joshua 10:10, 11). Finally, God chooses Mount Zion as His temple (Psalm 68:16).

"God Himself, attended by the heavenly hosts, carrying with Him all the majesty and glory that were displayed at Sinai, is now established in Mt. Zion. What a glorious conclusion to the historic retrospect!"[2] "The psalm closes with an invitation to all nations to praise the Supreme God who has so gloriously manifested His power and goodness in leading Israel on its triumphal march from Egypt to Mt. Zion. When Christ ascended to His Father, the angels received Him into the heavenly courts singing in triumph the words of vs. 32–34."[3] Blessed be God (v. 35)! "The contemplation of God's character as depicted in this poem elicits this tribute of praise from the heart of every grateful child of God (see Ps. 66:20)."[4]

"The God of Abraham praise, / Who reigns enthroned above; / Ancient of everlasting days, / And God of love; / Jehovah! Great I am! / By earth and heaven confessed; / I bow and bless the sacred name, / Forever blest."[5]

---

1. Francis D. Nichol, ed., *The Seventh-day Adventist Bible Commentary*, vol. 3 (Washington, DC: Review and Herald®, 1977), 789.

2. Nichol, 791.

3. Nichol, 792.

4. Nichol, 792.

5. Thomas Olivers, "The God of Abraham Praise" (1770), in *The Seventh-day Adventist Hymnal* (Hagerstown, MD: Review and Herald®, 1985), hymn 11.

PSALM 108: A NATIONAL HYMN

I will praise thee, O LORD, among the people:
and I will sing praises unto thee among the nations.
—Psalm 108:3

Psalm 108 would appear to be a compilation of Psalms 57 and 60. The first five verses of Psalm 108 mirror Psalm 57:7–11. The last eight verses of Psalm 108 replicate Psalm 60:5–12. It is possible these two psalms were combined into one song to be sung during temple services. The song may also have been sung during national festivals to recount the mercies of God to Israel.

David's heart is fixed firmly on obedience to the Lord (Psalm 108:1). This psalm is difficult to place in the historical context of David's life as it combines several earlier psalms into this new one. David here offers up all his talent—"my glory"—to praise the Lord (v. 1). Early in the morning, he rises to sing praises to the Lord. "The early hours of the morning spent in private devotion provide strength for the day's duties and a safeguard against temptation. The Saviour often rose to pray a great while before day [Mark 3:13]."[1] David cannot hold back his songs of praise and sings them in public. He is not ashamed of his devotion to God. He therefore praises God to the high heavens. Likewise, God's mercy cannot be contained to just the earth (Psalm 108:3–5).

God had often interposed to deliver David from peril. David sings of deliverance by Him who loves all humankind (v. 6). God had defeated Israel's enemies. The haughty nation of Moab, having been brought low, is compared to a vessel used to wash one's feet (v. 9). The Philistines had been conquered and no longer threatened Israel (2 Samuel 8:1). David had conquered the strong cities of the Edomites and placed garrisons (v. 14). God had not forsaken His people. He had come to their aid whenever they were in trouble. God had inspired them to triumph over their enemies (Psalm 108:10–13). Likewise, we have nothing to fear though our battles against sin are fierce. In Christ, the victory has already been won!

"Lead on, O King Eternal, / The day of march has come; / Henceforth in fields of conquest / Thy tents shall be our home; / Through days of preparation / Thy grace has made us strong, / And now, O King Eternal, / We lift our battle song."[2]

---

1. Francis D. Nichol, ed., *The Seventh-day Adventist Bible Commentary*, vol. 3 (Washington, DC: Review and Herald®, 1977), 877.
2. Ernest W. Shurtleff, "Lead On, O King Eternal" (1888), in *The Seventh-day Adventist Hymnal* (Hagerstown, MD: Review and Herald®, 1985), hymn 619.

PSALM 131: A PRAYER FOR ISRAEL

Let Israel hope in the LORD from henceforth and for ever.

—Psalm 131:3

Psalm 131 is a short prayer for the nation of Israel. David speaks from a position of power and humility (v. 1). He knew all he had came from God. "In the school of experience the psalmist had to renounce pride and selfishness and to develop a meek and lowly spirit. The great men in God's sight are men of deep humility. Christ stated that among those born of women there had not arisen a greater than John the Baptist (Matt. 11:11), and yet he was one of the humblest of men. John reached the height of self-abnegation (see John 3:30). 'Nearest the throne itself shall be, the footstool of humility' (see Jer. 45:5). None but the sincerely humble are truly great."[1]

"To be great in God's kingdom is to be a little child in humility, in simplicity of faith, and in the purity of love. All pride must perish, all jealousy be overcome, all ambition for supremacy be given up, and the meekness and trust of the child be encouraged."[2] "Nothing is more essential to communion with God than the most profound humility. 'I dwell,' says the High and Holy One, 'with him also that is of a contrite and humble spirit.' While you are so eagerly striving to be first, remember that you will be last in the favor of God if you fail to cherish a meek and lowly spirit."[3] Jesus said, "Take my yoke upon you, and learn of me; for I am meek and lowly in heart: and ye shall find rest unto your souls" (Matthew 11:29).

Heaven prizes humility. "He hath shewed thee, O man, what is good; and what doth the LORD require of thee, but to do justly, and to love mercy, and to walk humbly with thy God?" (Micah 6:8). David does not boast of his exalted position or vast wealth (Psalm 131:2). Rather, he has found peace in his relationship with God. He trusts Him and rests all his hopes on Him. David wants Israel to hope in the Lord and find the same peace and contentment he enjoys (v. 3).

"My hope is built on nothing less / Than Jesus' blood and righteousness; / I dare not trust the sweetest frame, / But wholly lean on Jesus' name."[4]

---

1. Francis D. Nichol, ed., *The Seventh-day Adventist Bible Commentary*, vol. 3 (Washington, DC: Review and Herald®, 1977), 916.

2. Ellen G. White, *Testimonies for the Church* (Mountain View, CA: Pacific Press®, 1948), 5:130.

3. White, 50.

4. Edward Mote, "My Hope Is Built on Nothing Less" (1834), in *The Seventh-day Adventist Hymnal* (Hagerstown, MD: Review and Herald®, 1985), hymn 522.

PSALM 146: HALLELUJAH—TRUST GOD

Put not your trust in princes, nor in the son of man,
in whom there is no help. His breath goeth forth, he
returneth to his earth; in that very day his thoughts perish.

—Psalm 146:3, 4

Psalm 146 is the first of five "Hallelujah" psalms—the last songs in the book of Psalms. These five, together with Psalm 145, are also known as "triumphant hymns."[1] In ten short verses, David extols the benefits of having the Lord as our helper. He warns against putting faith or trust in any human, no matter how powerful that individual might appear (Psalm 146:3). God is our only refuge.

While the psalmist lived, he lived to praise the Lord (v. 2). "This mortal life is of short duration, but all its days should be spent in blessing and extolling the name of God. 'Praise' is the theme of the anthems to God that are sung by the inhabitants of heaven. 'Let us learn the song of the angels now, that we may sing it when we join their shining ranks.'. . . The songs of heaven will bring joy and strength to lighten the burdens of this life [v. 2]."[2]

When humans die, consciousness ceases (v. 4). "The Bible lends no support to the popular doctrine of a conscious state between death and the resurrection and furthermore emphatically refutes such a teaching (see Ps. 115:17; Eccl. 9:5). A common metaphor for death is 'sleep' (Deut. 31:16; 2 Sam. 7:12; 1 Kings 11:43; Job 14:12; Dan. 12:2; John 11:11, 12; 1 Cor. 15:51; 1 Thess. 4:13–17; etc.). That such a 'sleep' is not a conscious fellowship with the Lord on the part of the righteous is clearly implied in the statement of Jesus, who comforted His disciples with the thought that at the second advent, not at death, the disciples would be united with their Lord (John 14:1–3). Paul similarly pointed to the second advent as the time when all the righteous, those living at the time of the advent, and the dead who will be raised at that moment, will together be united with Christ, with no precedence on the part of the living (1 Thess. 4:16, 17).[3] Only God has the power to save. Put your trust in Him!

"I've found a Friend; oh, such a Friend! / He loved me ere I knew Him; / He drew me with the cords of love, / And thus He bound me to Him."[4]

---

1. Francis D. Nichol, ed., *The Seventh-day Adventist Bible Commentary*, vol. 3 (Washington, DC: Review and Herald®, 1977), 936.
2. Nichol, 936.
3. Nichol, 937.
4. J. G. Small, "I've Found a Friend" (1863), in *The Seventh-day Adventist Hymnal* (Hagerstown, MD: Review and Herald®, 1985), hymn 186.

Psalm 147: Hallelujah—God Provides

He sendeth forth his commandment upon
earth: his word runneth very swiftly.

—Psalm 147:15

P salm 147 continues the Hallelujah psalms. Praising God as Creator of all reality shows appreciation for His ongoing blessings (v. 1). The human family owes everything to God. He controls the mechanisms that give us life. He is the Great Physician to our soul (v. 3). The vast universe is known to Him (v. 4). He regulates the orbits of a myriad of stars and constellations (v. 4). The farther we gaze into the heavens, the more systems appear beyond our view. God "made the night, marshaling the shining stars in the firmament. He calls them all by name. The heavens declare the glory of God, and the firmament showeth his handiwork, showing man that this little world is but a jot in God's creation."[1]

All nature responds to God's commands (vv. 8, 16–18). "God furnishes the matter and the properties with which to carry out his plans. He employs his agencies that vegetation may flourish. He sends the dew and the rain and the sunshine, that verdure may spring forth, and spread its carpet over the earth; that the shrubs and fruit-trees may bud and blossom and bring forth. It is not to be supposed that a law is set in motion for the seed to work itself, that the leaf appears because it must do so of itself. God has laws that he has instituted, but they are only the servants through which he effects results. It is through the immediate agency of God that every tiny seed breaks through the earth, and springs into life. Every leaf grows, every flower blooms, by the power of God."[2]

Psalm 147 speaks of God covering the heavens with clouds, preparing the rain, and making the grass grow on the mountains (v. 8). He sends the snow and scatters the frost (v. 16). He casts forth hail (v. 17) and causes the winds to blow and the waters to flow (see v. 18). All creation is subject to His command.

"All things bright and beautiful, / All creatures great and small, / All things wise and wonderful, / The Lord God made them all."[3]

---

1. Ellen G. White, "Lessons From the Life of Daniel," *Youth's Instructor*, April 4, 1905, 1.
2. Ellen G. White, "The Revelation of God," *Review and Herald*, November 8, 1898, 2.
3. Cecil F. Alexander, "All Things Bright and Beautiful" (1848), in *The Seventh-day Adventist Hymnal* (Hagerstown, MD: Review and Herald®, 1985), hymn 93.

PSALM 148: HALLELUJAH— PRAISE GOD IN HEAVEN AND EARTH

Praise ye the LORD.
—Psalm 148:1

P salm 148 is the third Hallelujah psalm. It calls all heaven (vv. 1–6) and earth to praise the Lord (vv. 7–14). "Not only heavenly beings, but, poetically, the heavenly bodies themselves are invited to join in praising God. The psalmist extends the invitation to every living creature on earth and to inanimate nature. No one is left out of this universal call to ascribe praise to the Creator and Sustainer of all things."[1]

God's reign is universal. All inhabitants of the universe should therefore recognize His authority and praise Him (v. 4, 5). The heavenly hosts respond to His command and offer Him praise (v. 2). The sun, moon, and stars are called upon to praise Him (v. 3). God created and ordained the movements of these celestial bodies. "The heavenly bodies owe their stability and permanence to the omnipotent will of God, their Sustainer. ". . . God has marked out the orbits in which the heavenly bodies move. They perform their revolutions with unerring accuracy within the bounds that He has prescribed [vv. 5, 6]."[2]

Animals and creatures of the deep should praise the Lord (v. 7). The elements—fire, hail, snow, fog, and wild winds—should praise Him (v. 8). The plant and animal kingdoms, including wild as well as domesticated birds and animals, should praise Him (vv. 9, 10). All humanity should praise Him (vv. 11, 12).

David ends by calling humankind to praise God. "Both young men, and maidens; old men, and children: Let them praise the name of the LORD: for his name alone is excellent; his glory is above the earth and heaven" (vv. 12, 13). Israel, as a nation, had reason to praise God, for He had strengthened and greatly blessed them (v. 14). David calls on all creation to praise the Lord. He ends this psalm as he did Psalms 146 and 147: "Praise ye the LORD!" (Psalm 148:14).

"Praise Him! praise Him! Jesus, our blessed Redeemer! | Sing, O earth—His wonderful love proclaim! | Hail Him! hail Him! highest archangels in glory; | Strength and honor give to His holy name!"[3]

---

1. Francis D. Nichol, ed., *The Seventh-day Adventist Bible Commentary*, vol. 3 (Washington, DC: Review and Herald®, 1977), 939.

2. Nichol, 940.

3. Fanny J. Crosby, "Praise Him! Praise Him!" (1869), in *The Seventh-day Adventist Hymnal* (Hagerstown, MD: Review and Herald®, 1985), hymn 249.

PSALM 149: HALLELUJAH—
PRAISE GOD DAILY WITH JOY

Praise ye the LORD. Sing unto the LORD a new song,
and his praise in the congregation of saints.

—Psalm 149:1

Psalm 149 is the fourth Hallelujah psalm. This is a short but happy song telling how to worship God. Our prayers should not be rote chanting. As God's blessings are fresh and new each day, so should our praise be tailored to those unique gifts (v. 1). We should sing and dance unto the Lord, playing musical instruments as accompaniment (v. 3). Dancing, as we know it today, is totally different from the way it was practiced in David's time (2 Samuel 6:14). "The sacred dance of holy joy was a thing apart from the frivolous or debasing dances of the present day."[1] "By this means David expressed his grateful praise and thus gave honor and glory to God's holy name. There was nothing in the dancing of David that is comparable to or that will justify the modern dance. The popular dance draws no one nearer to God, nor does it inspire to purer thoughts or holier living."[2] There is no inappropriate time to praise God with vigor (Psalm 149:5).

The psalm takes an abrupt turn and speaks of Israel as God's "two-edged sword" of justice (vv. 6–9). "Death and destruction are horrible thoughts to contemplate under any circumstances, and the most God-fearing and Bible-believing individual may willingly admit that he is filled with distressing thoughts as he reads of the destruction of the wicked at different times in the history of the world, and as he contemplates the final destruction of all evildoers. But it would be far more distressing to contemplate the kind of world and the kind of universe we would be forced to live in, if summary destruction were not ultimately meted out to all who were stubbornly determined to continue on in their sinful, corrupting ways."[3] Rejoice! God has given us a way out (John 3:16).

"Rejoice, ye pure in heart! | Rejoice, give thanks, and sing; | Your festal banner wave on high, | The cross of Christ your King."[4]

---

1. Francis D. Nichol, ed., *The Seventh-day Adventist Bible Commentary*, vol. 3 (Washington, DC: Review and Herald®, 1977), 941.
2. Francis D. Nichol, ed., *The Seventh-day Adventist Bible Commentary*, vol. 2 (Washington, DC: Review and Herald®, 1976), 627.
3. Nichol, 2:201, 202.
4. Edward H. Plumptre, "Rejoice, Ye Pure in Heart!" (1865), in *The Seventh-day Adventist Hymnal* (Hagerstown, MD: Review and Herald®, 1985), hymn 27.

PSALM 150: HALLELUJAH—
EVERYTHING WITH BREATH PRAISE GOD!

*Praise ye the LORD. Praise God in his sanctuary: praise him
in the firmament of his power. Praise him for his mighty
acts: praise him according to his excellent greatness.*
—Psalm 150:1, 2

P salm 150, the final Hallelujah psalm, calls all living beings to raise a
song of praise to the great Jehovah! All heaven and earth are called to
praise the Lord (v. 1). Praise God for "his excellent greatness" (v. 2).
Praise God on a myriad of instruments. Praise Him with the shofar, the
psaltery, and the harp (v. 3). Praise Him with "the timbrel and with dance"
(v. 4). "Praise him with stringed instruments and organs" (v. 5). Praise Him
with "loud cymbals," with "high sounding cymbals" (v. 5). The psalm ends
with David imploring everything that has breath to praise the Lord (v. 6)!

"With one final grand 'hallelujah' . . . the greatest book of songs ever
composed, closes. In the great audience chamber of the psalms, where our
hearts have thrilled with many soul-stirring choruses, we rise and stand in
reverence as the great symphony reaches its climax. We would fain join our
voices in the last great 'hallelujah' to the Lamb."[1] "The melody of praise is
the atmosphere of heaven; and when heaven comes in touch with the earth
there is music and song—'thanksgiving, and the voice of melody.'

"Above the new-created earth, as it lay, fair and unblemished, under
the smile of God, 'the morning stars sang together, and all the sons of
God shouted for joy.' So human hearts, in sympathy with heaven, have
responded to God's goodness in notes of praise. . . .

". . . Heaven's communion begins on earth. We learn here the keynote
of its praise."[2] "God is worshiped with song and music in the courts
above, and as we express our gratitude, we are approximating to the
worship of the heavenly hosts."[3] The Lord deserves our continual praise.

*"Praise Him! praise Him! Jesus, our blessed Redeemer! / Heavenly portals,
loud with hosannas ring! / Jesus, Savior, reigneth forever and ever; / Crown
Him! Crown Him! Prophet, and Priest, and King!"*[4]

---

1. Francis D. Nichol, ed., *The Seventh-day Adventist Bible Commentary*, vol. 3 (Washington, DC: Review and Herald®, 1977), 941.
2. Ellen G. White, *Messages to Young People* (Washington, DC: Review and Herald®, 1930), 291, 292.
3. Ellen G. White, *My Life Today* (Washington, DC: Review and Herald®, 1952), 33.
4. Fanny J. Crosby, "Praise Him! Praise Him!" (1869), in *The Seventh-day Adventist Hymnal* (Hagerstown, MD: Review and Herald®, 1985), hymn 249.

PSALM 45: A VISION OF CHRIST

*Thou art fairer than the children of men: grace is poured
into thy lips: therefore God hath blessed thee for ever.*

—Psalm 45:2

Psalm 45 "is a marriage hymn, celebrating the marriage of a king to a princess. Some commentators incline to the view that the psalm is entirely Messianic. That portions of it are, there can be no doubt. Verses 6 and 7 are quoted in Heb. 1:8, 9 as the words God the Father addressed to the Son. [Psalm 45:2] has also been declared to be Messianic: 'The divine beauty of the character of Christ, . . . of whom David, seeing Him in prophetic vision, said, "Thou art fairer than the children of men." ' . . . This statement also sets forth the fact that David was the author of the psalm."[1] David's vision of Christ compelled him to respond in song (v. 1).

In verses 2–9, "the king is portrayed as a man, as a warrior, as a ruler, and finally as a bridegroom on the wedding day."[2] David speaks of Christ's speech as being graceful (v. 2). This is in keeping with other scriptures that state the same detail (Song of Solomon 5:16; Isaiah 50:4; Matthew 7:29; 13:54; Luke 2:47; 4:22). The king is bold in battle, majestic and glorious (Psalm 45:3–5). Yet Christ's kingdom is founded on meekness, humility, and gentleness, not haughtiness (v. 4). "Thy throne, O God, is for ever and ever: the sceptre of thy kingdom is a right sceptre" (v. 6). The Messiah is to be exalted above the angels (v. 7; Hebrews 1:8, 9). The king's robe is fragrant with spices, and royal princesses stand at his right hand (Psalm 45:8, 9).

The psalm now shifts to the bride. She is urged to consider her new life seriously (v. 10). She must devote herself to the king, forsaking her former home and anything that might stand between her and her new husband (v. 10). The bride is a princess already and is adorned in a golden gown (v. 13). The descendants of this union will be greater than either kingdom that came before (vv. 16, 17). They will be princes of the earth and will praise God eternally.

"Fairest Lord Jesus, / Ruler of all nature, / O Thou of God and man the Son! / Thee will I cherish, / Thee will I honor, / Thou art my glory, joy, and crown."[3]

---

1. Francis D. Nichol, ed., *The Seventh-day Adventist Bible Commentary*, vol. 3 (Washington, DC: Review and Herald®, 1977), 741.
2. Nichol, 741.
3. Anonymous, "Fairest Lord Jesus," in *The Seventh-day Adventist Hymnal* (Hagerstown, MD: Review and Herald®, 1985), hymn 240.

DAVID SEES CHRIST

*And he shall be as the light of the morning, when the
sun riseth, even a morning without clouds; as the tender
grass springing out of the earth by clear shining after rain.*
—2 Samuel 23:4

D avid's last words, inspired by the Holy Spirit (2 Samuel 23:2), constitute a psalm. This humble shepherd boy had risen to become king and prophet of a great theocracy. His fame as a singer and composer was widely recognized. The trials of life revealed his most enduring character trait: David never lost trust in the Lord! His experiences with danger, betrayal, temptation, lust, sin, sorrow, disappointment, and grief have benefited many facing similar situations. "Great had been David's fall, but deep was his repentance, ardent was his love, and strong his faith. He had been forgiven much, and therefore he loved much. Luke 7:47.

"The psalms of David pass through the whole range of experience, from the depths of conscious guilt and self-condemnation to the loftiest faith and the most exalted communing with God. His life record declares that sin can bring only shame and woe, but that God's love and mercy can reach to the deepest depths, that faith will lift up the repenting soul to share the adoption of the sons of God. Of all the assurances which His word contains, it is one of the strongest testimonies to the faithfulness, the justice, and the covenant mercy of God."[1]

"Because David endeavored to rule justly and wisely, in the constant fear of God, the Lord promised to establish his house forever. The promise was conditional, and the conditions were not met by his literal posterity. Hence only through Christ as the seed of David will these promises now meet fulfillment."[2] In contrast to an everlasting kingdom, those who follow Satan will be "thrust away" and "utterly burned with fire" (2 Samuel 23:6, 7). No more will the wicked be allowed to harm others. The difference between the two outcomes is stark and final. David's conclusion is still relevant: obey God's commands and trust His willingness to forgive our sins (2 Peter 3:9).

Obedience to all God's commandments and faith in Jesus as humankind's Savior will ultimately define a true follower of Christ (Revelation 14:12)!

---

1. Ellen G. White, *Patriarchs and Prophets* (Mountain View, CA: Pacific Press®, 1943), 754.
2. Francis D. Nichol, ed., *The Seventh-day Adventist Bible Commentary*, vol. 2 (Washington, DC: Review and Herald®, 1976), 705, 706.

THE DEATH OF DAVID

And he [David] died in a good old age, full of days, riches,
and honour: and Solomon his son reigned in his stead.
—1 Chronicles 29:28

Glorious are the promises made to David and his house, promises that look forward to the eternal ages, and find their complete fulfillment in Christ. The Lord declared:

" 'I have sworn unto David My servant . . . with whom My hand shall be established: Mine arm also shall strengthen him. . . . My faithfulness and My mercy shall be with him: and in My name shall his horn be exalted. . . . Also I will make him My first-born, higher than the kings of the earth. My mercy will I keep for him forevermore, and My covenant shall stand fast with him.' Psalm 89:3-28.

" 'His seed also will I make to endure forever,

And his throne as the days of heaven.' Psalm 89:29. . . .

" 'For unto us a Child is born, unto us a Son is given: and the government shall be upon His shoulder: and His name shall be called Wonderful, Counselor, The mighty God, The everlasting Father, The Prince of Peace.' 'He shall be great, and shall be called the Son of the Highest; and the Lord God shall give unto Him the throne of His father David: and He shall reign over the house of Jacob forever; and of His kingdom there shall be no end.' Isaiah 9:6; Luke 1:32, 33."[1]

"David's reign is distinguished by an unbroken chain of military victories. He defeated the Philistines repeatedly (2 Sam. 5:17–25; 21:15–22; 23:13–17) and was able to free Israel completely from their influence. . . . He also subjugated the Moabites, Ammonites, and Edomites (2 Sam. 8:2, 14; 10:6 to 11:1; 12:26–31; 1 Chron. 18:2, 11–13; 19:1 to 20:3), and made the Aramaeans of Damascus and Zobah tributary (2 Sam. 8:3–13; 1 Chron. 18:5–10)."[2] Through all the turmoil, David prevailed with the Lord's help. Then he slept with his fathers (1 Kings 2:10).

"Death shows no partiality. . . . Worldly distinctions are only for a moment, and the glories of kings disappear wherever death holds sway."[3]

---

1. Ellen G. White, *Patriarchs and Prophets* (Mountain View, CA: Pacific Press®, 1943), 754, 755.
2. Francis D. Nichol, ed., *The Seventh-day Adventist Bible Commentary*, vol. 2 (Washington, DC: Review and Herald®, 1976), 74.
3. Nichol, 730, 731.

DAVID SLEEPS

*Men and brethren, let me freely speak unto you of the patriarch David,
that he is both dead and buried, and his sepulchre is with us unto this day.*
—Acts 2:29

S o David slept with his fathers, and was buried in the city of David"
(1 Kings 2:10). David's tomb was "evidently in Mt. Zion, on royal
ground near David's palace (2 Sam. 5:9). The 'sepulchres of David,'
the tombs of the successors of David, are mentioned by Nehemiah (Neh.
3:16), and were probably south of the Temple (Eze. 43:7–9). . . . It was in
existence in NT [New Testament] times (Acts 2:29), but its exact location
is at present unknown."[1]

Christ and David both describe death as an unconscious "sleep"
(Psalm 13:3; Luke 8:52; John 11:11–14). Peter made reference to King David during his sermon on the Day of Pentecost (Acts 2:29–36). Peter was
explaining the resurrection of Christ. His point was that the tomb could
not hold Christ, for He had risen from the dead (v. 24)! David, on the
other hand, was still asleep in the grave, awaiting the resurrection of the
saints. "Men and brethren, let me freely speak unto you of the patriarch
David, that he is both dead and buried, and his sepulchre is with us unto
this day. Therefore being a prophet, and knowing that God had sworn
with an oath to him, that of the fruit of his loins, according to the flesh,
he would raise up Christ to sit on his throne; He seeing this before spake
of the resurrection of Christ, that his soul was not left in hell, neither
his flesh did see corruption. This Jesus hath God raised up, whereof we
all are witnesses" (vv. 29–32). Peter's argument was unambiguous. David was dead and buried; therefore, the statement made in Psalm 16:10
could not pertain to him.

Peter plainly preached that man does not ascend to heaven at death
but rather "sleeps" (see also 1 Thessalonians 4:14–17). "For David is
not ascended into the heavens" (Acts 2:34). God welcomed His Son to
heaven and placed Him at His right hand. David rejoiced in vision at
the coronation of Christ and rested in the promised hope of his own
resurrection at Christ's second coming (Psalm 16:9).

We share this hope—hope in the soon coming of our Lord!

---

1. Francis D. Nichol, ed., *The Seventh-day Adventist Bible Commentary*, vol. 2 (Washington,
DC: Review and Herald®, 1976), 733.

DAVID'S LEGACY

1 Kings 2–11;
2 Chronicles 1–9

Prophets and Kings, chapters 1–5

ADONIJAH EXECUTED

Therefore, as the LORD liveth, which hath established me, and set me on the throne of David my father, and who hath made me an house, as he promised, Adonijah shall be put to death this day.

—1 Kings 2:24

I t is appropriate to consider the reign of Solomon as an addendum to that of David, for Solomon had many loose ends to wrap up. Solomon was still a young man, and there existed in Israel undercurrents of discontent threatening his rule. Adonijah, older brother to Solomon and rival for the throne, approached Bath-sheba with a request. His appearance in the palace following his failed coup against Solomon was highly suspicious. He wanted Bath-sheba to ask Solomon to grant him marriage to Abishag the Shunammite. He believed Solomon could refuse his mother nothing. To Adonijah's seemingly innocent request, Bath-sheba agreed.

She straightway presented herself to Solomon in the throne room. Solomon rose, bowed to his mother, and seated her to his right on the dais; then she presented Adonijah's appeal. "The request of Adonijah was tantamount to treason and as such was punishable by death."[1] Solomon immediately detected the underlying purpose hidden in the request. "Abishag was doubtless looked upon as the last wife, or at least the last concubine, of David. For Adonijah now to ask for Abishag could be construed as asking for the throne itself. . . .

". . . To have granted Adonijah's request would have provided strong encouragement to his pretensions. Those sympathetic with him would have a firm footing on which to rest the elder brother's claims."[2]

Solomon was disappointed that his mother had unwittingly made herself an accomplice to Adonijah's subtle attempt to claim the throne. "The scheming of Adonijah was directed not only against man but also against God. It was the Lord who had established Solomon upon the throne as the successor of his father David, but now Adonijah was apparently making plans to found a dynasty through union with Abishag. That must not be permitted."[3] This new attempt against God's directions could not stand, and Solomon ordered Benaiah to execute his traitorous brother.

"A friend loveth at all times, and a brother is born for adversity" (Proverbs 17:17).

---

1. Francis D. Nichol, ed., *The Seventh-day Adventist Bible Commentary*, vol. 2 (Washington, DC: Review and Herald®, 1976), 734.

2. Nichol, 733.

3. Nichol, 734.

Abiathar Banished

*So Solomon thrust out Abiathar from being priest
unto the Lord; that he might fulfil the word of the Lord,
which he spake concerning the house of Eli in Shiloh.*

—1 Kings 2:27

Solomon had finally dealt with his traitorous brother. It was apparent that others were involved in this latest attempt to seize the throne. Abiathar, the high priest, was evidently an accomplice, urging Adonijah to circumvent Solomon as God's choice to succeed David. Because he supported the traitor, Abiathar deserved death for treason.

Calling Abiathar before him, Solomon said, "Get thee to Anathoth, unto thine own fields; for thou art worthy of death: but I will not at this time put thee to death, because thou barest the ark of the Lord God before David my father, and because thou hast been afflicted in all wherein my father was afflicted" (1 Kings 2:26). "Abiathar received mercy because of his long friendship with David in his adversity. Instead of forfeiting his life, he would merely be deprived of his office and sent home."[1] Abiathar must have been relieved because exile was better than death.

"The prophecy fulfilled was that of 1 Sam. 2:30–35; 3:11–14. Abiathar was a descendant of the house of Eli and was the sole survivor of the slaughter of the sons of Ahimelech by Doeg (1 Sam. 22:9–23; 23:6). With the deposition of Abiathar, the high priesthood passed from the house of Ithamar to the house of Eleazar, the elder son of Aaron, to which Zadok belonged (Num. 25:11–13; 1 Chron. 24:1–6). Both Abiathar and Zadok had hitherto acted as priests, with some measure of coordination between the two while the tabernacle was at Gibeon under Zadok's charge, and the ark in Mt. Zion under Abiathar. After the disgrace of Abiathar the dignity of the office of the high priesthod passed to Zadok.

"It must not be thought that the purpose of Solomon in humbling Abiathar was merely for the purpose of bringing about the fulfillment of prophecy. His act was prompted solely by the merits of the case. God decrees because He foresees."[2]

*"The eyes of the Lord are in every place, beholding the evil and the good"
(Proverbs 15:3).*

---

1. Francis D. Nichol, ed., *The Seventh-day Adventist Bible Commentary*, vol. 2 (Washington, DC: Review and Herald®, 1976), 734.
2. Nichol, 734.

JOAB EXECUTED

Tidings came to Joab: for Joab had turned after Adonijah,
though he turned not after Absalom. And Joab fled unto the
tabernacle of the LORD, and caught hold on the horns of the altar.
—1 Kings 2:28

The day of reckoning had come. Joab received word that Adonijah was dead. Realizing he was probably next on the list of coconspirators, he sought refuge at the tabernacle. Grasping the horns of the altar, he claimed sanctuary. Word reached Solomon of Joab's location, and he sent Benaiah, son of Jehoiada, to slay him. Benaiah ordered Joab to come out of the tabernacle grounds. Joab answered, "Nay; but I will die here" (1 Kings 2:30). Benaiah reported these words back to Solomon. Solomon instructed Benaiah to return to the tabernacle and honor the words of Joab, for Joab had shed the innocent blood of Abner, son of Ner, captain of the host of Israel, and Amasa, the son of Jether, captain of the host of Judah.

If Joab "had felt himself entirely free from complicity in the recent conspiracy, he would hardly have feared for his life. Solomon's words in pronouncing sentence upon him make no reference to anything except the old crimes mentioned in the dying charge of David. One of the reasons, no doubt, was that sanctuary was denied in cases of willful murder (Ex. 21:14). The laws against the shedding of blood were so rigid that it is doubtful whether a murderer could be pardoned according to law (Num. 35:16–34; Deut. 19:11–13). If sentence against willful murder were not executed, the land would carry the guilt of blood (Num. 35:33). The altar provided asylum only for those who had killed unwittingly, but this was not the case with Joab. Knowing well the law, Joab knew the fate in store for him. . . . He was guilty of crimes for which he knew he could present no defense."[1]

Here ended the complicated life of the warrior who had once been commander of all David's men. Joab had not thought his actions through. He had conspired not just against Solomon but also against God. He had shed innocent blood to protect his position and conspired against Solomon. These crimes could not remain unpunished.

"Take away the wicked from before the king, and his throne shall be established in righteousness" (Proverbs 25:5).

---

1. Francis D. Nichol, ed., *The Seventh-day Adventist Bible Commentary*, vol. 2 (Washington, DC: Review and Herald®, 1976), 734.

SHIMEI EXECUTED

*It shall be, that on the day thou goest out, and passest
over the brook Kidron, thou shalt know for certain that thou
shalt surely die: thy blood shall be upon thine own head.*
—1 Kings 2:37

Solomon needed to keep a close eye on those who might instigate
trouble. David had warned him about Shimei the Benjamite, who had
demonstrated his bitter opposition to the house of David. It made
sense to restrict his movements. "The reference to crossing the Kidron
shows that it was for the purpose of preventing him from returning to his
native domain, Bahurim (2 Sam. 16:5), where he would have the greatest
influence and the best opportunity of stirring up trouble. Bahurim was in
the vicinity of the Mt. of Olives on the way from Jerusalem to the Jordan."[1]

For three years, Shimei followed this restraining order. Two of his servants ran away to the city of Gath. When Shimei heard where they were, he
went after them and returned with them to Jerusalem. The news of Shimei's
violation soon reached Solomon. He, therefore, called Shimei to appear before him to explain his actions. Shimei had disobeyed the king's decree and
had violated his solemn oath to obey the king's restraining order. "If Shimei
had wished to remain true to his oath, he should have informed the king of
the circumstances, made request for permission to go and bring his servants
back, and awaited the king's command. But by taking matters into his own
hands, and by venturing into a foreign land that had often been at war with
Solomon's father, Shimei was certainly laying himself open to suspicion."[2]

Solomon did not jump to a quick conclusion in the matter but rather
wanted to hear from Shimei's own mouth a defense for his actions. Shimei had no defense, and his silence became his death sentence (1 Kings
2:46). "God is not an arbitrary executioner of the sentence against transgression. Sinners reap in judgment what they themselves have sown. It
was Shimei's own iniquity, not merely the judgment of an earthly king,
that condemned him to death."[3]

*"The way of a fool is right in his own eyes: but he that hearkeneth unto
counsel is wise" (Proverbs 12:15).*

---

1. Francis D. Nichol, ed., *The Seventh-day Adventist Bible Commentary*, vol. 2 (Washington,
DC: Review and Herald®, 1976), 735.
2. Nichol, 735.
3. Nichol, 735.

SEEDS OF RUIN

But king Solomon loved many strange women.

—1 Kings 11:1

Once Solomon secured the throne from internal threats, he turned his attention to the nations surrounding Israel, and he made a political alliance with the pharaoh by marrying his daughter. "The marriage was in direct violation of the command of God. Though Pharaoh's daughter forsook the religion of her native Egypt and threw in her lot with the Hebrews, among whom she had come to live . . . , this salutary result did not justify the foreign marriage."[1]

Solomon "reasoned that political and commercial alliances with the surrounding nations would bring these nations to a knowledge of the true God; and he entered into unholy alliance with nation after nation. Often these alliances were sealed by marriages with heathen princesses. The commands of Jehovah were set aside for the customs of surrounding peoples.

"Solomon flattered himself that his wisdom and the power of his example would lead his wives from idolatry to the worship of the true God, and also that the alliances thus formed would draw the nations round about into close touch with Israel. Vain hope! Solomon's mistake in regarding himself as strong enough to resist the influence of heathen associates was fatal. And fatal, too, the deception that led him to hope that notwithstanding a disregard of God's law on his part, others might be led to revere and obey its sacred precepts."[2]

Solomon eventually had "seven hundred wives . . . and three hundred concubines: and his wives turned away his heart" (1 Kings 11:3). By following the customs of the nations surrounding Israel, Solomon forgot Israel was not like those nations and needed to honor the true source of their wealth and power. It was by small steps and seemingly innocent trespasses that Solomon gradually came to believe he alone was the source of Israel's power and position. "More and more the king came to regard luxury, self-indulgence, and the favor of the world as indications of greatness."[3] What started out as a time of plenty would end in sorrow and disaster.

"Keep thy heart with all diligence; for out of it are the issues of life" (Proverbs 4:23).

---

1. Francis D. Nichol, ed., *The Seventh-day Adventist Bible Commentary*, vol. 2 (Washington, DC: Review and Herald®, 1976), 736, 737.

2. Ellen G. White, *Prophets and Kings* (Mountain View, CA: Pacific Press®, 1943), 54.

3. White, 56.

Solomon Builds Walls

*And Solomon made affinity with Pharaoh king of Egypt, and
took Pharaoh's daughter, and brought her into the city of David,
until he had made an end of building his own house, and the
house of the Lord, and the wall of Jerusalem round about.*

—1 Kings 3:1

Solomon had several construction projects pending—the most important was a house for the Lord. The fact there was no central place in which to worship caused the Israelites to begin worshiping and sacrificing on various hilltops. This was problematic. "Two prime reasons may be given for the prohibition of sacrifices at high places: (1) to keep the Israelites from the places where the corrupting idolatrous worship of the land was carried on; (2) to prevent the springing up of unauthorized sanctuaries of the Lord, where false practices might be developed."[1] "Solomon . . . knew that it would take much time to carry out the grand designs given for the building of the temple; and before building the house of the Lord or the walls about Jerusalem, he should have prepared a temporary place of worship for the people of God. He should not have encouraged them, by his own example, to go to the high places to offer sacrifice."[2]

Solomon's act of "sacrificing in a place not made sacred by the presence of the Lord, but dedicated to the worship of idols, removed from the minds of the people something of the repulsion with which they should have regarded the horrible performances practiced by idolaters. This mingling of the sacred and the profane was the first step in the practice of Solomon which led him to suppose that the Lord was not so particular in regard to the worship of His people. Thus he was educating himself to make still greater departures from God and His work."[3]

"Let not the wise man glory in his wisdom, neither let the mighty man glory in his might, let not the rich man glory in his riches: But let him that glorieth glory in this, that he understandeth and knoweth me, that I am the Lord which exercise lovingkindness, judgment, and righteousness, in the earth: for in these things I delight, saith the Lord" (Jeremiah 9:23, 24).

"Ponder the path of thy feet, and let all thy ways be established" (Proverbs 4:26).

1. Francis D. Nichol, ed., *The Seventh-day Adventist Bible Commentary*, vol. 2 (Washington, DC: Review and Herald®, 1976), 737.

2. Ellen G. White, "Ellen G. White Comments" in *The Seventh-day Adventist Bible Commentary*, vol. 2 (Washington, DC: Review and Herald®, 1976), 1025.

3. Ellen G. White, MS 5, 1912.

GIVE ME WISDOM

In Gibeon the LORD appeared to Solomon in a dream
by night: and God said, Ask what I shall give thee.

—1 Kings 3:5

G od knew well what Solomon needed, but He bade him ask. The incident was to be a test to the young king. By the nature of his request Solomon would reveal the nature of his heart."[1] Solomon realized he was inexperienced and in need of knowledge, so he asked for wisdom to rule. "Give therefore thy servant an understanding heart to judge thy people, that I may discern between good and bad: for who is able to judge this thy so great a people?" (1 Kings 3:9).

"One who is placed in a position of authority needs to understand the problems of others and how to solve them. In the administration of justice and the conduct of the affairs of state, he needs much of practical wisdom, keenness of insight, and clearness of judgment. One of Solomon's major functions would be the hearing of difficult cases that would be referred to him. . . . Standing at the head of the people of God, he sensed his great need of wisdom from God. No better understanding of the basic nature of wisdom is found anywhere than in the words written by him: 'The fear of the Lord is the beginning of wisdom' (Prov. 9:10)."[2]

Solomon's request pleased the Lord as he had not asked for riches, honor, long life, or his enemies' destruction. God granted Solomon not only wisdom but all besides (1 Kings 3:13, 14). "This is a lesson for us. Our petitions to God should not proceed from hearts that are filled with selfish aspirations. God exhorts us to choose those gifts that will redound to his glory. He would have us choose the heavenly instead of the earthly. He throws open before us the possibilities and advantages of a heavenly commerce. He gives encouragement to our loftiest aims, security to our choicest treasure. When the worldly possession is swept away, the believer will rejoice in his heavenly treasure, the riches that can not be lost in any earthly disaster."[3]

"Happy is the man that findeth wisdom, and the man that getteth understanding" (Proverbs 3:13).

---

1. Francis D. Nichol, ed., *The Seventh-day Adventist Bible Commentary*, vol. 2 (Washington, DC: Review and Herald®, 1976), 738.

2. Nichol, 738.

3. Ellen G. White, "Witnesses for Christ," *Review and Herald*, August 16, 1898, 2.

WAS IT REALLY A DREAM FROM GOD?

And Solomon awoke; and, behold, it was a dream.

—1 Kings 3:15

H ow did Solomon know he had received a message from the Lord and not simply imagined it?

First, notice the reference to God's dealings with David. "And Solomon said, Thou hast shewed unto thy servant David my father great mercy, according as he walked before thee in truth, . . . and thou hast kept for him this great kindness, that thou hast given him a son to sit on his throne, as it is this day" (1 Kings 3:6). Solomon personalized the merciful relationship that had existed between David and the Lord. "There is enough contained in these words to silence every skeptic in regard to God's sanctioning the sins of David and Solomon. God was merciful to them according as they walked before him in truth, righteousness, and uprightness of heart."[1]

Second, "in the days of Solomon's father David, the will of the Lord had been revealed to men through the prophets Nathan and Gad (2 Sam. 7:2–17; 12:1–14; 24:11–14), and through special services rendered by the priests (1 Sam. 23:9–12; 30:7, 8). In addition, David himself also frequently spoke under inspiration. . . . Solomon received his communication by a dream. God frequently chose dreams as a method of revealing Himself to His servants, for example, to Abraham (Gen. 15:12), Jacob (Gen. 28:12–16), Joseph (Gen. 37:5–10), and Daniel (Dan. 2:19; 7:1). He also spoke by dreams to those outside the ranks of Israel, for example, to Abimelech (Gen. 20:3–7), Laban (Gen. 31:24), Pharaoh and his servants (Gen. 40:5; 41:1–8), the Midianite (Judges 7:13), and Nebuchadnezzar (Dan. 2:1; 4:10–18)."[2]

Third, "Solomon had every assurance that the dream was of divine inspiration, and that he had come in touch with God. So certain was he that this was the case that immediately upon his return to the capital, he went before the ark and offered sacrifices to God."[3]

"For the LORD *giveth wisdom: out of his mouth cometh knowledge and understanding" (Proverbs 2:6).*

---

1. Ellen G. White, *The Spirit of Prophecy*, vol. 1 (Battle Creek, MI: Seventh-day Adventist Pub. Assn., 1870), 395.

2. Francis D. Nichol, ed., *The Seventh-day Adventist Bible Commentary*, vol. 2 (Washington, DC: Review and Herald®, 1976), 738.

3. Nichol, 739.

BRING ME A SWORD

And all Israel heard of the judgment which the king
had judged; and they feared the king: for they saw
that the wisdom of God was in him, to do judgment.

—1 Kings 3:28

An example of Solomon's wisdom is given in his ruling in the case of the disputed child. Two women living in the same house had each given birth to a child. During the night, one of the mothers had rolled on her baby, and the baby suffocated. She took her dead infant and switched it for the living one, still sleeping beside its mother in her bed. Arising in the morning to nurse her baby, the second mother discovered the dead infant. On closer examination, she realized a switch had been made.

The first woman denied the allegation and claimed the living child was hers. "Both disputants were of questionable character. The word of neither could be trusted. Their testimonies were evenly balanced, the stout affirmation of the one being met by the equally stout denial of the other. It seemed impossible to arrive at any certain or just decision. . . . Would the king have to admit that the matter was too difficult for him to handle? Inference, calculation, deduction, hypothesis—what were these but cumbersome weights to retard the wheels of justice in such a case as this?"[1]

Solomon called for a sword. "And the king said, Divide the living child in two, and give half to the one, and half to the other" (1 Kings 3:25). The real mother pleaded for the life of the child and asked the king to give the infant to the other woman. The other woman said, "Let it be neither mine nor thine, but divide it" (v. 26). Solomon pronounced his verdict based on the protective nature of a mother for her own child. "Give her the living child, and in no wise slay it: she is the mother thereof" (v. 27). Solomon "gave a swift and certain verdict, the justice of which was beyond dispute. The child was returned to its mother, justice had had its way, and Solomon's fame for wisdom and judgment was ensured for all time to come."[2]

"To do justice and judgment is more acceptable to the Lord *than sacrifice"* *(Proverbs 21:3).*

---

1. Francis D. Nichol, ed., *The Seventh-day Adventist Bible Commentary*, vol. 2 (Washington, DC: Review and Herald®, 1976), 739.

2. Nichol, 739.

TIMES OF PLENTY

*Judah and Israel were many, as the sand which is by the
sea in multitude, eating and drinking, and making merry.*
—1 Kings 4:20

F inally, the nation was strong and secure. Surrounding nations had
been subdued and no longer posed a threat to the very existence
of Israel. The population was increasing, and food was plentiful.
"For many years Solomon's life was marked with devotion to God, with
uprightness and firm principle, and with strict obedience to God's commands. He directed in every important enterprise and managed wisely
the business matters connected with the kingdom. His wealth and wisdom, the magnificent buildings and public works that he constructed
during the early years of his reign, the energy, piety, justice, and magnanimity that he revealed in word and deed, won the loyalty of his subjects
and the admiration and homage of the rulers of many lands.

"The name of Jehovah was greatly honored during the first part of Solomon's reign. The wisdom and righteousness revealed by the king bore
witness to all nations of the excellency of the attributes of the God whom
he served. For a time Israel was as the light of the world, showing forth
the greatness of Jehovah. Not in the surpassing wisdom, the fabulous
riches, the far-reaching power and fame that were his, lay the real glory
of Solomon's early reign; but in the honor that he brought to the name of
the God of Israel through a wise use of the gifts of Heaven."[1]

"And Solomon reigned over all kingdoms from the river unto the land
of the Philistines, and unto the border of Egypt: they brought presents,
and served Solomon all the days of his life" (1 Kings 4:21). "Solomon's
empire consisted, in part, of a group of small, semi-independent vassal
states that were ruled by their own kings but acknowledged the suzer-
ainty of the Hebrew king and paid him an annual tribute."[2] From Dan to
Beersheba and even beyond Israel's borders, all lived in peace and plenty.

"*Honour the* LORD *with thy substance, and with the firstfruits of all thine
increase*" (Proverbs 3:9).

---

1. Ellen G. White, *Prophets and Kings* (Mountain View, CA: Pacific Press®, 1943), 32, 33.
2. Francis D. Nichol, ed., *The Seventh-day Adventist Bible Commentary*, vol. 2 (Washington,
DC: Review and Herald®, 1976), 742.

THE WISDOM OF SOLOMON

*And there came of all people to hear the wisdom of Solomon,
from all kings of the earth, which had heard of his wisdom.*
—1 Kings 4:34

S olomon "sought to honor God by adding to his mental and spiritual strength. . . . None understood better than he that it was through the favor of Jehovah that he had come into possession of power and wisdom and understanding, and that these gifts were bestowed that he might give to the world a knowledge of the King of kings.

"Solomon took an especial interest in natural history, but his researches were not confined to any one branch of learning. Through a diligent study of all created things, . . . he gained a clear conception of the Creator. In the forces of nature, in the mineral and the animal world, and in every tree and shrub and flower, he saw a revelation of God's wisdom; and as he sought to learn more and more, his knowledge of God and his love for Him constantly increased.

"Solomon's divinely inspired wisdom found expression in songs of praise and in many proverbs. . . .

"In the proverbs of Solomon are outlined principles of holy living and high endeavor, principles that are heaven-born and that lead to godliness, principles that should govern every act of life. It was the wide dissemination of these principles, and the recognition of God as the One to whom all praise and honor belong, that made Solomon's early reign a time of moral uplift as well as of material prosperity."[1]

Of Solomon's proverbs, only some are preserved. Of his songs, only Song of Solomon and perhaps one or two of his psalms still exist. Of his scientific and secular writings, none are known to exist. Even so, Solomon's reputation for wisdom is firmly established in Scripture.

"The fear of the LORD is the beginning of knowledge: but fools despise wisdom and instruction" (Proverbs 1:7).

---

1. Ellen G. White, *Prophets and Kings* (Mountain View, CA: Pacific Press®, 1943), 33, 34.

DAVID'S FRIENDSHIP PAYS DIVIDENDS

And Hiram king of Tyre sent his servants unto Solomon;
for he had heard that they had anointed him king in the
room of his father: for Hiram was ever a lover of David.
—1 Kings 5:1

During his reign, David had developed a close friendship with Hiram, king of Tyre (2 Samuel 5:11; 1 Chronicles 14:1). In a gesture of friendship, Hiram sent costly cedarwood and other valuable materials to Jerusalem (2 Samuel 5:11). Additionally, Tyre formed an alliance with Israel, thus protecting Israel's northern flank. The influence of Israel for good even saw some of the residents of Tyre and Sidon give up idol worship. The relationship between David and Hiram was so close that Hiram acknowledged Jehovah as the only true God.

"Josephus cites Menander of Ephesus, who wrote, in Greek . . . to the effect that Hiram was the son of Abibaal and that he reigned 34 years, dying at the age of 53, and being succeeded by his son Baleazar (*Against Apion* 1. 18). According to Josephus the Temple was built in the 11th (*Antiquities* viii. 3. 1) or the 12th (*Against Apion* 1. 18) year of Hiram. Since the founding of the Temple took place in the fourth year of Solomon (1 King 6:1), the reign of Hiram must have overlapped that of David by some seven or eight years."[1]

Hearing Solomon had succeeded David, Hiram sent servants to congratulate the new king. Solomon took this opportunity to remind Hiram of David's desire to build a house for the Lord, and he asked Hiram for materials and skilled carpenters (1 Kings 5:6; 2 Chronicles 2:8). Hiram agreed to cut cedars of Lebanon as well as fir trees (1 Kings 5:8, 10) and float them down the coast to Joppa (2 Chronicles 2:16), which was around thirty-four miles from Jerusalem. In return, Solomon agreed to pay the workers with wheat, barley, wine, and pure oil and provide for Hiram's household on a year-by-year basis (v. 10; 1 Kings 5:11). The agreement was mutually beneficial: Solomon needed timber, and Hiram needed food. "There seems to have been a genuine friendship between Hiram and Solomon, going back, no doubt, to the sincere friendship between Hiram and David."[2]

"A man that hath friends must shew himself friendly: and there is a friend that sticketh closer than a brother" (Proverbs 18:24).

---

1. Francis D. Nichol, ed., *The Seventh-day Adventist Bible Commentary*, vol. 2 (Washington, DC: Review and Herald®, 1976), 745.

2. Nichol, 746.

FURTHER SEEDS OF RUIN

And Solomon's builders and Hiram's builders did hew them, and the stonesquarers: so they prepared timber and stones to build the house.
—1 Kings 5:18

S olomon's second mistake was employing foreigners to erect the temple. While Solomon tasked a crew of Israelite laborers to construct the temple (1 Kings 5:13, 14), these men were not skilled stonemasons or carpenters. They could not successfully handle the raw materials. This conscription of Israelites was not well received by those pressed into service one month out of every three, and it caused a good deal of disgust toward Solomon (1 Kings 12:4).

King Hiram sent Huram, a man from Tyre (1 Kings 7:13), to be the chief supervisor of the temple project (2 Chronicles 2:14). Solomon agreed to hire this master craftsman at high wages. The king should have looked to God for consecrated workers possessing the special talents needed to build to exact specifications. Instead, he lost this opportunity to exercise faith in God. "The baleful influences set in operation by the employment of this man of a grasping spirit, permeated all branches of the Lord's service, and extended throughout Solomon's kingdom. The high wages demanded and received gave many an opportunity to indulge in luxury and extravagance. In the far-reaching effects of these influences, may be traced one of the principal causes of the terrible apostasy of him who once was the wisest of mortals. . . . The poor were oppressed by the rich; the spirit of self-sacrifice in God's service was well nigh lost."[1]

"Solomon prepared the way for his own ruin when he sought for wise men from other nations to build the temple. God had been the educator of his people, and he designed that they should stand in his wisdom, and with his imparted talents should be second to none. If they had the clean hands, the pure heart, and the noble, sanctified purpose, the Lord would communicate to them his grace. But Solomon looked to man instead of God, and he found his supposed strength to be weakness. He brought to Jerusalem the leaven of the evil influences which were perpetuated in polygamy and idolatry."[2]

"In all thy ways acknowledge him, and he shall direct thy paths" (Proverbs 3:6).

---

1. Ellen G. White, "Lessons From the Life of Solomon—No. 16," *Review and Herald*, January 4, 1906, 8.
2. Ellen G. White, "Communication From Mrs. E. G. White," *General Conference Bulletin*, February 25, 1895, 340.

BUILDING THE HOUSE OF GOD

And it came to pass in the four hundred and eightieth year after the children of Israel were come out of the land of Egypt, in the fourth year of Solomon's reign over Israel, in the month Zif, which is the second month, that he began to build the house of the LORD.
—1 Kings 6:1

A full account of the building of the temple is recorded in 2 Chronicles 3 and 4. A more detailed description is found in 1 Kings 6. The temple was exactly twice the size of the wilderness tabernacle. The pattern shown to Moses on the mount was followed precisely. Solomon also had detailed instructions given to him by David. A front porch stretched the width of the building. High in the walls were placed slit windows that were wider on the interior than the exterior. Surrounding the temple on three sides were chambers that did not contact the main building.

Massive stones were shaped at the quarry, so noise was kept at a minimum at the temple site. This required more skill and quite a bit more labor but was done to preserve reverence. Cedarwood covered both the roof and interior stone walls. The interior was divided into the Holy Place, being forty cubits long, and the Most Holy Place, being twenty cubits square (1 Kings 6:16, 17). A cedar partition, reaching floor to ceiling, separated the rooms. The most significant object in the temple was the ark containing the tables of the law of the covenant (Exodus 34:1, 4, 10, 27, 28). Two cherubim with outstretched wings reached across the Most Holy Place (1 Kings 6:23–28; Exodus 37:6–9). An altar of incense was constructed in front of the opening to the Most Holy Place (Exodus 30:1–6; 40:26). Two carved olive wood doors separated the rooms.

The cedar walls were intricately carved with cherubims, palm trees, and open flowers (1 Kings 6:29). Gold covered the walls and floor as well as the interior portion of the front porch (2 Chronicles 3:4). "Of surpassing beauty and unrivaled splendor was the palatial building which Solomon and his associates erected for God and His worship. Garnished with precious stones, surrounded by spacious courts with magnificent approaches, and lined with carved cedar and burnished gold, the temple structure, with its broidered hangings and rich furnishings, was a fit emblem of the living church of God on earth."[1]

"And let them make me a sanctuary; that I may dwell among them" (Exodus 25:8).

---

1. Ellen G. White, *Prophets and Kings* (Mountain View, CA: Pacific Press®, 1943), 36.

A HOUSE OF GOLD

*So Solomon overlaid the house within with pure
gold: and he made a partition by the chains of gold
before the oracle; and he overlaid it with gold.*

—1 Kings 6:21

T he spot on which the temple was built had long been regarded as a consecrated place. It was here that Abraham, the father of the faithful, had revealed his willingness to sacrifice his only son in obedience to the command of Jehovah. Here God had renewed with Abraham the covenant of blessing, which included the glorious Messianic promise to the human race of deliverance through the sacrifice of the Son of the Most High. See Genesis 22:9, 16-18. Here it was that when David offered burnt offerings and peace offerings to stay the avenging sword of the destroying angel, God had answered him by fire from heaven. See 1 Chronicles 21."[1]

Solomon's temple was destroyed by Nebuchadnezzar, and a second temple was rebuilt five hundred years before Christ. It was inferior to the first and did not contain the visible tokens of God's presence. "The excellent construction of the building gave assurance that it would withstand the elements indefinitely. The city of Jerusalem itself was held to be, for all practical purposes, impregnable, but Jesus predicted that it would be destroyed by force."[2]

"And Jesus went out, and departed from the temple: and his disciples came to him for to shew him the buildings of the temple. And Jesus said unto them, See ye not all these things? verily I say unto you, There shall not be left here one stone upon another, that shall not be thrown down" (Matthew 24:1, 2). The prophecy came true in AD 70. The Roman general Titus had tried to save the building from destruction following his siege of Jerusalem. But Jews, using the building as a fortress, attacked the Roman soldiers one night and during the fight a firebrand was thrown into the building. The cedar walls immediately caught fire and gold ran down into the spaces between stones. "That magnificent structure fell. Angels of God were sent to do the work of destruction, so that one stone was not left one upon another that was not thrown down."[3]

God's prophecies always come true (Amos 3:7; Micah 3:10–12).

---

1. Ellen G. White, *Prophets and Kings* (Mountain View, CA: Pacific Press®, 1943), 37.

2. Francis D. Nichol, ed., *The Seventh-day Adventist Bible Commentary*, vol. 5 (Washington, DC: Review and Herald®, 1980), 496.

3. Ellen G. White, "The Judgments of God," in *Letters and Manuscripts*, vol. 21 (Silver Spring, MD: Ellen G. White Estate, n.d.), MS 35, 1906 (April 27, 1906).

DAVID'S CONTRIBUTION

*So was ended all the work that king Solomon made for the house
of the LORD. And Solomon brought in the things which David
his father had dedicated; even the silver, and the gold, and the
vessels, did he put among the treasures of the house of the LORD.*
—1 Kings 7:51

For seven years Jerusalem was filled with busy workers engaged in leveling the chosen site, in building vast retaining walls, in laying broad foundations. . . .

"Simultaneously with the preparation of wood and stone, to which task many thousands were bending their energies, the manufacture of the furnishings for the temple was steadily progressing under the leadership of Huram of Tyre. . . . 2 Chronicles 2:13, 14.

"Thus as the building on Mount Moriah was noiselessly upreared with 'stone made ready before it was brought thither: so that there was neither hammer nor ax nor any tool of iron heard in the house, while it was in building,' the beautiful fittings were perfected according to the patterns committed by David to his son, 'all the vessels that were for the house of God.' 1 Kings 6:7; 2 Chronicles 4:19. These included the altar of incense, the table of shewbread, the candlestick and lamps, with the vessels and instruments connected with the ministrations of the priests in the holy place, all 'of gold, and that perfect gold.' 2 Chronicles 4:21. "These furnishings were provided in abundance, that there should be no lack."[1]

Although known as "Solomon's temple," David bought the land, drew the design, collected the funds, and passed the information on to his son (2 Samuel 7; 1 Chronicles 21:18–22:5). "It was his [David's] hope and purpose to build the Temple, but that task, he was told, was not for him. Humbly he submitted to the divine will, accepting those tasks that God had for him, and not permitting himself to become sullen and morose because he was not permitted to carry out his own purpose."[2]

Would you surrender your treasured plans to God's will as graciously as David?

---

1. Ellen G. White, *Prophets and Kings* (Mountain View, CA: Pacific Press®, 1943), 35, 36.
2. Francis D. Nichol, ed., *The Seventh-day Adventist Bible Commentary*, vol. 2 (Washington, DC: Review and Herald®, 1976), 633.

THE ARK OF THE COVENANT

*And the priests brought in the ark of the covenant of
the LORD unto his place, into the oracle of the house, to the
most holy place, even under the wings of the cherubims.*

—1 Kings 8:6

A great feast was prepared, and elders from each tribe assembled in Jerusalem for the temple's dedication. Sacrifices were offered, and the ark was carried by Levite priests into the Most Holy Place of the temple. "All priests were Levites (Joshua 3:3), but not all the descendants of Levi were priests. The bearing of the ark on its journeys was properly the responsibility of the Levites of the family of Kohath (Num. 3:31; 4:15; 1 Chron. 15:2–15)."[1] The ark was oriented crosswise from north to south, and the staves used to carry it were drawn out so they were visible from the Holy Place beyond the ends of a separating veil (2 Chronicles 3:14) through the open wooden doors in the separating wall (1 Kings 6:16, 31).

The ark held the tablets of stone that Moses had placed there at Horeb (1 Kings 8:9). "The ark was brought into the most holy place, where, between the cherubim, was to be manifested the presence of God. This showed the sacredness of the law of God. The law is a transcript of the character of God. As God is holy, so are His commandments holy, just, and pure."[2] "There is something singularly impressive in this special hallowing of the two tables of the law. By being thus placed within the ark, directly above which God was to meet with His people (Ex. 25:22), the law is indissolubly bound together with God Himself. The most sacred place in the Temple was the holy of holies, and its most sacred item was the ark containing the law of God. As God by His very nature is holy and eternal, so likewise is His law. Everything that could possibly be done to impress upon His children the eternal sanctity of His law was done by God in the appointments of His holy Temple. This law, under the old covenant, was written upon two tables of stone; under the new covenant it is written upon the hearts of the righteous (Jer. 31:31–33)."[3] God has always desired transformed hearts in His people.

When God chose David to lead His people, He looked not on outward appearances but upon his heart (1 Samuel 16:7).

1. Francis D. Nichol, ed., *The Seventh-day Adventist Bible Commentary*, vol. 2 (Washington, DC: Review and Herald®, 1976), 762.
2. Nichol, 763.
3. Nichol, 763, 764.

A CLOUD OF GLORY

And it came to pass, when the priests were come out of
the holy place, that the cloud filled the house of the LORD,
So that the priests could not stand to minister because of the
cloud: for the glory of the LORD had filled the house of the LORD.
—1 Kings 8:10, 11

It was during a great lifting up of the voices of the assembled priests in an anthem of praise to God that His glory appeared in the form of a cloud (2 Chron. 5:13)."[1] "So great was the overpowering glory of God's presence that the officiating priests were forced temporarily to withdraw. So also when the tabernacle was first set up, Moses was not able to enter because of the glory of God which filled the sacred tent (Ex. 40:35). When Isaiah had his vision of God, the train of divine glory filled the Temple, and Isaiah felt himself undone because of having come so near to the presence of the Lord (Isa. 6:1–5). The disciples of Jesus likewise trembled as the cloud of God's glory overshadowed them on the mount of transfiguration (Luke 9:34). Why do men experience such reactions when in the presence of God? It is because of the very nature of God, His greatness and His holiness, His grandeur and sublimity, His majesty and might. . . . Sinful man cannot come into His sublime presence and continue to exist. God is like a consuming fire, which unholy men cannot approach without being destroyed.

"The cloud in the Temple was not God, but it was a means by which the Lord veiled His presence to the end that man might not be consumed. So great was the divine glory on the occasion of the dedication of the Temple that in spite of the enveloping cloud, the ministering priests were forced to draw back in holy awe."[2] "Witnessing the combined darkness and glory before him, the mingled shadow and light, Solomon was assured that the Lord was there (Eze. 48:35). . . . This is evidence of the very presence of God; He is with us; we have nothing to fear, but we have everything to be thankful for on this glorious occasion."[3]

"The LORD reigneth; let the people tremble: he sitteth between the cherubims; let the earth be moved" (Psalm 99:1).

---

1. Francis D. Nichol, ed., *The Seventh-day Adventist Bible Commentary*, vol. 2 (Washington, DC: Review and Herald®, 1976), 764.
2. Nichol, 764.
3. Nichol, 764.

A Prayer of Dedication

Lord God of Israel, there is no God like thee, in heaven
above, or on earth beneath, who keepest covenant and mercy
with thy servants that walk before thee with all their heart.
—1 Kings 8:23

The time chosen for the dedication was a most favorable one—the seventh month, when the people from every part of the kingdom were accustomed to assemble at Jerusalem to celebrate the Feast of Tabernacles. This feast was preeminently an occasion of rejoicing. The labors of the harvest being ended and the toils of the new year not yet begun, the people were free from care and could give themselves up to the sacred, joyous influences of the hour."[1]

With uplifted hands, Solomon blessed the immense crowd facing him. "And all the congregation of Israel stood. And he said, Blessed be the Lord God of Israel, who hath with his hands fulfilled that which he spake with his mouth to my father David" (2 Chronicles 6:3, 4). Solomon knelt and prayed the prayer recorded in 1 Kings 8 and 2 Chronicles 6. "But when Solomon contemplated the greatness and the grandeur of God, the One who inhabiteth eternity, who had 'measured the waters in the hollow of his hand, and meted out heaven with the span, and comprehended the dust of the earth in a measure, and weighed the mountains in scales, and the hills in a balance' (Isa. 40:12), it seemed incomprehensible that such a God would take up His abode on earth, in such a house as Solomon had made. . . . It will never cease to be a source of wonderment that One so mighty and so transcendently great should . . . come to dwell in sanctuaries of mere wood and stone, and within the human heart."[2]

"Solomon prays that God may still take cognizance of this structure on earth, by night and day, and from heaven, His true dwelling place, give ear to the earnest prayers of men."[3] He lists seven cases in which a supplicant might need God's mercy, and each time he repeats the same phrase: "Hear thou in heaven" (1 Kings 8:30, 32, 34, 36, 39, 43, 45).

"Hear, O Lord, when I cry with my voice: have mercy also upon me, and answer me" (Psalm 27:7).

---

1. Ellen G. White, *Prophets and Kings* (Mountain View, CA: Pacific Press®, 1943), 37.
2. Francis D. Nichol, ed., *The Seventh-day Adventist Bible Commentary*, vol. 2 (Washington, DC: Review and Herald®, 1976), 766.
3. Nichol, 766.

EXILE FORETOLD?

And forgive thy people that have sinned against thee, and all their transgressions wherein they have transgressed against thee, and give them compassion before them who carried them captive, that they may have compassion on them.

—1 Kings 8:50

Solomon recognized the possibility that Israel would sin so grievously that the Lord would be forced to withdraw His protection, and he prayed God would not forget His people and would show them compassion. "This prayer of Solomon, offered three and a half centuries before the Exile, is very similar to the prayer of Daniel at the time the captivity in Babylon was drawing to its close (Dan. 9:2–19). As the Temple was being dedicated there seemed little need for such a prayer as this. But with inspired foresight, Solomon envisioned an hour when that splendid Temple would lie in ruins, when the Land of Promise would be a land of bitterness and distress, and the children of Israel would be outcasts in an alien land. There is a touching pathos in the fact that at the hour of Israel's greatest glory, Solomon prayed the same kind of prayer that Daniel prayed at the hour of his nation's greatest shame. Both prayers were needed and both were heard. The first was not only a prayer, it was also a message of warning that would help to avert the doom that transgression would bring. The other would rise to a God in heaven who waited only for a genuine repentance on the part of His people before permitting their return from captivity."[1]

Solomon believed the deliverance from Egyptian bondage was proof God would not desert His people should they fall captive to another nation. Israel was God's inheritance and His chosen people (Deuteronomy 4:20; 9:26, 29). God chose them from among all nations of the earth and made a covenant with them. He established them in the Promised Land (Exodus 19:4–6; Deuteronomy 9:29; 2 Samuel 7:23; Psalm 135:4). To reject them in the future would bring dishonor to His name (Psalm 79:9, 10; Daniel 9:19; Ezekiel 20:9, 14, 22). But God's promise of protection was always conditional on His people keeping His commandments. Solomon's touching prayer stands for all who need grace and redemption!

"If we confess our sins, he is faithful and just to forgive us our sins, and to cleanse us from all unrighteousness" (1 John 1:9).

---

1. Francis D. Nichol, ed., *The Seventh-day Adventist Bible Commentary*, vol. 2 (Washington, DC: Review and Herald®, 1976), 768.

A BENEDICTION

The LORD our God be with us, as he was with our fathers: let him not leave us, nor forsake us: That he may incline our hearts unto him, to walk in all his ways, and to keep his commandments, and his statutes, and his judgments, which he commanded our fathers.

—1 Kings 8:57, 58

Solomon blessed the people and reminded them of God's promise to Abraham and that only their rejection of Him would lead to His withdrawal (2 Kings 17:7–23; Jeremiah 7:3–15; 25:4–9). "As a God of love, the Lord desires to be with His people. The Temple was built that He might dwell among them (Ex. 25:8; 1 Kings 6:12, 13). Jesus came to the world as Immanuel, 'God with us' (Matt. 1:23), and . . . His promise was that He would be with His people 'always, even unto the end of the world' (Matt.28:20). In the heart of every true child of God there is no higher desire, no deeper longing, than to realize the presence of God (Ps. 42:1, 2; Rev. 22:20, 21)."[1]

"The Spirit of God leads men to obey and inclines them to keep the commands of the law, but it does not do this against man's will. . . . The closer a man draws to the Lord, the more fully do God's thoughts become his thoughts, and God's ways his ways. When man comes to the Lord with humbleness of spirit and willingness of heart, desirous of learning His ways and of walking therein (Ps. 119:26, 27, 30, 32–36), he begins to find obedience to God to be a matter of pleasure rather than duty and the law of God to be a law of liberty (Ps. 119:45, 47, 97; James 1:25; James 2:12)."[2] "The Scriptures make clear that perfection of character is prerequisite to entrance into the kingdom of heaven. The standard of perfection is found in those principles of righteousness and love set forth in the commandments of God (Matt. 19:16–21; Luke 10:25–28; Deut. 5:2–22, 29–33; 6:3–5). The gospel, revealed in types in the OT [Old Testament] and in full clarity in the NT [New Testament], shows how we may obtain the perfection of which Solomon spoke."[3]

"Let your heart therefore be perfect with the LORD our God, to walk in his statutes, and to keep his commandments, as at this day" (1 Kings 8:61).

---

1. Francis D. Nichol, ed., *The Seventh-day Adventist Bible Commentary*, vol. 2 (Washington, DC: Review and Herald®, 1976), 769.

2. Nichol, 769, 770.

3. Nichol, 770.

THE HOUSE OF THE FOREST OF LEBANON

He built also the house of the forest of Lebanon.
—1 Kings 7:2

S olomon's early reign was busy from the standpoint of construction. Not only did he have the temple built but he also erected executive buildings within his capital. Construction took place on two hills— Mount Moriah and Mount Zion, which lay between the valleys of Kidron and Tyropoeon.[1] This required much filling and leveling of construction sites before actual work on structures could proceed. Unlike the temple, no stockpile of construction materials existed for these buildings. Building on such a grand scale was both costly and time consuming.

Little is known about the location of these buildings or the manner of their construction. We are told one of them was called "the house of the forest of Lebanon." It is believed this was descriptive of the building and not its location. "Built as it was with four rows of cedar pillars, it would have the appearance of a cedar forest, and from that resemblance probably achieved its name. Because of the statement in 1 Kings 10:16, 17, some conclude that the building served chiefly, if not altogether, as an armory, for Solomon placed in it 'two hundred targets of beaten gold,' each target made of 600 golden shekels, together with 'three hundred shields of beaten gold,' 3 lb. of gold going into each shield. But such 'targets' and 'shields' certainly were hardly for the purpose of war. . . . The hall was large, 146 by 73 ft. (44.5 by 22.3 m.), yet it was not as large as some of the great Assyrian palace halls unearthed by modern excavation. Portions of the house may, however, have been used for the storage of arms, for Isa. 22:8 speaks of the 'armour of the house of the forest.'

"Of the four rows of cedar pillars, the first and the fourth were probably set as pilasters against the walls, thus providing for three great aisles down the length of the building.

". . . Perhaps at the ends of each of the three aisles [windows were placed in three rows—1 Kings 7:3]. . . . If these were placed high on the walls, near the ceiling, a striking effect could be achieved by the rays of light coming in among the pillars like sunlight in a cedar forest."[2]

"When the LORD *shall build up Zion, he shall appear in his glory"* (Psalm 102:16).

---

1. Francis D. Nichol, ed., *The Seventh-day Adventist Bible Commentary*, vol. 2 (Washington, DC: Review and Herald®, 1976), 754–756.
2. Nichol, 756.

BLESSINGS ARE CONDITIONAL

And it came to pass . . . that the LORD
appeared to Solomon the second time.

—1 Kings 9:1, 2

The Lord appeared to Solomon in a second dream following the completion of his construction projects. The dream at Gibeon had been one of encouragement and promise. This dream differed significantly from the first. This dream presented dire warnings of what might be expected if Solomon failed to walk in uprightness and integrity. God's promise to establish David's lineage on an eternal throne was contingent upon Solomon keeping God's commandments and statutes. God had heard Solomon's prayer and had sanctified the temple with His presence. Now He reminded Solomon that obedience was necessary for His promise to be fulfilled. Obedience would bring joy and blessings, but transgression only sorrow, disaster, and death.

"God did not choose the children of Israel for the purpose of later casting them off. He did not choose David with the purpose of later rejecting his house. Every choice of God is a wise choice, and has behind it basic reasons that prove it good. It was His plan that the throne of David and the nation of Israel should be established forever. In spite of the failure of the descendants of David and of Israel after the flesh, God's purpose will yet be accomplished through spiritual Israel (Rom. 2:28, 29; 4:16; Gal. 3:29) and through Jesus the Son of David (Micah 5:2; Acts 2:34–36; Rom. 1:3)."[1]

The worship of false gods was singled out as being a particularly grievous sin against the Lord Himself. "Repeatedly through His prophets the Lord warned Israel of the tragic consequences of transgression, and His solemn warnings seem to have been multiplied in the closing days of Israel's and Judah's history, when transgression brought the people face to face with doom (Isa. 1:19–24, 28; Jer. 7:9–15; Eze. 20:7–24; Dan. 9:9–17; Hosea 4:1–9; Amos 2:4–6; 4:1–12; Micah 1:3–5; Zeph. 3:1–8)."[2] God delivered Israel from Egyptian bondage. He led them through the wilderness to their Promised Land. He bestowed upon them divine favor. How, then, could such a blessed nation be so ungrateful as to turn to idol worship?

"Righteousness exalteth a nation: but sin is a reproach to any people" (Proverbs 14:34).

---

1. Francis D. Nichol, ed., *The Seventh-day Adventist Bible Commentary*, vol. 2 (Washington, DC: Review and Herald®, 1976), 773.
2. Nichol, 773.

A Rejected Gift

And Hiram came out from Tyre to see the cities which
Solomon had given him; and they pleased him not.
—1 Kings 9:12

Now the temple was completed, but Solomon's coffers were depleted. Turning again to Hiram, Solomon asked if he would consider trading gold for land. Hiram sent him 120 talents of gold. Hiram's contribution would be roughly equivalent to 327 bars of gold today.

"The gold that Hiram gave to Solomon may not have been provided at the time the Temple was built, but was probably the 120 talents mentioned in [1 Kings 9:14]."[1] In exchange for this infusion of gold, Solomon ceded to Hiram twenty cities in the region of Galilee. "These cities are not mentioned in the compact made between Solomon and Hiram, whereby Hiram was to furnish timber and labor for activities connected with the building of the Temple, and was to receive in return certain provisions of food (1 Kings 5:5–11). Nor is anything said in the original agreement about Hiram's providing Solomon with gold. According to the strict provisions of the Mosaic code, Solomon had no right to give away these cities (Lev. 25:23). But such are the necessities of a worldly policy that technical provisions of the law are easily set aside.

". . . It appears that at the time the compact was made, these cities were populated by native inhabitants of the land rather than Israelites, for it was 20 years after the return of these cities to Solomon that men of Israel were caused by their king to dwell there (2 Chron. 8:2)."[2] Hiram came out to see the cities he had been given and was unhappy with what he received. He probably thought he would get land bordering the Mediterranean or perhaps some fertile valley area that might grow needed grain. Instead, he "received a group of inferior inland towns. It seems that Hiram refused Solomon's gift, and never even took possession of the cities."[3] Hiram called the land "Cabul," which, interpreted by Josephus, means "what does not please."[4]

"Therefore all things whatsoever ye would that men should do to you, do ye even so to them: for this is the law and the prophets" (Matthew 7:12).

---

1. Francis D. Nichol, ed., *The Seventh-day Adventist Bible Commentary*, vol. 2 (Washington, DC: Review and Herald®, 1976), 774.

2. Nichol, 774.

3. Nichol, 774.

4. Nichol, 774.

BUILDING A NAVY

And king Solomon made a navy of ships in Eziongeber, which is beside Eloth, on the shore of the Red sea, in the land of Edom.
—1 Kings 9:26

The Israelites engaged in fishing as a commercial endeavor, but the skills needed to cross the sea were not something they possessed. Solomon, therefore, used the Phoenicians to manage his navy. "And Hiram sent in the navy his servants, shipmen that had knowledge of the sea, with the servants of Solomon" (1 Kings 9:27). Apparently, the displeasure at the gift of worthless cities in the region of Galilee was not enough to destroy the alliance between Tyre and Israel. The number of ships built by Solomon, their size, and their type are not known. First Kings 9:26 relates the location of the port from which these ships sailed, and verse 28 states their destination.

Ezion-geber "is at the head of the Gulf of Aqabah, a seaport of Edom on an arm of the Arabian Gulf. The Israelites camped near here on their journeys through the wilderness (Num. 33:35; Deut. 2:8). . . . Solomon apparently controlled the overland trade route from Palestine to Arabia and the sea route to Ophir. The ambition to control these routes was probably one of the major causes of the struggles between Israel and Edom. Saul fought against Edom (1 Sam. 14:47), and David placed garrisons there (2 Sam. 8:14; 1 Chron. 18:13)."[1]

The destination for these ships was Ophir. The ships plied their trade across the Arabian Sea to the northeast coast of Africa once every three years (1 Kings 10:22). "In addition to gold the products obtained from there were almug trees and precious stones ([1 Kings] 10:11), and possibly also silver, ivory, apes, and peacocks ([v.] 22). There is a record of the Egyptian queen Hatshepsut sending an expedition to Punt to bring back myrrh trees for her temple. The ships of the Egyptian queen also brought back from there ebony, ivory, gold, cinnamonwood, panther skins, monkeys, and baboons."[2] "So king Solomon exceeded all the kings of the earth for riches and for wisdom" (1 Kings 10:23).

"For riches are not for ever: and doth the crown endure to every generation?" (Proverbs 27:24).

---

1. Francis D. Nichol, ed., *The Seventh-day Adventist Bible Commentary*, vol. 2 (Washington, DC: Review and Herald®, 1976), 777.
2. Nichol, 778.

A ROYAL VISITOR

And when the queen of Sheba heard of the fame of Solomon concerning the name of the LORD, she came to prove him with hard questions.

—1 Kings 10:1

hen the queen of Sheba heard rumors of Solomon's wealth and wisdom, she resolved to learn firsthand if the rumors were true. "Attended by a retinue of servants, and with camels bearing 'spices, and gold in abundance, and precious stones,' she made the long journey to Jerusalem. . . . She talked with him of the mysteries of nature; and Solomon taught her of the God of nature, the great Creator, who dwells in the highest heaven and rules over all. 'Solomon told her all her questions: there was not anything hid from the king, which he told her not.' 1 Kings 10:1-3; 2 Chronicles 9:1, 2."[1]

There is a question among Bible scholars as to the location of Sheba. Some place it in Arabia and others in Ethiopia. "Results of recent archeological researches in southern Arabia tend to identify the queen with this territory and her capital with Marib, in Yemen. The Arabian Sheba was a great spice country, and many are inclined to believe that this was the Sheba whose queen made a visit to Solomon."[2] Either location is a long distance from Jerusalem.

To her delight, the queen discovered the stories were not only true but had understated Solomon's wisdom and wealth. Solomon did more than share his knowledge and hospitality—he shared his faith with the queen as well. Had Israel remained true to God and worshiped Him alone, the nation would have been a beacon of salvation to the world. "By the time of the close of her visit the queen had been so fully taught by Solomon as to the source of his wisdom and prosperity that she was constrained, not to extol the human agent, but to exclaim, 'Blessed be the Lord thy God, which delighted in thee, to set thee on the throne of Israel: because the Lord loved Israel forever, therefore made He thee king, to do judgment and justice.' 1 Kings 10:9."[3]

"The true Christian will make God first and last and best in everything."[4]

---

1. Ellen G. White, *Prophets and Kings* (Mountain View, CA: Pacific Press®, 1943), 66, 67.

2. Francis D. Nichol, ed., *The Seventh-day Adventist Bible Commentary*, vol. 2 (Washington, DC: Review and Herald®, 1976), 779.

3. White, *Prophets and Kings*, 67.

4. White, 68, 69.

SOLOMON'S WEALTH AND WISDOM

Now the weight of gold that came to Solomon in one year
was six hundred threescore and six talents of gold.
—1 Kings 10:14

I n the pride of his ambition and prosperity Solomon engaged in very extensive building enterprises. A description of some of his ambitious projects is given in Eccl. 2:4–10, which included houses, gardens, orchards, pools of water—'whatsoever mine eyes desired.' Anxious to surpass the glorious achievements of all nations about him, Solomon's ambition carried him into enterprises that were against the purposes of Heaven and the best interests of the state. The heavy burdens placed upon the people soon became intolerable and led to discontent, bitterness, and ultimate revolt."[1] Solomon raised his annual revenue through tributes paid by subjugated nations, taxes, levies on international trade, and his own commercial transactions. Solomon's wooden throne was overlaid with an ivory and gold veneer. Silver was so plentiful that it ceased to be of any value (1 Kings 10:27).

"The gathering of chariots and horsemen is a sign of military conquest and extension of empire by force. The accumulation of horses was expressly against the purpose of God, who directed that Israel's future king should 'not multiply horses to himself' (Deut. 17:16). Gains secured in such ways would in the end prove to be only loss. Solomon realized it not."[2] Solomon sat squarely on the trade route from Egypt to Syria and acted as a middleman for horses and chariots. "Commerce is an honorable calling and brings many just and worth-while returns. But it also offers many temptations and often provides a swift road to ruin. As the people of Israel became more and more interested in worldly gain, they found themselves straying further and further away from God."[3]

"Better is the poor that walketh in his uprightness, than he that is perverse in his ways, though he be rich" (Proverbs 28:6).

---

1. Francis D. Nichol, ed., *The Seventh-day Adventist Bible Commentary*, vol. 2 (Washington, DC: Review and Herald®, 1976), 776.

2. Nichol, 782.

3. Nichol, 782.

A FALL FROM GRACE

And Solomon did evil in the sight of the LORD, and
went not fully after the LORD, as did David his father.
—1 Kings 11:6

Solomon for a time honored God by reverently pointing them [the kings of the earth] to the Creator of the heavens and the earth, the Ruler of the universe, the All-wise.

"Had Solomon continued in humility of mind to turn the attention of men from himself to the One who had given him wisdom and riches and honor, what a history might have been his! But while the pen of inspiration records his virtues, it also bears faithful witness to his downfall. Raised to a pinnacle of greatness and surrounded with the gifts of fortune, Solomon became dizzy, lost his balance, and fell. . . . He finally permitted men to speak of him as the one most worthy of praise for the matchless splendor of the building planned and erected for the honor of 'the name of the Lord God of Israel.'

"Thus it was that the temple of Jehovah came to be known throughout the nations as 'Solomon's temple.' "[1]

Commercialism and greed took hold of the kingdom. The demand for high wages resulted in extravagance. Heavy taxes were imposed in order to surpass all other nations in glory. "The conscientious, considerate spirit that had marked his [Solomon's] dealings with the people during the early part of his reign, was now changed. From the wisest and most merciful of rulers, he degenerated into a tyrant. Once the compassionate, God-fearing guardian of the people, he became oppressive and despotic."[2]

Solomon wed hundreds of foreign women who worshiped idols. "Infatuated with their beauty, the king neglected his duties to God and to his kingdom.

"His wives exerted a strong influence over him and gradually prevailed on him to unite with them in their worship. Solomon had disregarded the instruction that God had given to serve as a barrier against apostasy, and now he gave himself up to the worship of false gods. . . .

"Solomon's course brought its sure penalty. His separation from God through communication with idolaters was his ruin."[3]

"Pride goeth before destruction, and an haughty spirit before a fall" (Proverbs 16:18).

---

1. Ellen G. White, *Prophets and Kings* (Mountain View, CA: Pacific Press®, 1943), 68.
2. White, 55, 56.
3. White, 56, 57.

A SAD SPECTACLE

For Solomon went after Ashtoreth the goddess of the Zidonians,
and after Milcom the abomination of the Ammonites.

—1 Kings 11:5

Solomon's downfall came gradually. He compromised one principle after another until he became a shadow of the man he once was. "Thus far in the record of Solomon's wealth and glory many indications of moral weakness have become apparent. The excessive accumulation of silver and gold and the multiplication of horses were in violation of the warnings given by Moses (Deut. 17:16, 17). Solomon's shortcomings along these lines have not been specifically mentioned as such [1 Kings 10:23, 26]. . . . But in regard to the multiplication of wives, the excesses of Solomon were so outstanding that particular attention is called to the monarch's failings along this line [1 Kings 11:1]. The multiplication of wives is mentioned by Moses in the same connection with the multiplication of horses and silver and gold (Deut. 17:16, 17)."[1]

"And he had seven hundred wives, princesses, and three hundred concubines: and his wives turned away his heart" (1 Kings 11:3). The Lord had warned against marrying nonbelievers (Exodus 34:14–16; Deuteronomy 7:4), but Solomon chose to ignore it. His heathen wives' influence led Solomon to eventually join them in their worship of false gods. "Then did Solomon build an high place for Chemosh, the abomination of Moab, in the hill that is before Jerusalem, and for Molech, the abomination of the children of Ammon" (1 Kings 11:7).

"Solomon's course brought its sure penalty. His separation from God through communication with idolaters was his ruin. . . . He who in his early reign had displayed so much wisdom and sympathy in restoring a helpless babe to its unfortunate mother (see 1 Kings 3:16-28), fell so low as to consent to the erection of an idol to whom living children were offered as sacrifices."[2] Slowly, Solomon began to harbor atheistic doubts. He lost his sense of dependence on God and questioned whether God even existed!

"There is a way which seemeth right unto a man, but the end thereof are the ways of death" (Proverbs 14:12).

---

1. Francis D. Nichol, ed., *The Seventh-day Adventist Bible Commentary*, vol. 2 (Washington, DC: Review and Herald®, 1976), 784.
2. Ellen G. White, *Prophets and Kings* (Mountain View, CA: Pacific Press®, 1943), 57.

THE DEATH OF SOLOMON

And the time that Solomon reigned in Jerusalem over all Israel was forty years. And Solomon slept with his fathers, and was buried in the city of David his father: and Rehoboam his son reigned in his stead.
—1 Kings 11:42, 43

The lesson to be learned from the life of Solomon has a special moral bearing upon the life of the aged, of those who are no longer climbing the mountain but are descending and facing the western sun. . . . We see youth wavering between right and wrong, vacillating between fixed principle and the almost overpowering current of evil that is bearing them off their feet to ruin. But of those of mature age we expect better things. We look for the character to be established, for principles to be rooted, and for them to be beyond the danger of pollution. But the case of Solomon is before us as a beacon of warning. When thou, aged pilgrim who hast fought the battles of life, thinkest that thou standest take heed lest thou fall. How, in Solomon's case, was weak, vacillating character, naturally bold, firm, and determined, shaken like a reed in the wind under the tempter's power!. . . . What a lesson for all who desire to save their souls to watch unto prayer continually! What a warning to keep the grace of Christ ever in their heart, to battle with inward corruptions and outward temptations!"[1]

"The marks of Solomon's apostasy lived ages after him. In the days of Christ, the worshipers in the temple could look, just opposite them, upon the Mount of Offense, and be reminded that the builder of their rich and glorious temple, the most renowned of all kings, had separated himself from God, and reared altars to heathen idols; that the mightiest ruler on earth had failed in ruling his own spirit. Solomon went down to death a repentant man; but his repentance and tears could not efface from the Mount of Offense the signs of his miserable departure from God. Ruined walls and broken pillars bore silent witness for a thousand years to the apostasy of the greatest king that ever sat upon an earthly throne."[2] Solomon awakened to his dire position and, in his closing years, sought to lead others to avoid his mistakes.

Watch and pray, lest ye enter into temptation!

---

1. Ellen G. White, *Conflict and Courage* (Washington, DC: Review and Herald®, 1970), 197.
2. Ellen G. White, "The Apostasy of Solomon: His Idolatry and Dissipation," *Health Reformer*, May 1878, 142.

MY COVENANT SHALL STAND FAST

So all the generations from Abraham to David are fourteen generations; and from David until the carrying away into Babylon are fourteen generations; and from the carrying away into Babylon unto Christ are fourteen generations.

—Matthew 1:17

God extended great favors to David because he obeyed the Lord, keeping His commandments and statutes. "This commendation of David is remarkable in view of David's grievous errors, as in the matter of Uriah, the Hittite (2 Sam. 11) and in the act of numbering Israel (2 Sam. 24). Of both of these failings David sincerely repented, and through the provisions of grace was accepted as if he had never committed these infractions. Character is not finally determined by occasional deeds or misdeeds, but by the habitual tendency of the life."[1]

"Glorious are the promises made to David and his house, promises that look forward to the eternal ages, and find their complete fulfillment in Christ. The Lord declared:

" 'I have sworn unto David My servant . . . with whom My hand shall be established: Mine arm also shall strengthen him. . . . My faithfulness and My mercy shall be with him. . . . He shall cry unto Me, Thou art my Father, my God, and the Rock of my salvation. . . . My mercy will I keep for him forevermore, and My covenant shall stand fast with him.' Psalm 89:3-28.

" 'His seed also will I make to endure forever, / And his throne as the days of heaven.' Psalm 89:29.

" 'He shall judge the poor of the people, / He shall save the children of the needy, / And shall break in pieces the oppressor. / They shall fear thee while the sun endureth, / And so long as the moon, throughout all generations. . . . / He shall have dominion also from sea to sea, / And from the river unto the ends of the earth.' / 'His name shall endure forever: / His name shall be continued as long as the sun: / And men shall be blessed in him: / All nations shall call him blessed.' Psalm 72:4-8, R.V., 17.

" ' . . . And His name shall be called Wonderful, Counselor, The mighty God, The everlasting Father, The Prince of Peace.'. . . Isaiah 9:6."[2] Still, generations would pass before the promise was fulfilled (Isaiah 11:1).

God keeps His promises!

---

1. Francis D. Nichol, ed., *The Seventh-day Adventist Bible Commentary*, vol. 2 (Washington, DC: Review and Herald®, 1976), 787.
2. Ellen G. White, *Patriarchs and Prophets* (Mountain View, CA: Pacific Press®, 1943), 754, 755.

CHRIST FULFILLS THE PSALMS

And he shall be as the light of the morning.

—2 Samuel 23:4

I n his psalms, David prophesied the Messiah would

- have a distinguishing mission (Psalm 146:6–10; Luke 4:18; Matthew 4:16, 23, 24);
- fulfill the covenant (Psalm 89:3–28; Matthew 3:17);
- be declared the Son of God (Psalm 2:7; Matthew 3:17);
- bless the meek (Psalm 37:11; Matthew 5:5);
- speak in parables (Psalm 78:2; Matthew 13:13);
- calm the sea (Psalm 89:9; Matthew 8:24–26; 14:32);
- cleanse the temple (Psalm 69:9; Luke 19:45, 46);
- be betrayed by a trusted friend (Psalm 41:9; John 13:18);
- be rejected as the Cornerstone (Psalm 118:22; Matthew 21:42; Luke 20:17; Acts 4:11);
- be accused by false witnesses (Psalm 35:11; Mark 14:57, 58);
- be hated without reason (Psalm 35:19; John 15:24, 25);
- be scorned and mocked (Psalm 22:1, 6–8, 13–18; Luke 23:35);
- have soldiers gamble for His coat (Psalm 22:17, 18; Matthew 27:35, 36);
- be offered vinegar and gall (Psalm 69:21; Matthew 27:34);
- pray for His enemies (Psalm 109:4; Luke 23:34);
- say, "Into thine hand I commit my spirit," on the cross (Psalm 31:5; Luke 23:46);
- have no bones broken (Psalm 34:20; John 19:32, 33, 36);
- be buried and resurrected (Psalms 16:10; 49:15; Mark 16:6, 7; 1 Corinthians 15:4);
- ascend to God's right hand (Psalm 68:18; Mark 16:19; Ephesians 4:8);
- return in triumph to His Father (Psalm 24:7–10; John 14:28; 16:28);
- see every knee bow before Him (Psalm 72:4–8, 11, 17, 19; Romans 14:10, 11);
- be a priest after the order of Melchizedek (Psalm 110:4; Hebrews 5:5, 6); and
- be King of kings and inherit an everlasting kingdom (Psalm 89:27, 29; Revelation 11:15).

The theme of David's story is redemption. David was a man after God's "own heart" (1 Samuel 13:14)—humble, repentant, trusting, faithful, and obedient. May we follow his example.